SPIDER-MAN
and the
BLACK CAT

"The EVIL THAT MEN DO"

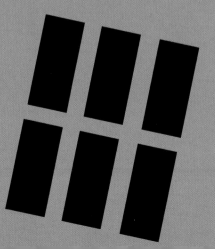

SPIDER-MAN
and the
BLACK CAT

"The EVIL THAT MEN DO"

WRITER: KEVIN SMITH

PENCILS: TERRY DODSON

INKS: RACHEL DODSON

COLORS: LEE LOUGHRIDGE & RACHEL DODSON
LETTERS: RICHARD STARKINGS & COMICRAFT

ASSISTANT EDITOR: JOHN MIESEGAES
ASSOCIATE EDITOR: WARREN SIMONS
EDITOR: AXEL ALONSO

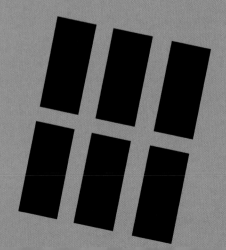

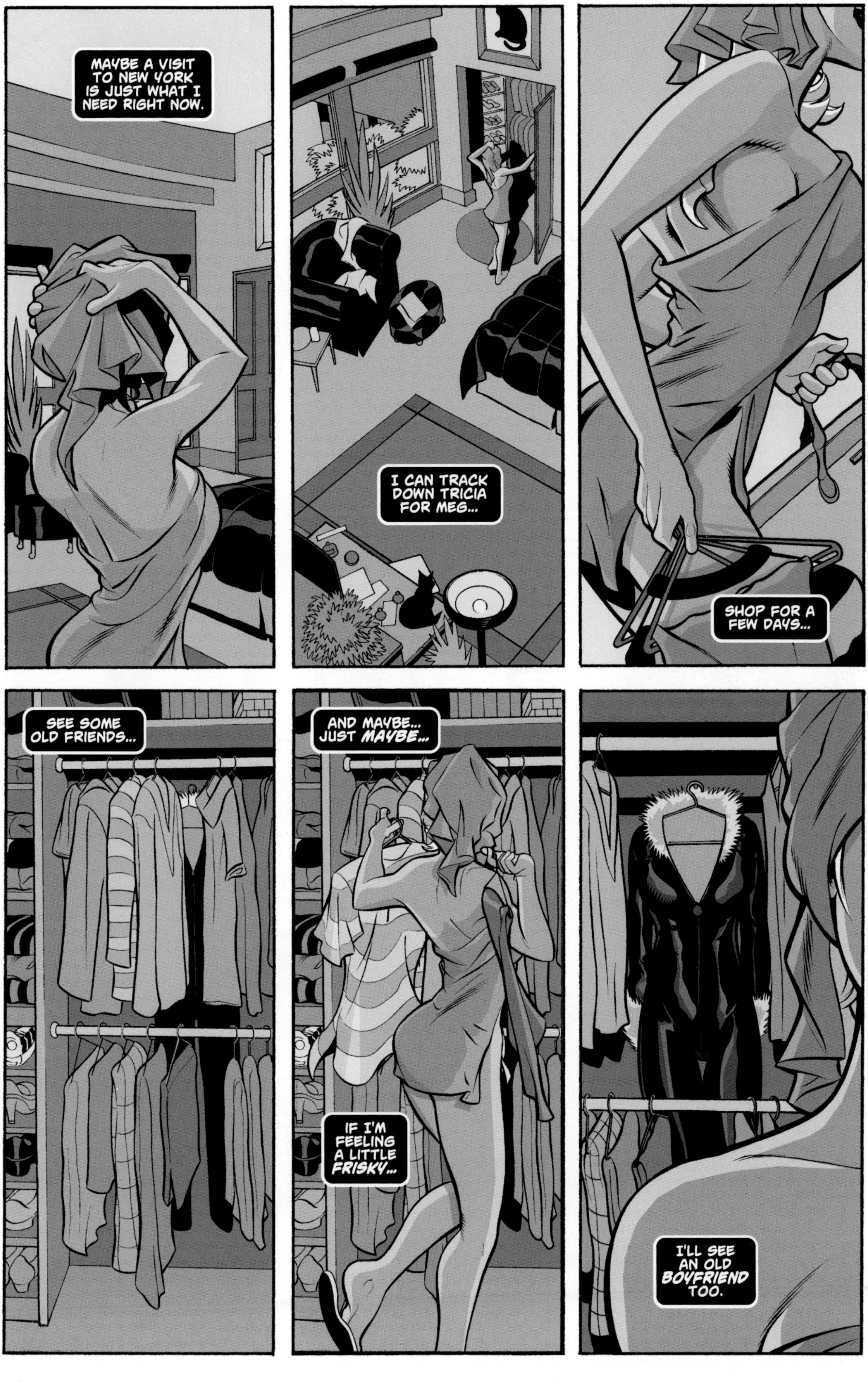
MAYBE A VISIT TO NEW YORK IS JUST WHAT I NEED RIGHT NOW.
I CAN TRACK DOWN TRICIA FOR MEG...
SHOP FOR A FEW DAYS...
SEE SOME OLD FRIENDS...
AND MAYBE... JUST MAYBE...
IF I'M FEELING A LITTLE FRISKY...
I'LL SEE AN OLD BOYFRIEND TOO.

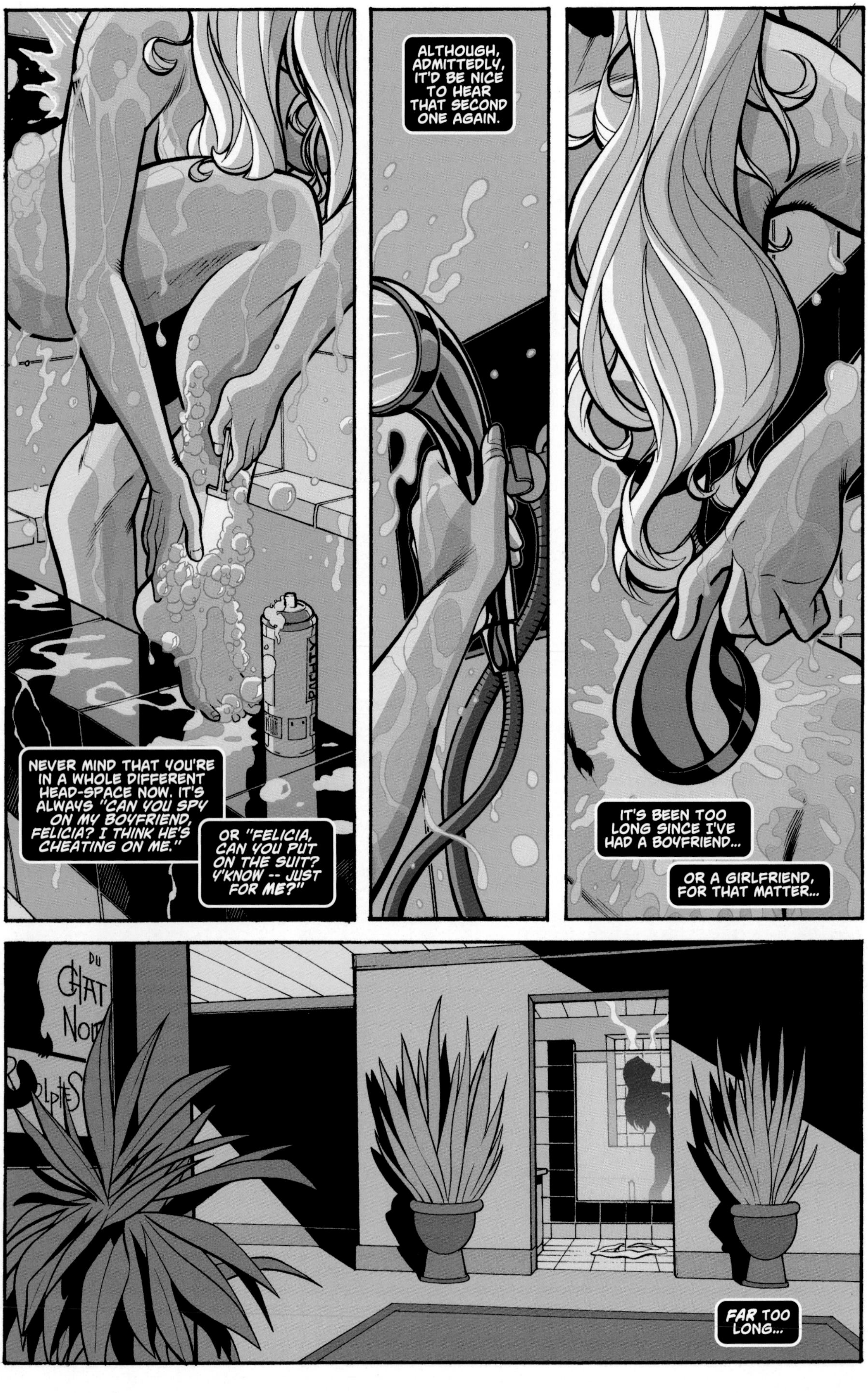
NEVER MIND THAT YOU'RE IN A WHOLE DIFFERENT HEAD-SPACE NOW. IT'S ALWAYS "CAN YOU SPY ON MY BOYFRIEND, FELICIA? I THINK HE'S CHEATING ON ME."
OR "FELICIA, CAN YOU PUT ON THE SUIT? Y'KNOW -- JUST FOR *ME*?"
ALTHOUGH, ADMITTEDLY, IT'D BE NICE TO HEAR THAT SECOND ONE AGAIN.
IT'S BEEN TOO LONG SINCE I'VE HAD A BOYFRIEND...
OR A GIRLFRIEND, FOR THAT MATTER...
FAR TOO LONG...

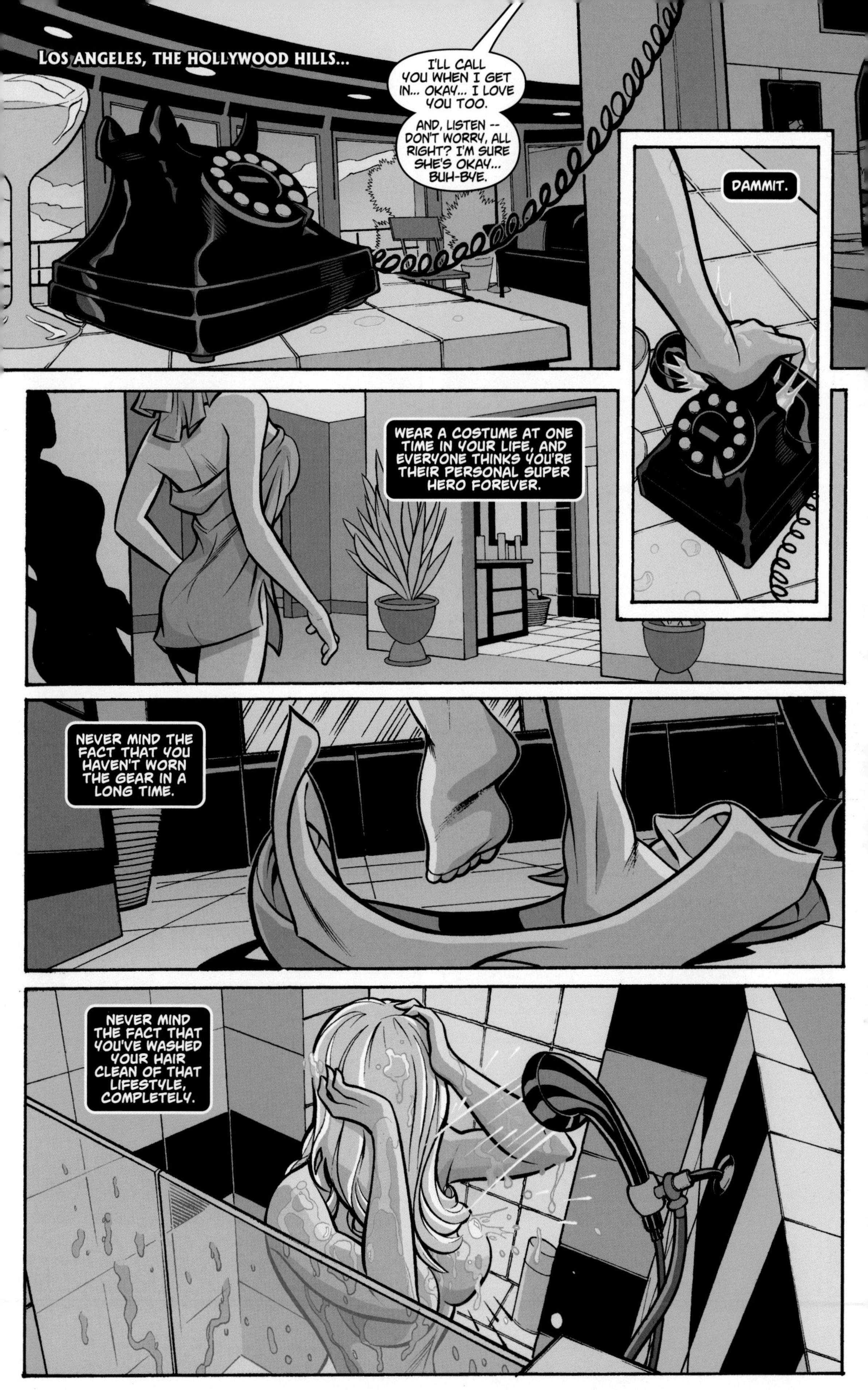
LOS ANGELES, THE HOLLYWOOD HILLS...
I'LL CALL YOU WHEN I GET IN... OKAY... I LOVE YOU TOO.
AND, LISTEN -- DON'T WORRY, ALL RIGHT? I'M SURE SHE'S OKAY... BUH-BYE.
DAMMIT.
WEAR A COSTUME AT ONE TIME IN YOUR LIFE, AND EVERYONE THINKS YOU'RE THEIR PERSONAL SUPER HERO FOREVER.
NEVER MIND THE FACT THAT YOU HAVEN'T WORN THE GEAR IN A LONG TIME.
NEVER MIND THE FACT THAT YOU'VE WASHED YOUR HAIR CLEAN OF THAT LIFESTYLE, COMPLETELY.

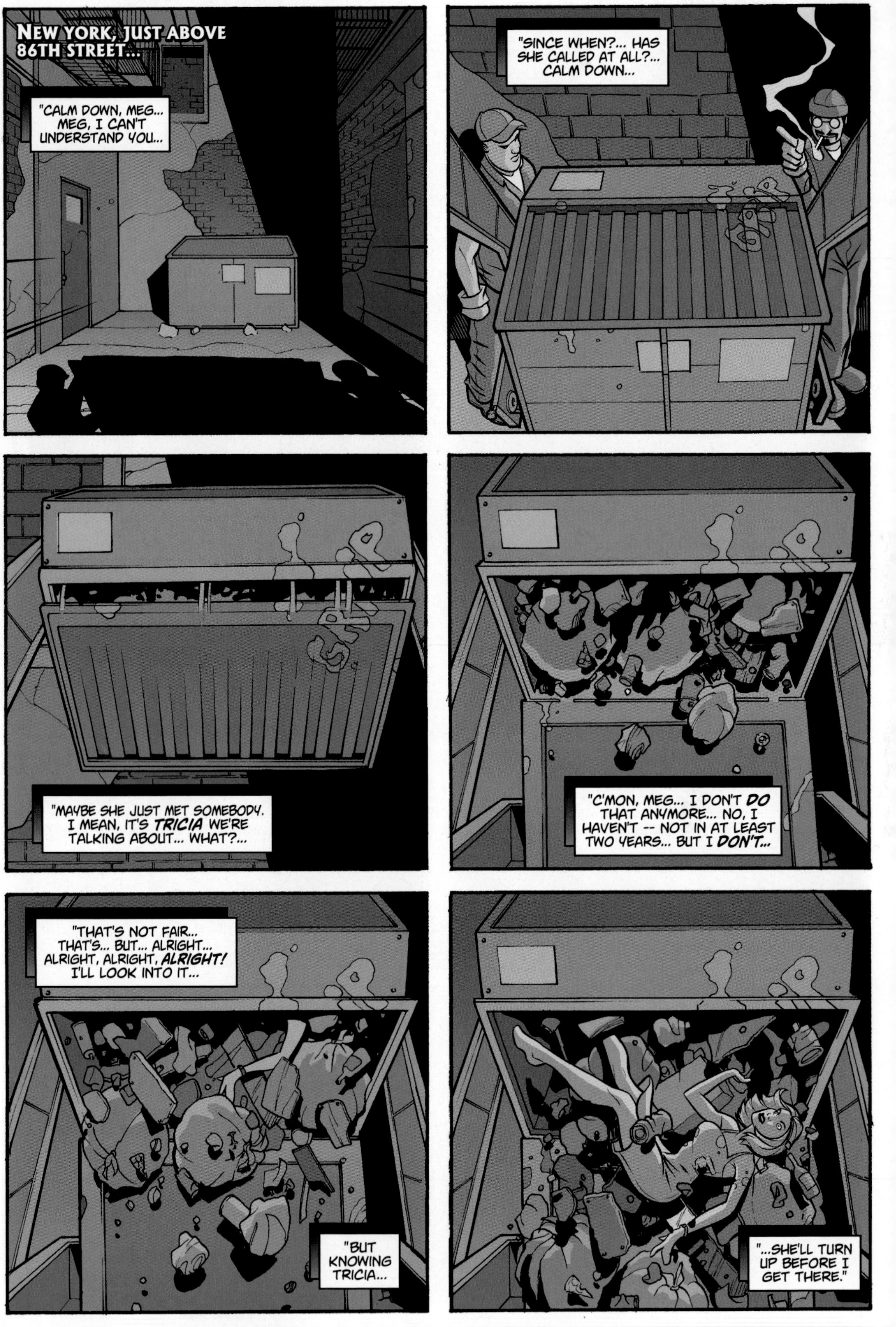
New York, just above 86th Street...
"Calm down, Meg... Meg, I can't understand you...
"Since when?... Has she called at all?... Calm down...
"Maybe she just met somebody. I mean, it's Tricia we're talking about... what?...
"C'mon, Meg... I don't do that anymore... no, I haven't -- not in at least two years... but I don't...
"That's not fair... that's... but... alright... alright, alright, alright! I'll look into it...
"But knowing Tricia...
"...she'll turn up before I get there."

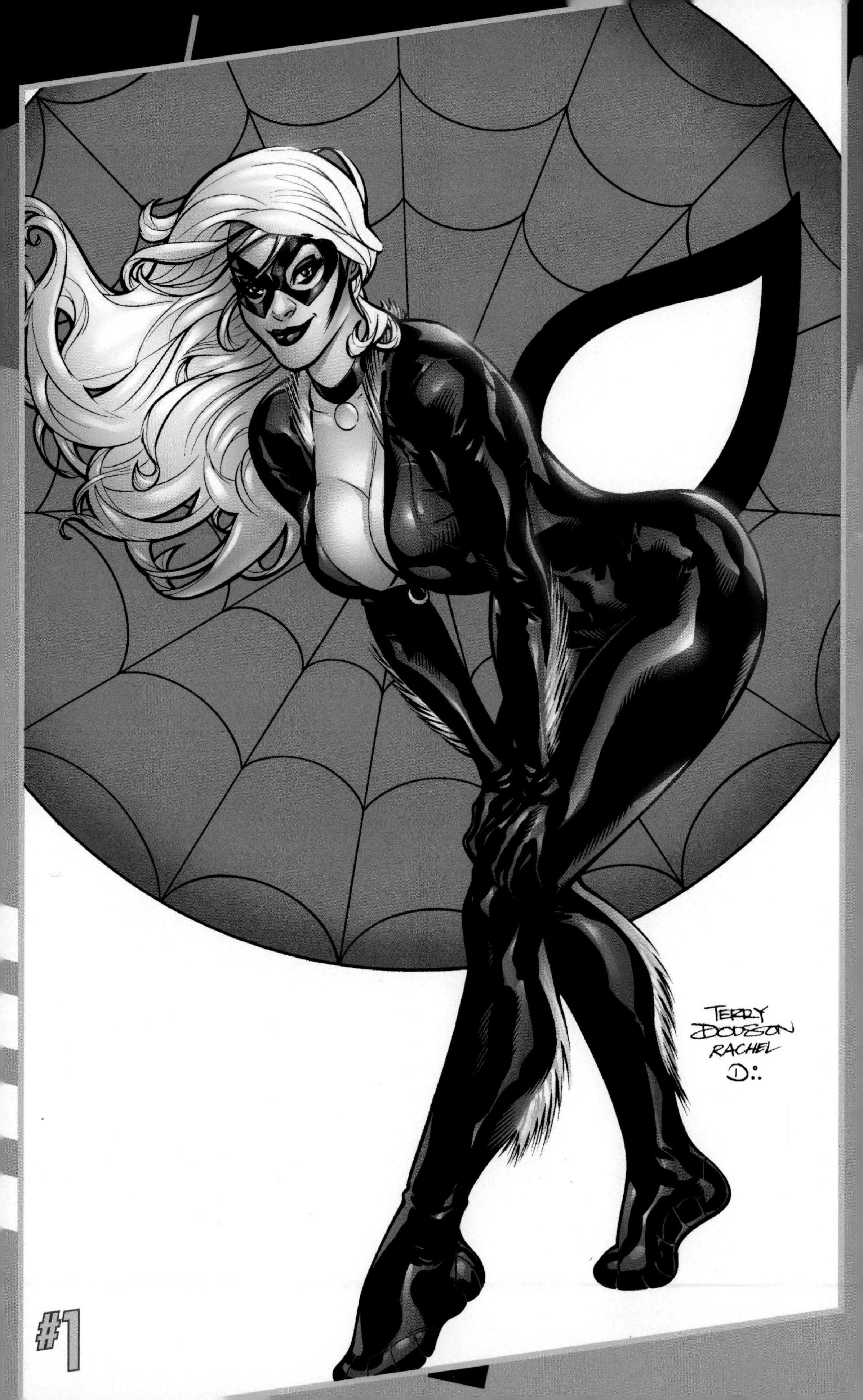

TERRY
DODSON
RACHEL
D.:
#1

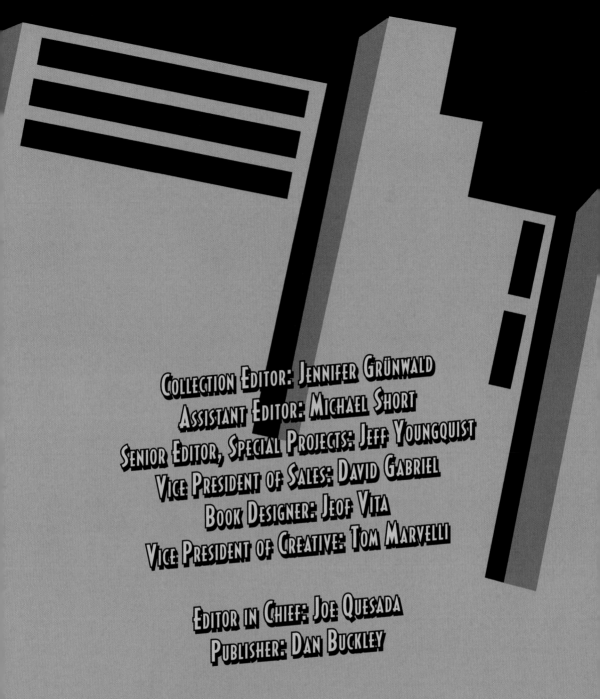

COLLECTION EDITOR: JENNIFER GRÜNWALD
ASSISTANT EDITOR: MICHAEL SHORT
SENIOR EDITOR, SPECIAL PROJECTS: JEFF YOUNGQUIST
VICE PRESIDENT OF SALES: DAVID GABRIEL
BOOK DESIGNER: JEOF VITA
VICE PRESIDENT OF CREATIVE: TOM MARVELLI

EDITOR IN CHIEF: JOE QUESADA
PUBLISHER: DAN BUCKLEY

SPIDER-MAN/BLACK CAT: THE EVIL THAT MEN DO. Contains material originally published in magazine form as SPIDER-MAN/BLACK CAT: THE EVIL THAT MEN DO #1-6. First printing 2006. ISBN# 0-7851-1095-X. Published by MARVEL PUBLISHING, INC., a subsidiary of MARVEL ENTERTAINMENT, INC. OFFICE OF PUBLICATION: 417 5th Avenue, New York, NY 10016. Copyright © 2002, 2005 and 2006 Marvel Characters, Inc. All rights reserved. $19.99 per copy in the U.S. and $32.00 in Canada (GST #R127032852); Canadian Agreement #40668537. All characters featured in this issue and the distinctive names and likenesses thereof, and all related indicia are trademarks of Marvel Characters, Inc. No similarity between any of the names, characters, persons, and/or institutions in this magazine with those of any living or dead person or institution is intended, and any such similarity which may exist is purely coincidental. **Printed in the U.S.A.** AVI ARAD, Chief Creative Officer; ALAN FINE, President & CEO Of Marvel Toys and Marvel Publishing, Inc.; DAVID BOGART, VP Of Publishing Operations; DAN CARR, Director of Production; JUSTIN F. GABRIE, Managing Editor; STAN LEE, Chairman Emeritus. For information regarding advertising in Marvel Comics or on Marvel.com, please contact Joe Maimone, Advertising Director, at jmaimone@marvel.com or 212-576-8534.

10 9 8 7 6 5 4 3 2 1

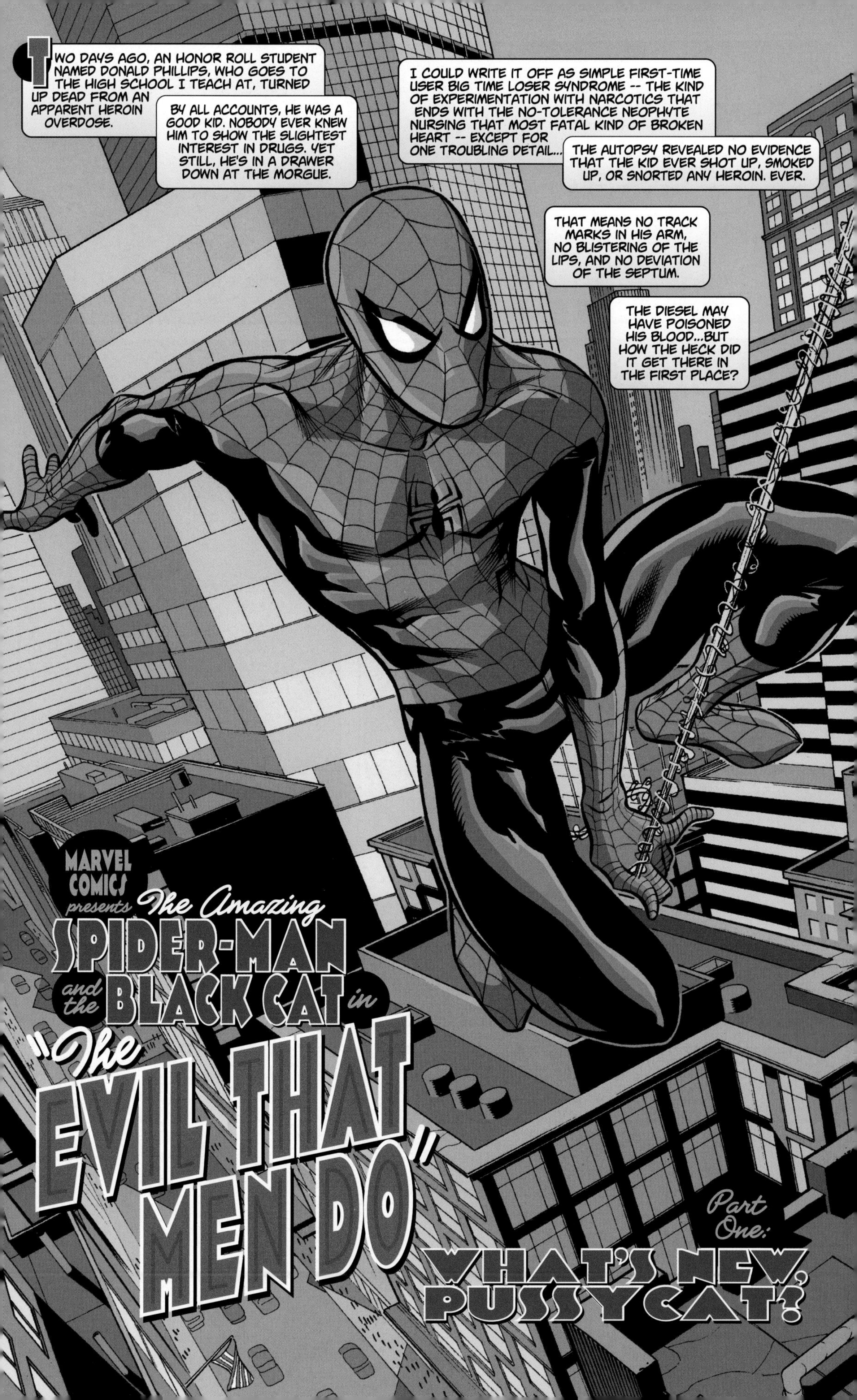
TWO DAYS AGO, AN HONOR ROLL STUDENT NAMED DONALD PHILLIPS, WHO GOES TO THE HIGH SCHOOL I TEACH AT, TURNED UP DEAD FROM AN APPARENT HEROIN OVERDOSE.
BY ALL ACCOUNTS, HE WAS A GOOD KID. NOBODY EVER KNEW HIM TO SHOW THE SLIGHTEST INTEREST IN DRUGS. YET STILL, HE'S IN A DRAWER DOWN AT THE MORGUE.
I COULD WRITE IT OFF AS SIMPLE FIRST-TIME USER BIG TIME LOSER SYNDROME -- THE KIND OF EXPERIMENTATION WITH NARCOTICS THAT ENDS WITH THE NO-TOLERANCE NEOPHYTE NURSING THAT MOST FATAL KIND OF BROKEN HEART -- EXCEPT FOR ONE TROUBLING DETAIL...
THE AUTOPSY REVEALED NO EVIDENCE THAT THE KID EVER SHOT UP, SMOKED UP, OR SNORTED ANY HEROIN. EVER.
THAT MEANS NO TRACK MARKS IN HIS ARM, NO BLISTERING OF THE LIPS, AND NO DEVIATION OF THE SEPTUM.
THE DIESEL MAY HAVE POISONED HIS BLOOD...BUT HOW THE HECK DID IT GET THERE IN THE FIRST PLACE?
MARVEL COMICS presents The Amazing SPIDER-MAN and the BLACK CAT in
"The EVIL THAT MEN DO"
Part One:
WHAT'S NEW, PUSSYCAT?

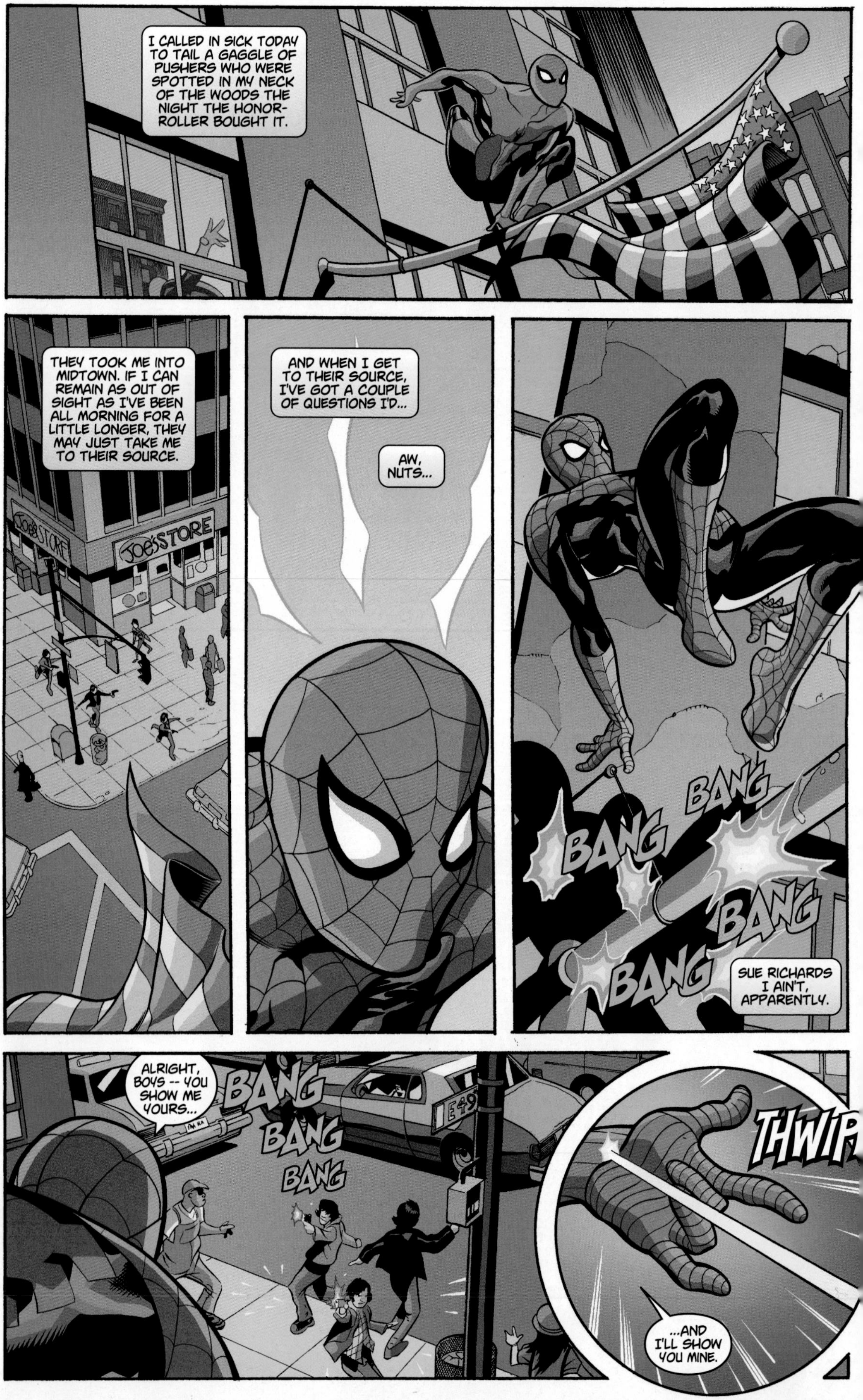
I CALLED IN SICK TODAY TO TAIL A GAGGLE OF PUSHERS WHO WERE SPOTTED IN MY NECK OF THE WOODS THE NIGHT THE HONOR-ROLLER BOUGHT IT.
THEY TOOK ME INTO MIDTOWN. IF I CAN REMAIN AS OUT OF SIGHT AS I'VE BEEN ALL MORNING FOR A LITTLE LONGER, THEY MAY JUST TAKE ME TO THEIR SOURCE.
JOE'S STORE
JOE'S STORE
AND WHEN I GET TO THEIR SOURCE, I'VE GOT A COUPLE OF QUESTIONS I'D...
AW, NUTS...
BANG
BANG
BANG
BANG
SUE RICHARDS I AIN'T, APPARENTLY.
ALRIGHT, BOYS -- YOU SHOW ME YOURS...
BANG
BANG
BANG
THWIP
...AND I'LL SHOW YOU MINE.

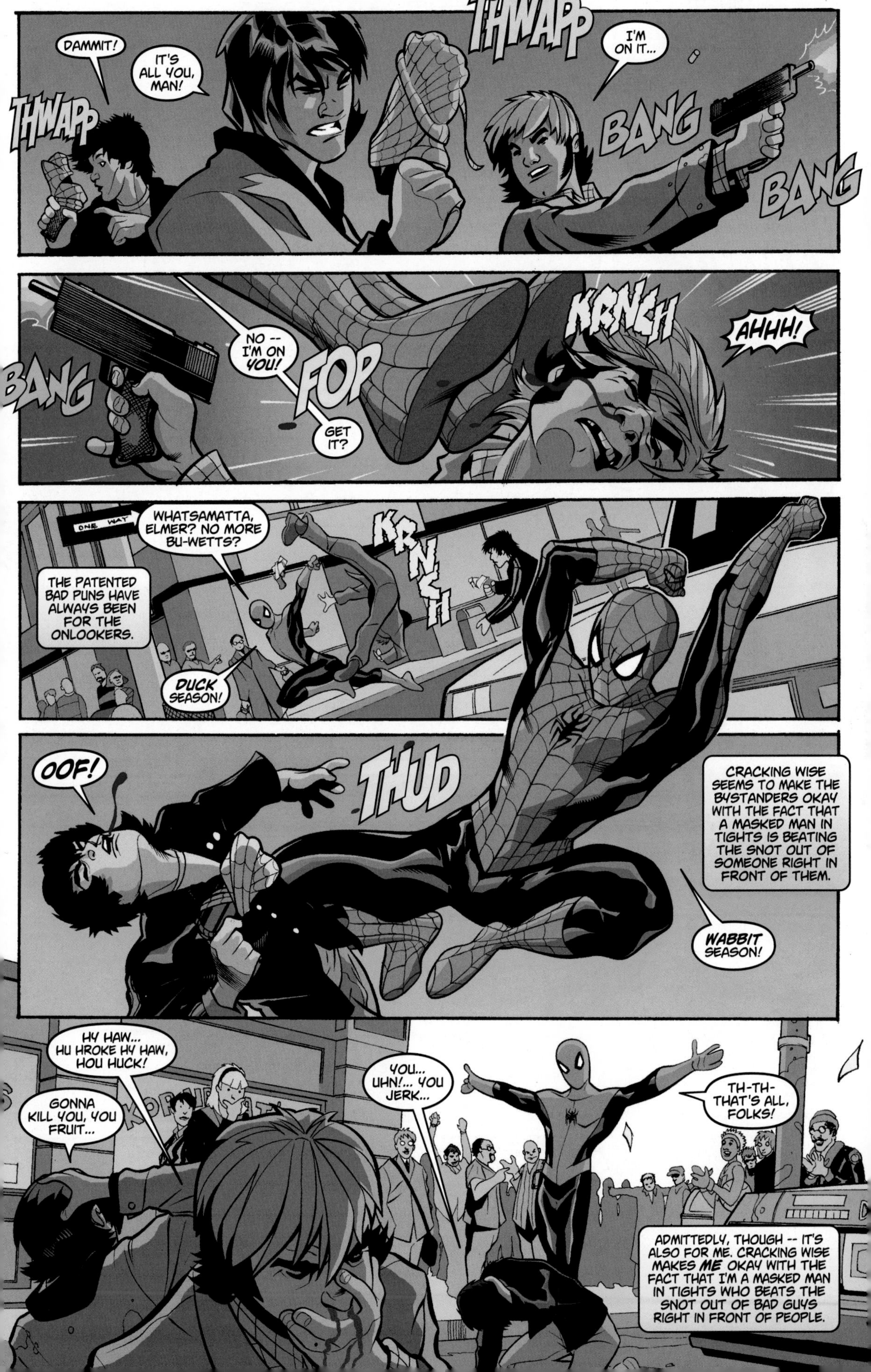
DAMMIT!
THWAPP
IT'S ALL YOU, MAN!
THWAPP
I'M ON IT...
BANG
BANG
BANG
NO -- I'M ON YOU!
FOP
GET IT?
KRNCH
AHHH!
ONE WAY
WHATSAMATTA, ELMER? NO MORE BU-WETTS?
KRNCH
THE PATENTED BAD PUNS HAVE ALWAYS BEEN FOR THE ONLOOKERS.
DUCK SEASON!
OOF!
THUD
CRACKING WISE SEEMS TO MAKE THE BYSTANDERS OKAY WITH THE FACT THAT A MASKED MAN IN TIGHTS IS BEATING THE SNOT OUT OF SOMEONE RIGHT IN FRONT OF THEM.
WABBIT SEASON!
HY HAW... HU HROKE HY HAW, HOU HUCK!
GONNA KILL YOU, YOU FRUIT...
YOU... UHN!... YOU JERK...
TH-TH-THAT'S ALL, FOLKS!
ADMITTEDLY, THOUGH -- IT'S ALSO FOR ME. CRACKING WISE MAKES ME OKAY WITH THE FACT THAT I'M A MASKED MAN IN TIGHTS WHO BEATS THE SNOT OUT OF BAD GUYS RIGHT IN FRONT OF PEOPLE.

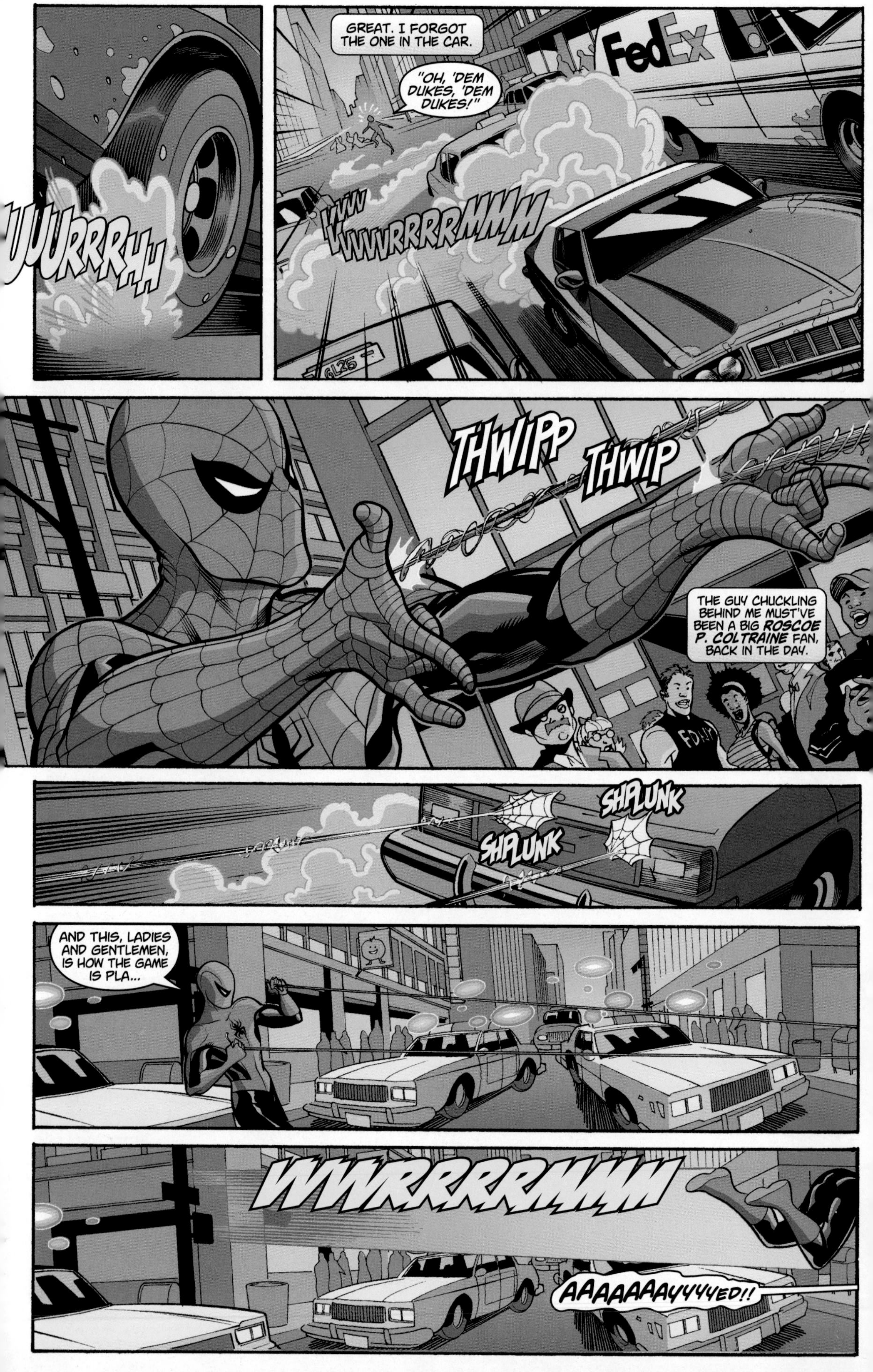
UUURRRHH
GREAT. I FORGOT THE ONE IN THE CAR.
"OH, 'DEM DUKES, 'DEM DUKES!"
FedEx
VVVVVVVRRRRMMMM
THWIPP
THWIP
THE GUY CHUCKLING BEHIND ME MUST'VE BEEN A BIG ROSCOE P. COLTRAINE FAN, BACK IN THE DAY.
SHPLUNK
SHPLUNK
AND THIS, LADIES AND GENTLEMEN, IS HOW THE GAME IS PLA...
VVVRRRRMMM
AAAAAAYYYYED!!

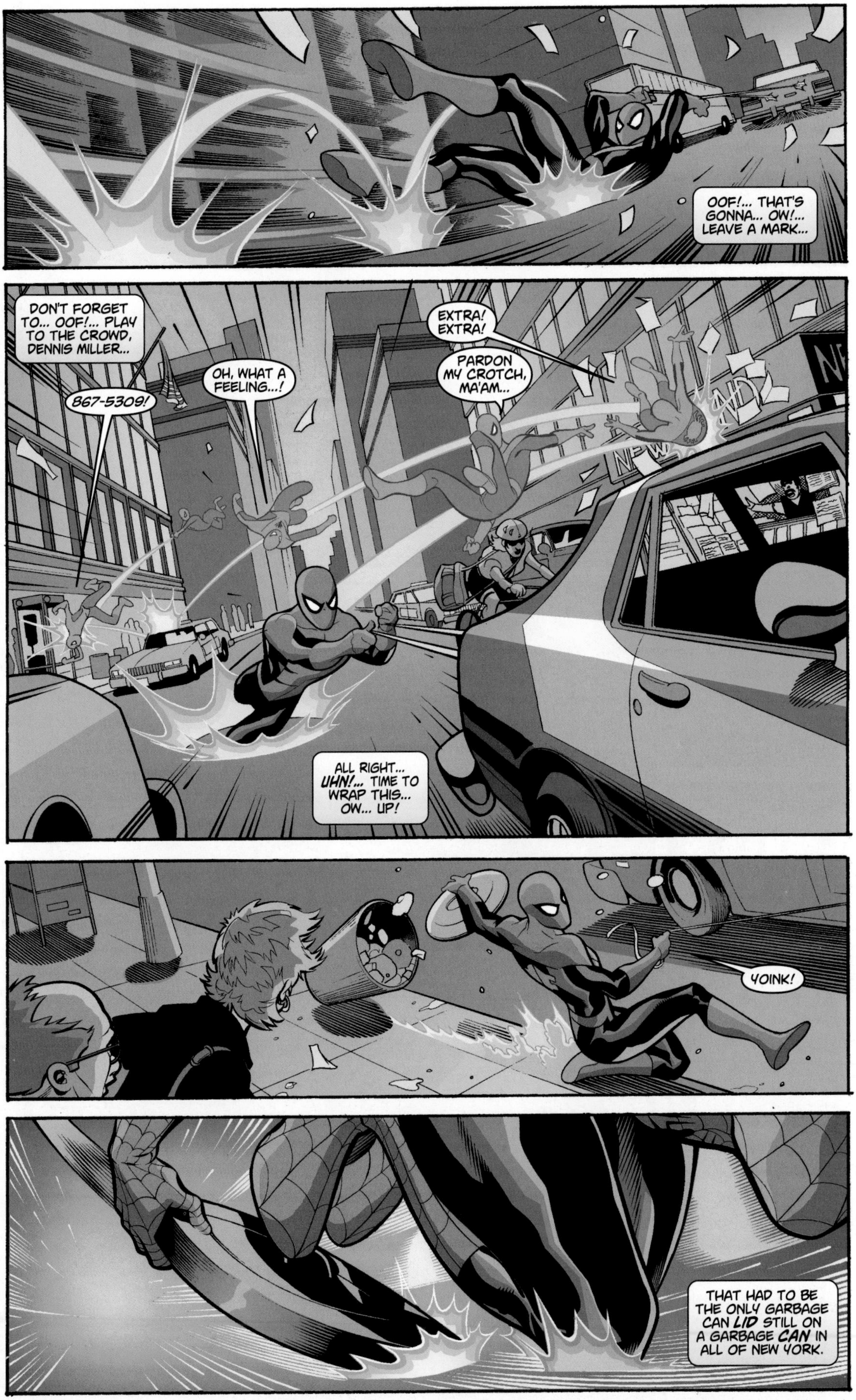
OOF!... THAT'S GONNA... OW!... LEAVE A MARK...
DON'T FORGET TO... OOF!... PLAY TO THE CROWD, DENNIS MILLER...
867-5309!
OH, WHAT A FEELING...!
EXTRA! EXTRA!
PARDON MY CROTCH, MA'AM...
ALL RIGHT... UHN!... TIME TO WRAP THIS... OW... UP!
YOINK!
THAT HAD TO BE THE ONLY GARBAGE CAN LID STILL ON A GARBAGE CAN IN ALL OF NEW YORK.

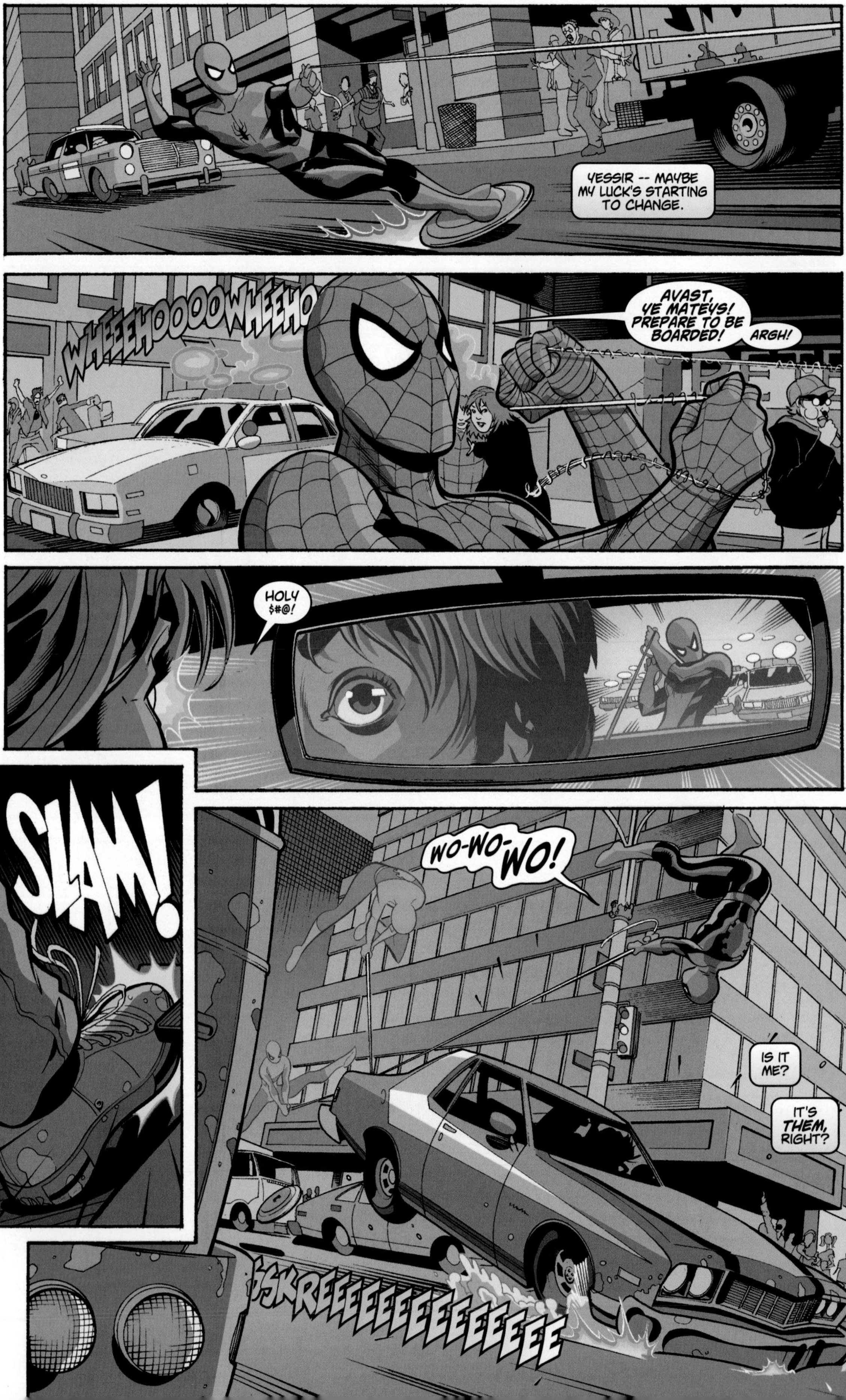
YESSIR -- MAYBE MY LUCK'S STARTING TO CHANGE.
WHEEEHOOOOWHEEHO
AVAST, YE MATEYS! PREPARE TO BE BOARDED!
ARGH!
HOLY $#@!
SLAM!
WO-WO-WO!
IS IT ME?
IT'S THEM, RIGHT?
SKREEEEEEEEEEEEEE

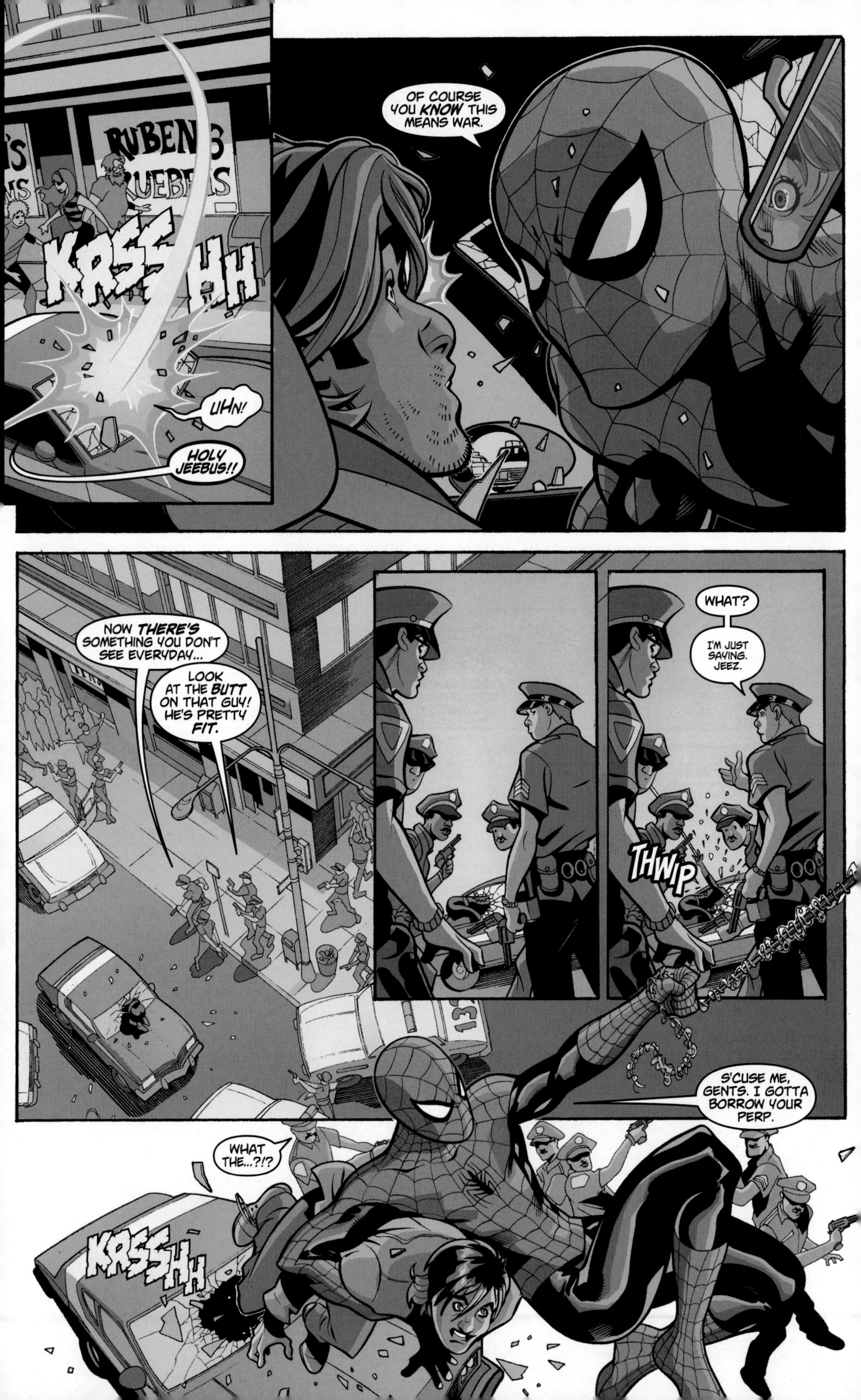
RUBEN'S
RUEBENS
KRSSHH
UHN!
HOLY JEEBUS!!
OF COURSE YOU KNOW THIS MEANS WAR.
NOW THERE'S SOMETHING YOU DON'T SEE EVERYDAY...
LOOK AT THE BUTT ON THAT GUY! HE'S PRETTY FIT.
WHAT?
I'M JUST SAYING. JEEZ.
THWIP
S'CUSE ME, GENTS. I GOTTA BORROW YOUR PERP.
WHAT THE...?!?
KRSSHH

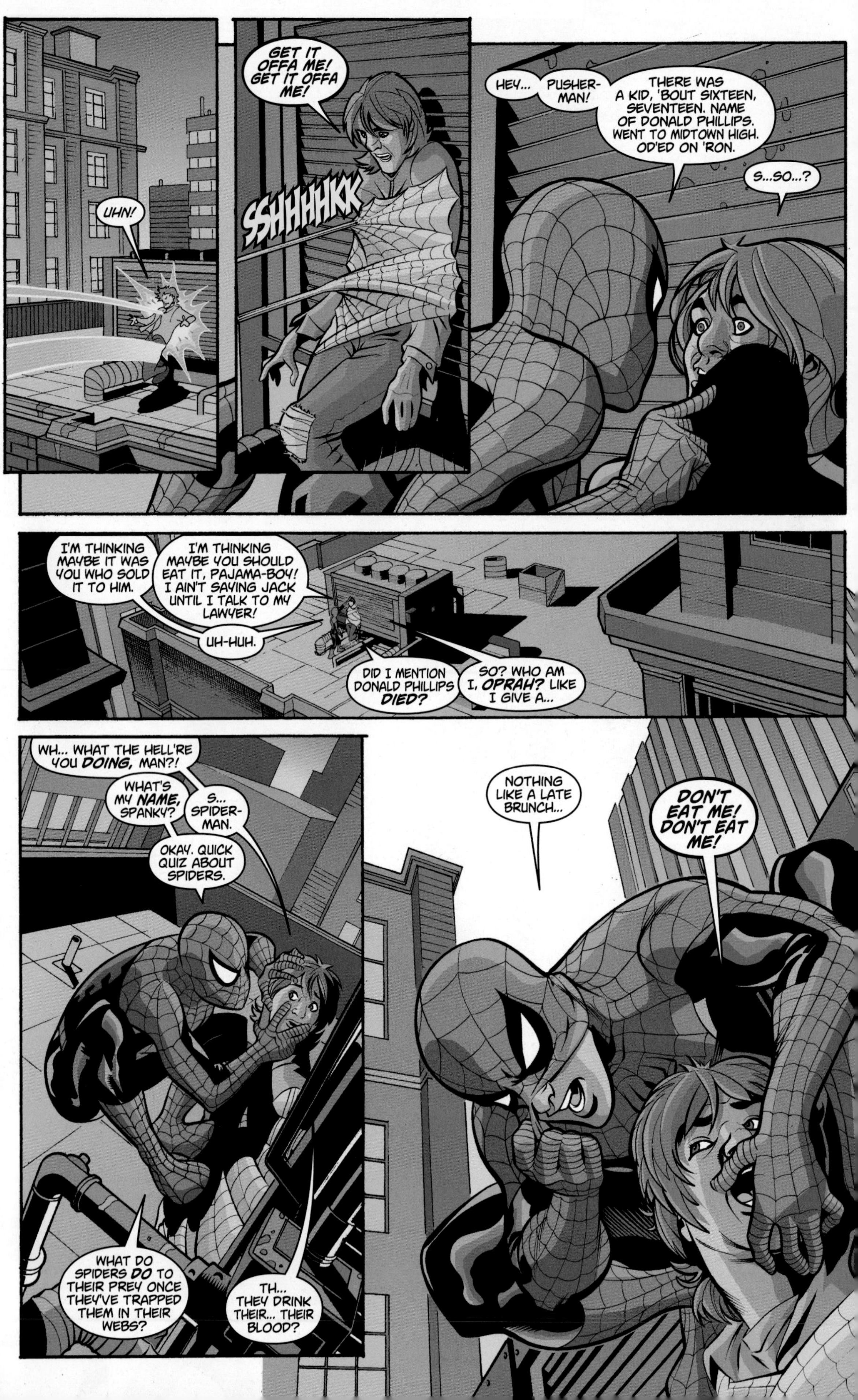
UHN!
GET IT OFFA ME! GET IT OFFA ME!
SSHHHHKK
HEY...
PUSHER-MAN!
THERE WAS A KID, 'BOUT SIXTEEN, SEVENTEEN. NAME OF DONALD PHILLIPS. WENT TO MIDTOWN HIGH. OD'ED ON 'RON.
S...SO...?
I'M THINKING MAYBE IT WAS YOU WHO SOLD IT TO HIM.
I'M THINKING MAYBE YOU SHOULD EAT IT, PAJAMA-BOY! I AIN'T SAYING JACK UNTIL I TALK TO MY LAWYER!
UH-HUH.
DID I MENTION DONALD PHILLIPS DIED?
SO? WHO AM I, OPRAH? LIKE I GIVE A...
WH... WHAT THE HELL'RE YOU DOING, MAN?!
WHAT'S MY NAME, SPANKY?
S... SPIDER-MAN.
OKAY. QUICK QUIZ ABOUT SPIDERS.
WHAT DO SPIDERS DO TO THEIR PREY ONCE THEY'VE TRAPPED THEM IN THEIR WEBS?
TH... THEY DRINK THEIR... THEIR BLOOD?
NOTHING LIKE A LATE BRUNCH...
DON'T EAT ME! DON'T EAT ME!

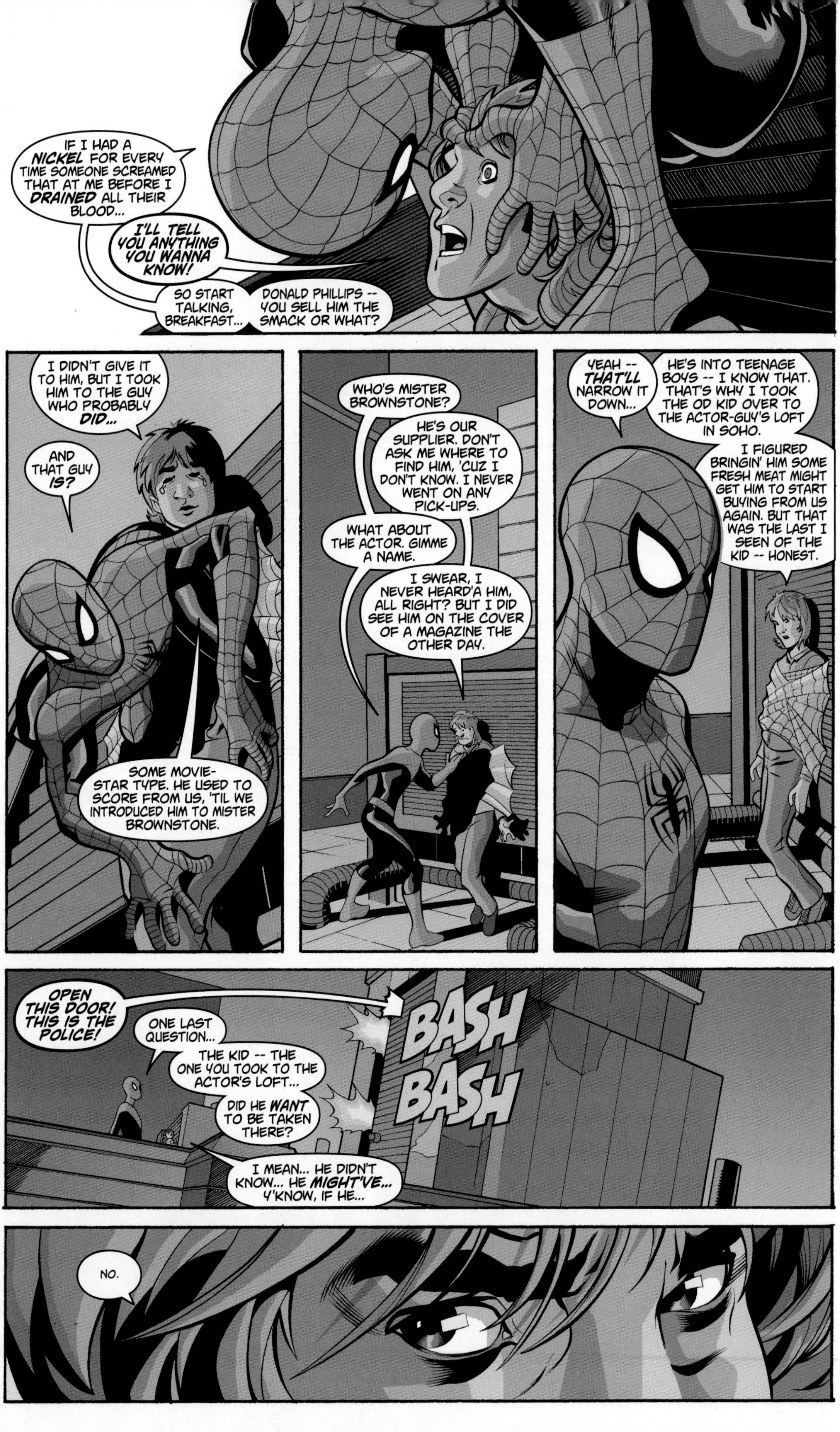
IF I HAD A NICKEL FOR EVERY TIME SOMEONE SCREAMED THAT AT ME BEFORE I DRAINED ALL THEIR BLOOD...
I'LL TELL YOU ANYTHING YOU WANNA KNOW!
SO START TALKING, BREAKFAST...
DONALD PHILLIPS -- YOU SELL HIM THE SMACK OR WHAT?
I DIDN'T GIVE IT TO HIM, BUT I TOOK HIM TO THE GUY WHO PROBABLY DID...
AND THAT GUY IS?
SOME MOVIE-STAR TYPE. HE USED TO SCORE FROM US, 'TIL WE INTRODUCED HIM TO MISTER BROWNSTONE.
WHO'S MISTER BROWNSTONE?
HE'S OUR SUPPLIER. DON'T ASK ME WHERE TO FIND HIM, 'CUZ I DON'T KNOW. I NEVER WENT ON ANY PICK-UPS.
WHAT ABOUT THE ACTOR. GIMME A NAME.
I SWEAR, I NEVER HEARD'A HIM, ALL RIGHT? BUT I DID SEE HIM ON THE COVER OF A MAGAZINE THE OTHER DAY.
HE'S INTO TEENAGE BOYS -- I KNOW THAT. THAT'S WHY I TOOK THE OD KID OVER TO THE ACTOR-GUY'S LOFT IN SOHO.
YEAH -- THAT'LL NARROW IT DOWN...
I FIGURED BRINGIN' HIM SOME FRESH MEAT MIGHT GET HIM TO START BUYING FROM US AGAIN. BUT THAT WAS THE LAST I SEEN OF THE KID -- HONEST.
OPEN THIS DOOR! THIS IS THE POLICE!
BASH
BASH
ONE LAST QUESTION...
THE KID -- THE ONE YOU TOOK TO THE ACTOR'S LOFT...
DID HE WANT TO BE TAKEN THERE?
I MEAN... HE DIDN'T KNOW... HE MIGHT'VE... Y'KNOW, IF HE...
NO.

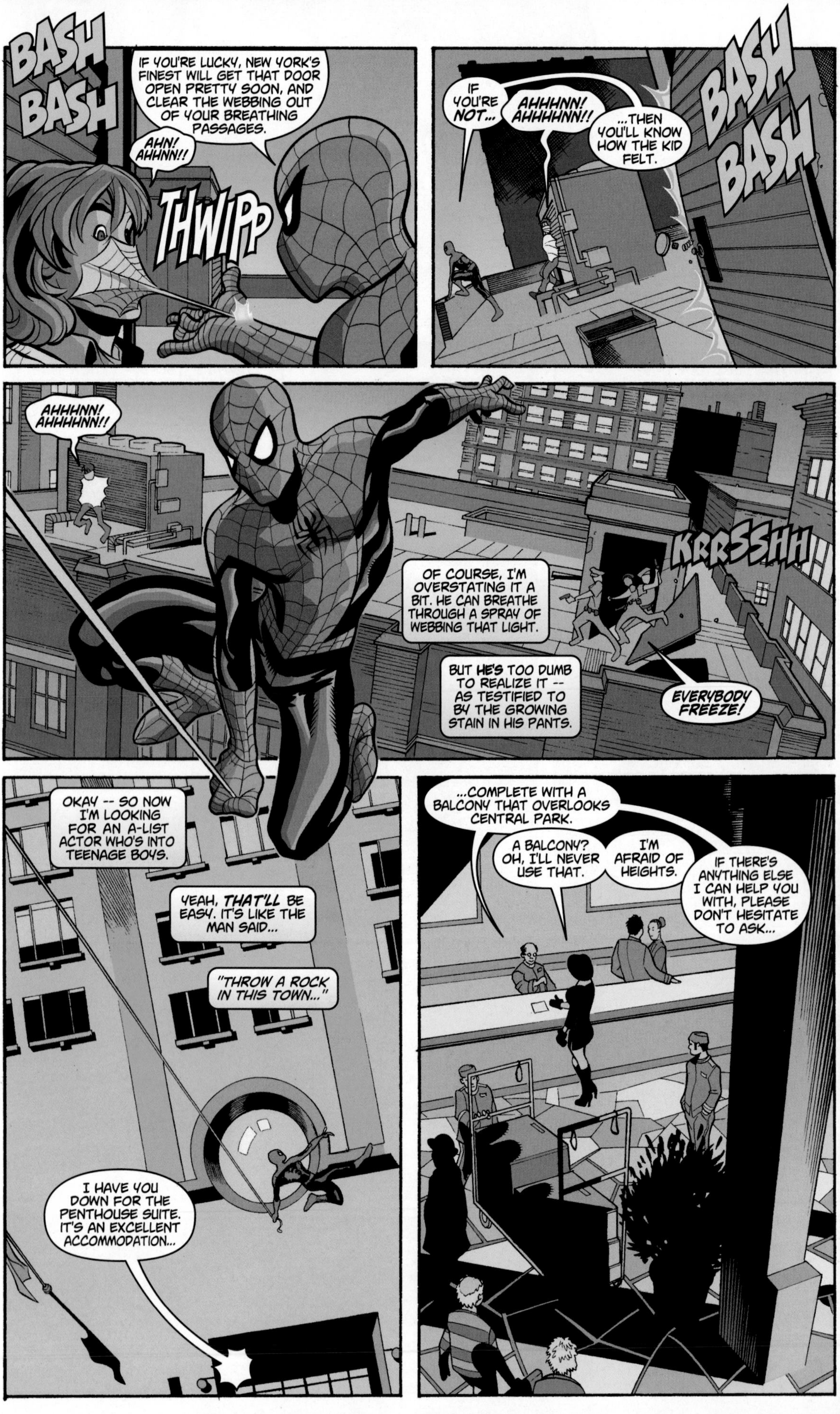
BASH BASH
IF YOU'RE LUCKY, NEW YORK'S FINEST WILL GET THAT DOOR OPEN PRETTY SOON, AND CLEAR THE WEBBING OUT OF YOUR BREATHING PASSAGES.
AHN! AHNNN!!
THWIPP
IF YOU'RE NOT...
AHHHNN! AHHHHNN!!
...THEN YOU'LL KNOW HOW THE KID FELT.
BASH BASH
AHHHNN! AHHHHNN!!
KRRSSHH
OF COURSE, I'M OVERSTATING IT A BIT. HE CAN BREATHE THROUGH A SPRAY OF WEBBING THAT LIGHT.
BUT HE'S TOO DUMB TO REALIZE IT -- AS TESTIFIED TO BY THE GROWING STAIN IN HIS PANTS.
EVERYBODY FREEZE!
OKAY -- SO NOW I'M LOOKING FOR AN A-LIST ACTOR WHO'S INTO TEENAGE BOYS.
YEAH, THAT'LL BE EASY. IT'S LIKE THE MAN SAID...
"THROW A ROCK IN THIS TOWN..."
I HAVE YOU DOWN FOR THE PENTHOUSE SUITE. IT'S AN EXCELLENT ACCOMMODATION...
...COMPLETE WITH A BALCONY THAT OVERLOOKS CENTRAL PARK.
A BALCONY? OH, I'LL NEVER USE THAT.
I'M AFRAID OF HEIGHTS.
IF THERE'S ANYTHING ELSE I CAN HELP YOU WITH, PLEASE DON'T HESITATE TO ASK...

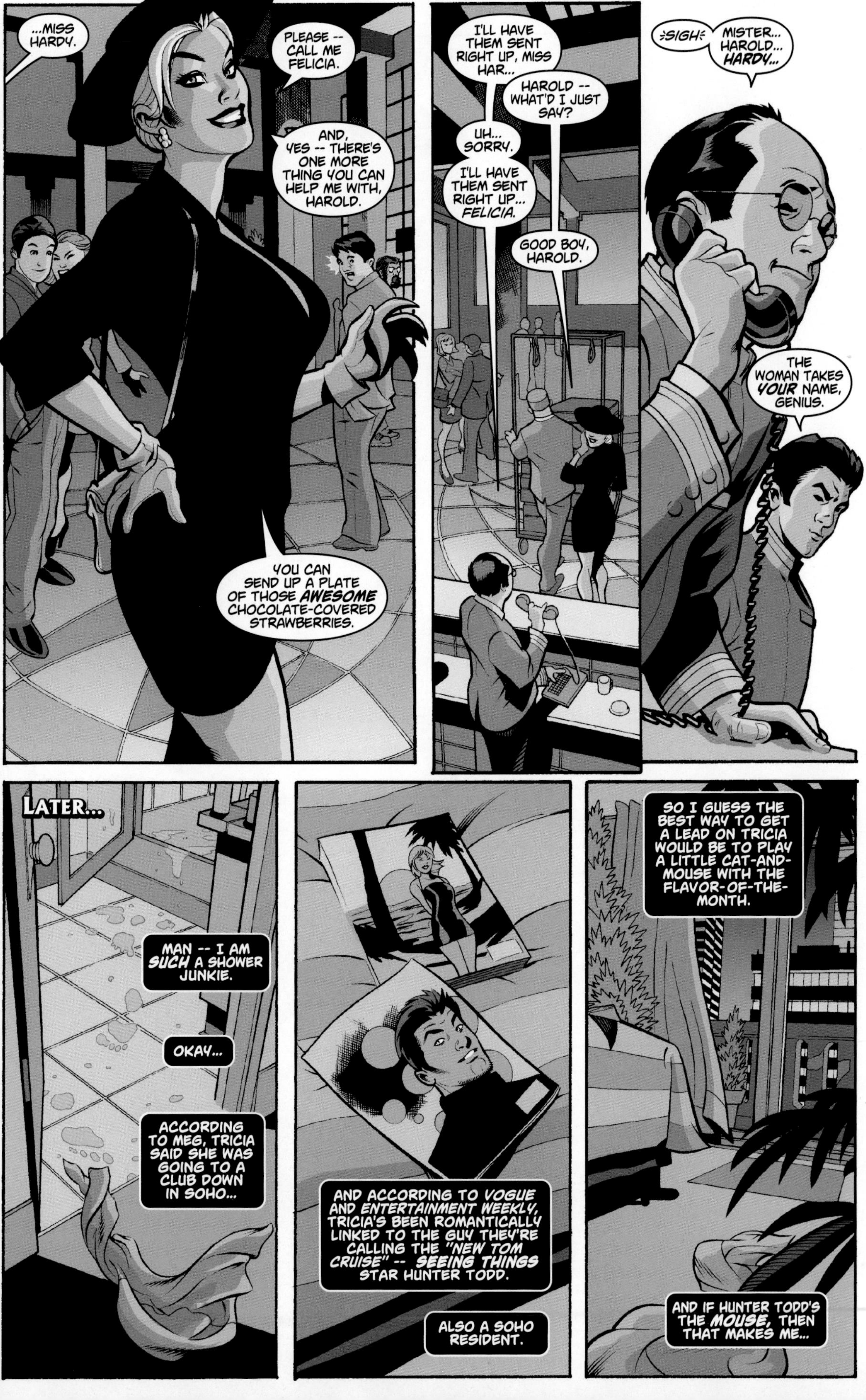
...MISS HARDY.
PLEASE -- CALL ME FELICIA.
AND, YES -- THERE'S ONE MORE THING YOU CAN HELP ME WITH, HAROLD.
YOU CAN SEND UP A PLATE OF THOSE AWESOME CHOCOLATE-COVERED STRAWBERRIES.
I'LL HAVE THEM SENT RIGHT UP, MISS HAR...
HAROLD -- WHAT'D I JUST SAY?
UH... SORRY.
I'LL HAVE THEM SENT RIGHT UP... FELICIA.
GOOD BOY, HAROLD.
SIGH
MISTER... HAROLD... HARDY...
THE WOMAN TAKES YOUR NAME, GENIUS.
LATER...
MAN -- I AM SUCH A SHOWER JUNKIE.
OKAY...
ACCORDING TO MEG, TRICIA SAID SHE WAS GOING TO A CLUB DOWN IN SOHO...
AND ACCORDING TO VOGUE AND ENTERTAINMENT WEEKLY, TRICIA'S BEEN ROMANTICALLY LINKED TO THE GUY THEY'RE CALLING THE "NEW TOM CRUISE" -- SEEING THINGS STAR HUNTER TODD.
ALSO A SOHO RESIDENT.
SO I GUESS THE BEST WAY TO GET A LEAD ON TRICIA WOULD BE TO PLAY A LITTLE CAT-AND-MOUSE WITH THE FLAVOR-OF-THE-MONTH.
AND IF HUNTER TODD'S THE MOUSE, THEN THAT MAKES ME...

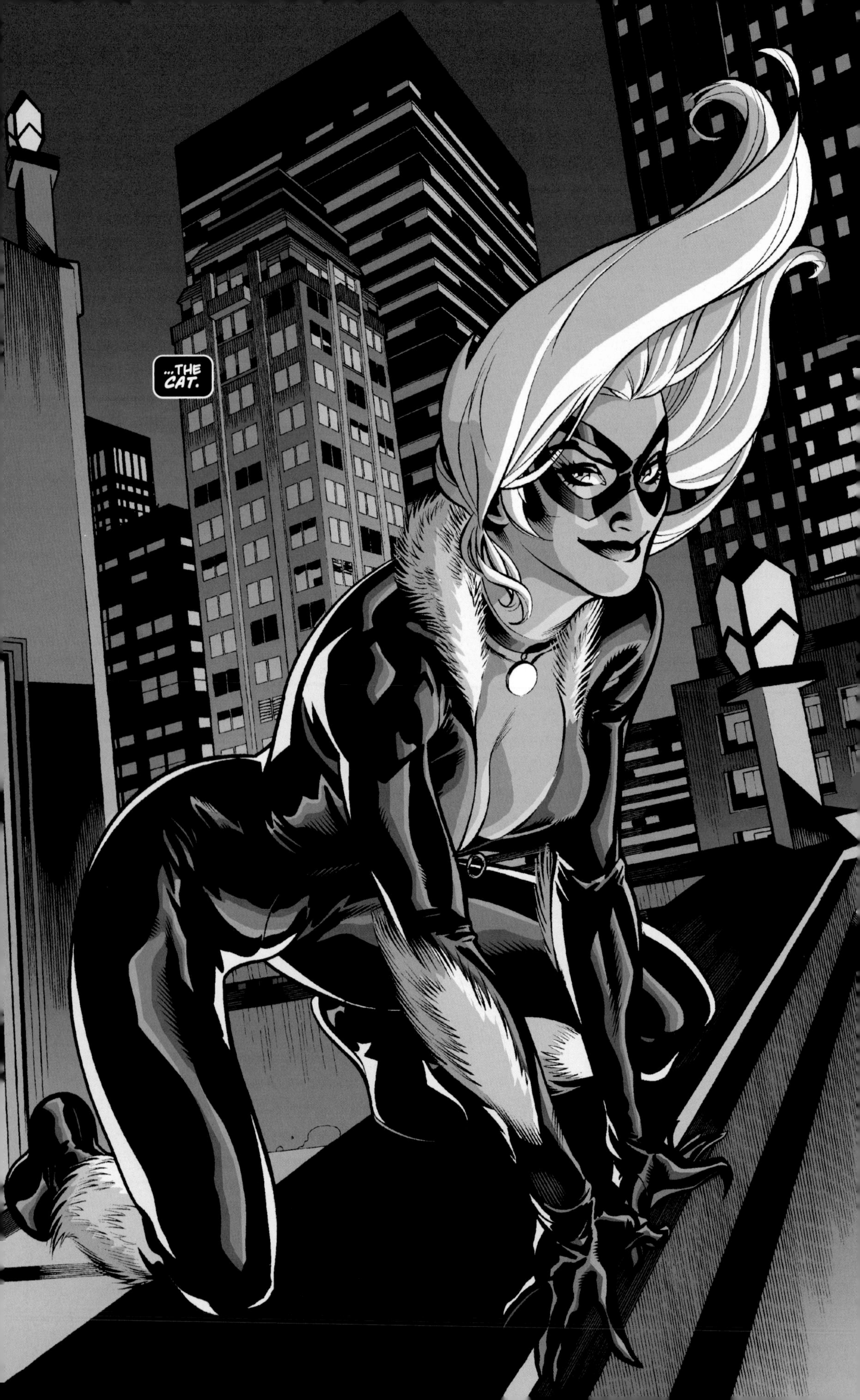
...THE CAT.

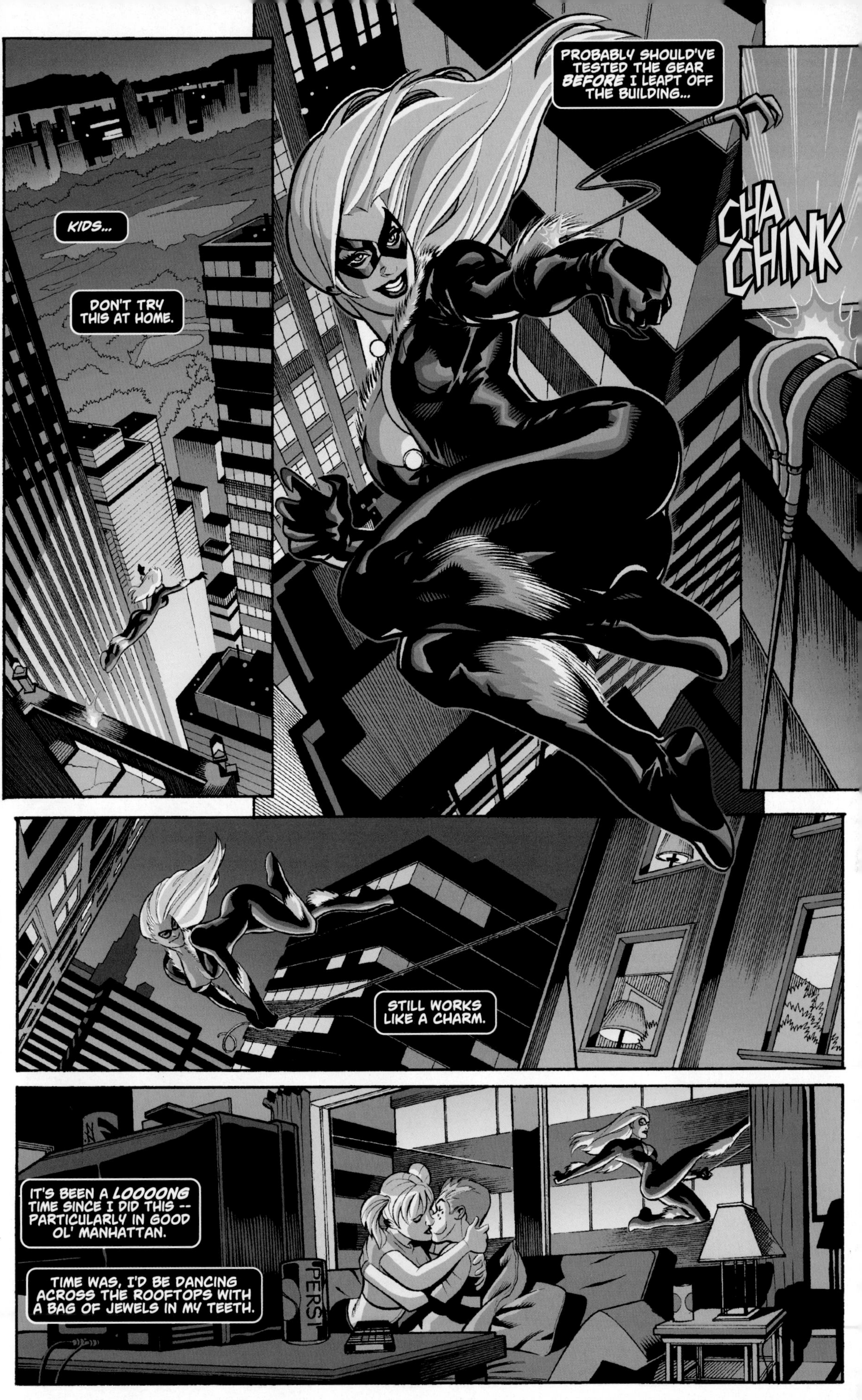
KIDS...
DON'T TRY THIS AT HOME.
PROBABLY SHOULD'VE TESTED THE GEAR *BEFORE* I LEAPT OFF THE BUILDING...
CHA CHINK
STILL WORKS LIKE A CHARM.
IT'S BEEN A *LOOOONG* TIME SINCE I DID THIS -- PARTICULARLY IN GOOD OL' MANHATTAN.
TIME WAS, I'D BE DANCING ACROSS THE ROOFTOPS WITH A BAG OF JEWELS IN MY TEETH.

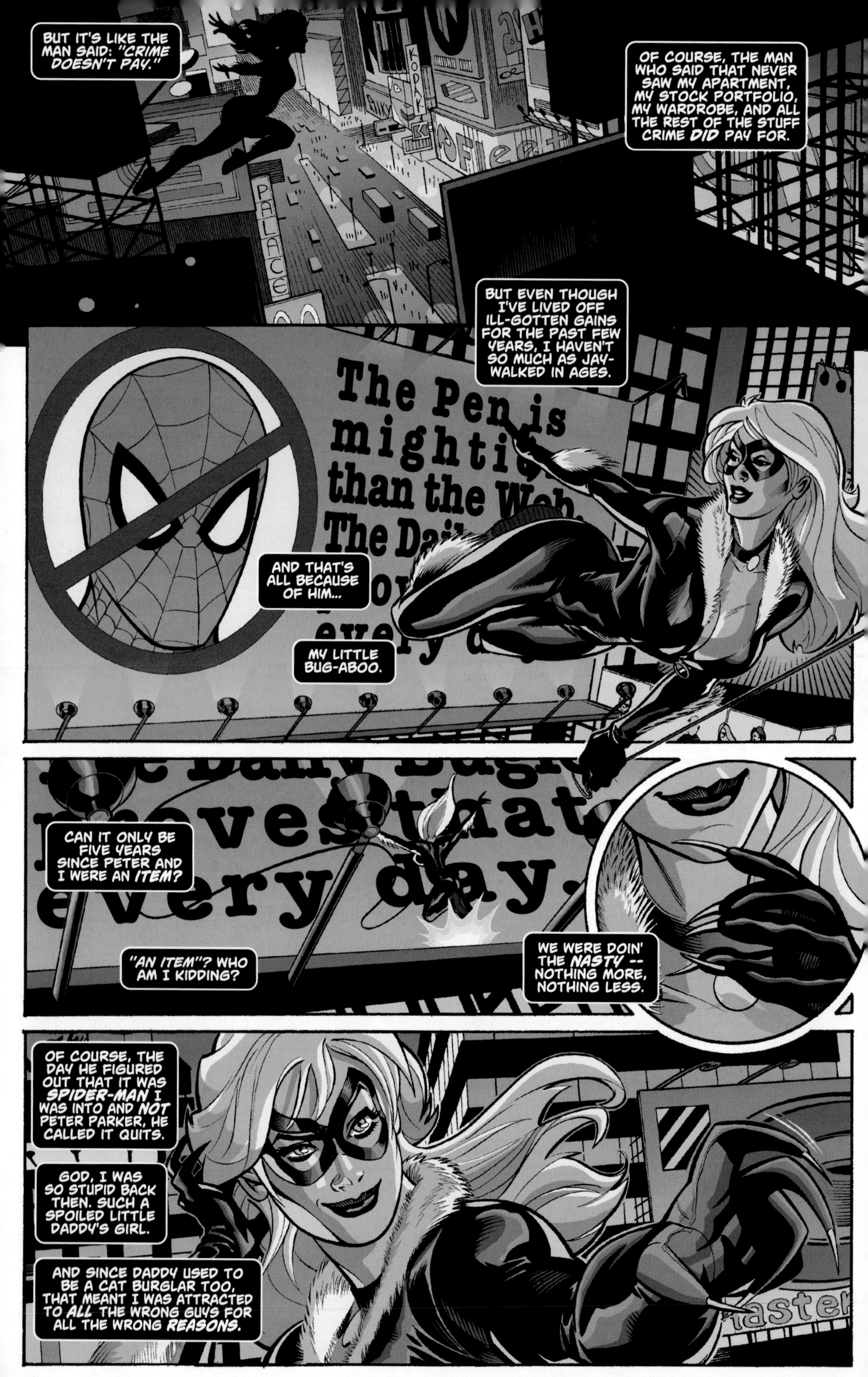
BUT IT'S LIKE THE MAN SAID: "CRIME DOESN'T PAY."
OF COURSE, THE MAN WHO SAID THAT NEVER SAW MY APARTMENT, MY STOCK PORTFOLIO, MY WARDROBE, AND ALL THE REST OF THE STUFF CRIME DID PAY FOR.
KODAK
PALACE
BUT EVEN THOUGH I'VE LIVED OFF ILL-GOTTEN GAINS FOR THE PAST FEW YEARS, I HAVEN'T SO MUCH AS JAY-WALKED IN AGES.
The Pen is
than the Web
AND THAT'S ALL BECAUSE OF HIM...
MY LITTLE BUG-ABOO.
every day.
CAN IT ONLY BE FIVE YEARS SINCE PETER AND I WERE AN ITEM?
"AN ITEM"? WHO AM I KIDDING?
WE WERE DOIN' THE NASTY -- NOTHING MORE, NOTHING LESS.
OF COURSE, THE DAY HE FIGURED OUT THAT IT WAS SPIDER-MAN I WAS INTO AND NOT PETER PARKER, HE CALLED IT QUITS.
GOD, I WAS SO STUPID BACK THEN. SUCH A SPOILED LITTLE DADDY'S GIRL.
AND SINCE DADDY USED TO BE A CAT BURGLAR TOO, THAT MEANT I WAS ATTRACTED TO ALL THE WRONG GUYS FOR ALL THE WRONG REASONS.

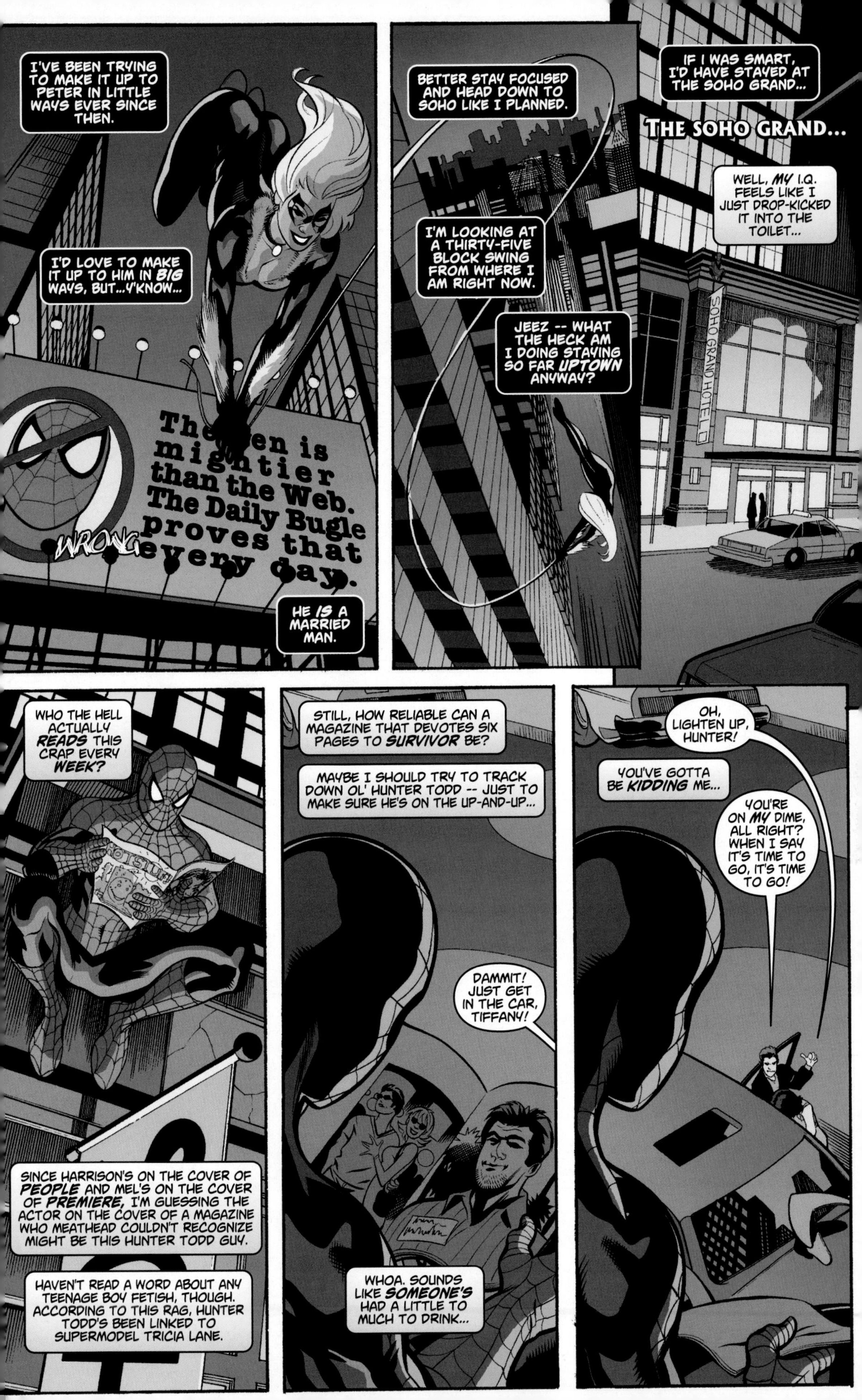
I'VE BEEN TRYING TO MAKE IT UP TO PETER IN LITTLE WAYS EVER SINCE THEN.
I'D LOVE TO MAKE IT UP TO HIM IN BIG WAYS, BUT...Y'KNOW...
The pen is mightier than the Web. The Daily Bugle proves that every day.
WRONG
HE IS A MARRIED MAN.
BETTER STAY FOCUSED AND HEAD DOWN TO SOHO LIKE I PLANNED.
I'M LOOKING AT A THIRTY-FIVE BLOCK SWING FROM WHERE I AM RIGHT NOW.
JEEZ -- WHAT THE HECK AM I DOING STAYING SO FAR UPTOWN ANYWAY?
IF I WAS SMART, I'D HAVE STAYED AT THE SOHO GRAND...
THE SOHO GRAND...
WELL, MY I.Q. FEELS LIKE I JUST DROP-KICKED IT INTO THE TOILET...
SOHO GRAND HOTEL
WHO THE HELL ACTUALLY READS THIS CRAP EVERY WEEK?
SINCE HARRISON'S ON THE COVER OF PEOPLE AND MEL'S ON THE COVER OF PREMIERE, I'M GUESSING THE ACTOR ON THE COVER OF A MAGAZINE WHO MEATHEAD COULDN'T RECOGNIZE MIGHT BE THIS HUNTER TODD GUY.
HAVEN'T READ A WORD ABOUT ANY TEENAGE BOY FETISH, THOUGH. ACCORDING TO THIS RAG, HUNTER TODD'S BEEN LINKED TO SUPERMODEL TRICIA LANE.
STILL, HOW RELIABLE CAN A MAGAZINE THAT DEVOTES SIX PAGES TO SURVIVOR BE?
MAYBE I SHOULD TRY TO TRACK DOWN OL' HUNTER TODD -- JUST TO MAKE SURE HE'S ON THE UP-AND-UP...
DAMMIT! JUST GET IN THE CAR, TIFFANY!
WHOA. SOUNDS LIKE SOMEONE'S HAD A LITTLE TO MUCH TO DRINK...
OH, LIGHTEN UP, HUNTER!
YOU'VE GOTTA BE KIDDING ME...
YOU'RE ON MY DIME, ALL RIGHT? WHEN I SAY IT'S TIME TO GO, IT'S TIME TO GO!

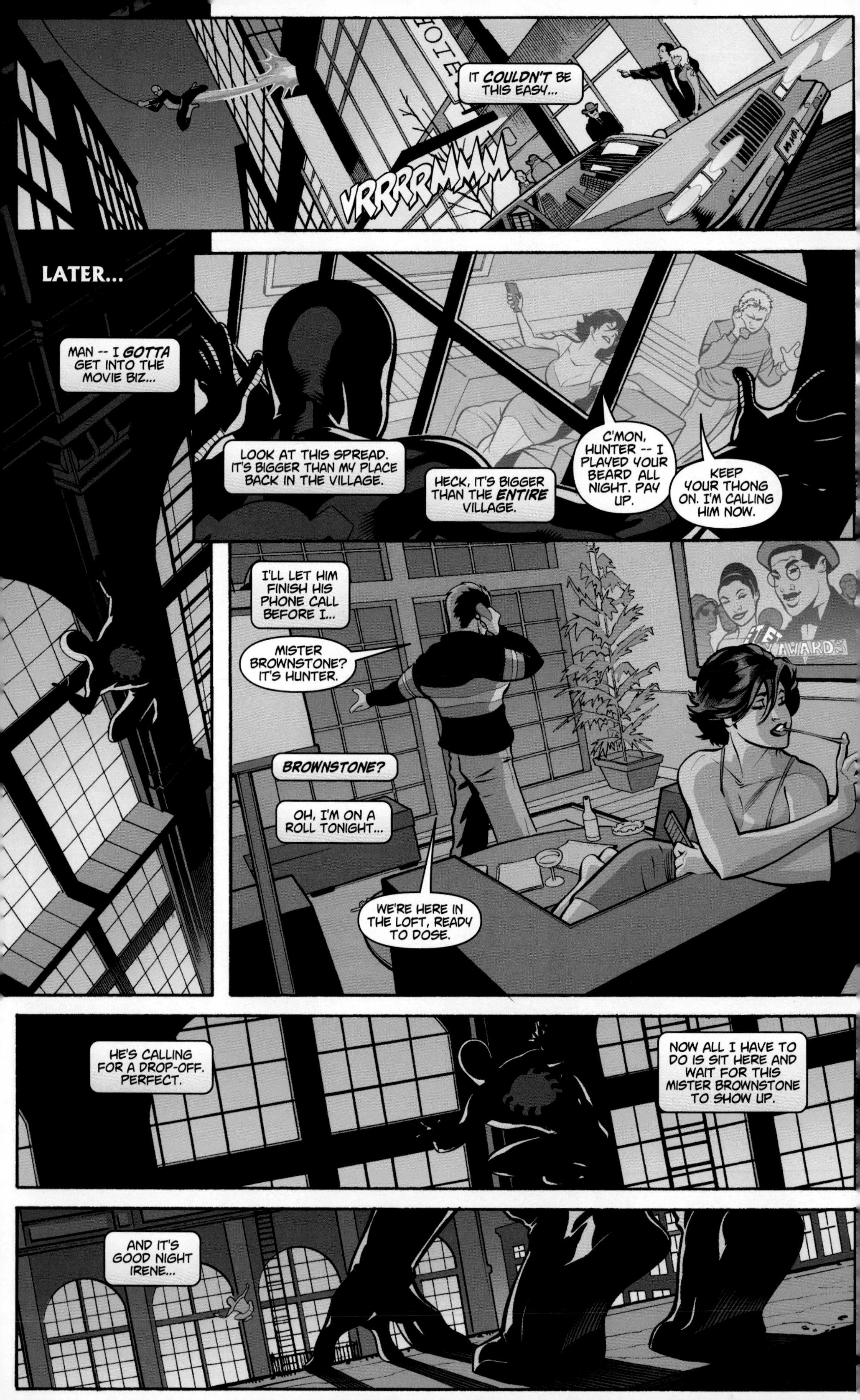

HOTE
IT COULDN'T BE THIS EASY...
VRRRRMMM
LATER...
MAN -- I GOTTA GET INTO THE MOVIE BIZ...
LOOK AT THIS SPREAD. IT'S BIGGER THAN MY PLACE BACK IN THE VILLAGE.
HECK, IT'S BIGGER THAN THE ENTIRE VILLAGE.
C'MON, HUNTER -- I PLAYED YOUR BEARD ALL NIGHT. PAY UP.
KEEP YOUR THONG ON. I'M CALLING HIM NOW.
I'LL LET HIM FINISH HIS PHONE CALL BEFORE I...
MISTER BROWNSTONE? IT'S HUNTER.
BROWNSTONE?
OH, I'M ON A ROLL TONIGHT...
WE'RE HERE IN THE LOFT, READY TO DOSE.
AWARDS
HE'S CALLING FOR A DROP-OFF. PERFECT.
NOW ALL I HAVE TO DO IS SIT HERE AND WAIT FOR THIS MISTER BROWNSTONE TO SHOW UP.
AND IT'S GOOD NIGHT IRENE...

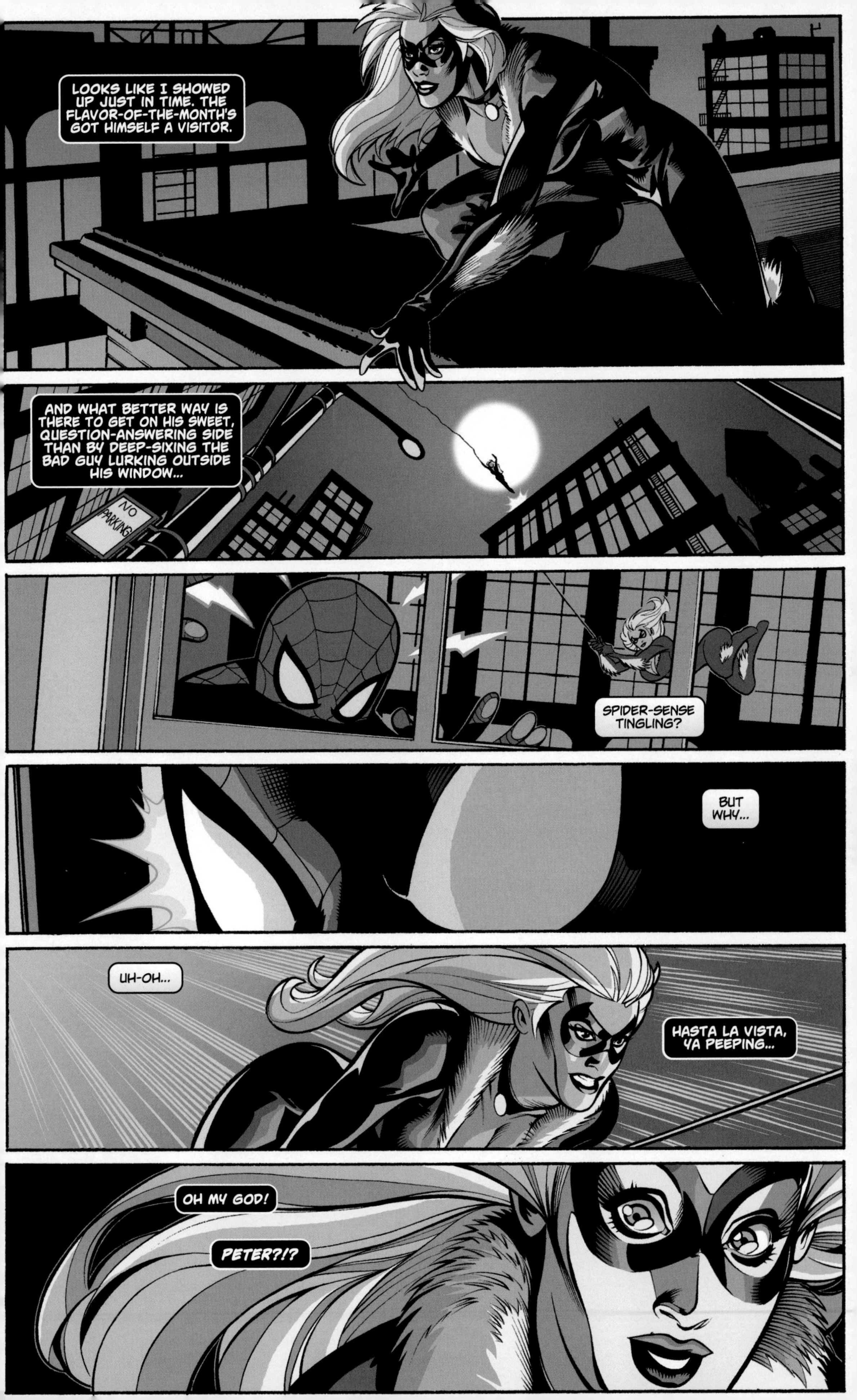
LOOKS LIKE I SHOWED UP JUST IN TIME. THE FLAVOR-OF-THE-MONTH'S GOT HIMSELF A VISITOR.
AND WHAT BETTER WAY IS THERE TO GET ON HIS SWEET, QUESTION-ANSWERING SIDE THAN BY DEEP-SIXING THE BAD GUY LURKING OUTSIDE HIS WINDOW...
NO PARKING
SPIDER-SENSE TINGLING?
BUT WHY...
UH-OH...
HASTA LA VISTA, YA PEEPING...
OH MY GOD!
PETER?!?

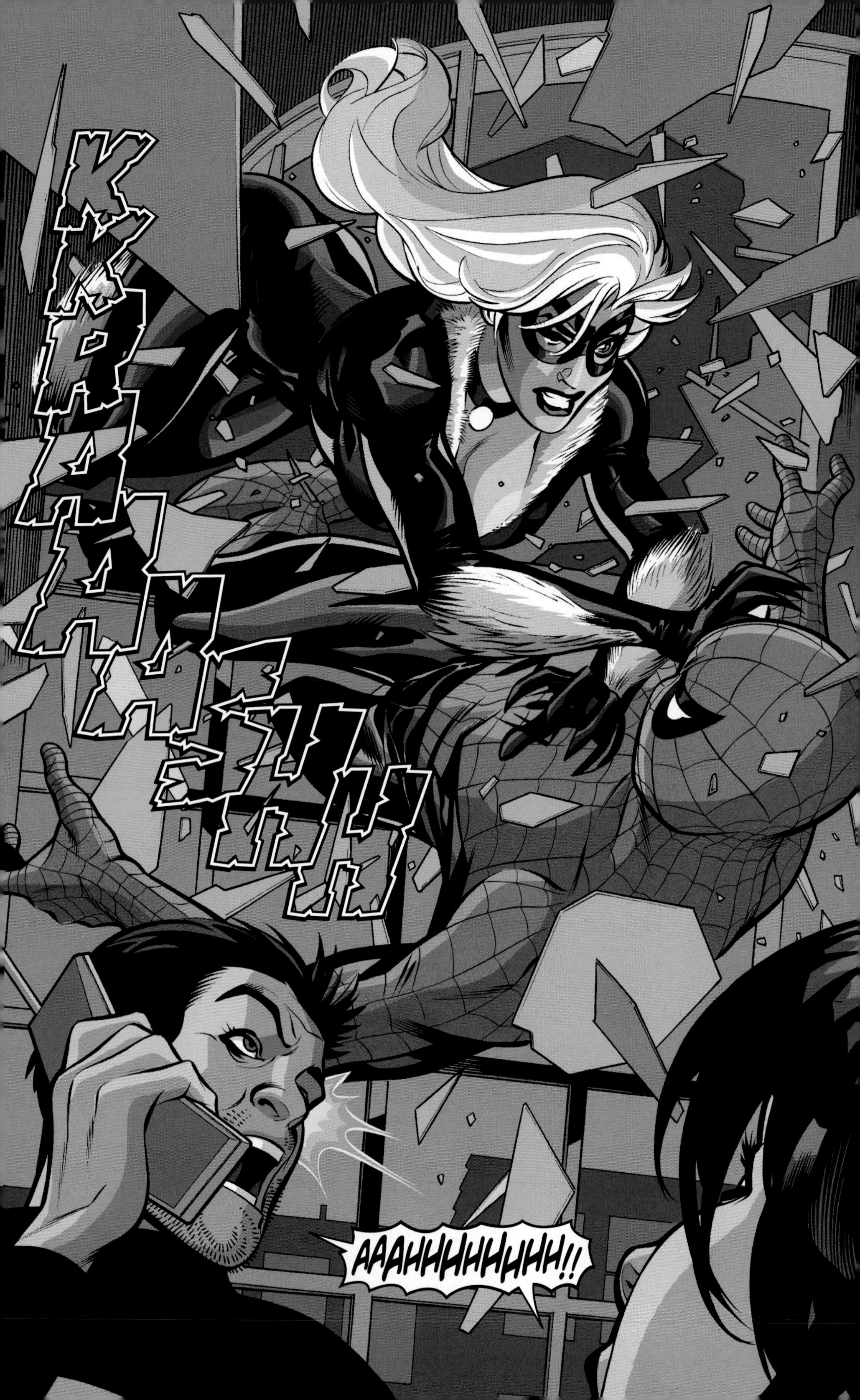
AAAHHHHHHHH!!

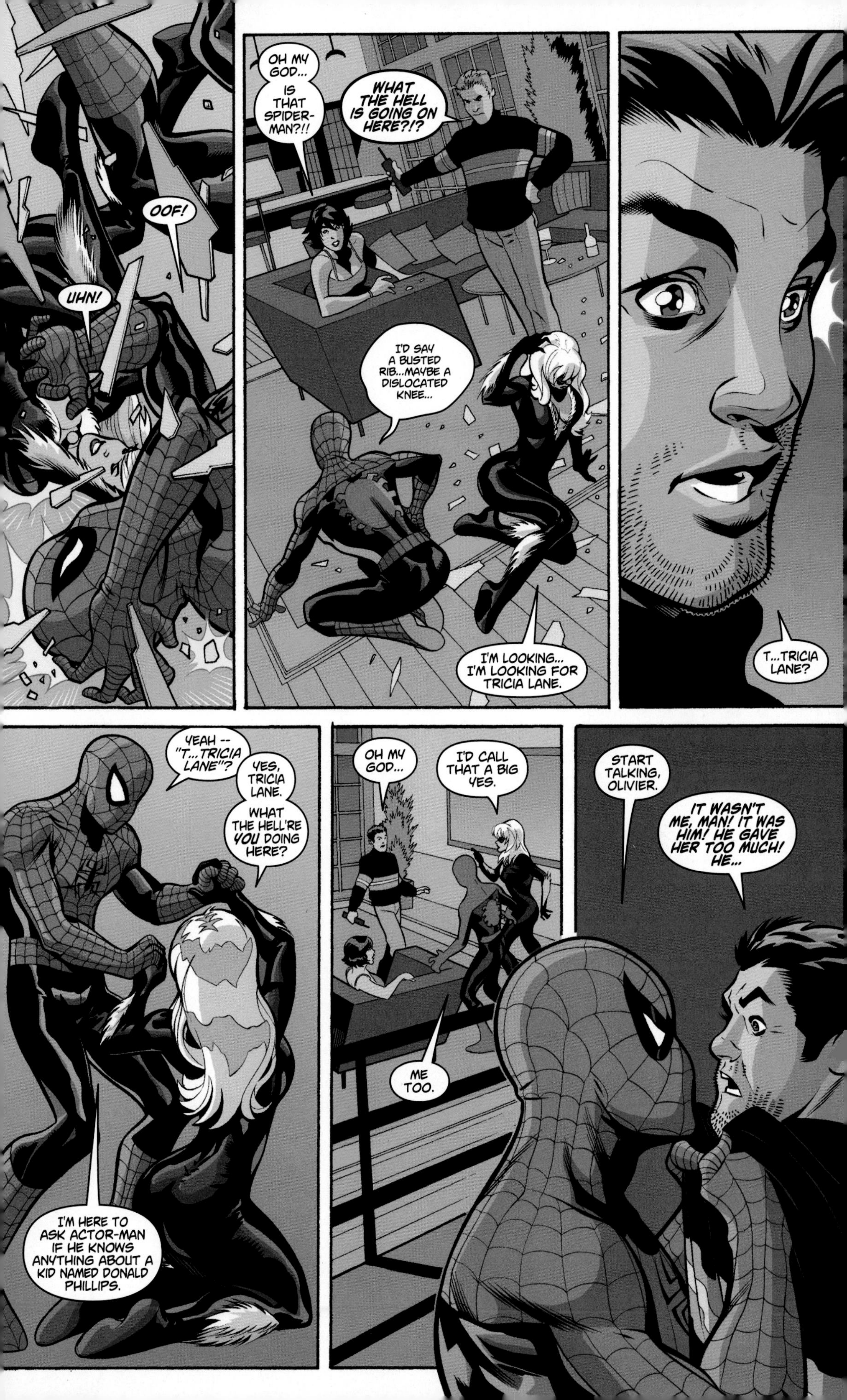
OOF!
UHN!
OH MY GOD...
IS THAT SPIDER-MAN?!!
WHAT THE HELL IS GOING ON HERE?!?
I'D SAY A BUSTED RIB...MAYBE A DISLOCATED KNEE...
I'M LOOKING... I'M LOOKING FOR TRICIA LANE.
T...TRICIA LANE?
YEAH -- "T...TRICIA LANE"?
YES, TRICIA LANE.
WHAT THE HELL'RE YOU DOING HERE?
I'M HERE TO ASK ACTOR-MAN IF HE KNOWS ANYTHING ABOUT A KID NAMED DONALD PHILLIPS.
OH MY GOD...
I'D CALL THAT A BIG YES.
ME TOO.
START TALKING, OLIVIER.
IT WASN'T ME, MAN! IT WAS HIM! HE GAVE HER TOO MUCH! HE...

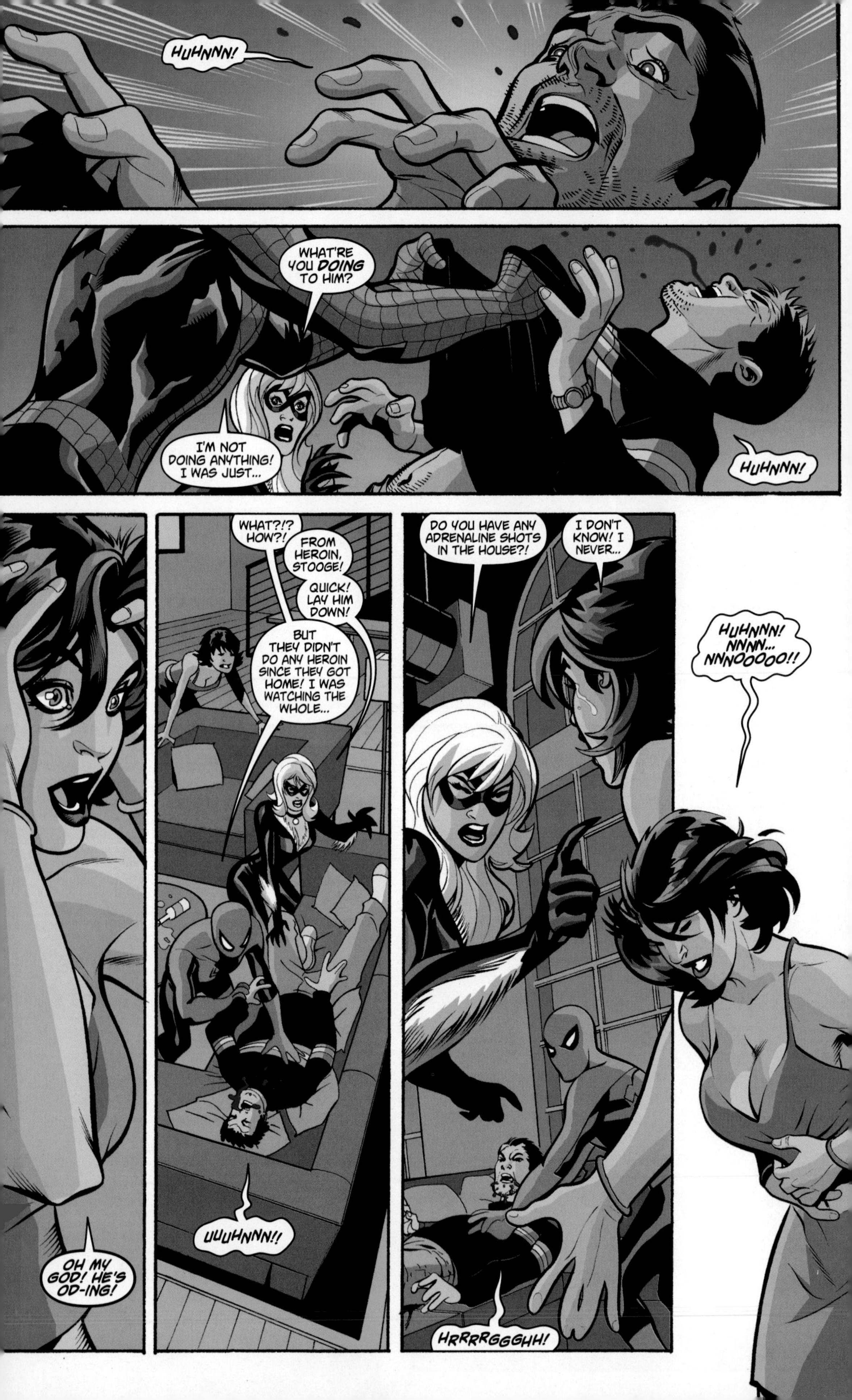
HUHNNN!
WHAT'RE YOU DOING TO HIM?
I'M NOT DOING ANYTHING! I WAS JUST...
HUHNNN!
OH MY GOD! HE'S OD-ING!
WHAT?!? HOW?!
FROM HEROIN, STOOGE!
QUICK! LAY HIM DOWN!
BUT THEY DIDN'T DO ANY HEROIN SINCE THEY GOT HOME! I WAS WATCHING THE WHOLE...
UUUHNNN!!
DO YOU HAVE ANY ADRENALINE SHOTS IN THE HOUSE?!
I DON'T KNOW! I NEVER...
HUHNNN! NNNN... NNNOOOOO!!
HRRRRGGGHH!

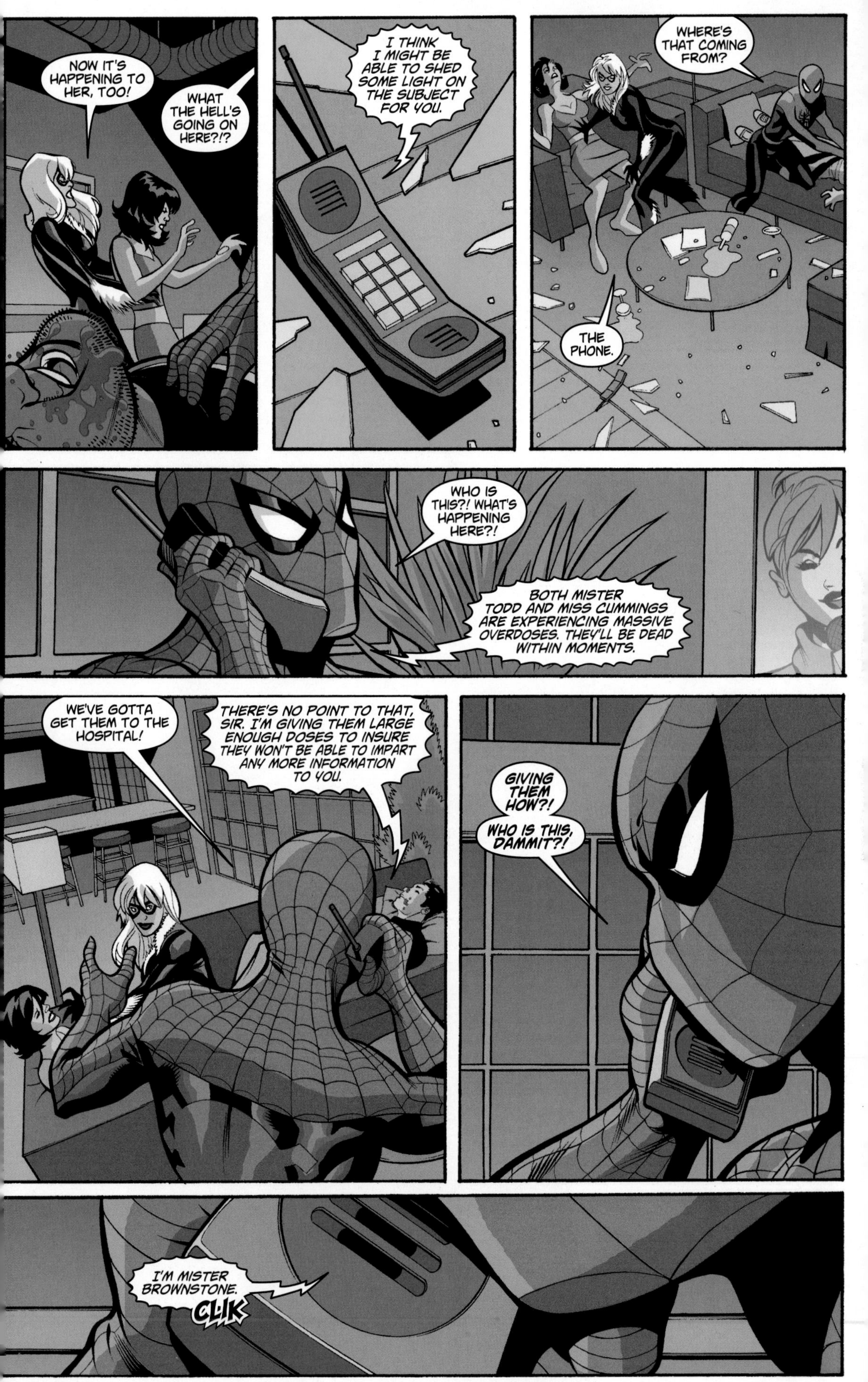
NOW IT'S HAPPENING TO HER, TOO!
WHAT THE HELL'S GOING ON HERE?!?
I THINK I MIGHT BE ABLE TO SHED SOME LIGHT ON THE SUBJECT FOR YOU.
WHERE'S THAT COMING FROM?
THE PHONE.
WHO IS THIS?! WHAT'S HAPPENING HERE?!
BOTH MISTER TODD AND MISS CUMMINGS ARE EXPERIENCING MASSIVE OVERDOSES. THEY'LL BE DEAD WITHIN MOMENTS.
WE'VE GOTTA GET THEM TO THE HOSPITAL!
THERE'S NO POINT TO THAT, SIR. I'M GIVING THEM LARGE ENOUGH DOSES TO INSURE THEY WON'T BE ABLE TO IMPART ANY MORE INFORMATION TO YOU.
GIVING THEM HOW?!
WHO IS THIS, DAMMIT?!
I'M MISTER BROWNSTONE.
CLIK

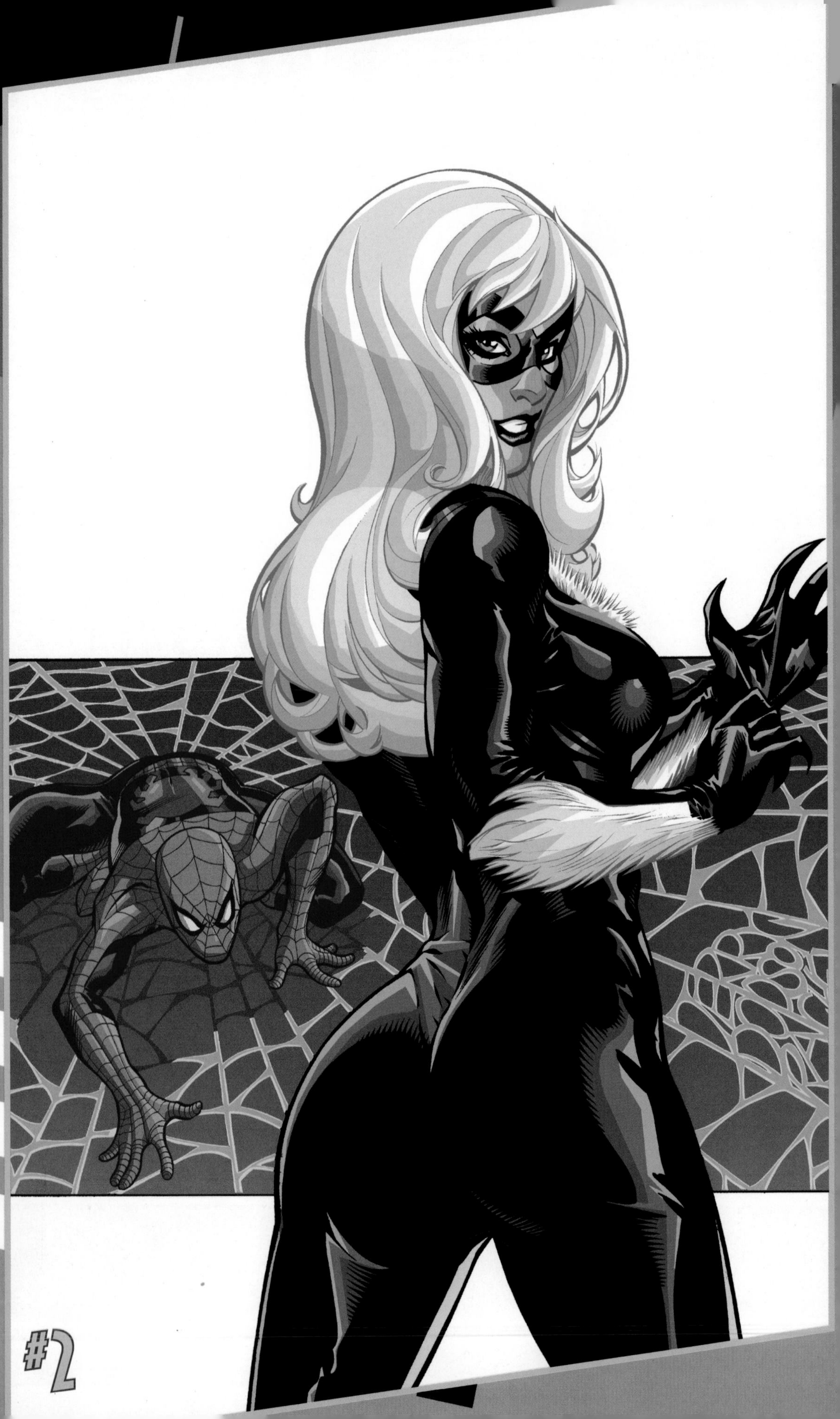
#2

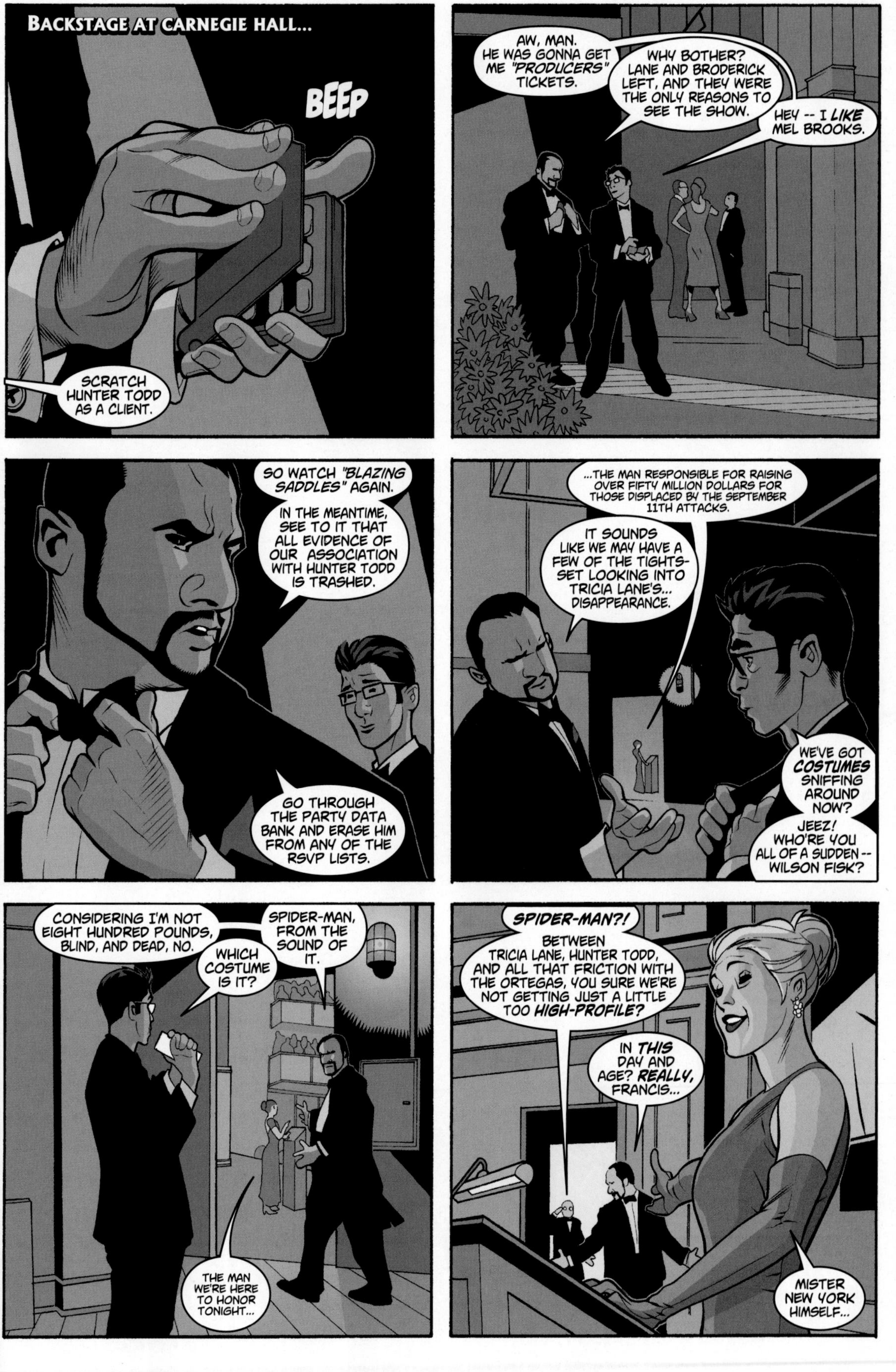
BACKSTAGE AT CARNEGIE HALL...
BEEP
SCRATCH HUNTER TODD AS A CLIENT.
AW, MAN. HE WAS GONNA GET ME "PRODUCERS" TICKETS.
WHY BOTHER? LANE AND BRODERICK LEFT, AND THEY WERE THE ONLY REASONS TO SEE THE SHOW.
HEY -- I LIKE MEL BROOKS.
SO WATCH "BLAZING SADDLES" AGAIN.
IN THE MEANTIME, SEE TO IT THAT ALL EVIDENCE OF OUR ASSOCIATION WITH HUNTER TODD IS TRASHED.
GO THROUGH THE PARTY DATA BANK AND ERASE HIM FROM ANY OF THE RSVP LISTS.
...THE MAN RESPONSIBLE FOR RAISING OVER FIFTY MILLION DOLLARS FOR THOSE DISPLACED BY THE SEPTEMBER 11TH ATTACKS.
IT SOUNDS LIKE WE MAY HAVE A FEW OF THE TIGHTS-SET LOOKING INTO TRICIA LANE'S... DISAPPEARANCE.
WE'VE GOT COSTUMES SNIFFING AROUND NOW?
JEEZ! WHO'RE YOU ALL OF A SUDDEN -- WILSON FISK?
CONSIDERING I'M NOT EIGHT HUNDRED POUNDS, BLIND, AND DEAD, NO.
WHICH COSTUME IS IT?
SPIDER-MAN, FROM THE SOUND OF IT.
THE MAN WE'RE HERE TO HONOR TONIGHT...
SPIDER-MAN?!
BETWEEN TRICIA LANE, HUNTER TODD, AND ALL THAT FRICTION WITH THE ORTEGAS, YOU SURE WE'RE NOT GETTING JUST A LITTLE TOO HIGH-PROFILE?
IN THIS DAY AND AGE? REALLY, FRANCIS...
MISTER NEW YORK HIMSELF...

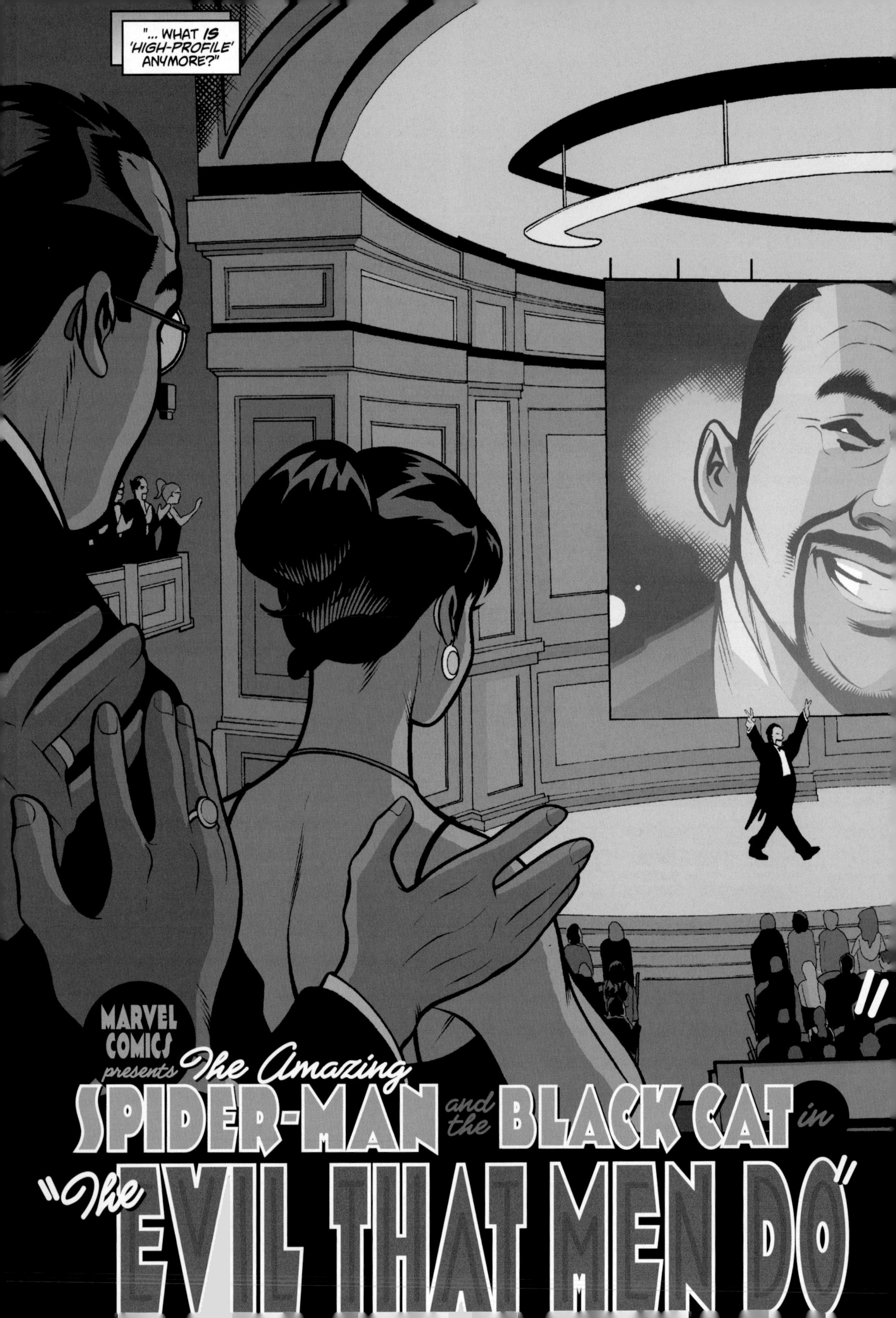
"... WHAT IS 'HIGH-PROFILE' ANYMORE?"
MARVEL COMICS presents The Amazing SPIDER-MAN and the BLACK CAT in
"The EVIL THAT MEN DO"

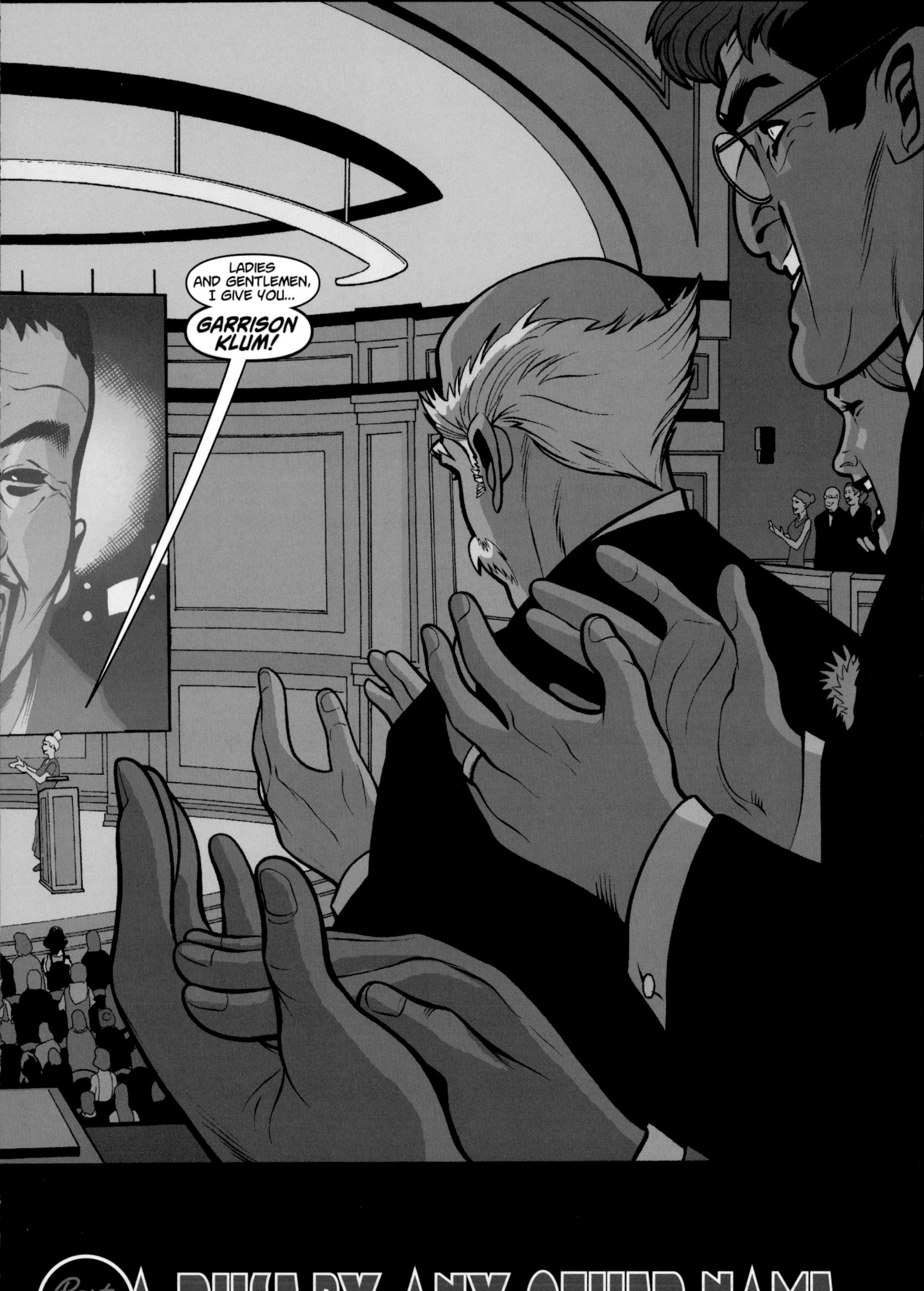
LADIES AND GENTLEMEN, I GIVE YOU...
GARRISON KLUM!

Part Two A RUSE BY ANY OTHER NAME...

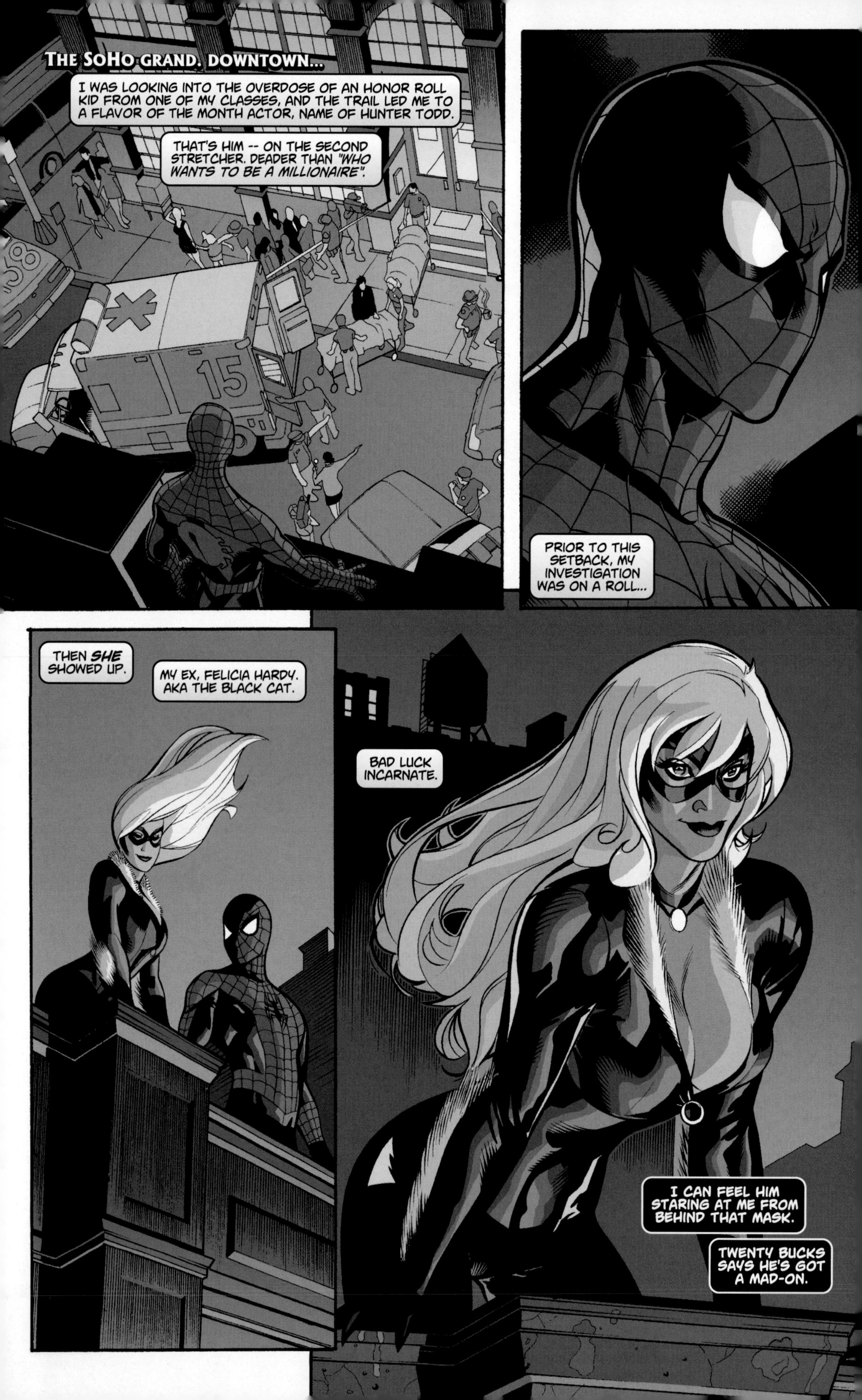
THE SOHO GRAND. DOWNTOWN...
I WAS LOOKING INTO THE OVERDOSE OF AN HONOR ROLL KID FROM ONE OF MY CLASSES, AND THE TRAIL LED ME TO A FLAVOR OF THE MONTH ACTOR, NAME OF HUNTER TODD.
THAT'S HIM -- ON THE SECOND STRETCHER. DEADER THAN "WHO WANTS TO BE A MILLIONAIRE".
PRIOR TO THIS SETBACK, MY INVESTIGATION WAS ON A ROLL...
THEN SHE SHOWED UP.
MY EX, FELICIA HARDY. AKA THE BLACK CAT.
BAD LUCK INCARNATE.
I CAN FEEL HIM STARING AT ME FROM BEHIND THAT MASK.
TWENTY BUCKS SAYS HE'S GOT A MAD-ON.

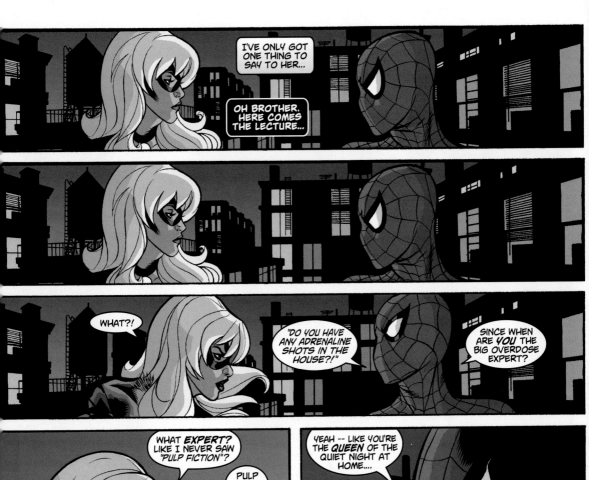

I'VE ONLY GOT ONE THING TO SAY TO HER...

OH BROTHER. HERE COMES THE LECTURE...

WHAT?!

"DO YOU HAVE ANY ADRENALINE SHOTS IN THE HOUSE?!"

SINCE WHEN ARE *YOU* THE BIG OVERDOSE EXPERT?

WHAT *EXPERT*? LIKE I NEVER SAW "PULP FICTION"?

PULP WHAT NOW?

GOOD GOD, PETER YOU CAN'T SPEND YOUR ENTIRE LIFE FIGHTING THE LIZARD OR ELECTRO. SOMETIMES, YOU'VE GOTTA TAKE A DAY OFF AND JUST GO TO THE MOVIES.

HELL, EVEN RENT ONE.

YEAH -- LIKE YOU'RE THE *QUEEN* OF THE QUIET NIGHT AT HOME....

WHAT'S *THAT* SUPPOSED TO MEAN?

IT MEANS THAT ONE OF US HERE...

AND I'M NOT NAMING NAMES...

BUT *ONE* OF US HERE CALLED IT QUITS ON OUR RELATIONSHIP BECAUSE SHE WAS IN LOVE WITH THE SPECTACULAR SPIDER-MAN -- NOT PLAIN OL' PETER PARKER.

GOOD GOD. *THIS* AGAIN...

I'M JUST SAYING, IS ALL.

WHAT DO YOU *WANT* FROM ME? I WAS A *CHILD.*

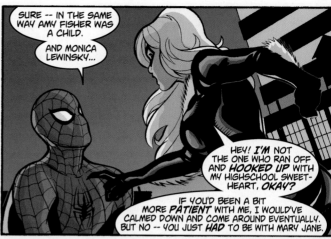

SURE -- IN THE SAME WAY AMY FISHER WAS A CHILD.

AND MONICA LEWINSKY...

HEY! *I'M* NOT THE ONE WHO RAN OFF AND *HOOKED UP* WITH MY HIGHSCHOOL SWEET-HEART, *OKAY?*

IF YOU'D BEEN A BIT MORE *PATIENT* WITH ME, I WOULD'VE CALMED DOWN AND COME AROUND EVENTUALLY. BUT NO -- YOU JUST *HAD* TO BE WITH MARY JANE.

BEST DECISION I'VE EVER MADE.

GOOD FOR *YOU.* BUT THEN DON'T GO BUSTING MY CHOPS ABOUT CRAP I DID TO YOU FIVE YEARS AGO, IF YOU'RE SO DAMN HAPPY WITH MARY *PLAIN.*

MAN OH MAN. IT'S NEVER "HEY, FELICIA -- YOU SURE SAVED MY BUTT THAT ONE TIME AGAINST SMYTHE'S SPIDER SLAYERS." OR "YOU KNOW, IT WAS SO SWEET WHEN YOU WENT THROUGH THAT SURGERY TO GET THOSE BAD LUCK POWERS JUST SO WE COULD PARTNER UP AND YOU COULD WATCH MY BACK IN THE FIELD."

ALL I EVER GET OUTTA YOU IS "YOU LOVED SPIDER-MAN, NOT ME! BOO-FRIGGIN'-HOO!"

MAN, I JUST WISH...

I JUST...

OOO, YOU CAN *REALLY* TICK ME OFF SOMETIMES!

HEY. FELICIA.

YOU SURE SAVED MY BUTT THAT ONE TIME AGAINST SMYTHE'S SPIDER SLAYERS.

AND Y'KNOW, IT WAS SO SWEET WHEN YOU WENT THROUGH THAT SURGERY TO GET BAD LUCK POWERS JUST SO WE COULD PARTNER UP AND YOU COULD WATCH MY BACK IN THE FIELD.

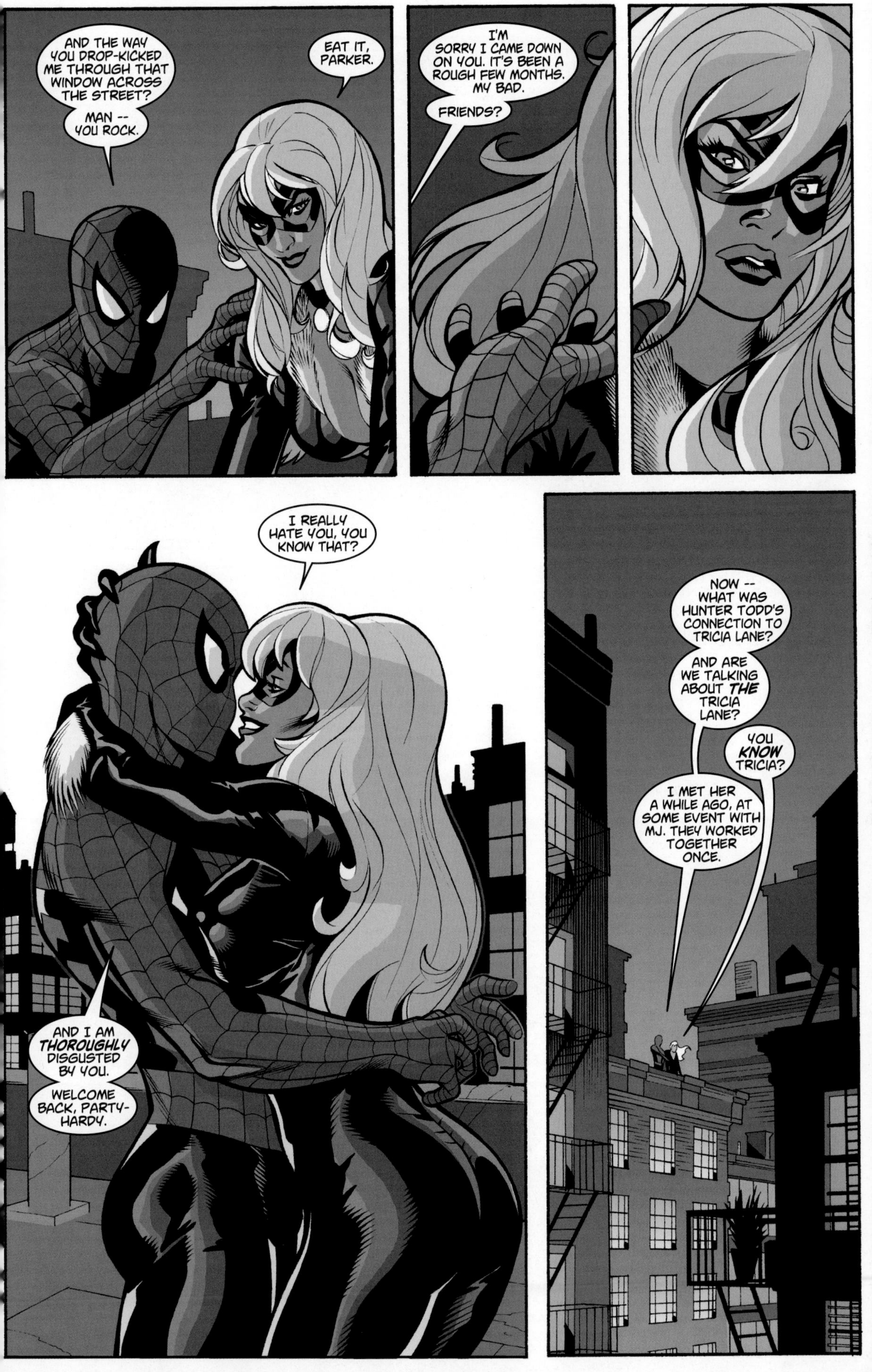
AND THE WAY YOU DROP-KICKED ME THROUGH THAT WINDOW ACROSS THE STREET?
MAN -- YOU ROCK.
EAT IT, PARKER.
I'M SORRY I CAME DOWN ON YOU. IT'S BEEN A ROUGH FEW MONTHS. MY BAD.
FRIENDS?
I REALLY HATE YOU, YOU KNOW THAT?
AND I AM *THOROUGHLY* DISGUSTED BY YOU.
WELCOME BACK, PARTY-HARDY.
NOW -- WHAT WAS HUNTER TODD'S CONNECTION TO TRICIA LANE?
AND ARE WE TALKING ABOUT *THE* TRICIA LANE?
YOU *KNOW* TRICIA?
I MET HER A WHILE AGO, AT SOME EVENT WITH MJ. THEY WORKED TOGETHER ONCE.

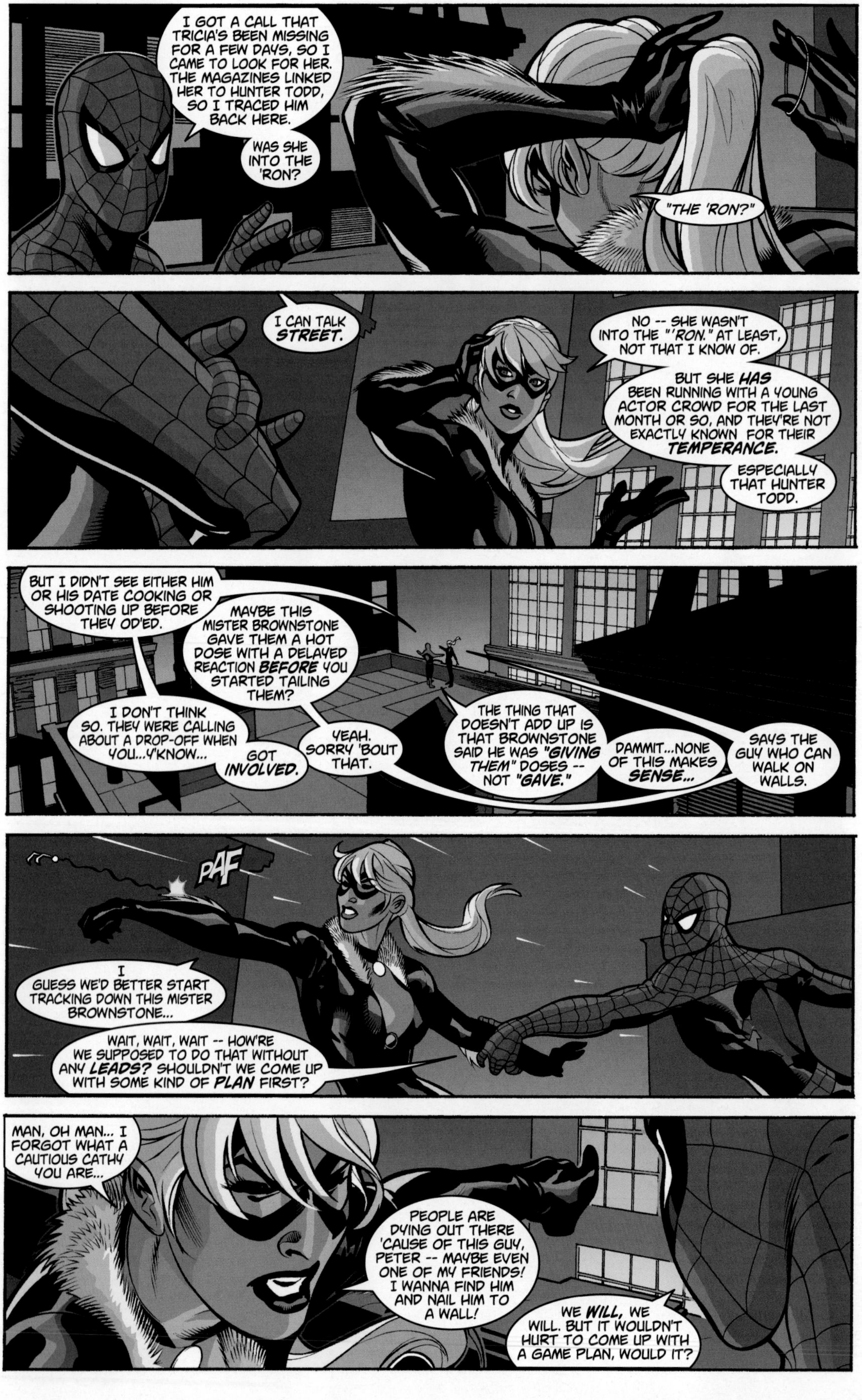

I GOT A CALL THAT TRICIA'S BEEN MISSING FOR A FEW DAYS, SO I CAME TO LOOK FOR HER. THE MAGAZINES LINKED HER TO HUNTER TODD, SO I TRACED HIM BACK HERE.
WAS SHE INTO THE 'RON?
"THE 'RON?"
I CAN TALK STREET.
NO -- SHE WASN'T INTO THE "'RON." AT LEAST, NOT THAT I KNOW OF.
BUT SHE HAS BEEN RUNNING WITH A YOUNG ACTOR CROWD FOR THE LAST MONTH OR SO, AND THEY'RE NOT EXACTLY KNOWN FOR THEIR TEMPERANCE.
ESPECIALLY THAT HUNTER TODD.
BUT I DIDN'T SEE EITHER HIM OR HIS DATE COOKING OR SHOOTING UP BEFORE THEY OD'ED.
MAYBE THIS MISTER BROWNSTONE GAVE THEM A HOT DOSE WITH A DELAYED REACTION BEFORE YOU STARTED TAILING THEM?
I DON'T THINK SO. THEY WERE CALLING ABOUT A DROP-OFF WHEN YOU...Y'KNOW...
GOT INVOLVED.
YEAH. SORRY 'BOUT THAT.
THE THING THAT DOESN'T ADD UP IS THAT BROWNSTONE SAID HE WAS "GIVING THEM" DOSES -- NOT "GAVE."
DAMMIT...NONE OF THIS MAKES SENSE...
SAYS THE GUY WHO CAN WALK ON WALLS.
PAF
I GUESS WE'D BETTER START TRACKING DOWN THIS MISTER BROWNSTONE...
WAIT, WAIT, WAIT -- HOW'RE WE SUPPOSED TO DO THAT WITHOUT ANY LEADS? SHOULDN'T WE COME UP WITH SOME KIND OF PLAN FIRST?
MAN, OH MAN... I FORGOT WHAT A CAUTIOUS CATHY YOU ARE...
PEOPLE ARE DYING OUT THERE 'CAUSE OF THIS GUY, PETER -- MAYBE EVEN ONE OF MY FRIENDS! I WANNA FIND HIM AND NAIL HIM TO A WALL!
WE WILL, WE WILL. BUT IT WOULDN'T HURT TO COME UP WITH A GAME PLAN, WOULD IT?

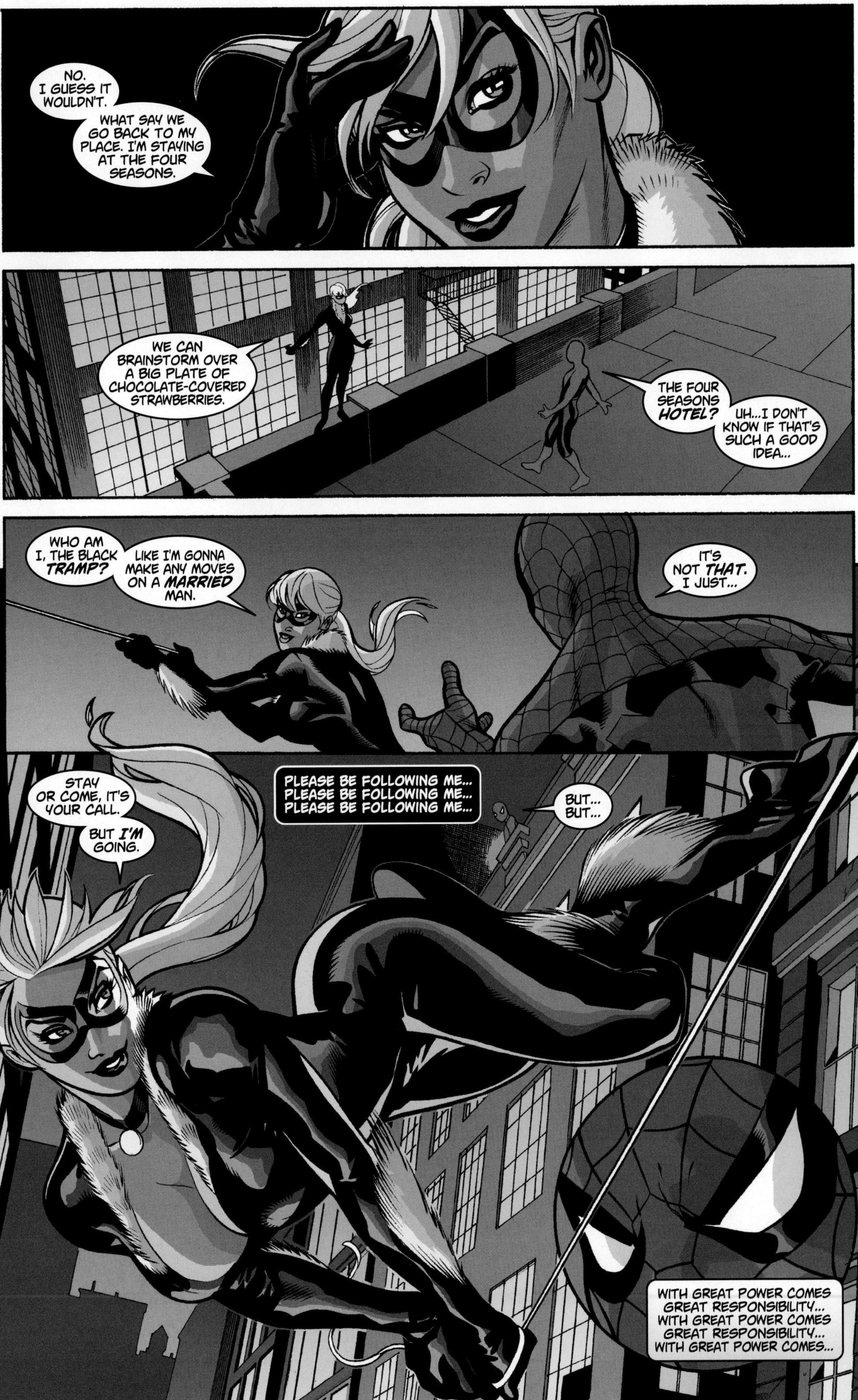
NO. I GUESS IT WOULDN'T.
WHAT SAY WE GO BACK TO MY PLACE. I'M STAYING AT THE FOUR SEASONS.
WE CAN BRAINSTORM OVER A BIG PLATE OF CHOCOLATE-COVERED STRAWBERRIES.
THE FOUR SEASONS HOTEL?
UH...I DON'T KNOW IF THAT'S SUCH A GOOD IDEA...
WHO AM I, THE BLACK TRAMP?
LIKE I'M GONNA MAKE ANY MOVES ON A MARRIED MAN.
IT'S NOT THAT. I JUST...
STAY OR COME, IT'S YOUR CALL.
BUT I'M GOING.
PLEASE BE FOLLOWING ME... PLEASE BE FOLLOWING ME... PLEASE BE FOLLOWING ME...
BUT... BUT...
WITH GREAT POWER COMES GREAT RESPONSIBILITY... WITH GREAT POWER COMES GREAT RESPONSIBILITY... WITH GREAT POWER COMES...

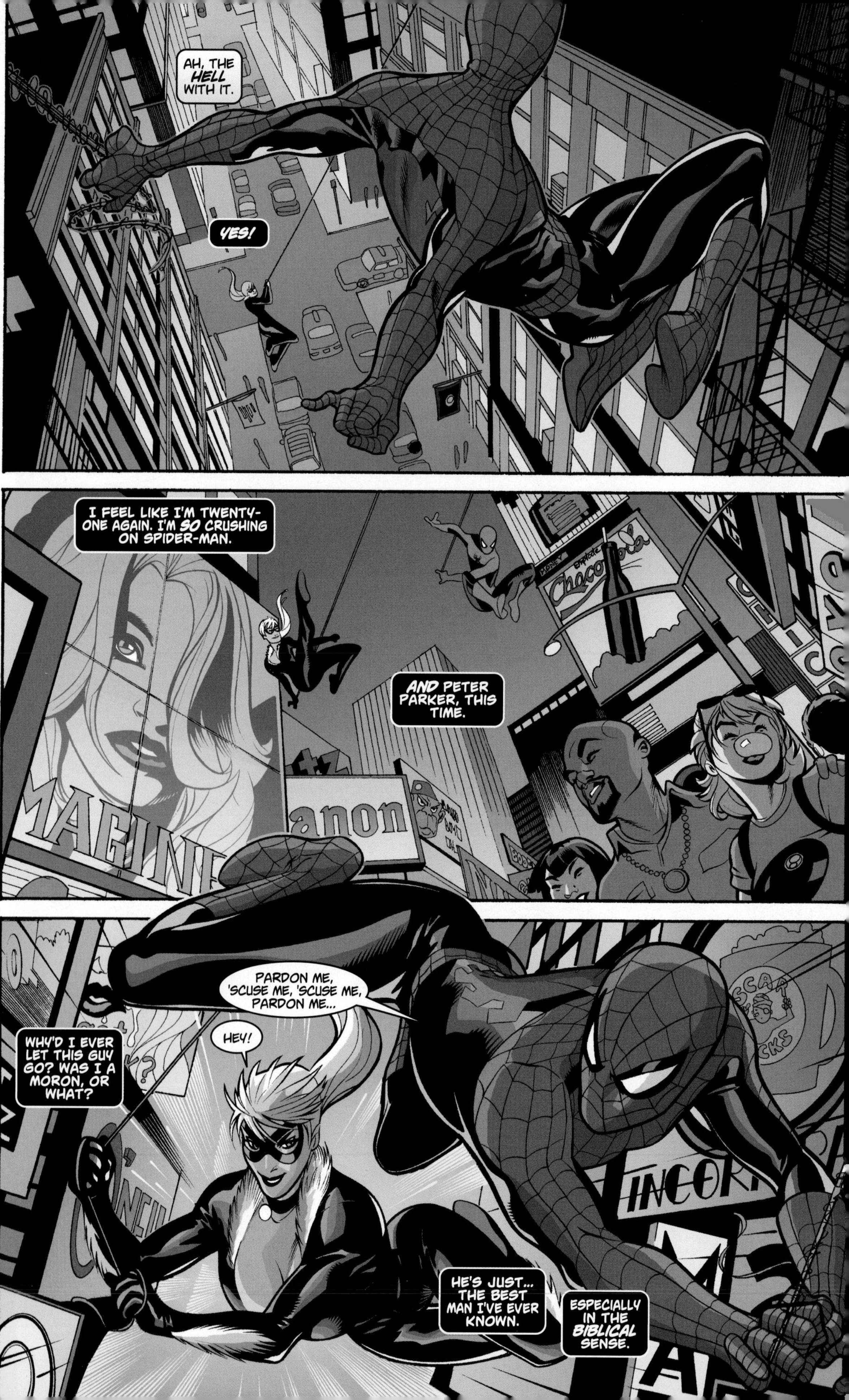
AH, THE HELL WITH IT.
YES!
I FEEL LIKE I'M TWENTY-ONE AGAIN. I'M SO CRUSHING ON SPIDER-MAN.
AND PETER PARKER, THIS TIME.
PARDON ME, 'SCUSE ME, 'SCUSE ME, PARDON ME...
HEY!
WHY'D I EVER LET THIS GUY GO? WAS I A MORON, OR WHAT?
HE'S JUST... THE BEST MAN I'VE EVER KNOWN.
ESPECIALLY IN THE BIBLICAL SENSE.

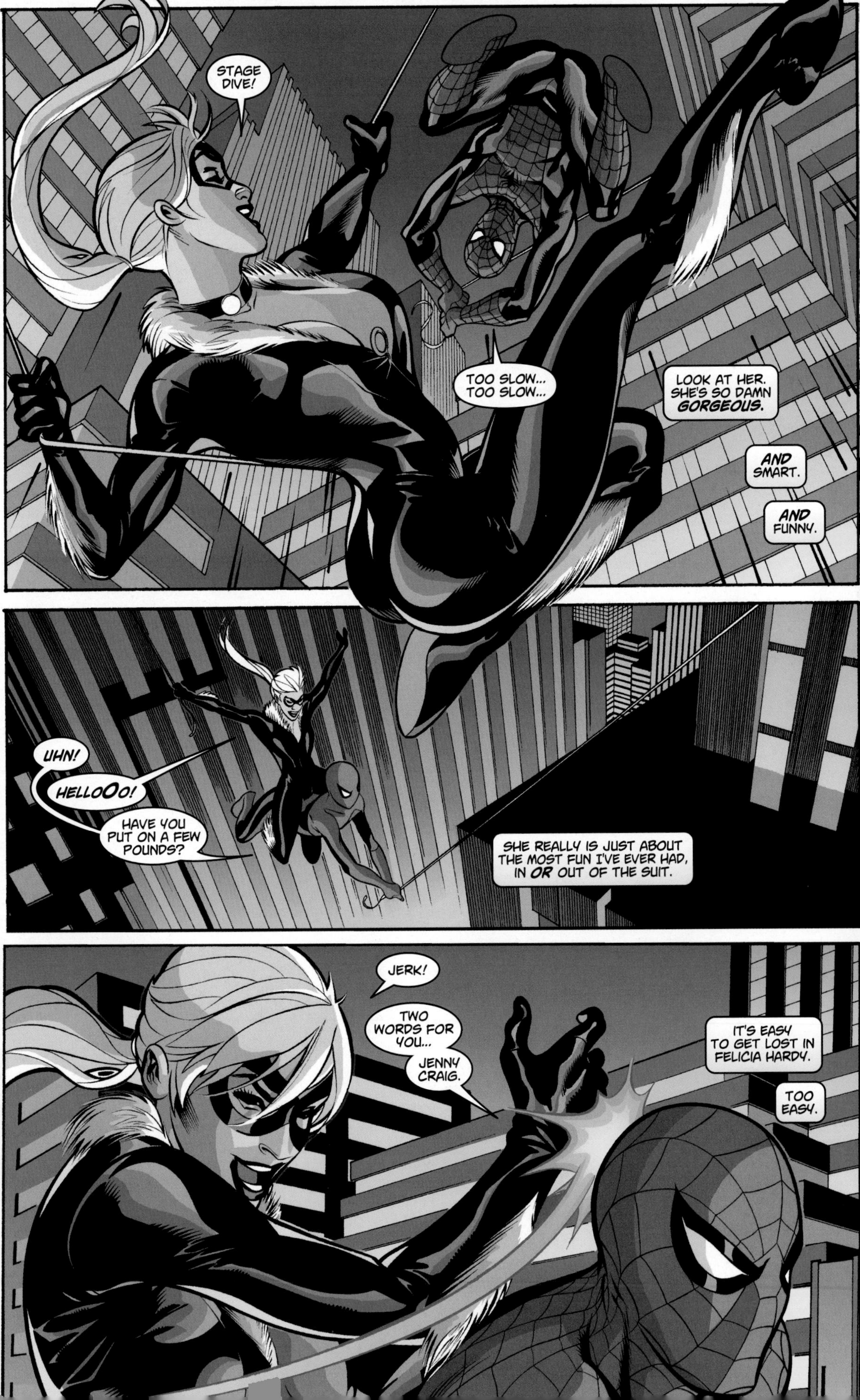
STAGE DIVE!
TOO SLOW... TOO SLOW...
LOOK AT HER. SHE'S SO DAMN GORGEOUS.
AND SMART.
AND FUNNY.
UHN!
HELLOOO!
HAVE YOU PUT ON A FEW POUNDS?
SHE REALLY IS JUST ABOUT THE MOST FUN I'VE EVER HAD, IN OR OUT OF THE SUIT.
JERK!
TWO WORDS FOR YOU...
JENNY CRAIG.
IT'S EASY TO GET LOST IN FELICIA HARDY.
TOO EASY.

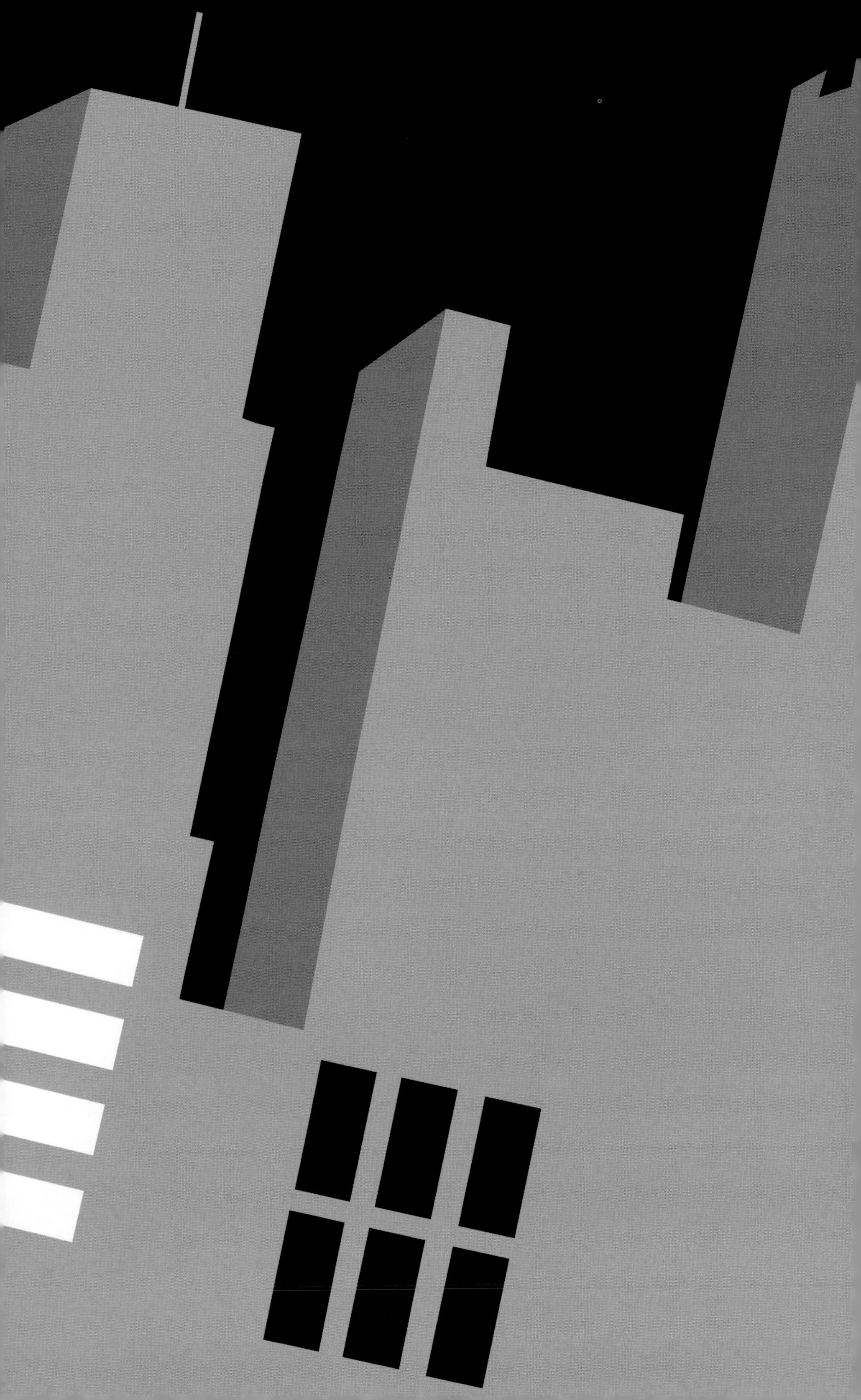

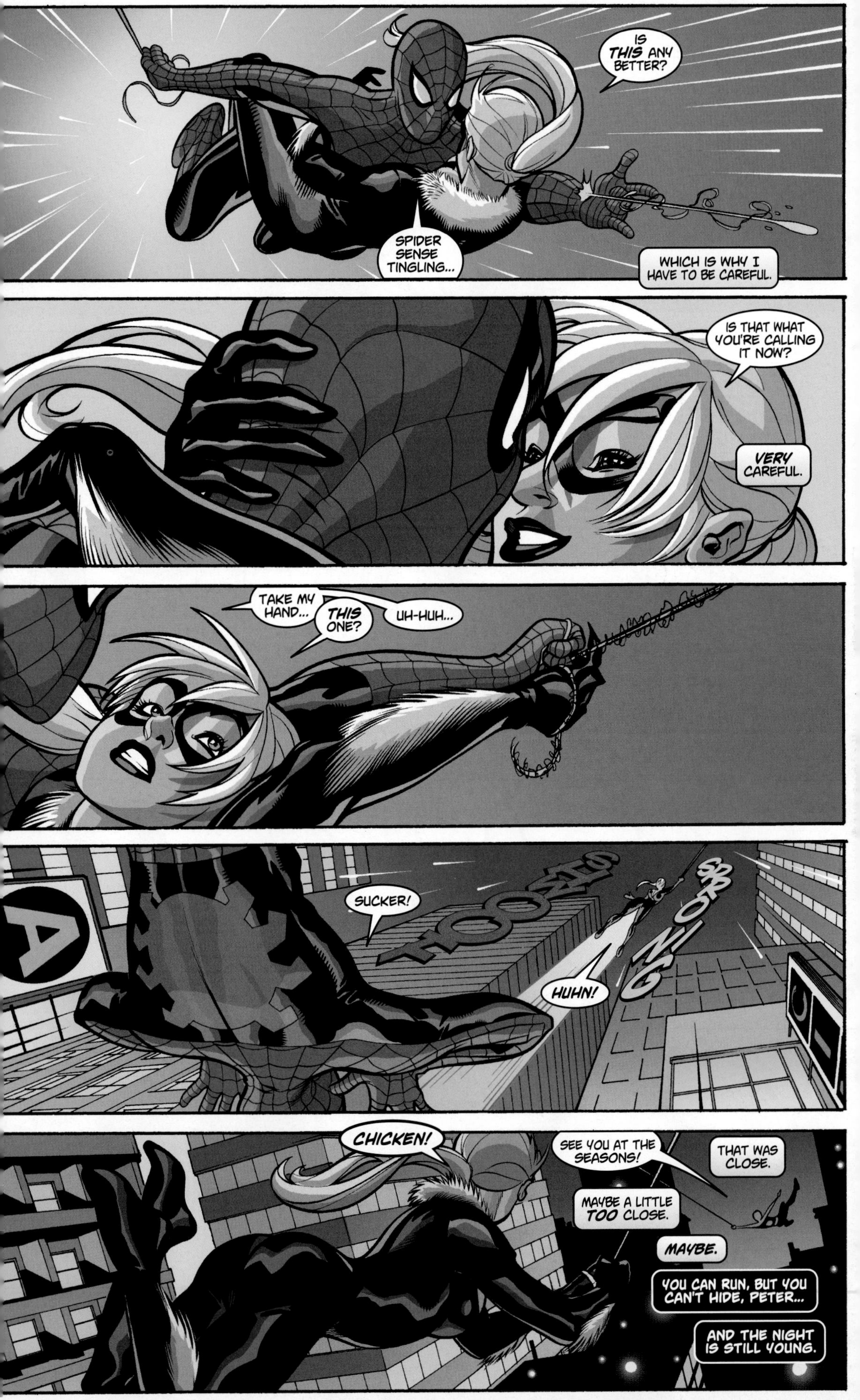
IS THIS ANY BETTER?
SPIDER SENSE TINGLING...
WHICH IS WHY I HAVE TO BE CAREFUL.
IS THAT WHAT YOU'RE CALLING IT NOW?
VERY CAREFUL.
TAKE MY HAND...
THIS ONE?
UH-HUH...
SUCKER!
SPROING
HUHN!
CHICKEN!
SEE YOU AT THE SEASONS!
THAT WAS CLOSE.
MAYBE A LITTLE TOO CLOSE.
MAYBE.
YOU CAN RUN, BUT YOU CAN'T HIDE, PETER...
AND THE NIGHT IS STILL YOUNG.

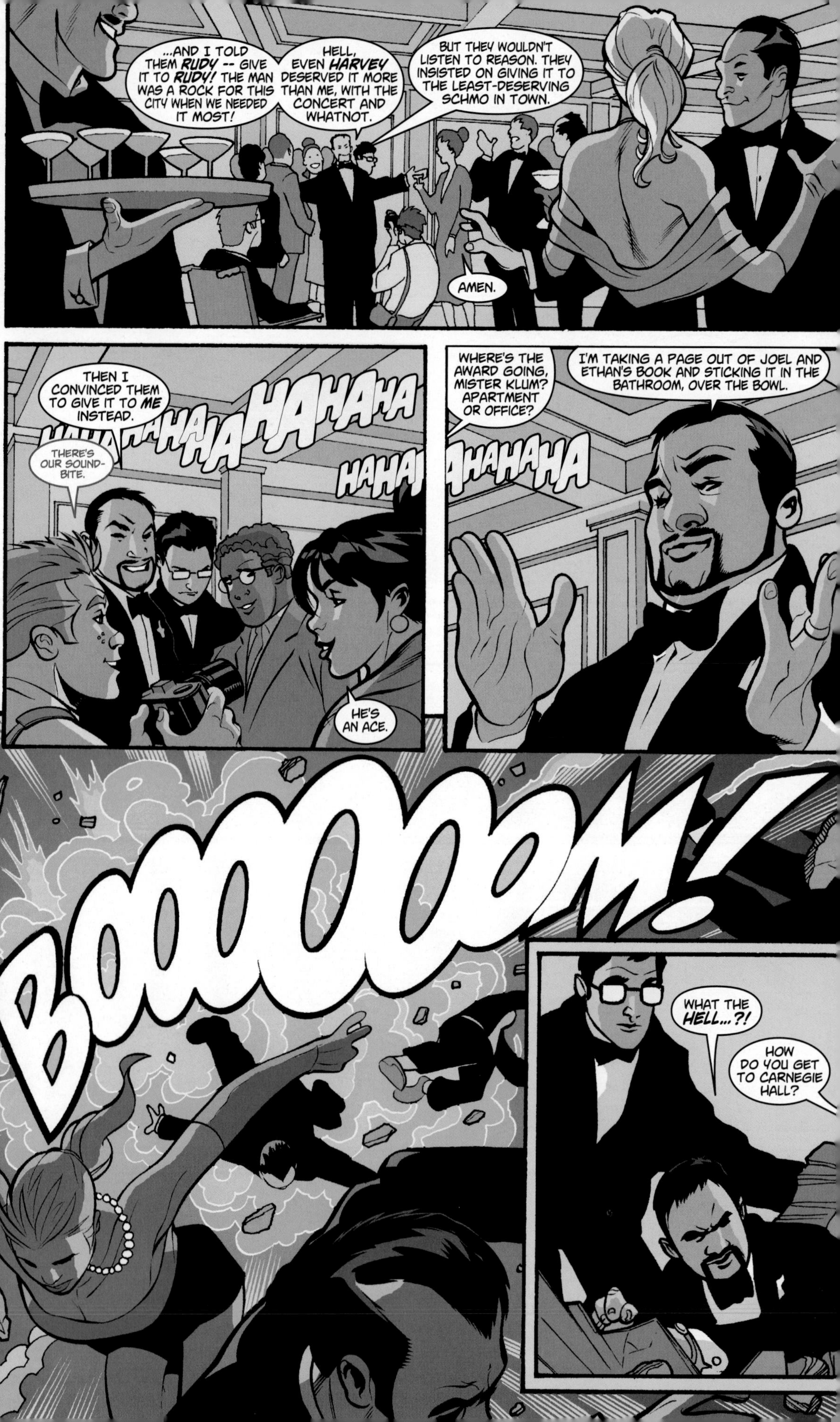
...AND I TOLD THEM RUDY -- GIVE IT TO RUDY! THE MAN WAS A ROCK FOR THIS CITY WHEN WE NEEDED IT MOST!
HELL, EVEN HARVEY DESERVED IT MORE THAN ME, WITH THE CONCERT AND WHATNOT.
BUT THEY WOULDN'T LISTEN TO REASON. THEY INSISTED ON GIVING IT TO THE LEAST-DESERVING SCHMO IN TOWN.
AMEN.
THEN I CONVINCED THEM TO GIVE IT TO ME INSTEAD.
HAHAHAHAHAHAHA
THERE'S OUR SOUND-BITE.
HE'S AN ACE.
WHERE'S THE AWARD GOING, MISTER KLUM? APARTMENT OR OFFICE?
HAHAHAHAHAHA
I'M TAKING A PAGE OUT OF JOEL AND ETHAN'S BOOK AND STICKING IT IN THE BATHROOM, OVER THE BOWL.
BOOOOOM!
WHAT THE HELL...?!
HOW DO YOU GET TO CARNEGIE HALL?

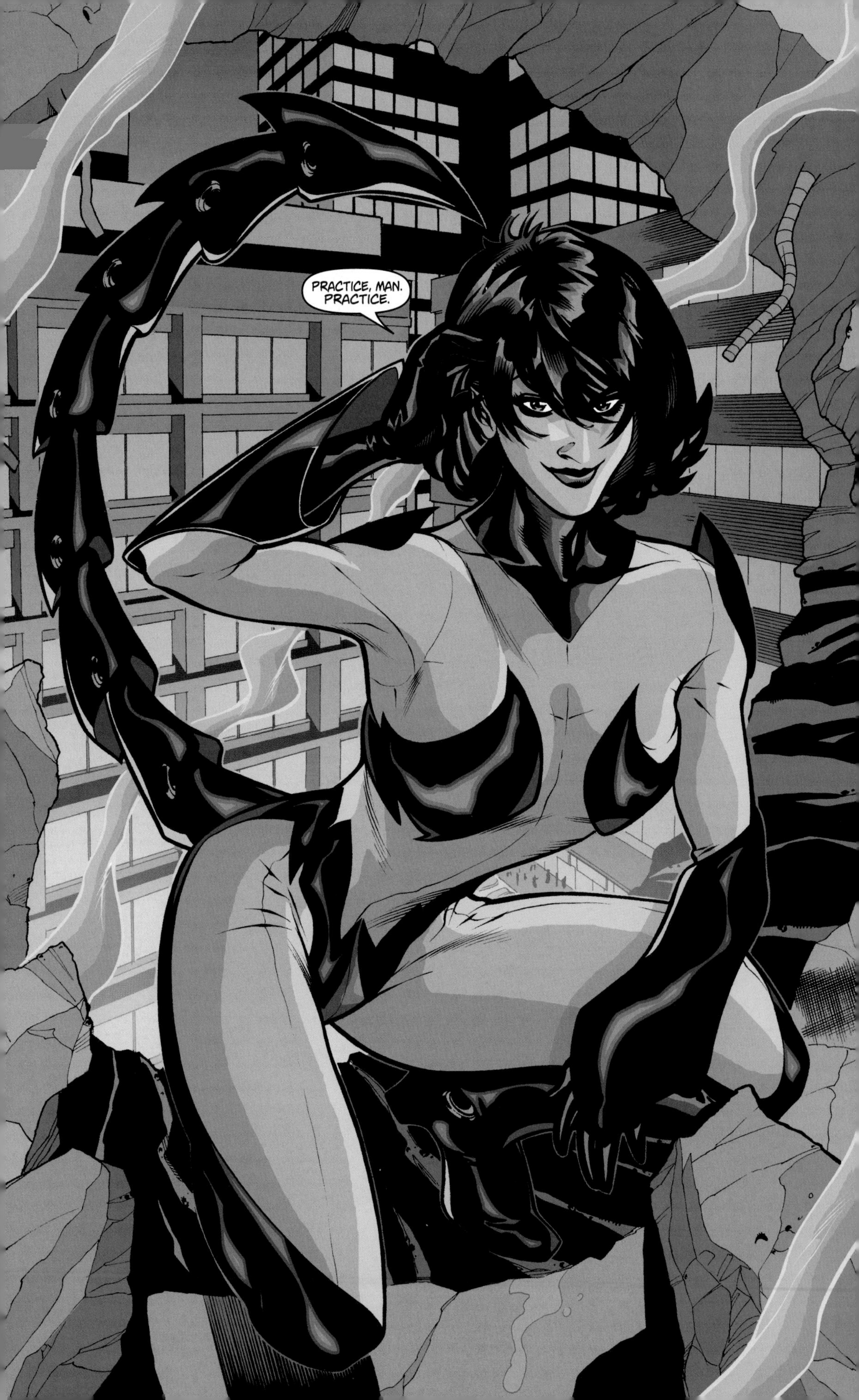
PRACTICE, MAN. PRACTICE.

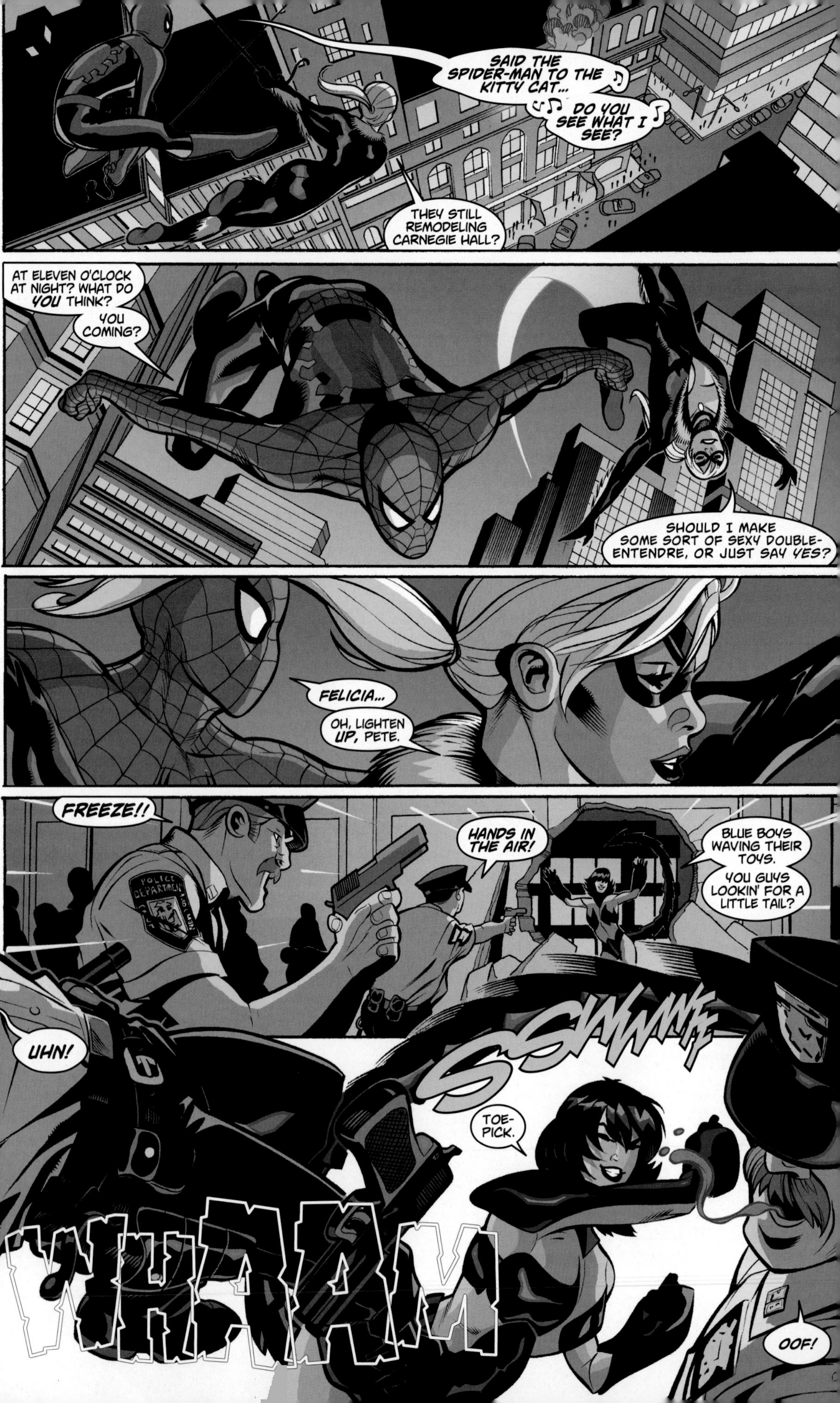
SAID THE SPIDER-MAN TO THE KITTY CAT...
DO YOU SEE WHAT I SEE?
THEY STILL REMODELING CARNEGIE HALL?
AT ELEVEN O'CLOCK AT NIGHT? WHAT DO YOU THINK?
YOU COMING?
SHOULD I MAKE SOME SORT OF SEXY DOUBLE-ENTENDRE, OR JUST SAY YES?
FELICIA...
OH, LIGHTEN UP, PETE.
FREEZE!!
HANDS IN THE AIR!
BLUE BOYS WAVING THEIR TOYS.
YOU GUYS LOOKIN' FOR A LITTLE TAIL?
UHN!
SSHWAAK
TOE-PICK.
VHRAM
OOF!

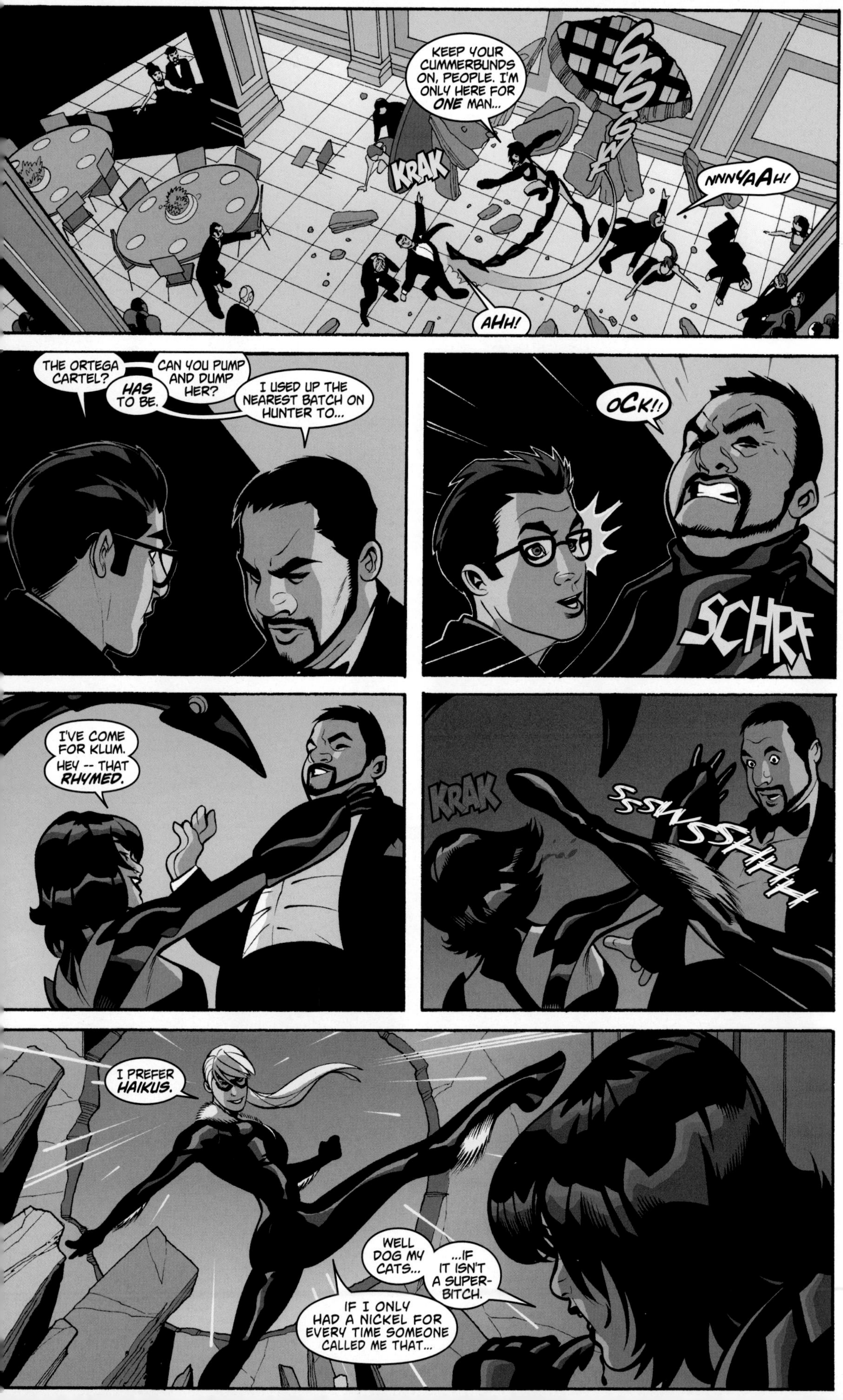
KEEP YOUR CUMMERBUNDS ON, PEOPLE. I'M ONLY HERE FOR ONE MAN...
KRAK
NNNYAAH!
AHH!
THE ORTEGA CARTEL?
HAS TO BE.
CAN YOU PUMP AND DUMP HER?
I USED UP THE NEAREST BATCH ON HUNTER TO...
OCK!!
SCHRF
I'VE COME FOR KLUM. HEY -- THAT RHYMED.
KRAK
SSSWSHHHH
I PREFER HAIKUS.
WELL DOG MY CATS...
...IF IT ISN'T A SUPER-BITCH.
IF I ONLY HAD A NICKEL FOR EVERY TIME SOMEONE CALLED ME THAT...

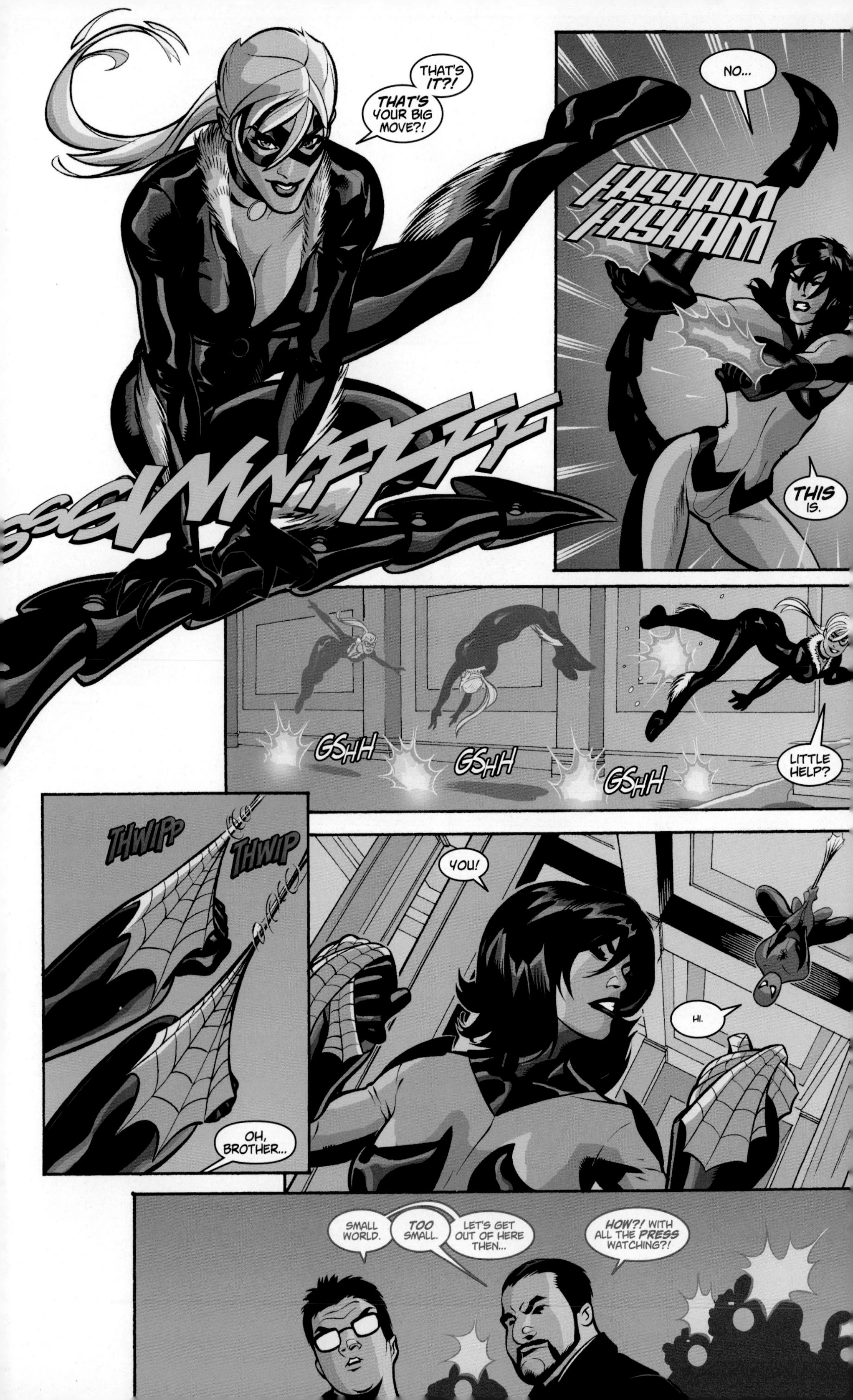
THAT'S IT?!
THAT'S YOUR BIG MOVE?!
NO...
FASHAM FASHAM
THIS IS.
GSHH
GSHH
GSHH
LITTLE HELP?
THWIPP
THWIP
OH, BROTHER...
YOU!
HI.
SMALL WORLD.
TOO SMALL.
LET'S GET OUT OF HERE THEN...
HOW?! WITH ALL THE PRESS WATCHING?!

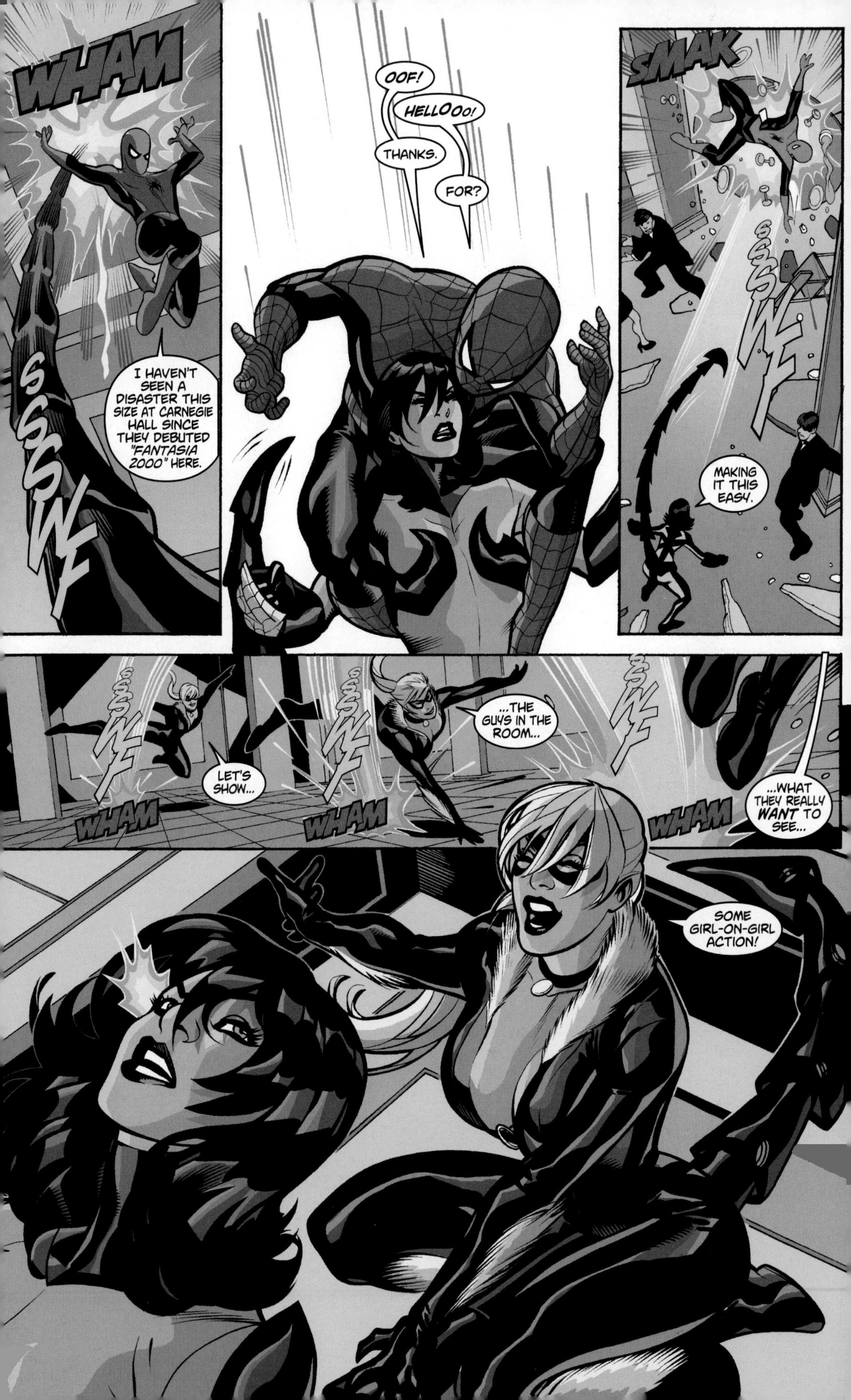
WHAM
I HAVEN'T SEEN A DISASTER THIS SIZE AT CARNEGIE HALL SINCE THEY DEBUTED "FANTASIA 2000" HERE.
SSSWF
OOF!
HELLOOO!
THANKS.
FOR?
SMAK
SSSWF
MAKING IT THIS EASY.
SSSWF
LET'S SHOW...
WHAM
SSSWF
...THE GUYS IN THE ROOM...
WHAM
SSSWF
...WHAT THEY REALLY WANT TO SEE...
WHAM
SOME GIRL-ON-GIRL ACTION!

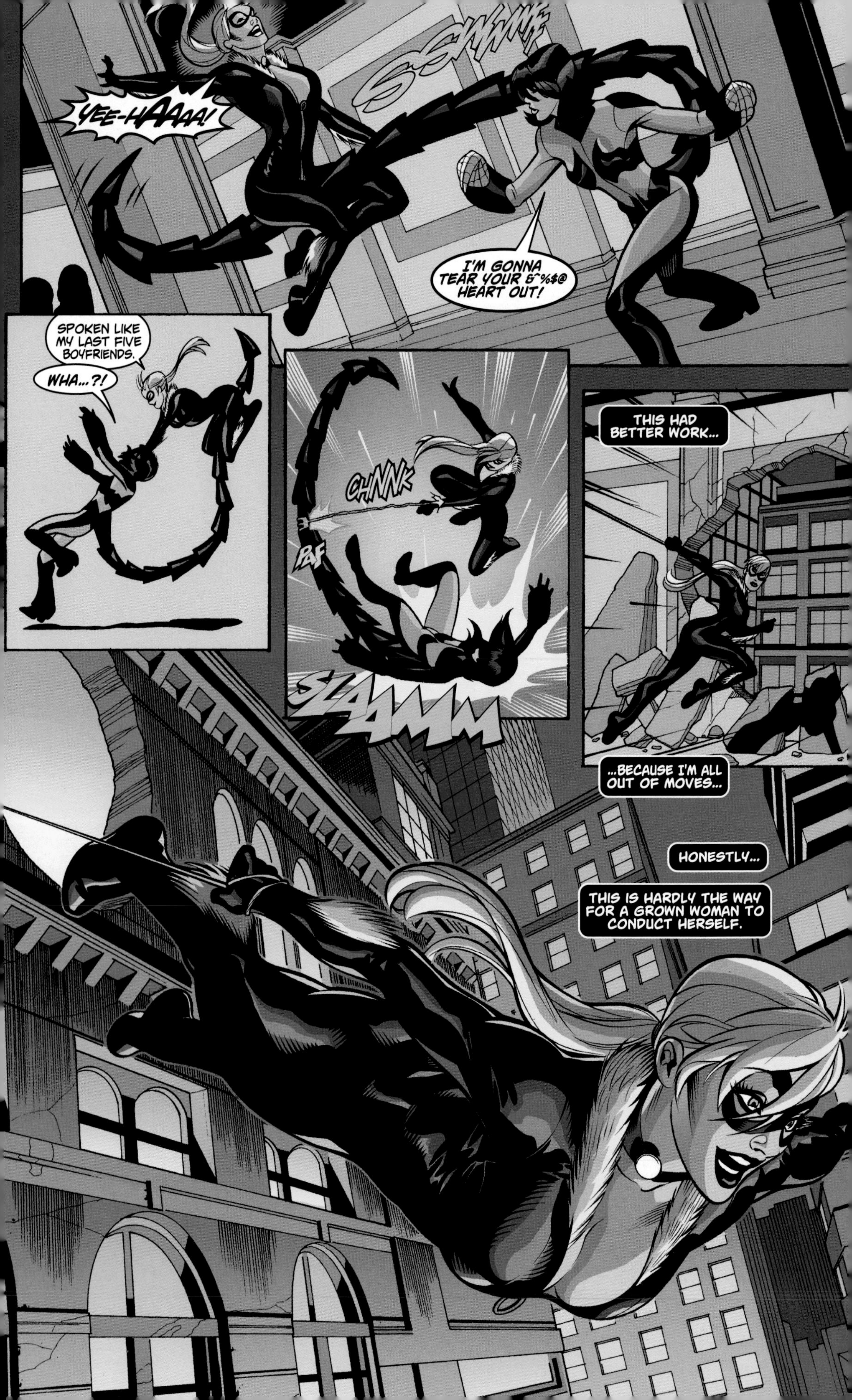
SSWMMF
YEE-HAAAA!
I'M GONNA TEAR YOUR &^%$@ HEART OUT!
SPOKEN LIKE MY LAST FIVE BOYFRIENDS.
WHA...?!
CHNNK
PAF
SLAMMM
THIS HAD BETTER WORK...
...BECAUSE I'M ALL OUT OF MOVES...
HONESTLY...
THIS IS HARDLY THE WAY FOR A GROWN WOMAN TO CONDUCT HERSELF.

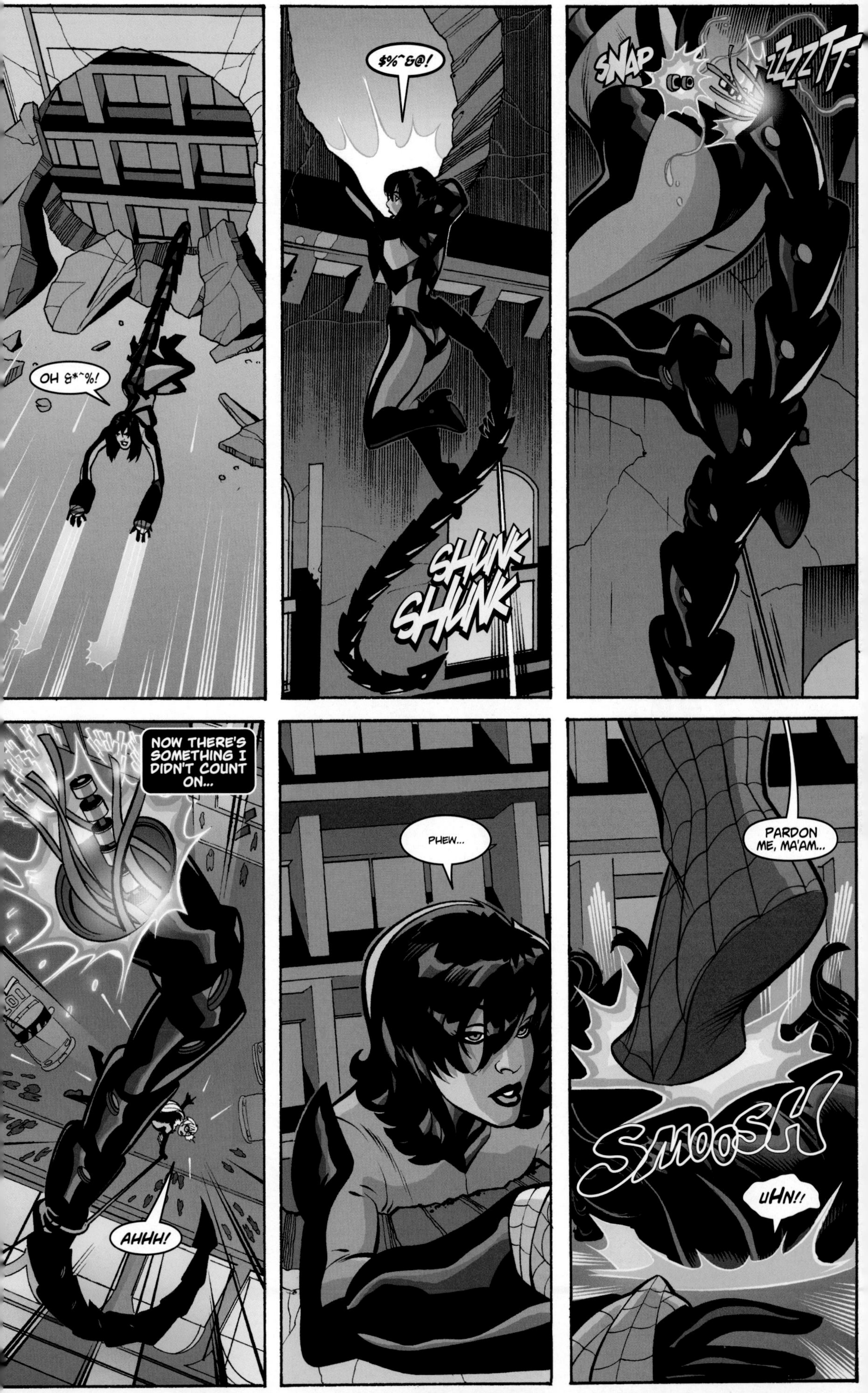
OH &*^%!
$%^&@!
SHUNK
SHUNK
SNAP
ZZZTT
NOW THERE'S SOMETHING I DIDN'T COUNT ON...
AHHH!
PHEW...
PARDON ME, MA'AM...
SMOOSH
UHN!!

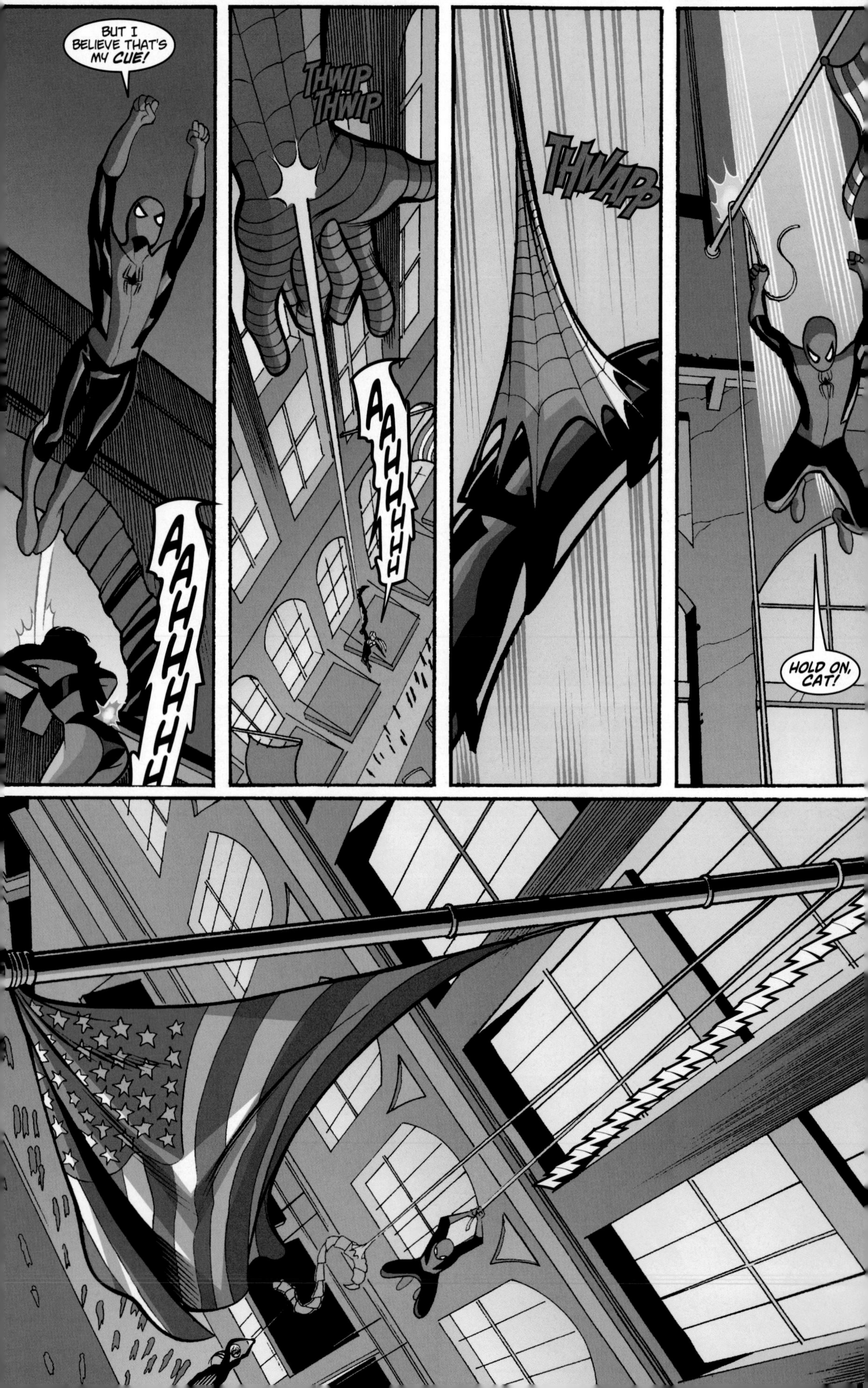
BUT I BELIEVE THAT'S MY CUE!
THWIP THWIP
THWAPP
HOLD ON, CAT!

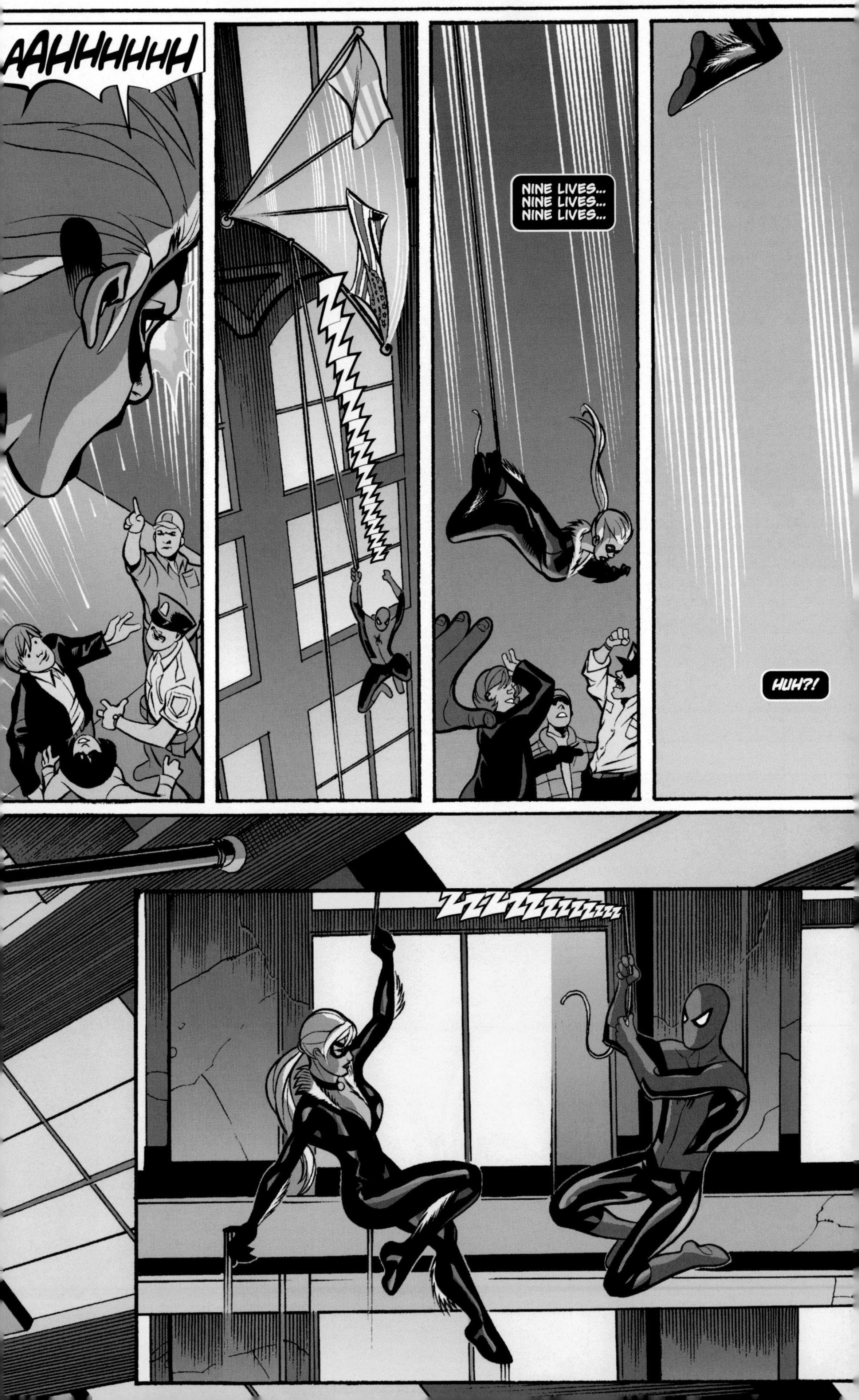

AAHHHHHH
NINE LIVES...
NINE LIVES...
NINE LIVES...
HUH?!
ZZZZZZZZZZZZZ

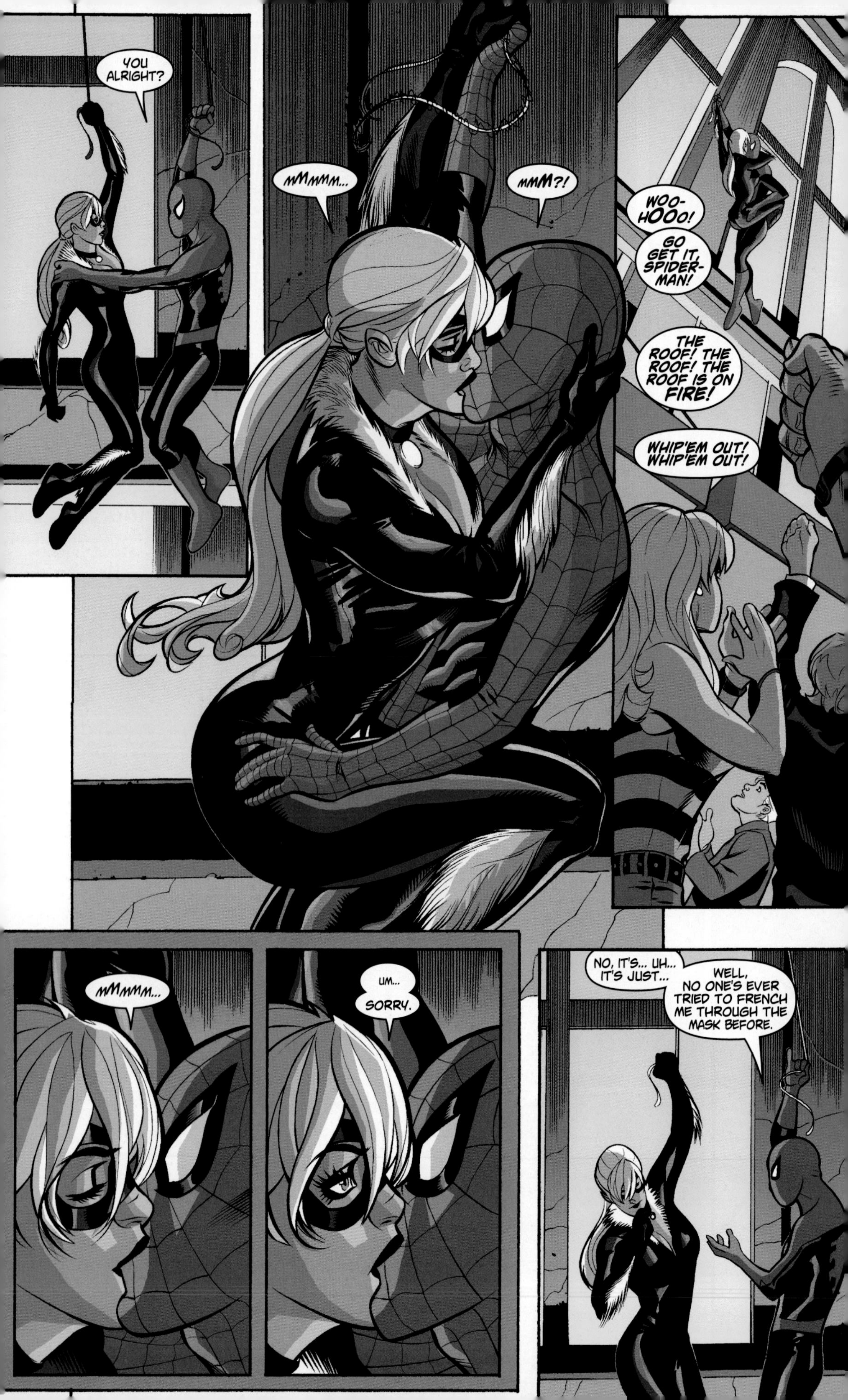
YOU ALRIGHT?
MMMMM...
MMM?!
WOO-HOOo!
GO GET IT, SPIDER-MAN!
THE ROOF! THE ROOF! THE ROOF IS ON FIRE!
WHIP'EM OUT! WHIP'EM OUT!
MMMMM...
UM...
SORRY.
NO, IT'S... UH... IT'S JUST...
WELL, NO ONE'S EVER TRIED TO FRENCH ME THROUGH THE MASK BEFORE.

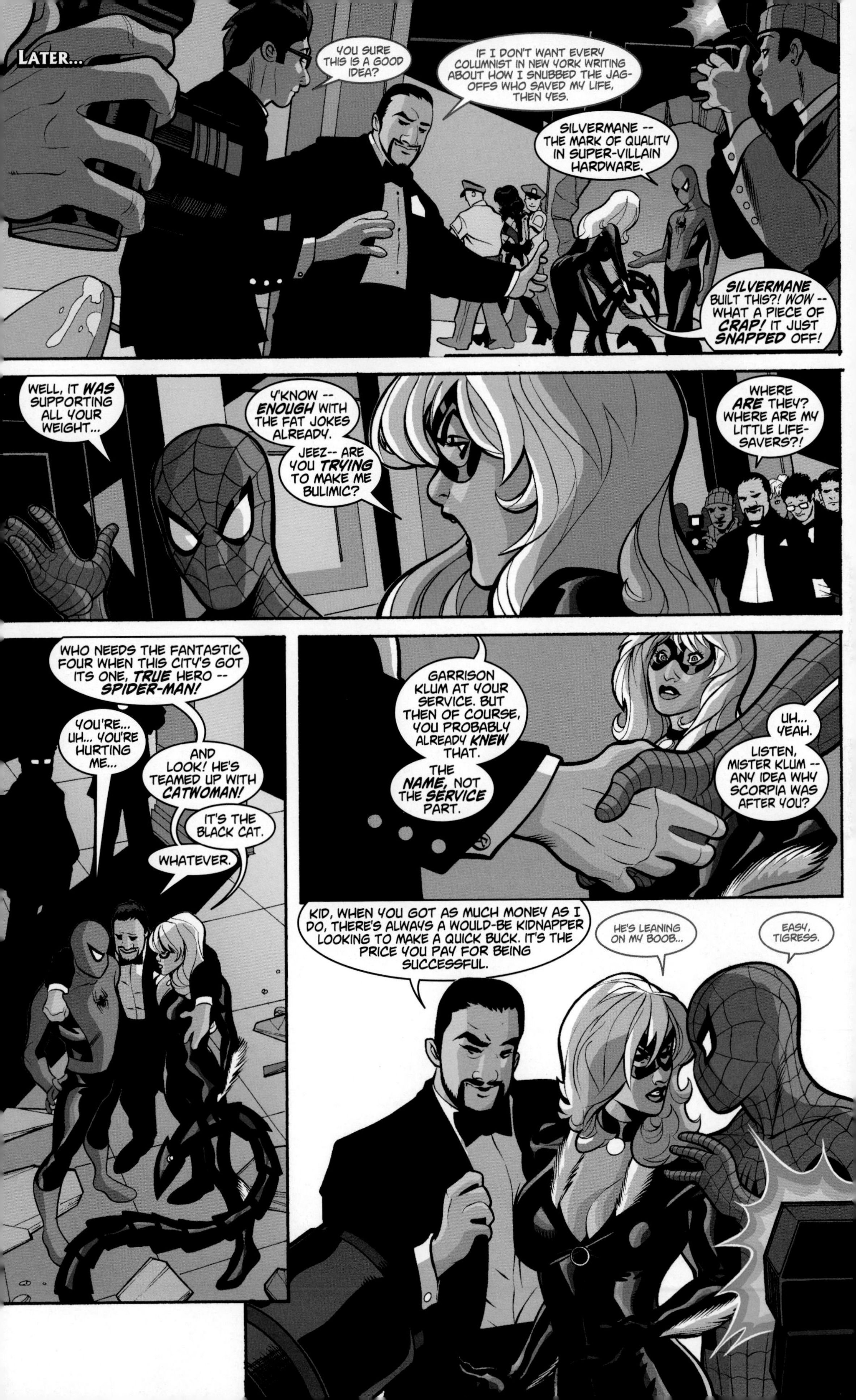
LATER...
YOU SURE THIS IS A GOOD IDEA?
IF I DON'T WANT EVERY COLUMNIST IN NEW YORK WRITING ABOUT HOW I SNUBBED THE JAG-OFFS WHO SAVED MY LIFE, THEN YES.
SILVERMANE -- THE MARK OF QUALITY IN SUPER-VILLAIN HARDWARE.
SILVERMANE BUILT THIS?! WOW -- WHAT A PIECE OF CRAP! IT JUST SNAPPED OFF!
WELL, IT WAS SUPPORTING ALL YOUR WEIGHT...
Y'KNOW -- ENOUGH WITH THE FAT JOKES ALREADY.
JEEZ-- ARE YOU TRYING TO MAKE ME BULIMIC?
WHERE ARE THEY? WHERE ARE MY LITTLE LIFE-SAVERS?!
WHO NEEDS THE FANTASTIC FOUR WHEN THIS CITY'S GOT ITS ONE, TRUE HERO -- SPIDER-MAN!
YOU'RE... UH... YOU'RE HURTING ME...
AND LOOK! HE'S TEAMED UP WITH CATWOMAN!
IT'S THE BLACK CAT.
WHATEVER.
GARRISON KLUM AT YOUR SERVICE. BUT THEN OF COURSE, YOU PROBABLY ALREADY KNEW THAT.
THE NAME, NOT THE SERVICE PART.
UH... YEAH.
LISTEN, MISTER KLUM -- ANY IDEA WHY SCORPIA WAS AFTER YOU?
KID, WHEN YOU GOT AS MUCH MONEY AS I DO, THERE'S ALWAYS A WOULD-BE KIDNAPPER LOOKING TO MAKE A QUICK BUCK. IT'S THE PRICE YOU PAY FOR BEING SUCCESSFUL.
HE'S LEANING ON MY BOOB...
EASY, TIGRESS.

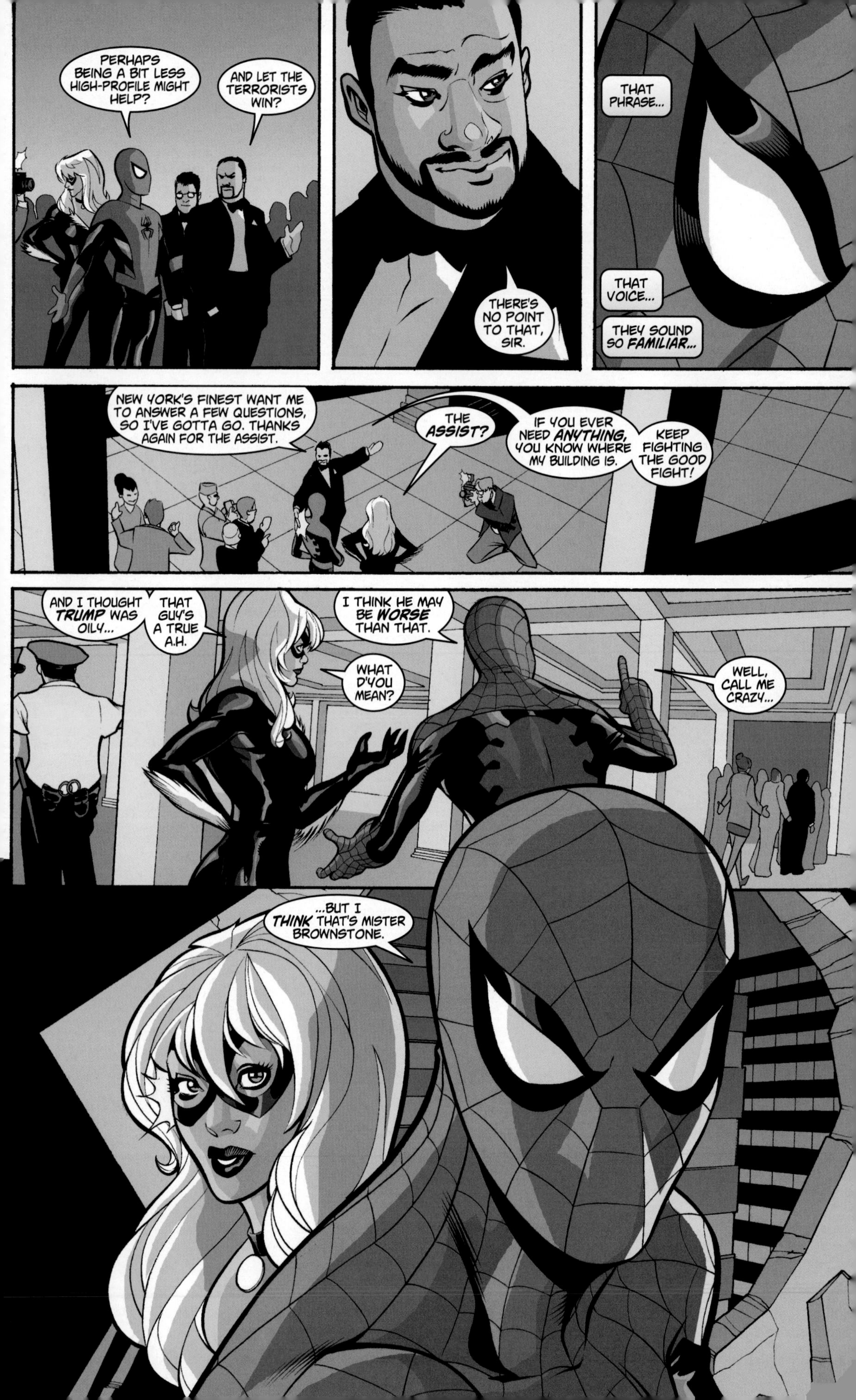

PERHAPS BEING A BIT LESS HIGH-PROFILE MIGHT HELP?
AND LET THE TERRORISTS WIN?
THERE'S NO POINT TO THAT, SIR.
THAT PHRASE...
THAT VOICE...
THEY SOUND SO **FAMILIAR...**
NEW YORK'S FINEST WANT ME TO ANSWER A FEW QUESTIONS, SO I'VE GOTTA GO. THANKS AGAIN FOR THE ASSIST.
THE **ASSIST?**
IF YOU EVER NEED **ANYTHING,** YOU KNOW WHERE MY BUILDING IS.
KEEP FIGHTING THE GOOD FIGHT!
AND I THOUGHT **TRUMP** WAS OILY...
THAT GUY'S A TRUE A.H.
I THINK HE MAY BE **WORSE** THAN THAT.
WHAT D'YOU MEAN?
WELL, CALL ME CRAZY...
...BUT I **THINK** THAT'S MISTER BROWNSTONE.

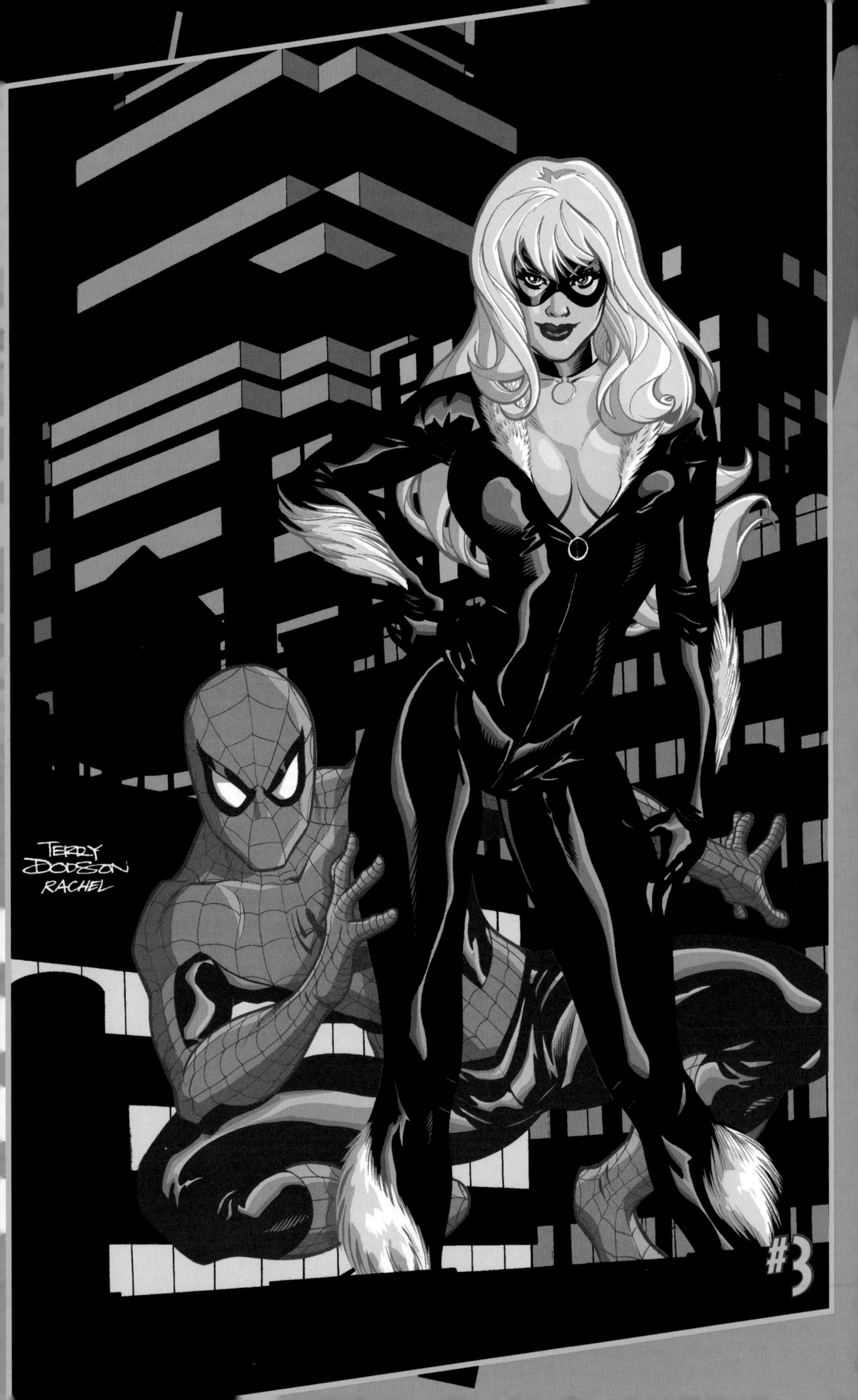
TERRY
DODSON
RACHEL
#3

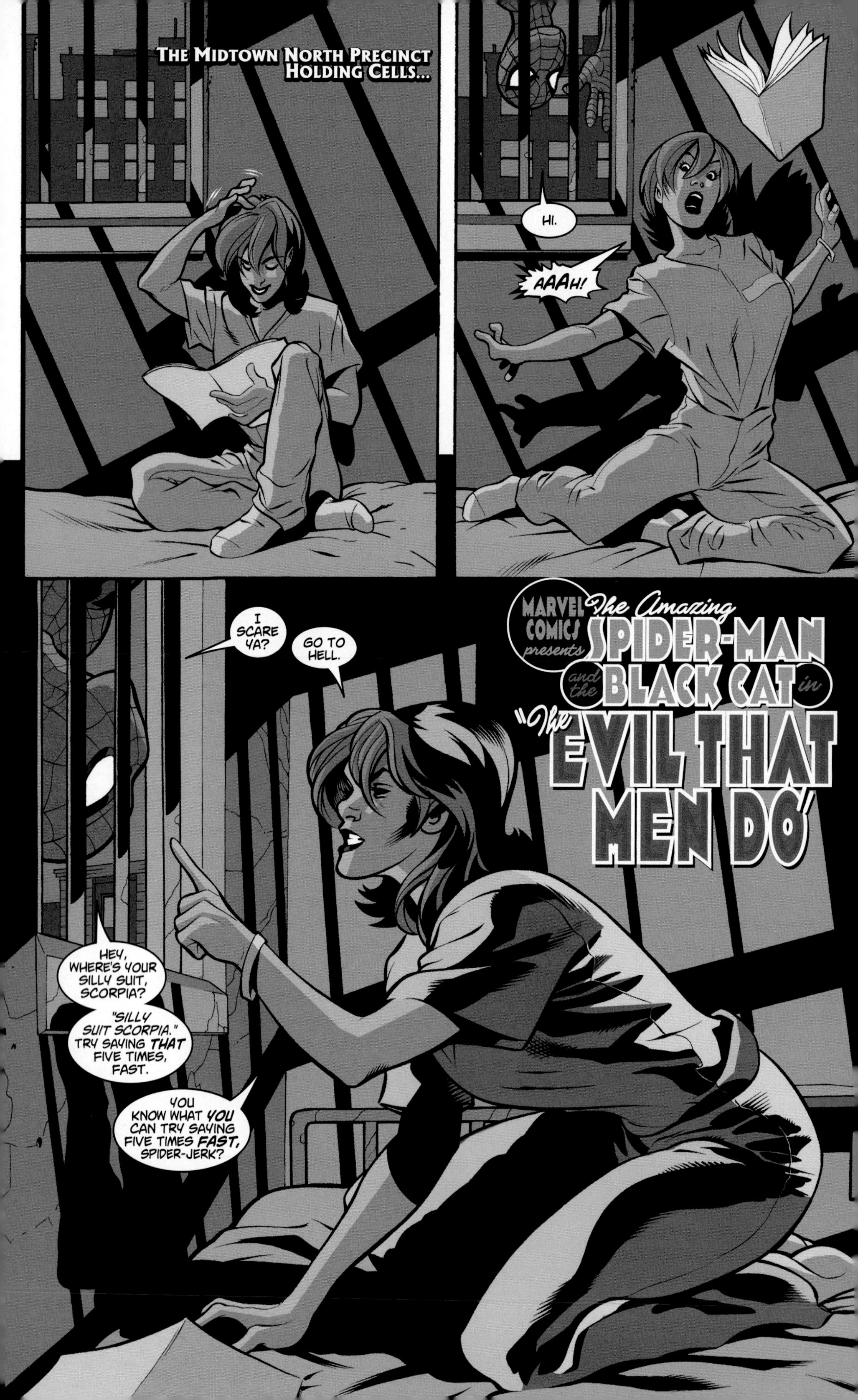
THE MIDTOWN NORTH PRECINCT HOLDING CELLS...
HI.
AAAH!
I SCARE YA?
GO TO HELL.
MARVEL COMICS presents The Amazing SPIDER-MAN and the BLACK CAT in "The EVIL THAT MEN DO"
HEY, WHERE'S YOUR SILLY SUIT, SCORPIA?
"SILLY SUIT SCORPIA." TRY SAYING THAT FIVE TIMES, FAST.
YOU KNOW WHAT YOU CAN TRY SAYING FIVE TIMES FAST, SPIDER-JERK?

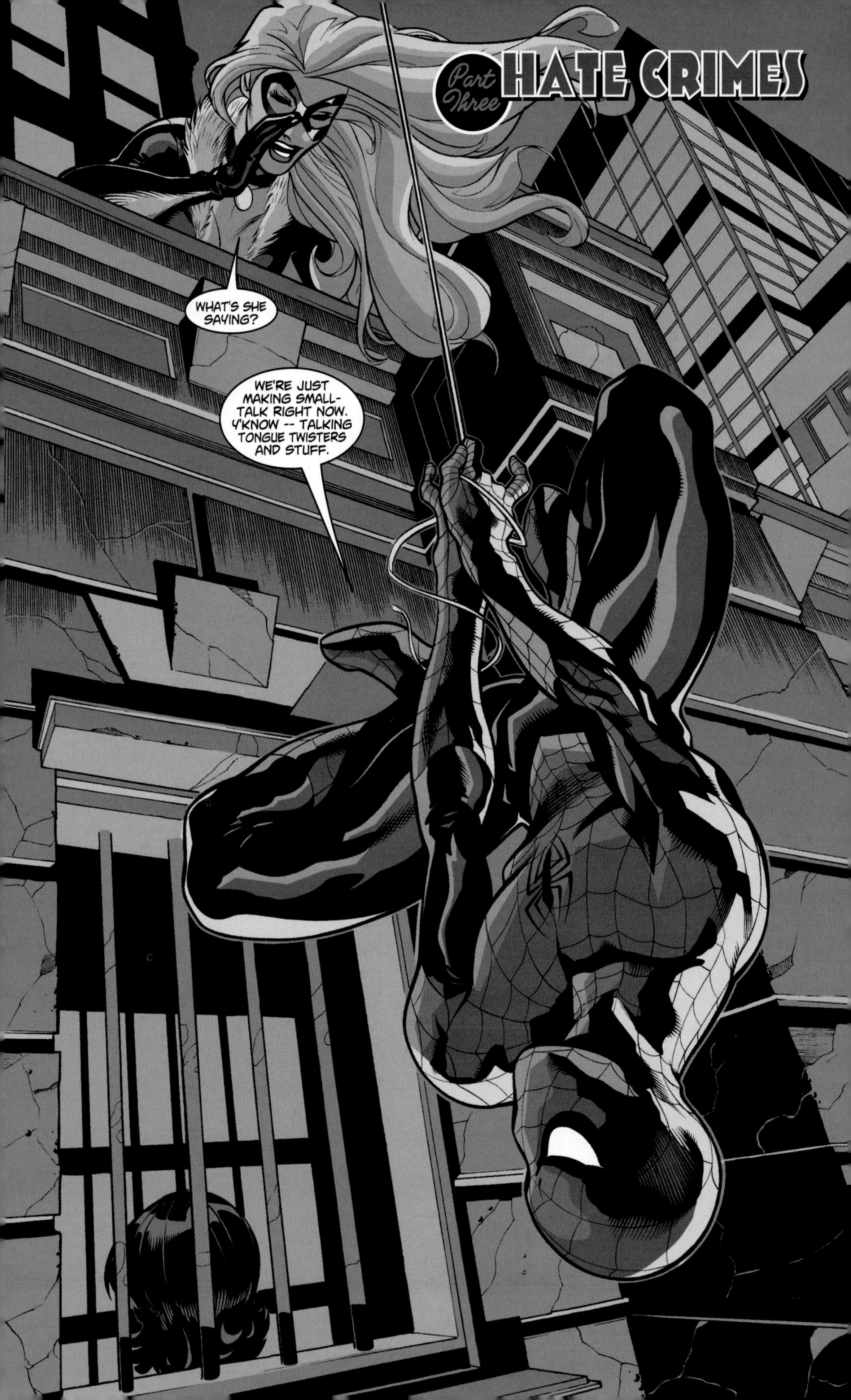
Part Three HATE CRIMES
WHAT'S SHE SAYING?
WE'RE JUST MAKING SMALL-TALK RIGHT NOW. Y'KNOW -- TALKING TONGUE TWISTERS AND STUFF.

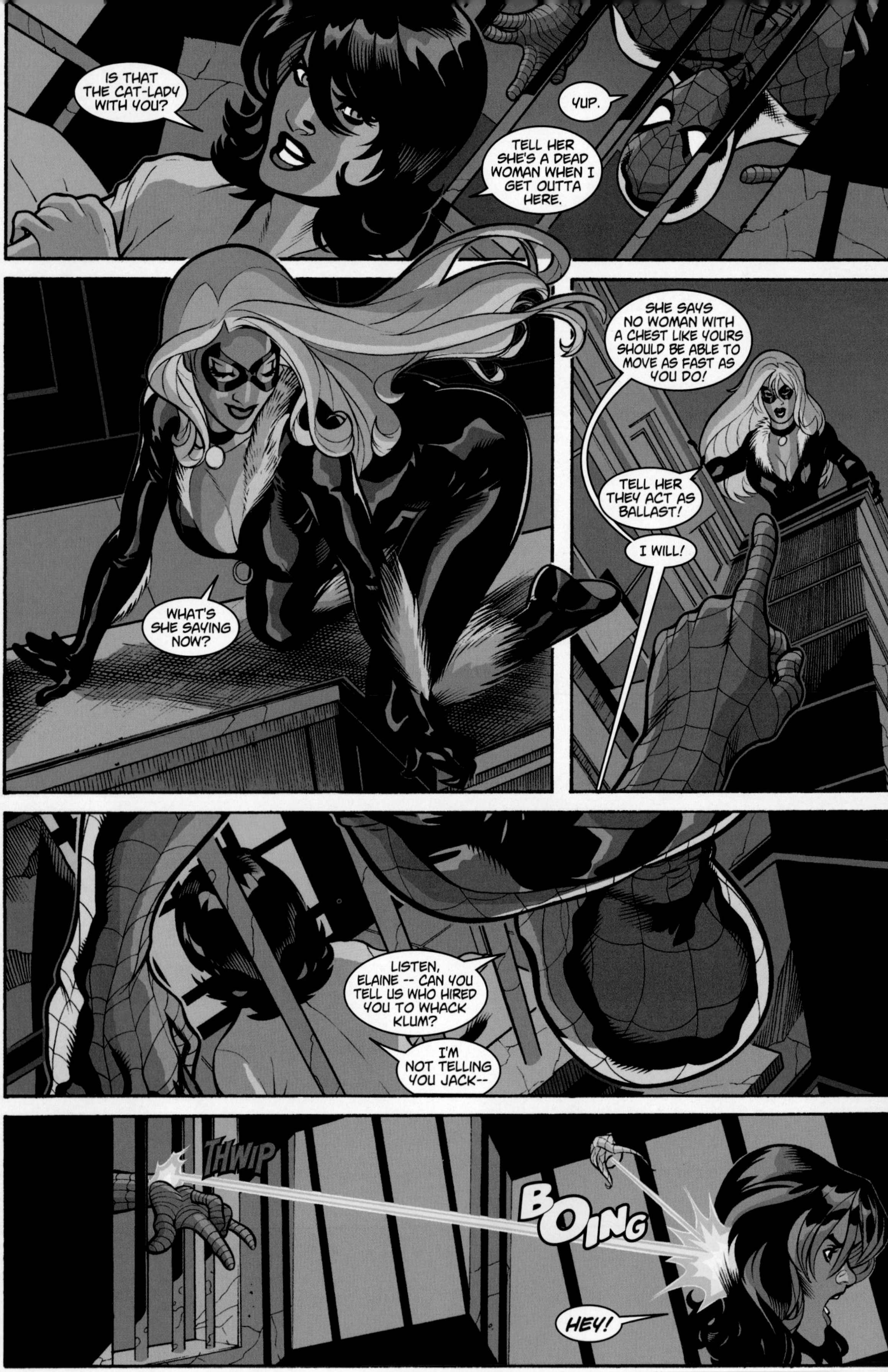
IS THAT THE CAT-LADY WITH YOU?
YUP.
TELL HER SHE'S A DEAD WOMAN WHEN I GET OUTTA HERE.
WHAT'S SHE SAYING NOW?
SHE SAYS NO WOMAN WITH A CHEST LIKE YOURS SHOULD BE ABLE TO MOVE AS FAST AS YOU DO!
TELL HER THEY ACT AS BALLAST!
I WILL!
LISTEN, ELAINE -- CAN YOU TELL US WHO HIRED YOU TO WHACK KLUM?
I'M NOT TELLING YOU JACK--
THWIP
BOING
HEY!

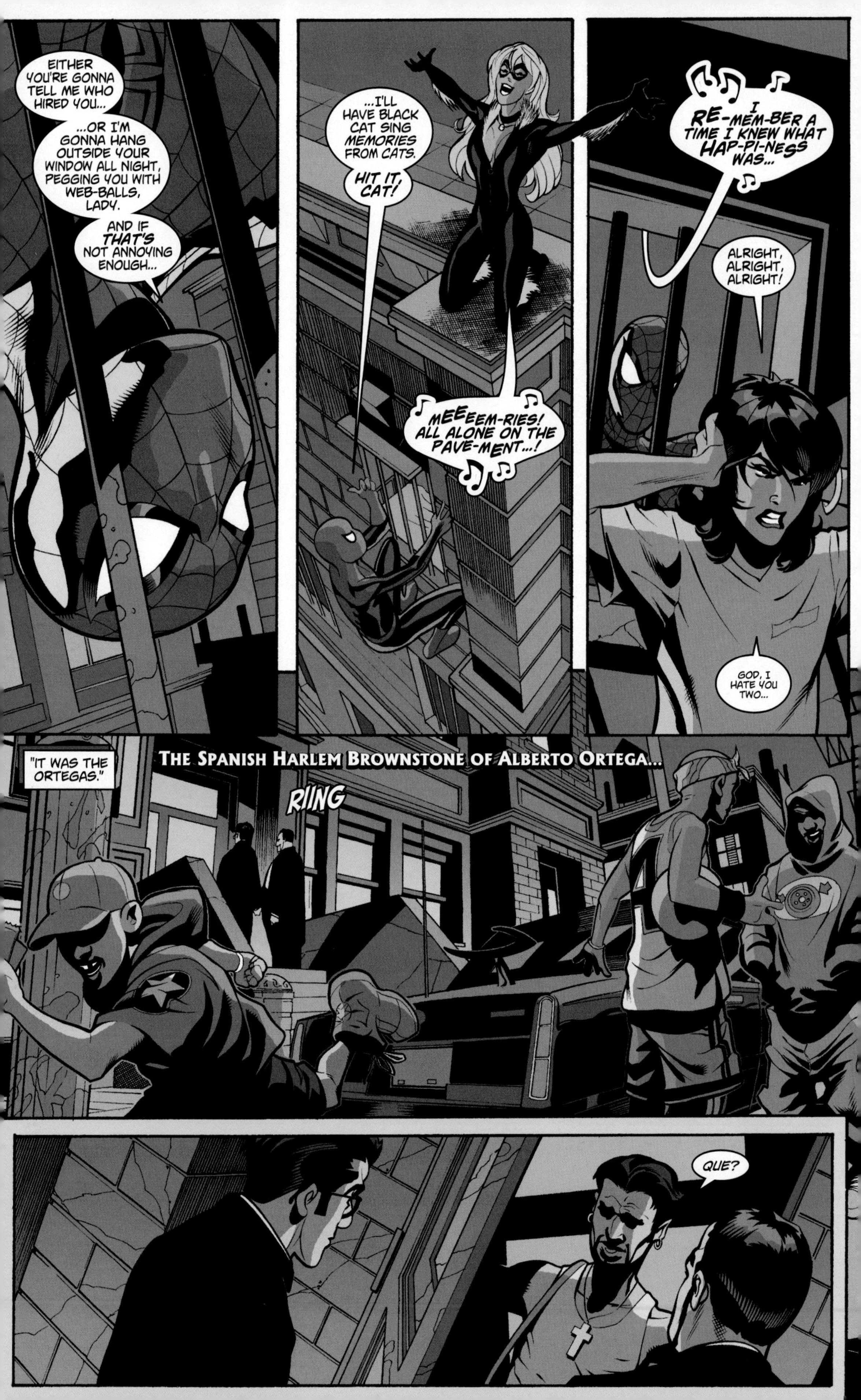
EITHER YOU'RE GONNA TELL ME WHO HIRED YOU...
...OR I'M GONNA HANG OUTSIDE YOUR WINDOW ALL NIGHT, PEGGING YOU WITH WEB-BALLS, LADY.
AND IF THAT'S NOT ANNOYING ENOUGH...
...I'LL HAVE BLACK CAT SING MEMORIES FROM CATS.
HIT IT, CAT!
MEEEEM-RIES! ALL ALONE ON THE PAVE-MENT...!
I RE-MEM-BER A TIME I KNEW WHAT HAP-PI-NESS WAS...
ALRIGHT, ALRIGHT, ALRIGHT!
GOD, I HATE YOU TWO...
"IT WAS THE ORTEGAS."
THE SPANISH HARLEM BROWNSTONE OF ALBERTO ORTEGA...
RIING
QUE?

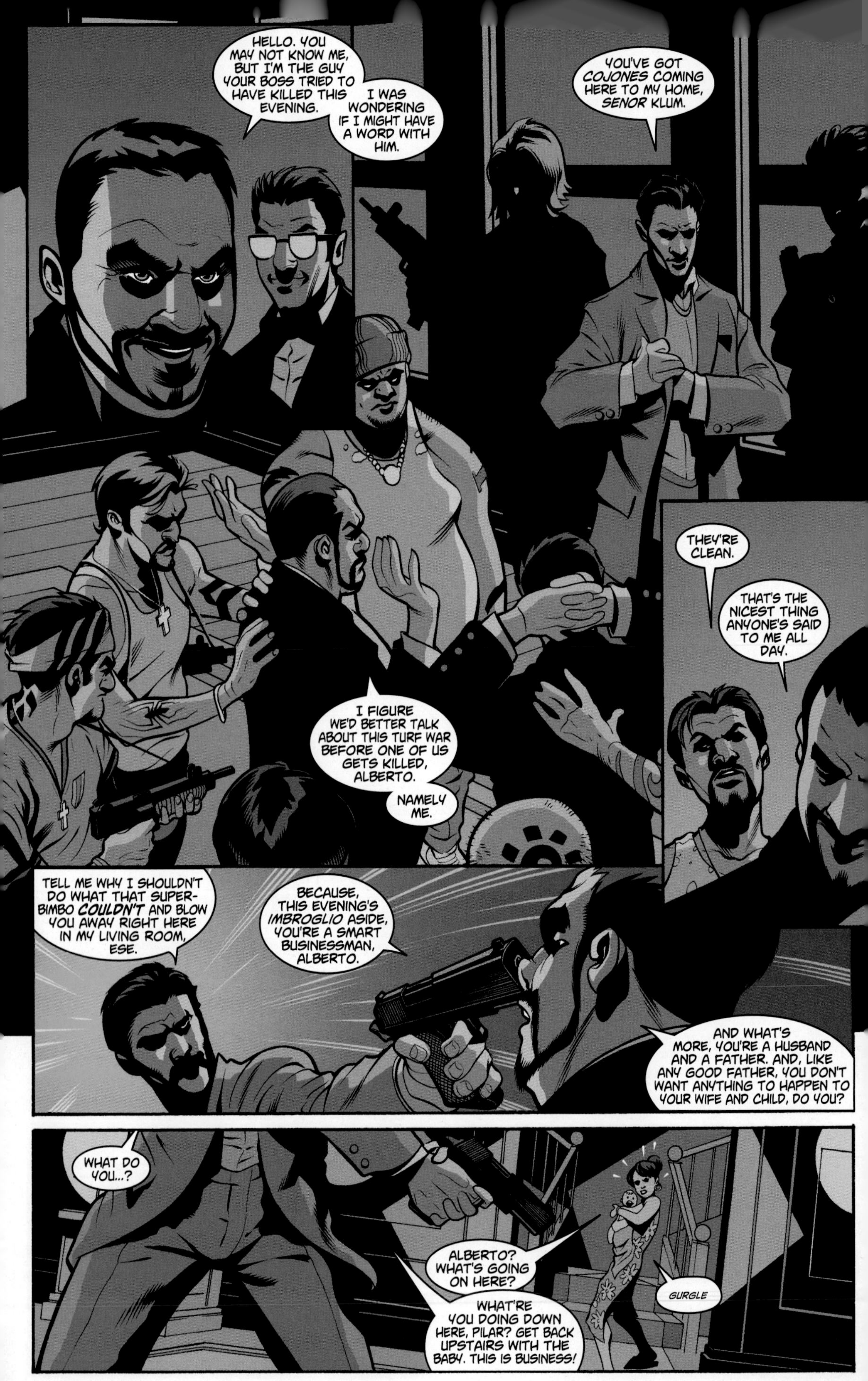
HELLO. YOU MAY NOT KNOW ME, BUT I'M THE GUY YOUR BOSS TRIED TO HAVE KILLED THIS EVENING.
I WAS WONDERING IF I MIGHT HAVE A WORD WITH HIM.
YOU'VE GOT COJONES COMING HERE TO MY HOME, SENOR KLUM.
THEY'RE CLEAN.
THAT'S THE NICEST THING ANYONE'S SAID TO ME ALL DAY.
I FIGURE WE'D BETTER TALK ABOUT THIS TURF WAR BEFORE ONE OF US GETS KILLED, ALBERTO.
NAMELY ME.
TELL ME WHY I SHOULDN'T DO WHAT THAT SUPER-BIMBO COULDN'T AND BLOW YOU AWAY RIGHT HERE IN MY LIVING ROOM, ESE.
BECAUSE, THIS EVENING'S IMBROGLIO ASIDE, YOU'RE A SMART BUSINESSMAN, ALBERTO.
AND WHAT'S MORE, YOU'RE A HUSBAND AND A FATHER. AND, LIKE ANY GOOD FATHER, YOU DON'T WANT ANYTHING TO HAPPEN TO YOUR WIFE AND CHILD, DO YOU?
WHAT DO YOU...?
ALBERTO? WHAT'S GOING ON HERE?
GURGLE
WHAT'RE YOU DOING DOWN HERE, PILAR? GET BACK UPSTAIRS WITH THE BABY. THIS IS BUSINESS!

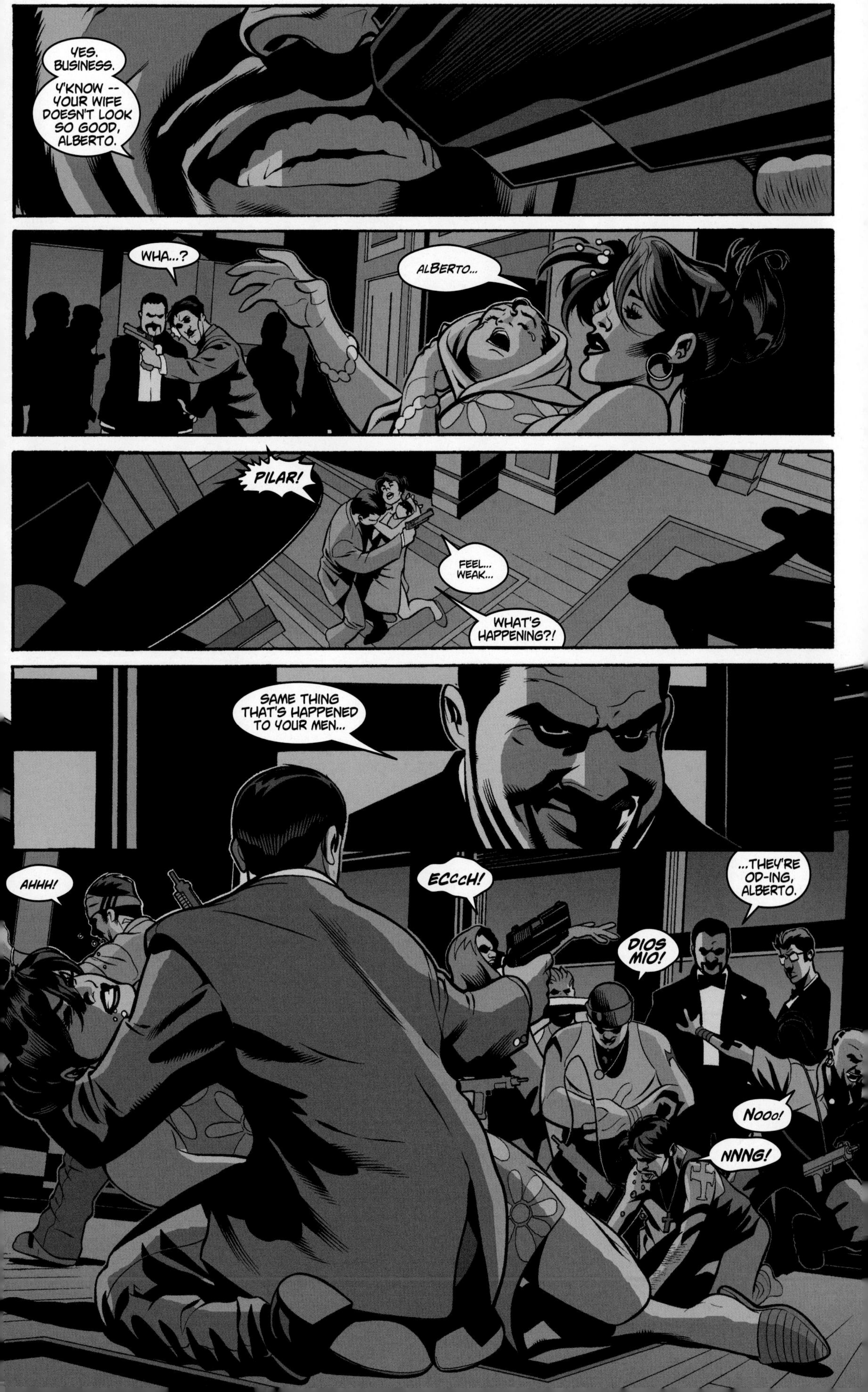
YES. BUSINESS.
Y'KNOW -- YOUR WIFE DOESN'T LOOK SO GOOD, ALBERTO.
WHA...?
ALBERTO...
PILAR!
FEEL... WEAK...
WHAT'S HAPPENING?!
SAME THING THAT'S HAPPENED TO YOUR MEN...
AHHH!
ECCCH!
...THEY'RE OD-ING, ALBERTO.
DIOS MIO!
NOOO!
NNNG!

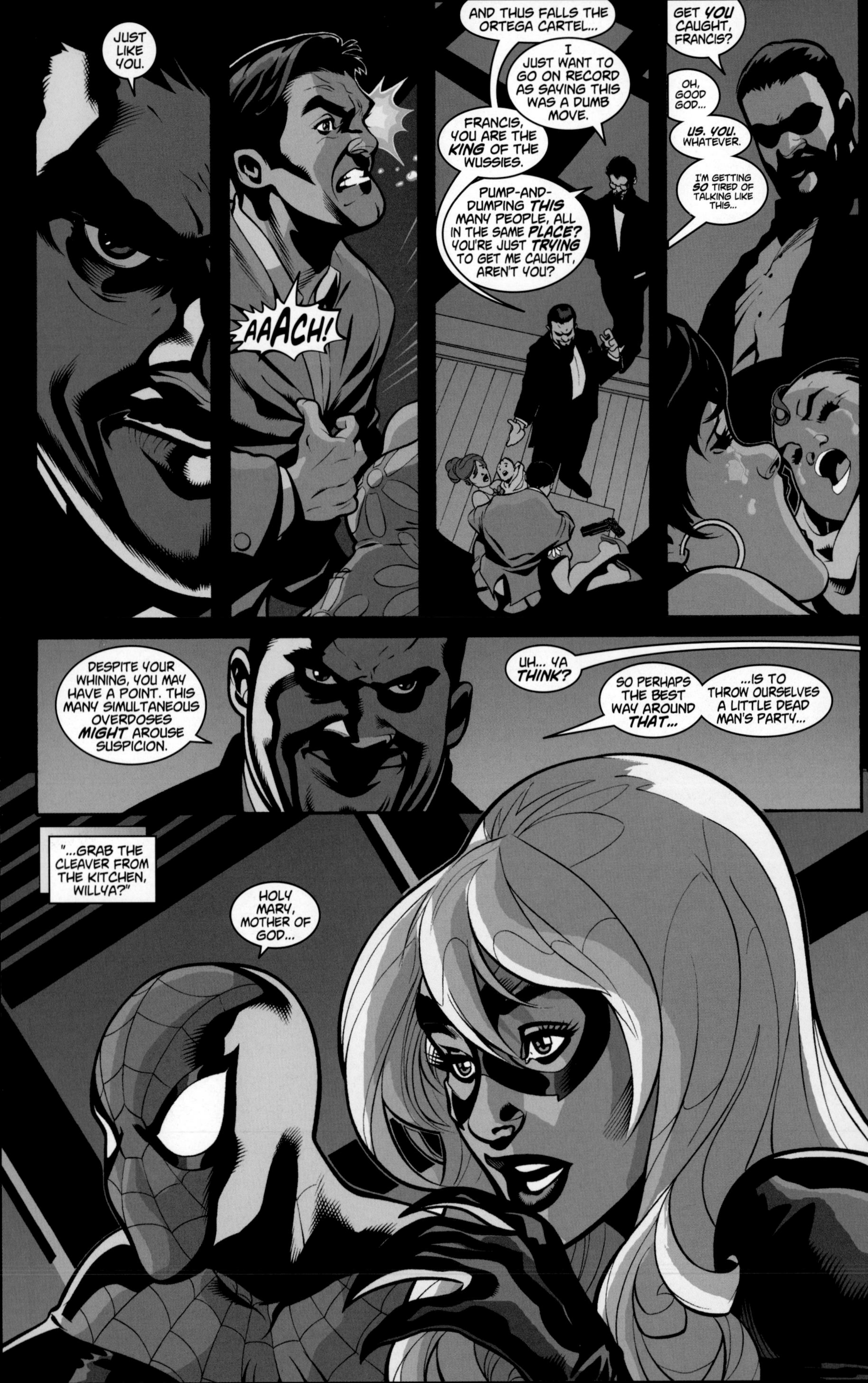
JUST LIKE YOU.
AAACH!
AND THUS FALLS THE ORTEGA CARTEL...
I JUST WANT TO GO ON RECORD AS SAYING THIS WAS A DUMB MOVE.
FRANCIS, YOU ARE THE KING OF THE WUSSIES.
PUMP-AND-DUMPING THIS MANY PEOPLE, ALL IN THE SAME PLACE? YOU'RE JUST TRYING TO GET ME CAUGHT, AREN'T YOU?
GET YOU CAUGHT, FRANCIS?
OH, GOOD GOD...
US. YOU. WHATEVER.
I'M GETTING SO TIRED OF TALKING LIKE THIS...
DESPITE YOUR WHINING, YOU MAY HAVE A POINT. THIS MANY SIMULTANEOUS OVERDOSES MIGHT AROUSE SUSPICION.
UH... YA THINK?
SO PERHAPS THE BEST WAY AROUND THAT...
...IS TO THROW OURSELVES A LITTLE DEAD MAN'S PARTY...
"...GRAB THE CLEAVER FROM THE KITCHEN, WILLYA?"
HOLY MARY, MOTHER OF GOD...

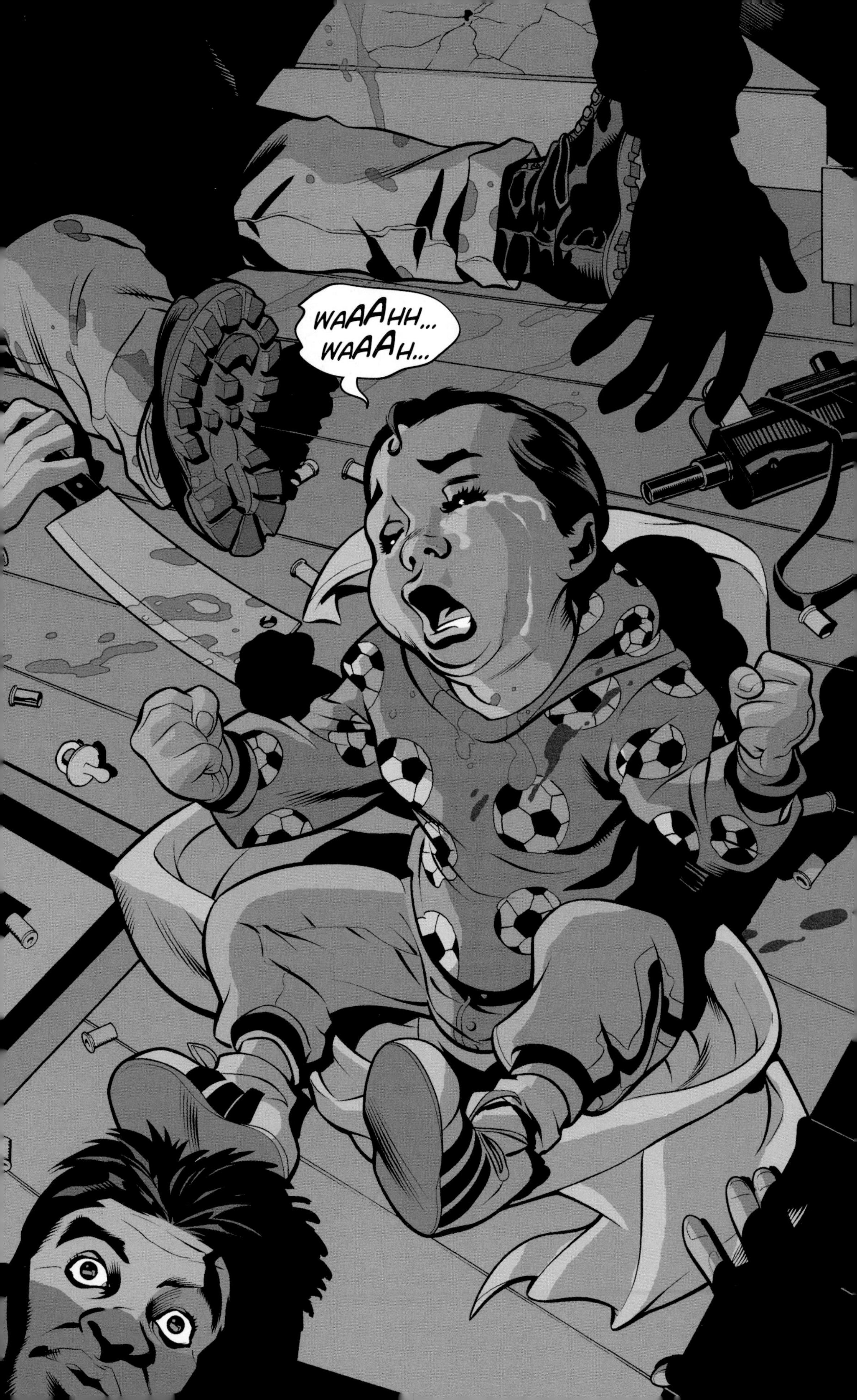
WAAAHH... WAAAH...

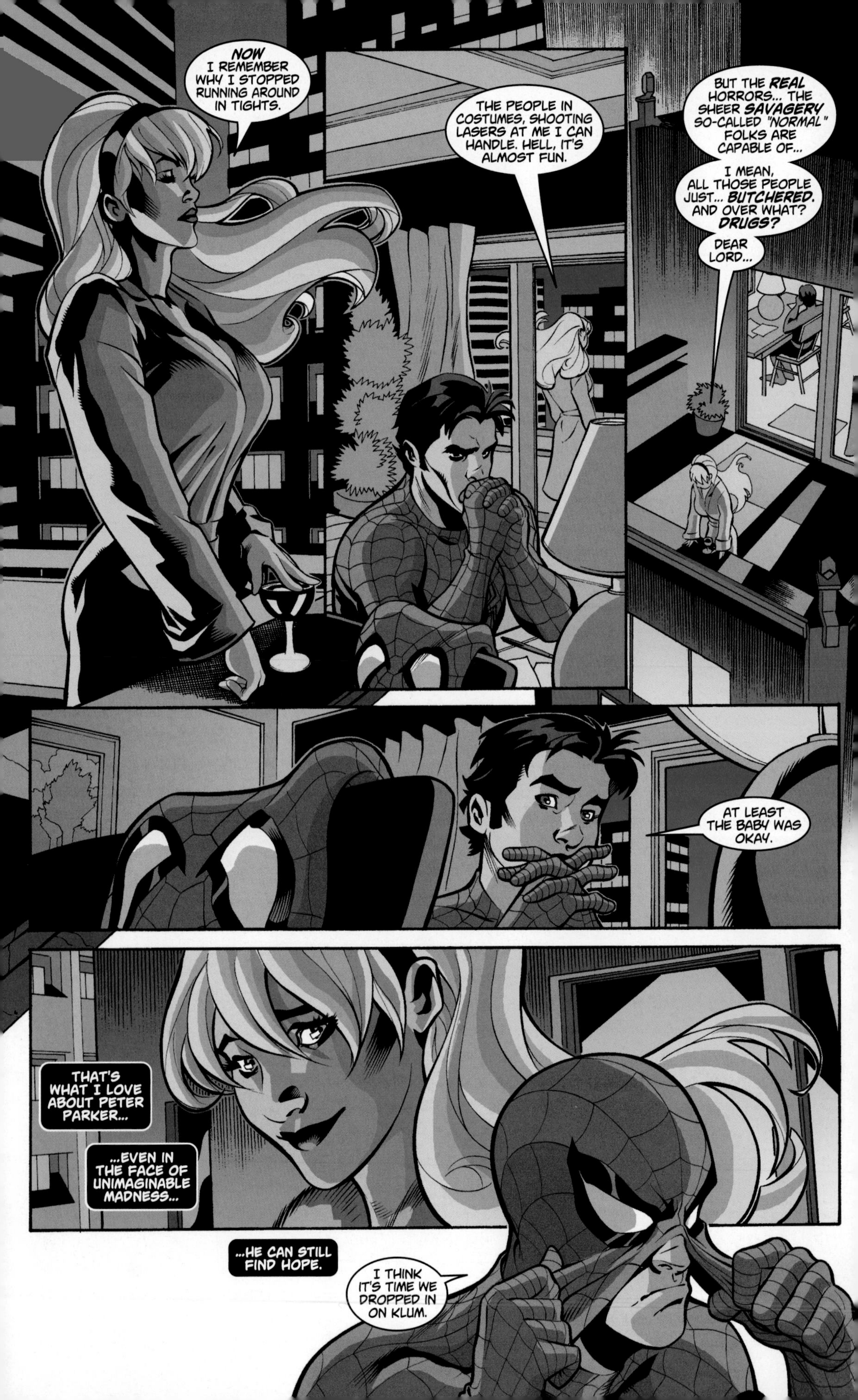
NOW I REMEMBER WHY I STOPPED RUNNING AROUND IN TIGHTS.
THE PEOPLE IN COSTUMES, SHOOTING LASERS AT ME I CAN HANDLE. HELL, IT'S ALMOST FUN.
BUT THE REAL HORRORS... THE SHEER SAVAGERY SO-CALLED "NORMAL" FOLKS ARE CAPABLE OF...
I MEAN, ALL THOSE PEOPLE JUST... BUTCHERED. AND OVER WHAT? DRUGS?
DEAR LORD...
AT LEAST THE BABY WAS OKAY.
THAT'S WHAT I LOVE ABOUT PETER PARKER...
...EVEN IN THE FACE OF UNIMAGINABLE MADNESS...
...HE CAN STILL FIND HOPE.
I THINK IT'S TIME WE DROPPED IN ON KLUM.

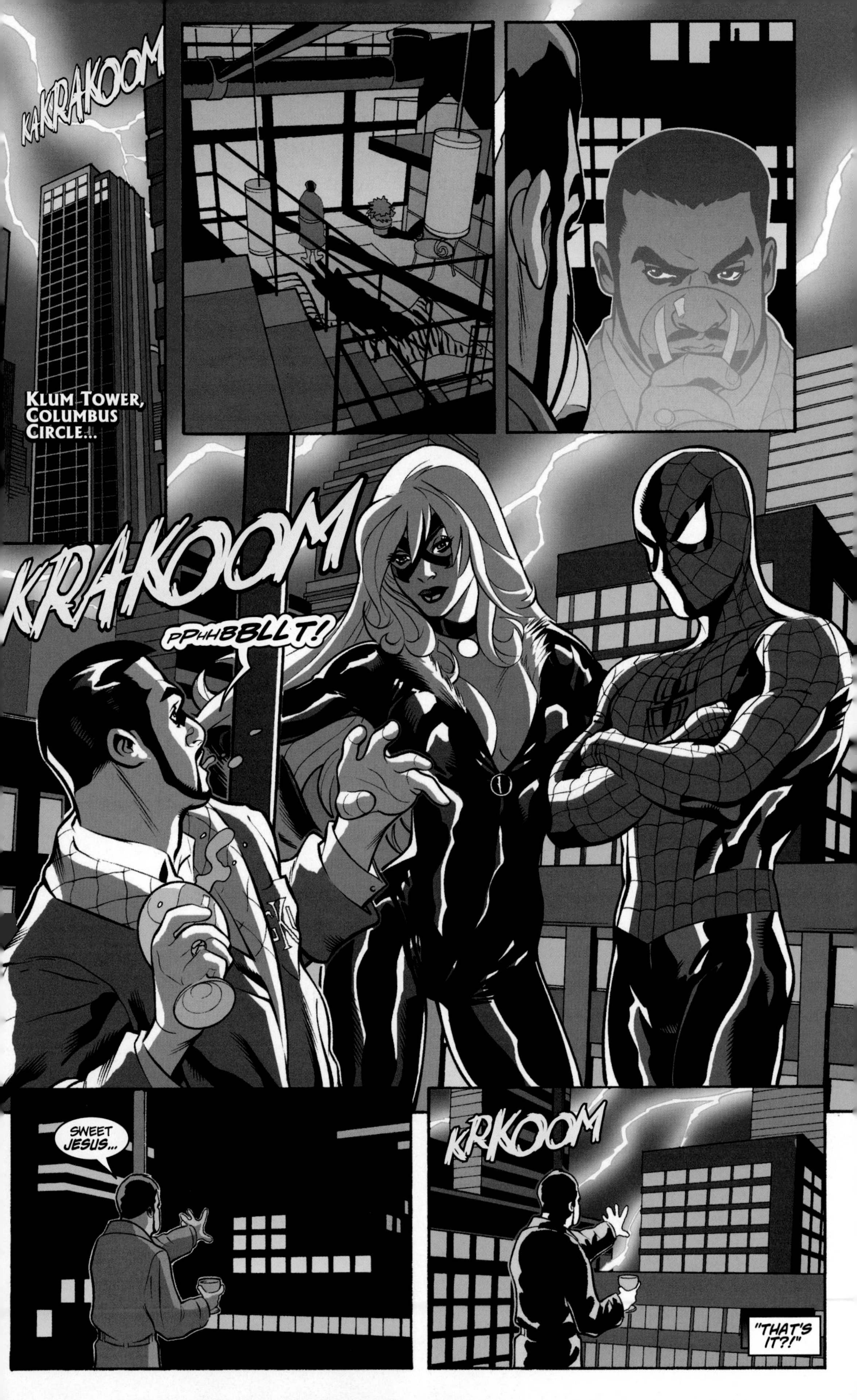
KAKRAKOOM
KLUM TOWER, COLUMBUS CIRCLE...
KRAKOOM
PPHHBBLLT!
SWEET JESUS...
KRKOOM
"THAT'S IT?!"

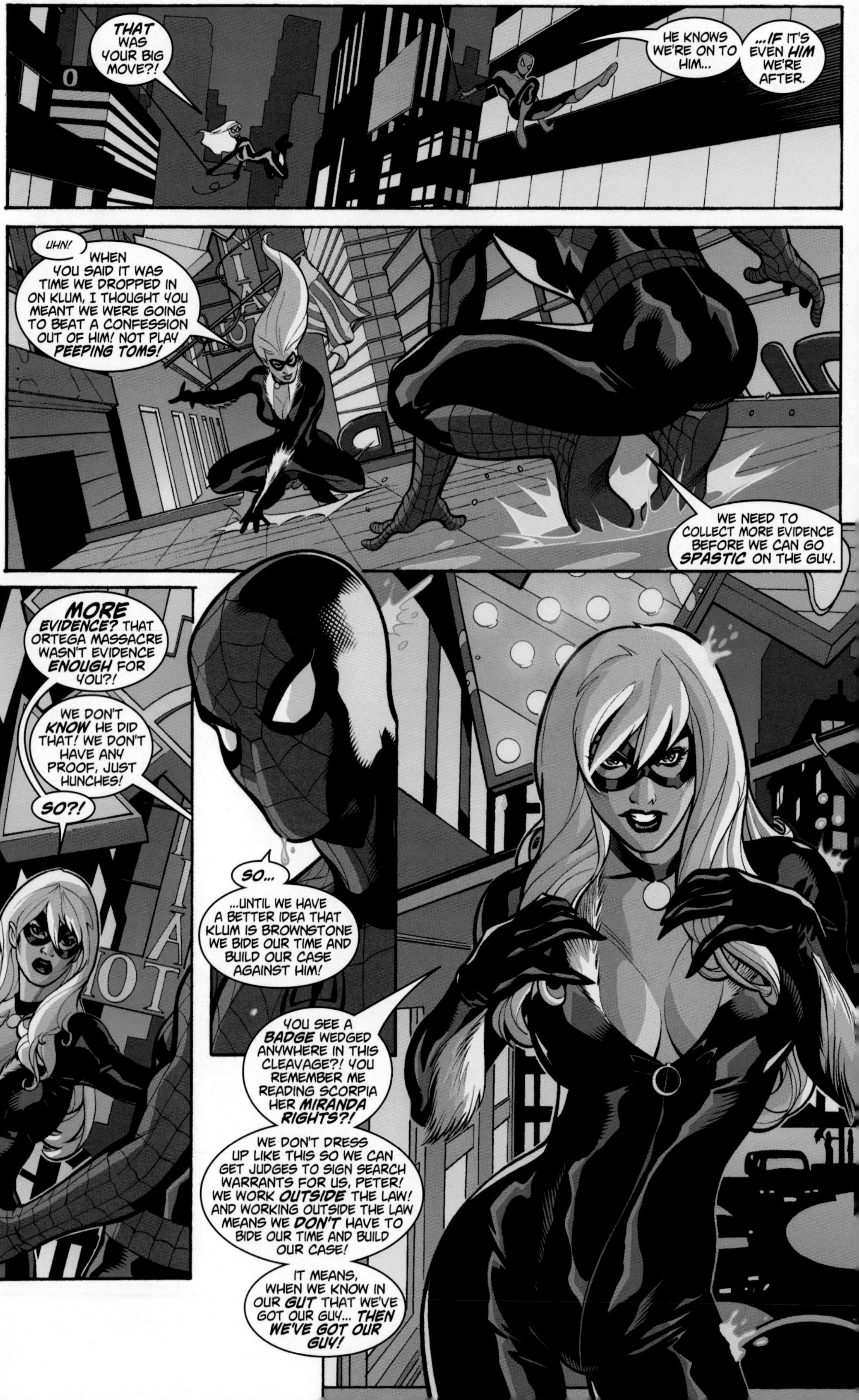
THAT WAS YOUR BIG MOVE?!
HE KNOWS WE'RE ON TO HIM...
...IF IT'S EVEN HIM WE'RE AFTER.
UHN!
WHEN YOU SAID IT WAS TIME WE DROPPED IN ON KLUM, I THOUGHT YOU MEANT WE WERE GOING TO BEAT A CONFESSION OUT OF HIM! NOT PLAY PEEPING TOMS!
WE NEED TO COLLECT MORE EVIDENCE BEFORE WE CAN GO SPASTIC ON THE GUY.
MORE EVIDENCE? THAT ORTEGA MASSACRE WASN'T EVIDENCE ENOUGH FOR YOU?!
WE DON'T KNOW HE DID THAT! WE DON'T HAVE ANY PROOF, JUST HUNCHES!
SO?!
SO...
...UNTIL WE HAVE A BETTER IDEA THAT KLUM IS BROWNSTONE WE BIDE OUR TIME AND BUILD OUR CASE AGAINST HIM!
YOU SEE A BADGE WEDGED ANYWHERE IN THIS CLEAVAGE?! YOU REMEMBER ME READING SCORPIA HER MIRANDA RIGHTS?!
WE DON'T DRESS UP LIKE THIS SO WE CAN GET JUDGES TO SIGN SEARCH WARRANTS FOR US, PETER! WE WORK OUTSIDE THE LAW! AND WORKING OUTSIDE THE LAW MEANS WE DON'T HAVE TO BIDE OUR TIME AND BUILD OUR CASE!
IT MEANS, WHEN WE KNOW IN OUR GUT THAT WE'VE GOT OUR GUY... THEN WE'VE GOT OUR GUY!

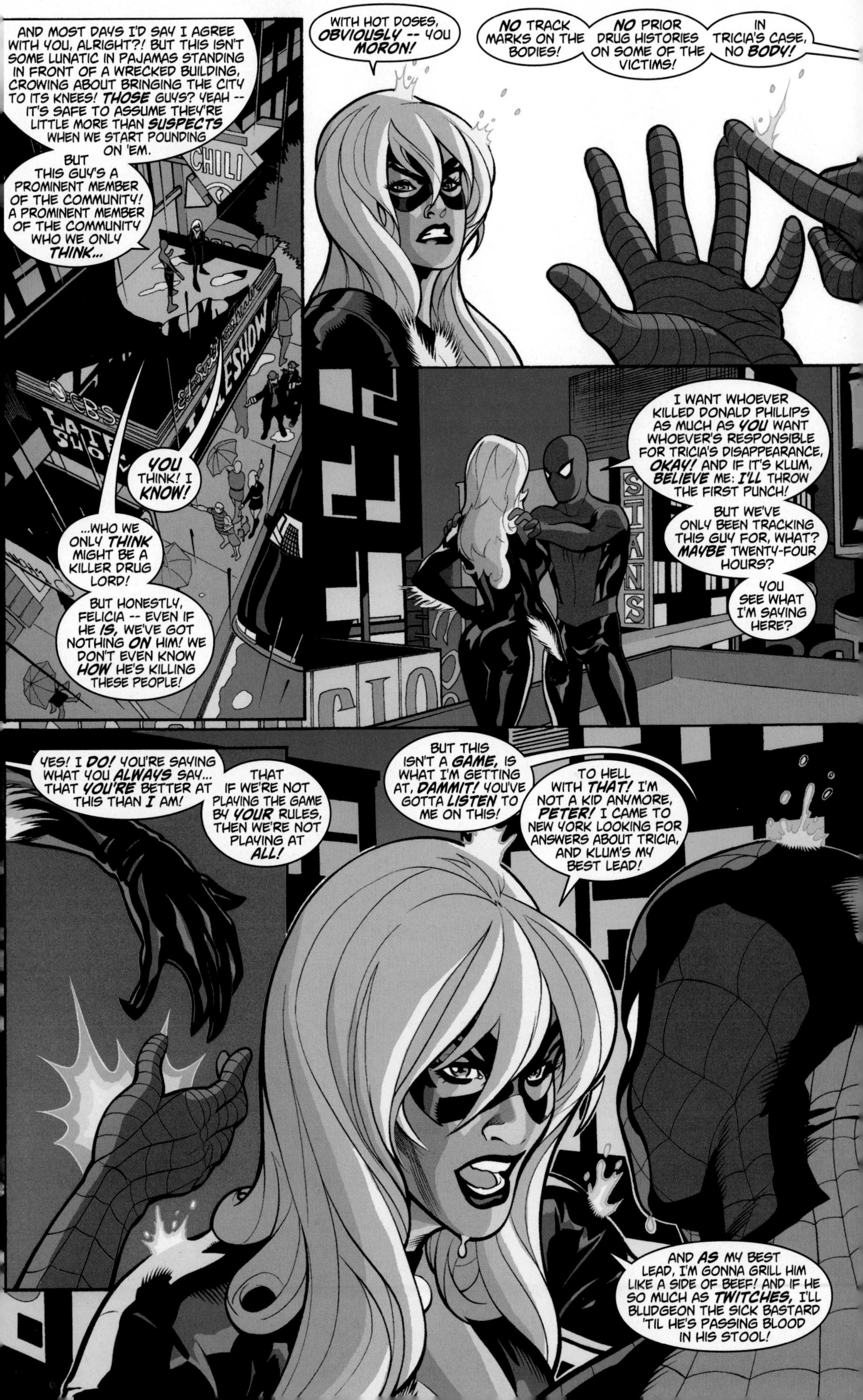

AND MOST DAYS I'D SAY I AGREE WITH YOU, ALRIGHT?! BUT THIS ISN'T SOME LUNATIC IN PAJAMAS STANDING IN FRONT OF A WRECKED BUILDING, CROWING ABOUT BRINGING THE CITY TO ITS KNEES! THOSE GUYS? YEAH -- IT'S SAFE TO ASSUME THEY'RE LITTLE MORE THAN SUSPECTS WHEN WE START POUNDING ON 'EM.
BUT THIS GUY'S A PROMINENT MEMBER OF THE COMMUNITY! A PROMINENT MEMBER OF THE COMMUNITY WHO WE ONLY THINK...
YOU THINK! I KNOW!
...WHO WE ONLY THINK MIGHT BE A KILLER DRUG LORD!
BUT HONESTLY, FELICIA -- EVEN IF HE IS, WE'VE GOT NOTHING ON HIM! WE DON'T EVEN KNOW HOW HE'S KILLING THESE PEOPLE!
WITH HOT DOSES, OBVIOUSLY -- YOU MORON!
NO TRACK MARKS ON THE BODIES!
NO PRIOR DRUG HISTORIES ON SOME OF THE VICTIMS!
IN TRICIA'S CASE, NO BODY!
I WANT WHOEVER KILLED DONALD PHILLIPS AS MUCH AS YOU WANT WHOEVER'S RESPONSIBLE FOR TRICIA'S DISAPPEARANCE, OKAY! AND IF IT'S KLUM, BELIEVE ME: I'LL THROW THE FIRST PUNCH!
BUT WE'VE ONLY BEEN TRACKING THIS GUY FOR, WHAT? MAYBE TWENTY-FOUR HOURS?
YOU SEE WHAT I'M SAYING HERE?
YES! I DO! YOU'RE SAYING WHAT YOU ALWAYS SAY... THAT YOU'RE BETTER AT THIS THAN I AM!
THAT IF WE'RE NOT PLAYING THE GAME BY YOUR RULES, THEN WE'RE NOT PLAYING AT ALL!
BUT THIS ISN'T A GAME, IS WHAT I'M GETTING AT, DAMMIT! YOU'VE GOTTA LISTEN TO ME ON THIS!
TO HELL WITH THAT! I'M NOT A KID ANYMORE, PETER! I CAME TO NEW YORK LOOKING FOR ANSWERS ABOUT TRICIA, AND KLUM'S MY BEST LEAD!
AND AS MY BEST LEAD, I'M GONNA GRILL HIM LIKE A SIDE OF BEEF! AND IF HE SO MUCH AS TWITCHES, I'LL BLUDGEON THE SICK BASTARD 'TIL HE'S PASSING BLOOD IN HIS STOOL!

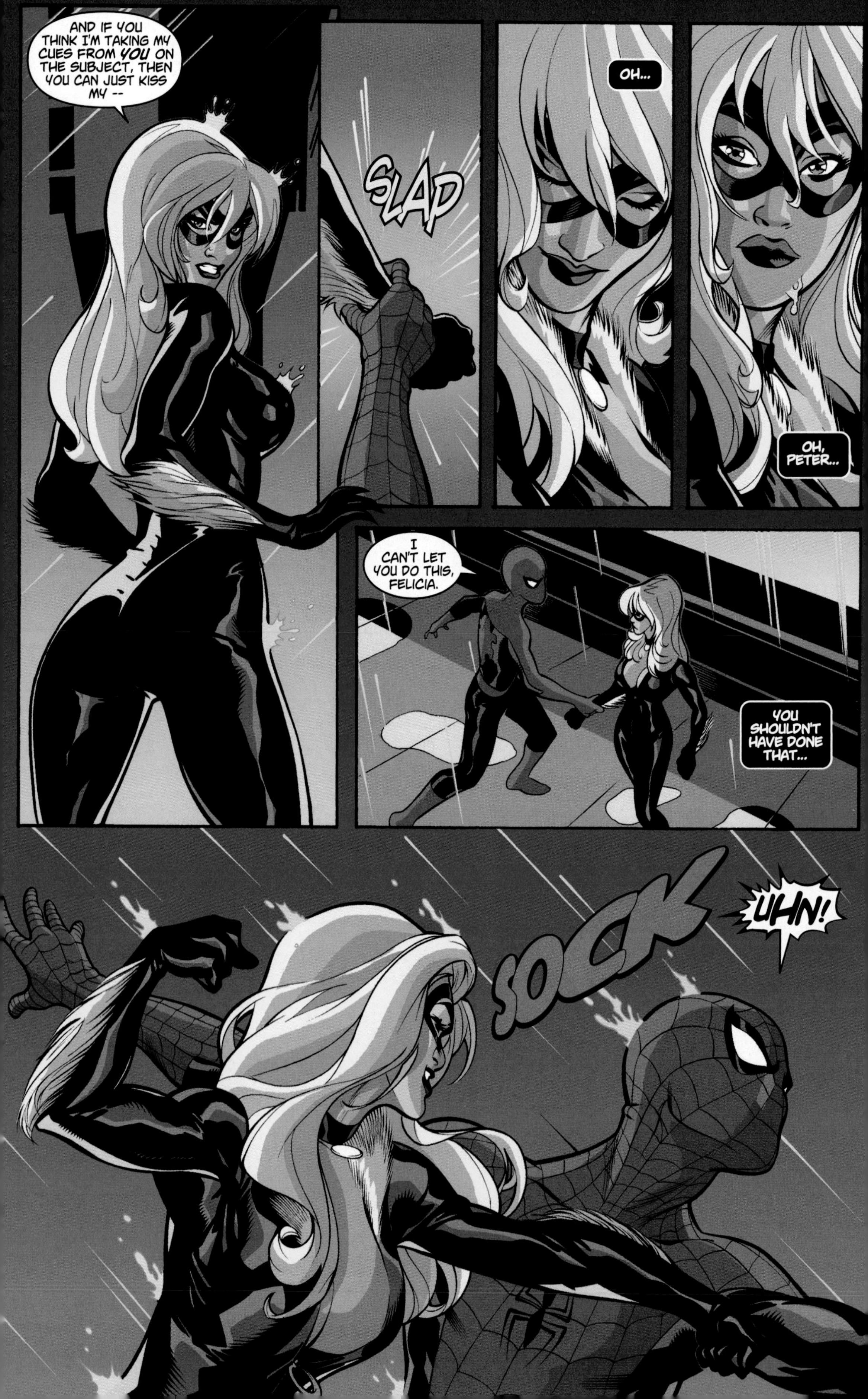
AND IF YOU THINK I'M TAKING MY CUES FROM YOU ON THE SUBJECT, THEN YOU CAN JUST KISS MY --
SLAP
OH...
OH, PETER...
I CAN'T LET YOU DO THIS, FELICIA.
YOU SHOULDN'T HAVE DONE THAT...
SOCK
UHN!

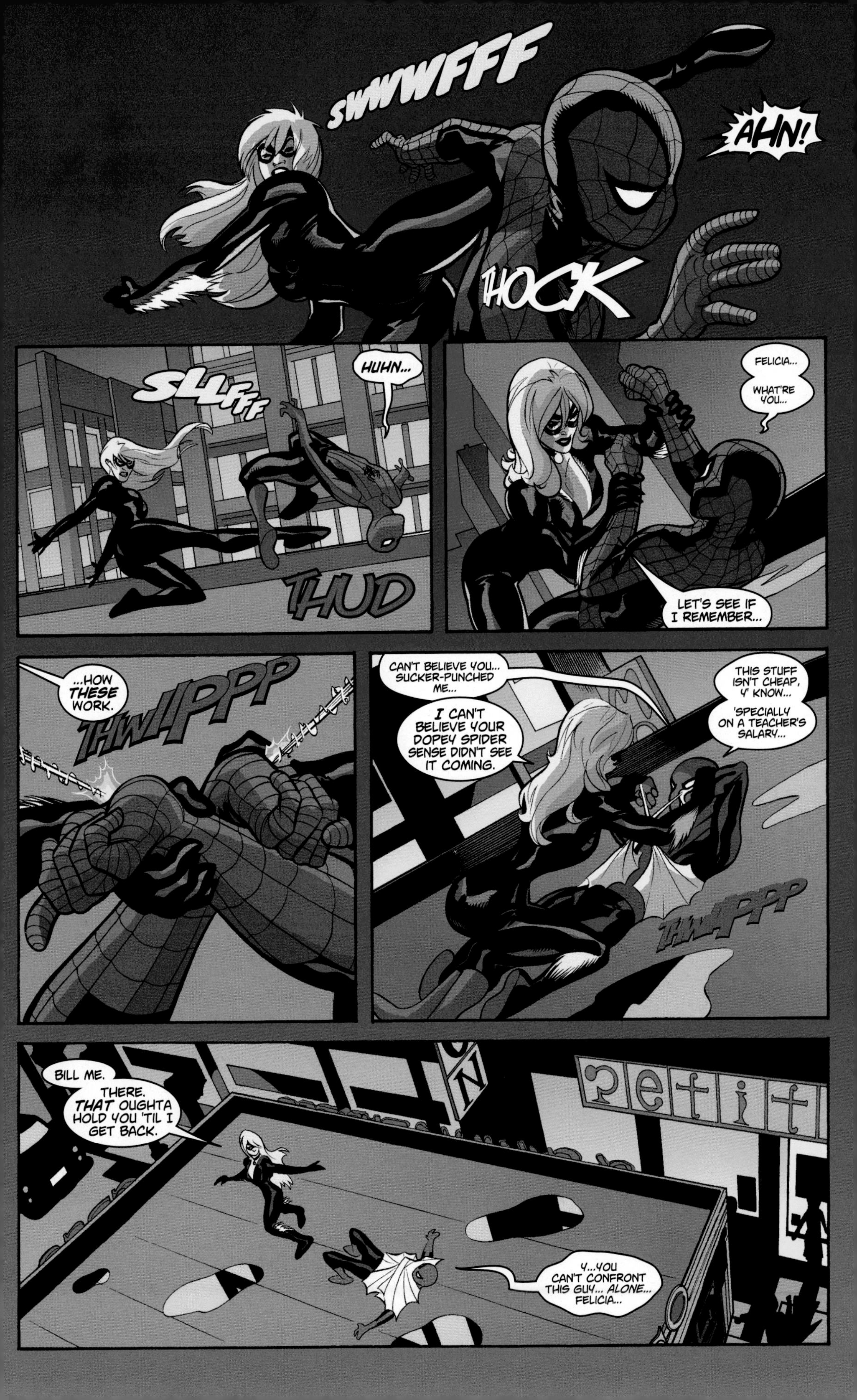
SWWWFFF
AHN!
THOCK
SLLFFF
HUHN...
THUD
FELICIA...
WHAT'RE YOU...
LET'S SEE IF I REMEMBER...
...HOW THESE WORK.
THWIPPP
CAN'T BELIEVE YOU... SUCKER-PUNCHED ME...
I CAN'T BELIEVE YOUR DOPEY SPIDER SENSE DIDN'T SEE IT COMING.
THIS STUFF ISN'T CHEAP, Y' KNOW...
'SPECIALLY ON A TEACHER'S SALARY...
THWIPPP
BILL ME.
THERE. THAT OUGHTA HOLD YOU 'TIL I GET BACK.
petit
Y...YOU CAN'T CONFRONT THIS GUY... ALONE... FELICIA...

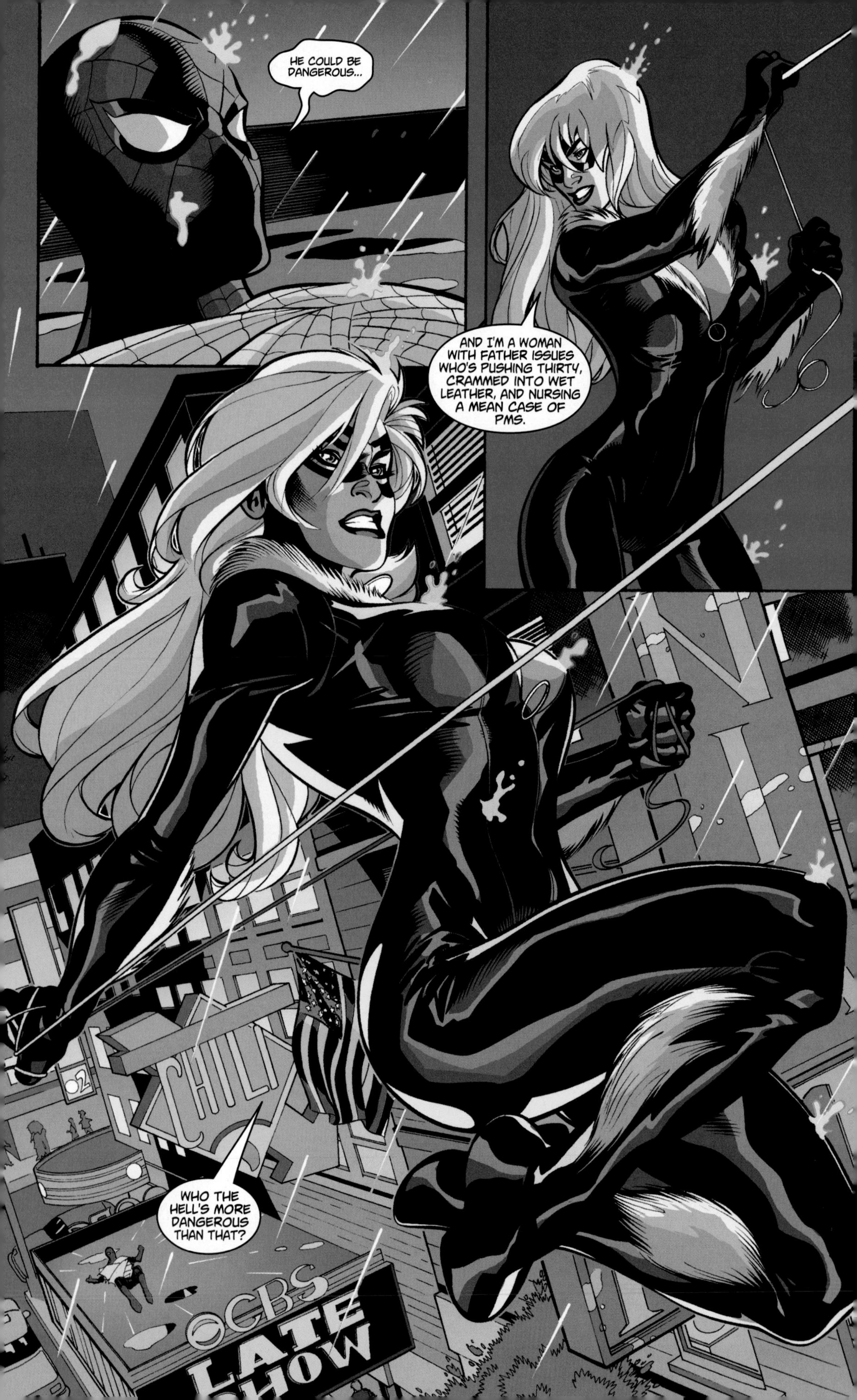
HE COULD BE DANGEROUS...
AND I'M A WOMAN WITH FATHER ISSUES WHO'S PUSHING THIRTY, CRAMMED INTO WET LEATHER, AND NURSING A MEAN CASE OF PMS.
WHO THE HELL'S MORE DANGEROUS THAN THAT?
CHILI
CBS
LATE SHOW

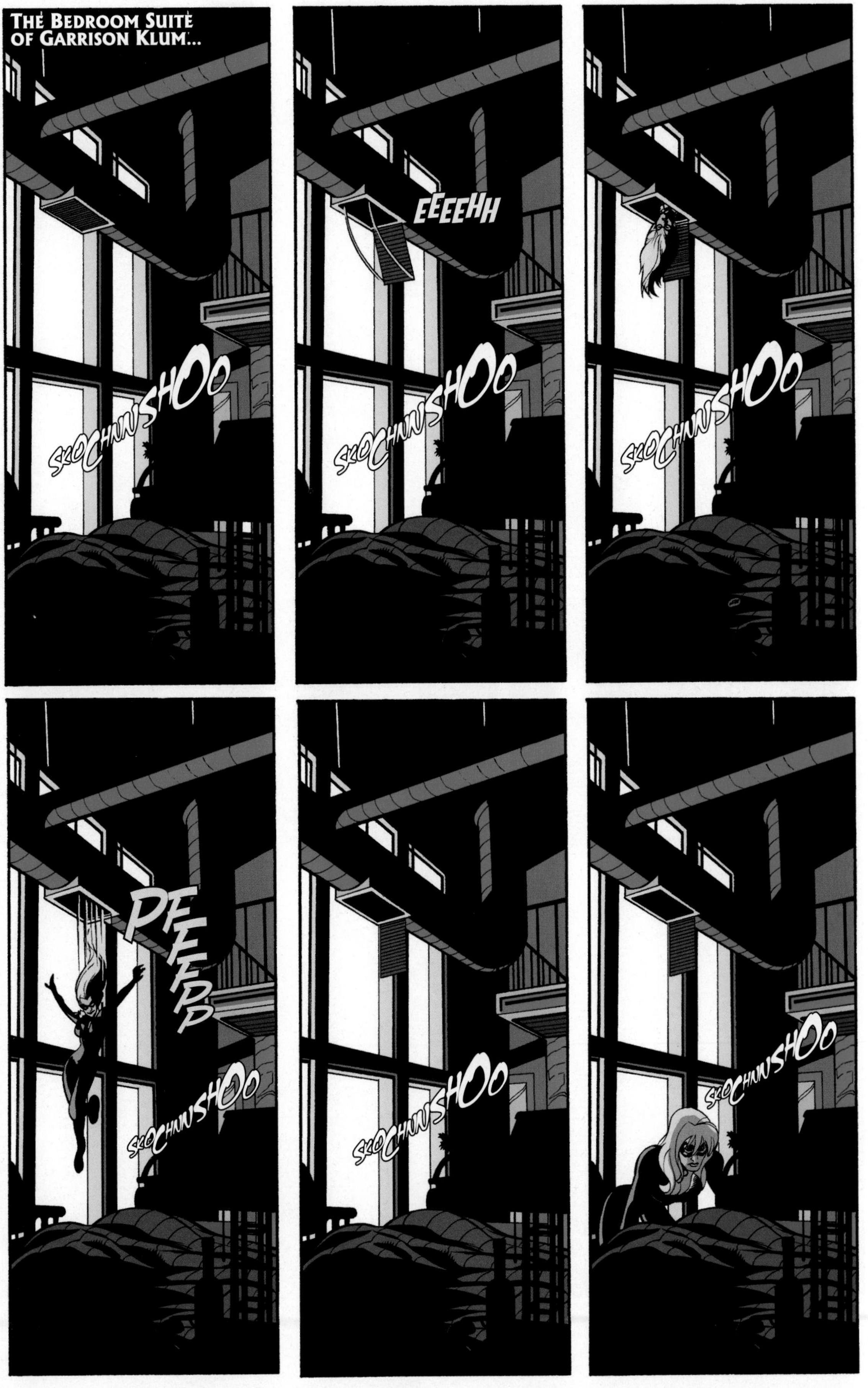
The Bedroom Suite of Garrison Klum...
SKOCHNNSHOO
EEEEHH
SKOCHNNSHOO
SKOCHNNSHOO
PFFFPP
SKOCHNNSHOO
SKOCHNNSHOO
SKOCHNNSHOO

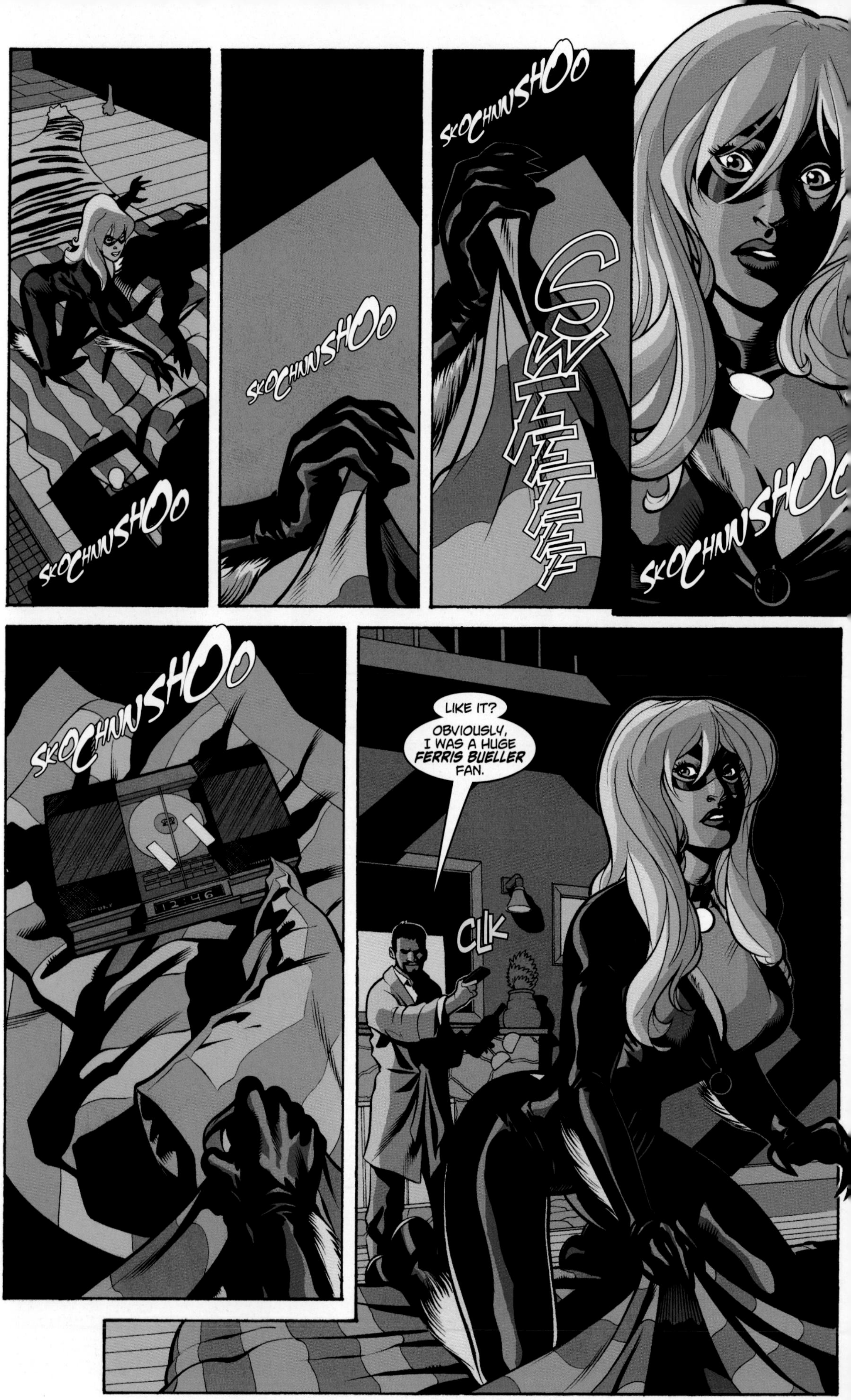

SKOCHNNSHOO
SKOCHNNSHOO
SKOCHNNSHOO
SWEEEEEE
SKOCHNNSHOO
SKOCHNNSHOO
12:46
LIKE IT?
OBVIOUSLY, I WAS A HUGE FERRIS BUELLER FAN.
CLIK

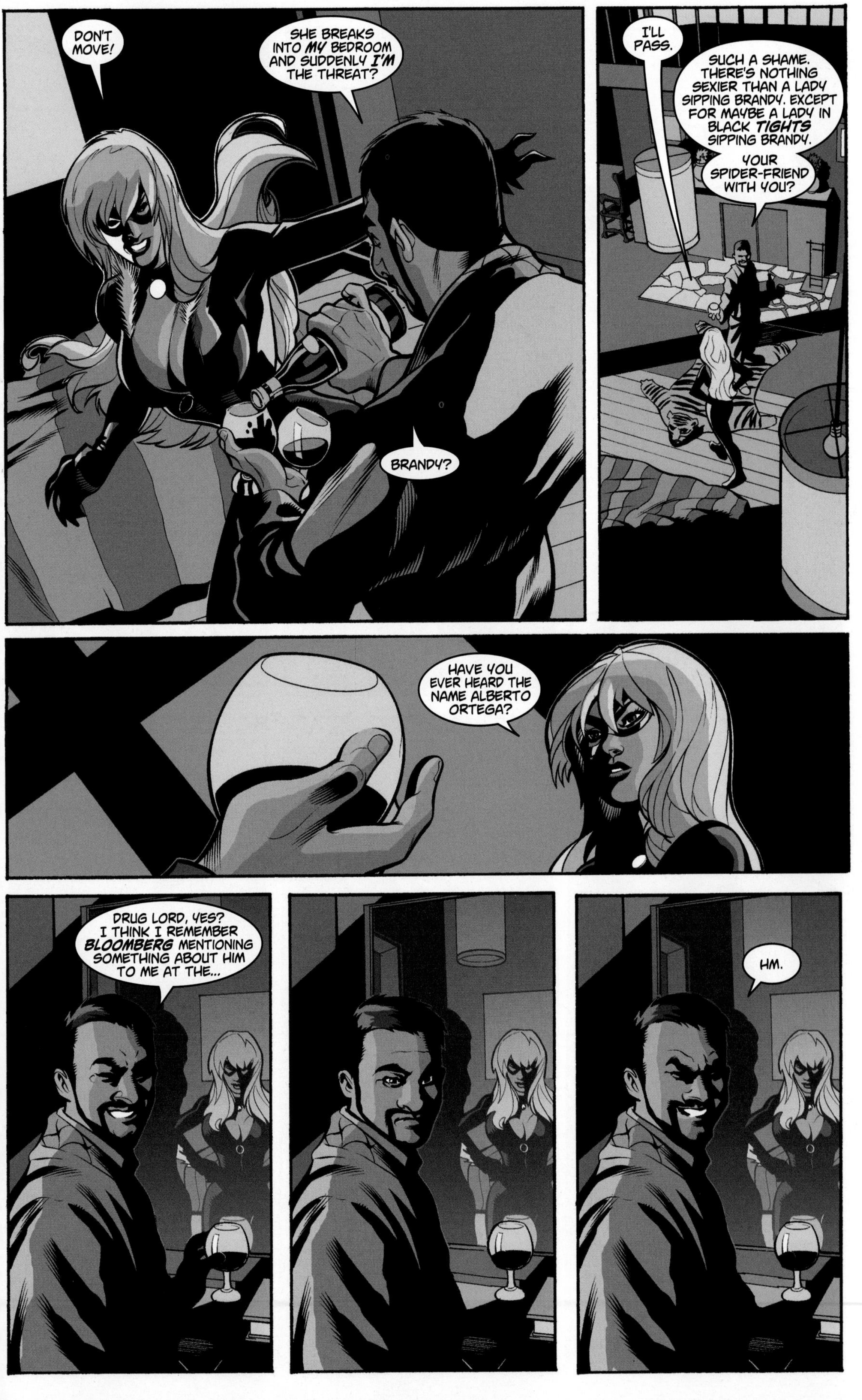
DON'T MOVE!
SHE BREAKS INTO MY BEDROOM AND SUDDENLY I'M THE THREAT?
BRANDY?
I'LL PASS.
SUCH A SHAME. THERE'S NOTHING SEXIER THAN A LADY SIPPING BRANDY. EXCEPT FOR MAYBE A LADY IN BLACK TIGHTS SIPPING BRANDY.
YOUR SPIDER-FRIEND WITH YOU?
HAVE YOU EVER HEARD THE NAME ALBERTO ORTEGA?
DRUG LORD, YES? I THINK I REMEMBER BLOOMBERG MENTIONING SOMETHING ABOUT HIM TO ME AT THE...
HM.

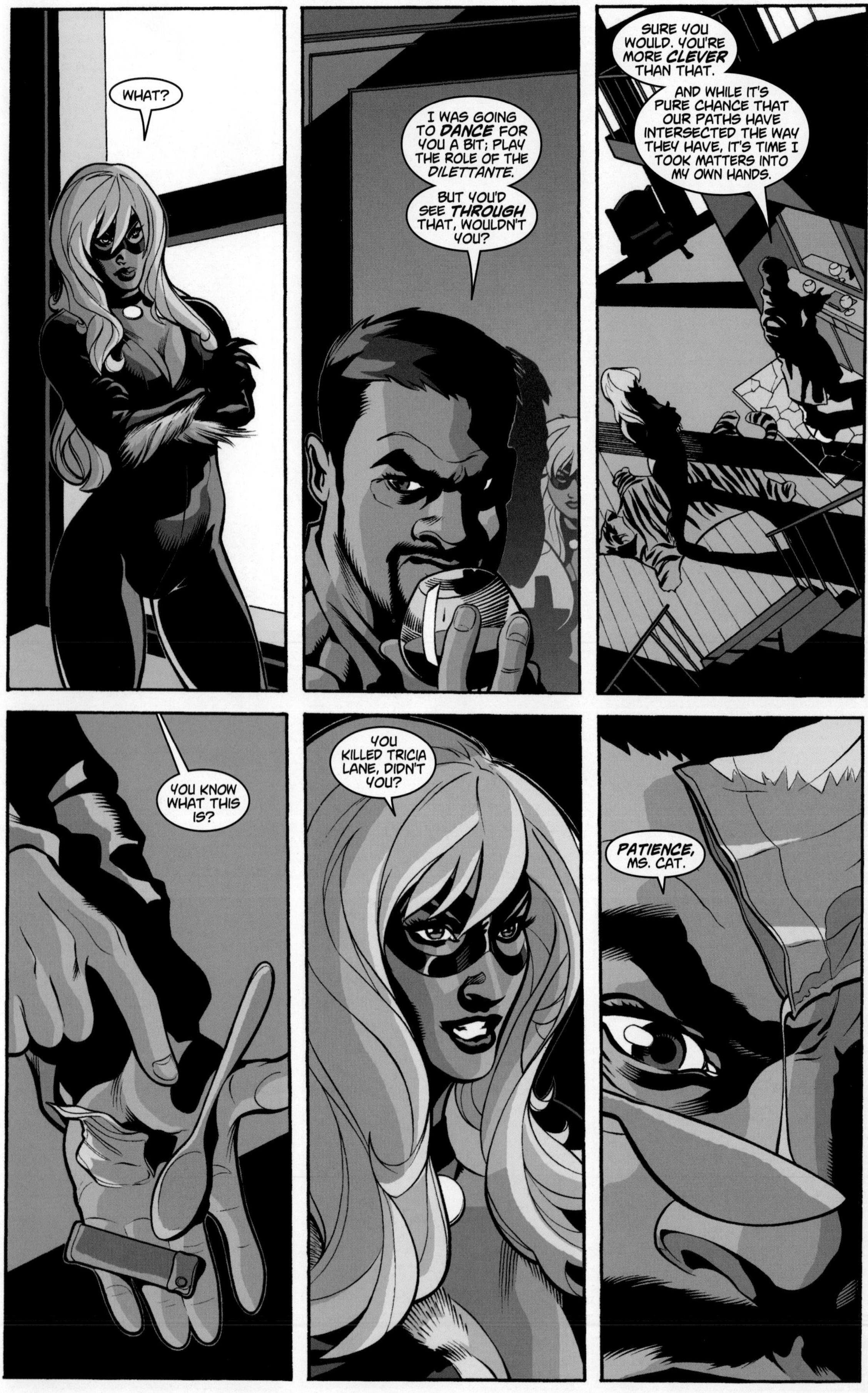
WHAT?
I WAS GOING TO DANCE FOR YOU A BIT; PLAY THE ROLE OF THE DILETTANTE.
BUT YOU'D SEE THROUGH THAT, WOULDN'T YOU?
SURE YOU WOULD. YOU'RE MORE CLEVER THAN THAT.
AND WHILE IT'S PURE CHANCE THAT OUR PATHS HAVE INTERSECTED THE WAY THEY HAVE, IT'S TIME I TOOK MATTERS INTO MY OWN HANDS.
YOU KNOW WHAT THIS IS?
YOU KILLED TRICIA LANE, DIDN'T YOU?
PATIENCE, MS. CAT.

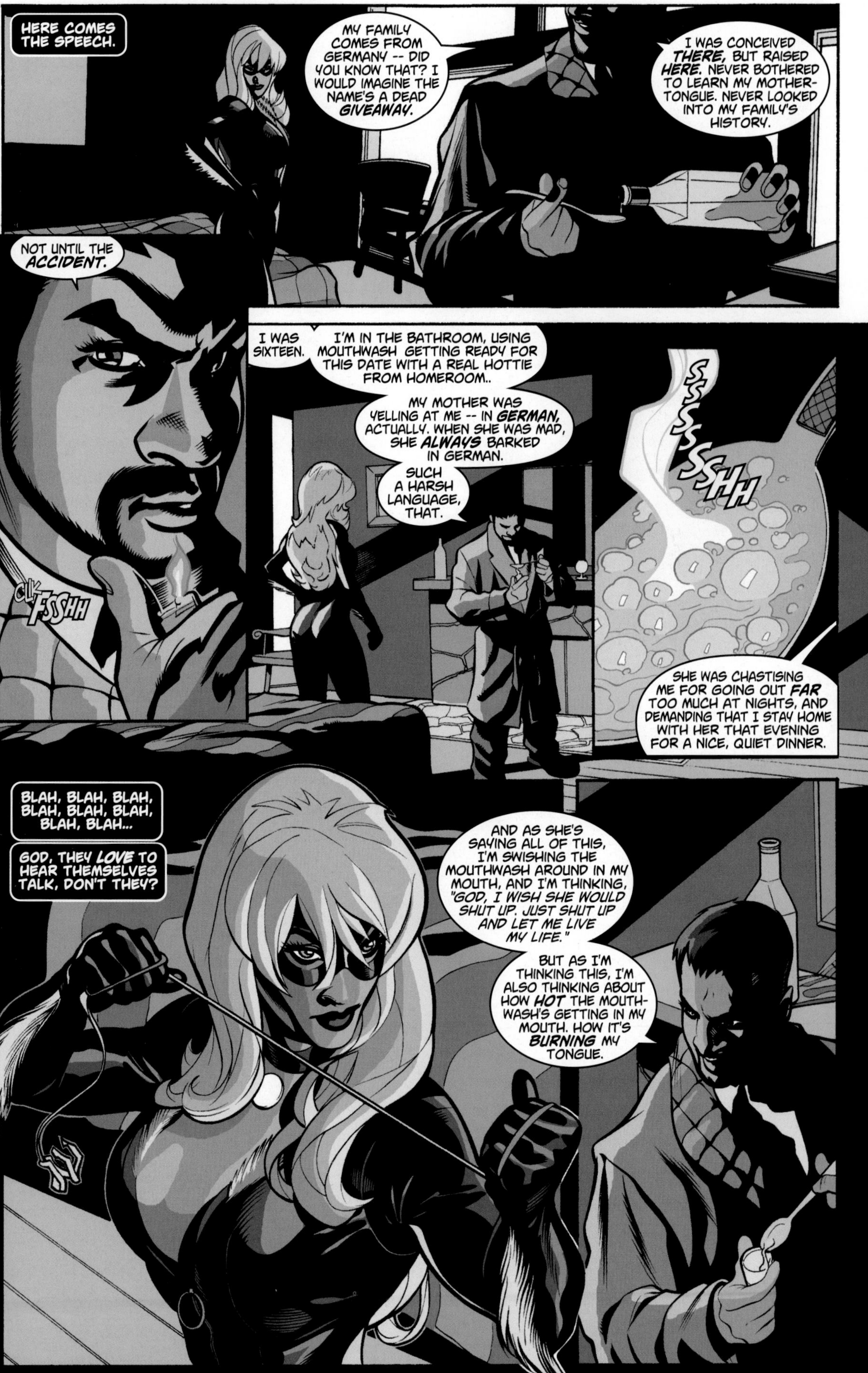
HERE COMES THE SPEECH.
MY FAMILY COMES FROM GERMANY -- DID YOU KNOW THAT? I WOULD IMAGINE THE NAME'S A DEAD GIVEAWAY.
I WAS CONCEIVED THERE, BUT RAISED HERE. NEVER BOTHERED TO LEARN MY MOTHER-TONGUE. NEVER LOOKED INTO MY FAMILY'S HISTORY.
NOT UNTIL THE ACCIDENT.
CLIK FSSHH
I WAS SIXTEEN.
I'M IN THE BATHROOM, USING MOUTHWASH GETTING READY FOR THIS DATE WITH A REAL HOTTIE FROM HOMEROOM..
MY MOTHER WAS YELLING AT ME -- IN GERMAN, ACTUALLY. WHEN SHE WAS MAD, SHE ALWAYS BARKED IN GERMAN.
SUCH A HARSH LANGUAGE, THAT.
SSSSSSHH
SHE WAS CHASTISING ME FOR GOING OUT FAR TOO MUCH AT NIGHTS, AND DEMANDING THAT I STAY HOME WITH HER THAT EVENING FOR A NICE, QUIET DINNER.
BLAH, BLAH, BLAH, BLAH, BLAH, BLAH, BLAH, BLAH...
GOD, THEY LOVE TO HEAR THEMSELVES TALK, DON'T THEY?
AND AS SHE'S SAYING ALL OF THIS, I'M SWISHING THE MOUTHWASH AROUND IN MY MOUTH, AND I'M THINKING, "GOD, I WISH SHE WOULD SHUT UP. JUST SHUT UP AND LET ME LIVE MY LIFE."
BUT AS I'M THINKING THIS, I'M ALSO THINKING ABOUT HOW HOT THE MOUTH-WASH'S GETTING IN MY MOUTH. HOW IT'S BURNING MY TONGUE.

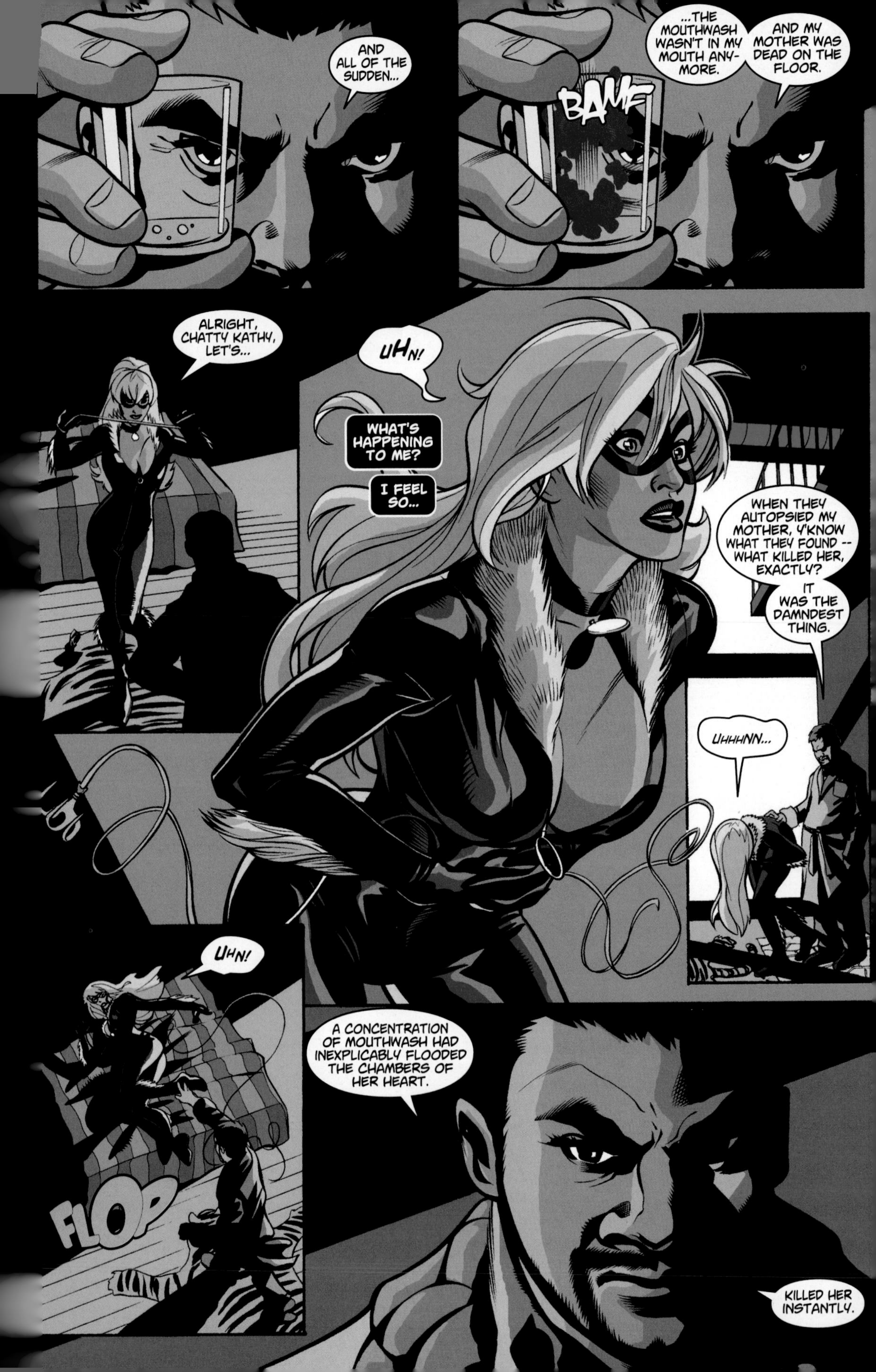
AND ALL OF THE SUDDEN...
BAMF
...THE MOUTHWASH WASN'T IN MY MOUTH ANY-MORE.
AND MY MOTHER WAS DEAD ON THE FLOOR.
ALRIGHT, CHATTY KATHY, LET'S...
UHN!
WHAT'S HAPPENING TO ME?
I FEEL SO...
WHEN THEY AUTOPSIED MY MOTHER, Y'KNOW WHAT THEY FOUND -- WHAT KILLED HER, EXACTLY?
IT WAS THE DAMNDEST THING.
UHHHNN...
UHN!
FLOP
A CONCENTRATION OF MOUTHWASH HAD INEXPLICABLY FLOODED THE CHAMBERS OF HER HEART.
KILLED HER INSTANTLY.

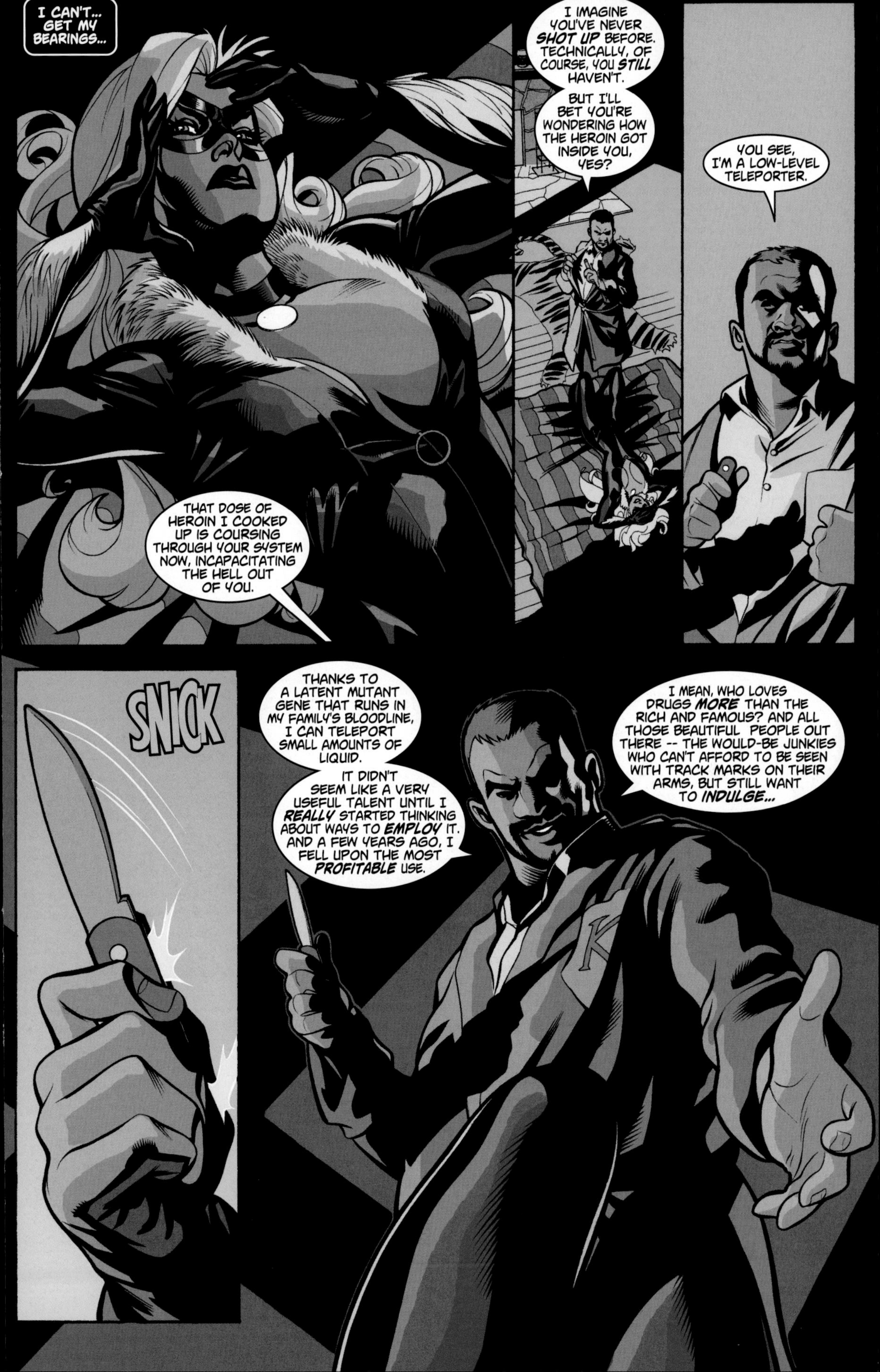
I CAN'T... GET MY BEARINGS...
THAT DOSE OF HEROIN I COOKED UP IS COURSING THROUGH YOUR SYSTEM NOW, INCAPACITATING THE HELL OUT OF YOU.
I IMAGINE YOU'VE NEVER SHOT UP BEFORE. TECHNICALLY, OF COURSE, YOU STILL HAVEN'T.
BUT I'LL BET YOU'RE WONDERING HOW THE HEROIN GOT INSIDE YOU, YES?
YOU SEE, I'M A LOW-LEVEL TELEPORTER.
SNICK
THANKS TO A LATENT MUTANT GENE THAT RUNS IN MY FAMILY'S BLOODLINE, I CAN TELEPORT SMALL AMOUNTS OF LIQUID.
IT DIDN'T SEEM LIKE A VERY USEFUL TALENT UNTIL I REALLY STARTED THINKING ABOUT WAYS TO EMPLOY IT. AND A FEW YEARS AGO, I FELL UPON THE MOST PROFITABLE USE.
I MEAN, WHO LOVES DRUGS MORE THAN THE RICH AND FAMOUS? AND ALL THOSE BEAUTIFUL PEOPLE OUT THERE -- THE WOULD-BE JUNKIES WHO CAN'T AFFORD TO BE SEEN WITH TRACK MARKS ON THEIR ARMS, BUT STILL WANT TO INDULGE...

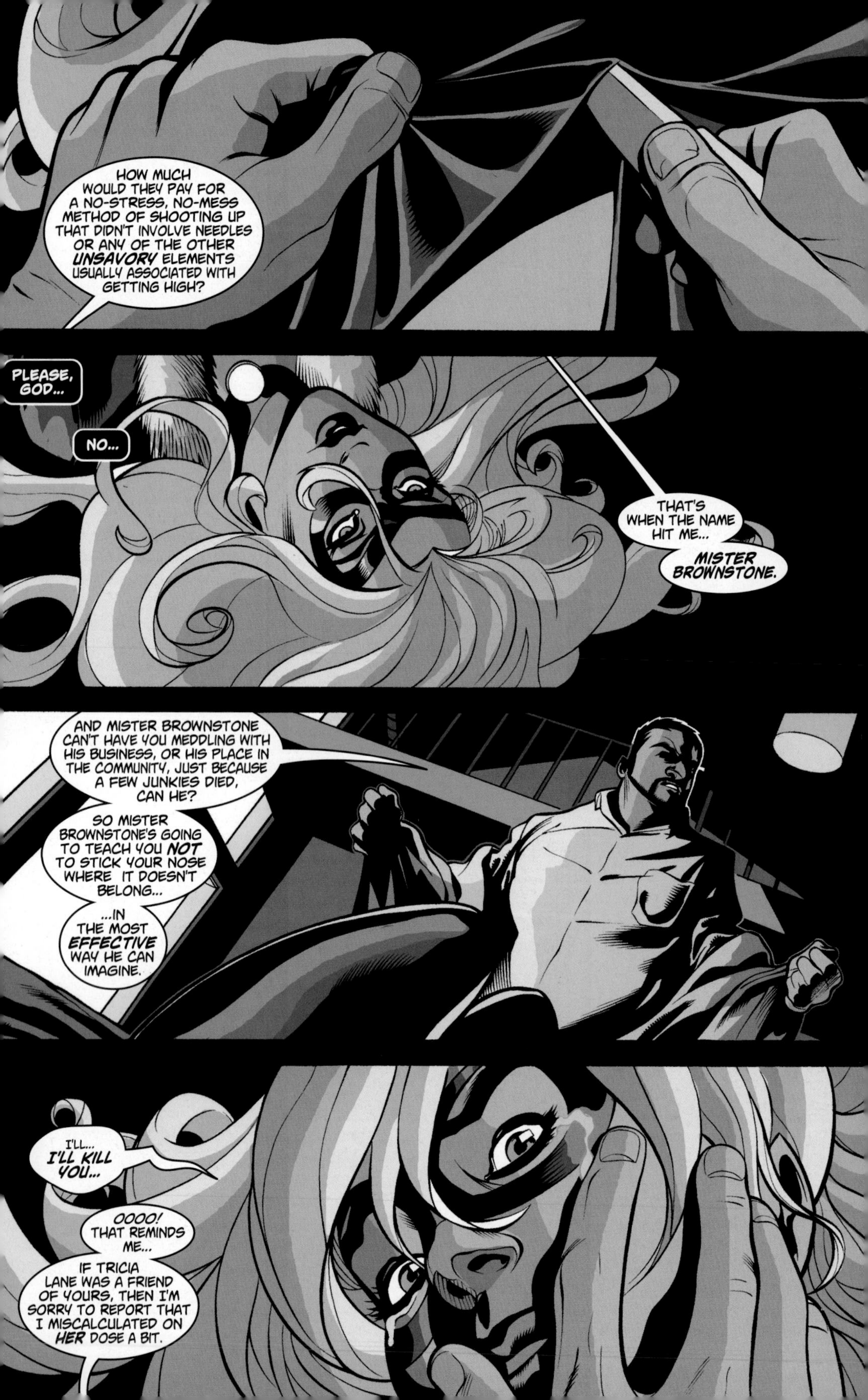
HOW MUCH WOULD THEY PAY FOR A NO-STRESS, NO-MESS METHOD OF SHOOTING UP THAT DIDN'T INVOLVE NEEDLES OR ANY OF THE OTHER UNSAVORY ELEMENTS USUALLY ASSOCIATED WITH GETTING HIGH?
PLEASE, GOD...
NO...
THAT'S WHEN THE NAME HIT ME...
MISTER BROWNSTONE.
AND MISTER BROWNSTONE CAN'T HAVE YOU MEDDLING WITH HIS BUSINESS, OR HIS PLACE IN THE COMMUNITY, JUST BECAUSE A FEW JUNKIES DIED, CAN HE?
SO MISTER BROWNSTONE'S GOING TO TEACH YOU NOT TO STICK YOUR NOSE WHERE IT DOESN'T BELONG...
...IN THE MOST EFFECTIVE WAY HE CAN IMAGINE.
I'LL... I'LL KILL YOU...
OOOO! THAT REMINDS ME...
IF TRICIA LANE WAS A FRIEND OF YOURS, THEN I'M SORRY TO REPORT THAT I MISCALCULATED ON HER DOSE A BIT.

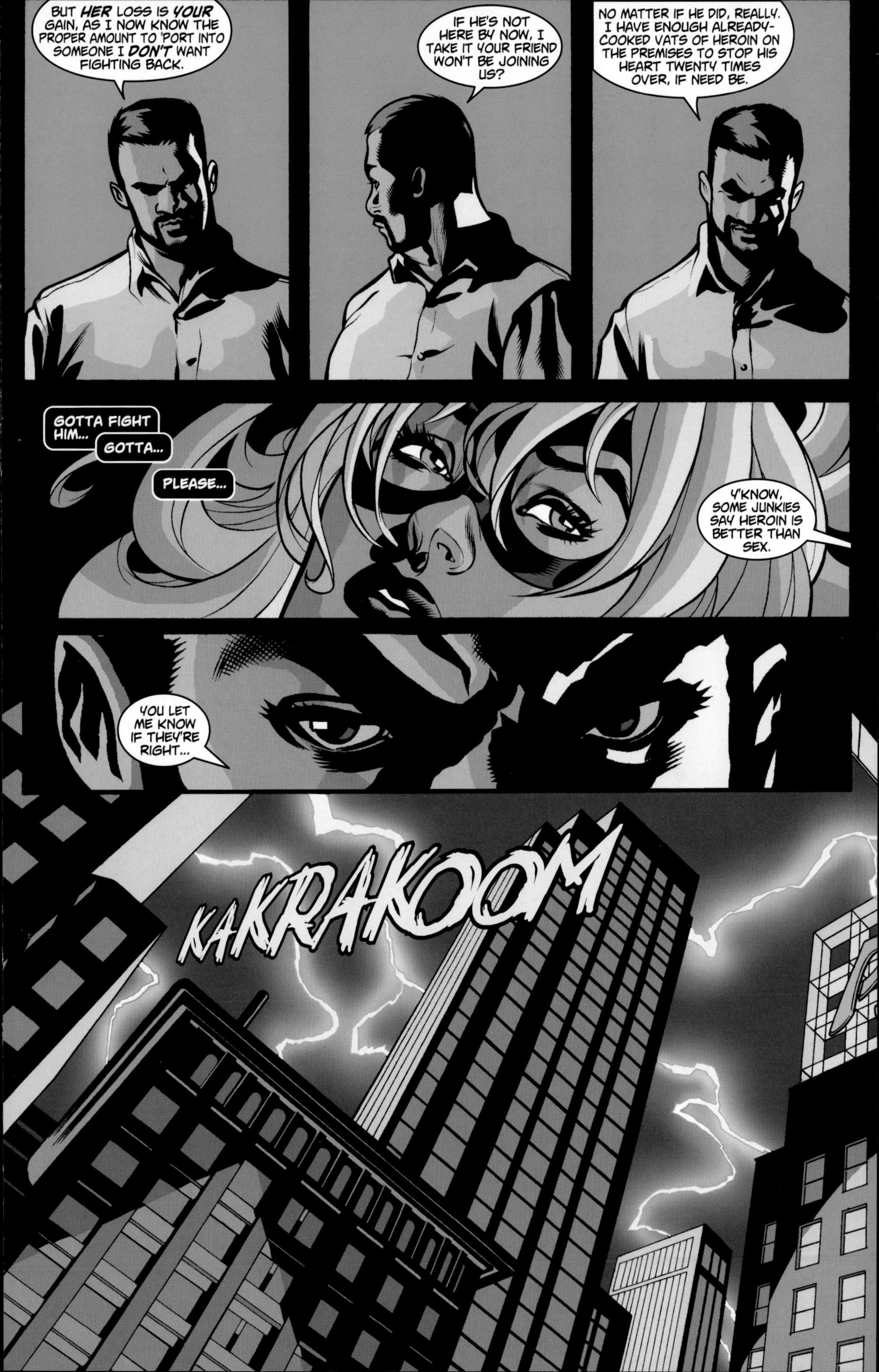
BUT HER LOSS IS YOUR GAIN, AS I NOW KNOW THE PROPER AMOUNT TO 'PORT INTO SOMEONE I DON'T WANT FIGHTING BACK.
IF HE'S NOT HERE BY NOW, I TAKE IT YOUR FRIEND WON'T BE JOINING US?
NO MATTER IF HE DID, REALLY. I HAVE ENOUGH ALREADY-COOKED VATS OF HEROIN ON THE PREMISES TO STOP HIS HEART TWENTY TIMES OVER, IF NEED BE.
GOTTA FIGHT HIM...
GOTTA...
PLEASE...
Y'KNOW, SOME JUNKIES SAY HEROIN IS BETTER THAN SEX.
YOU LET ME KNOW IF THEY'RE RIGHT...
KAKRAKOOM

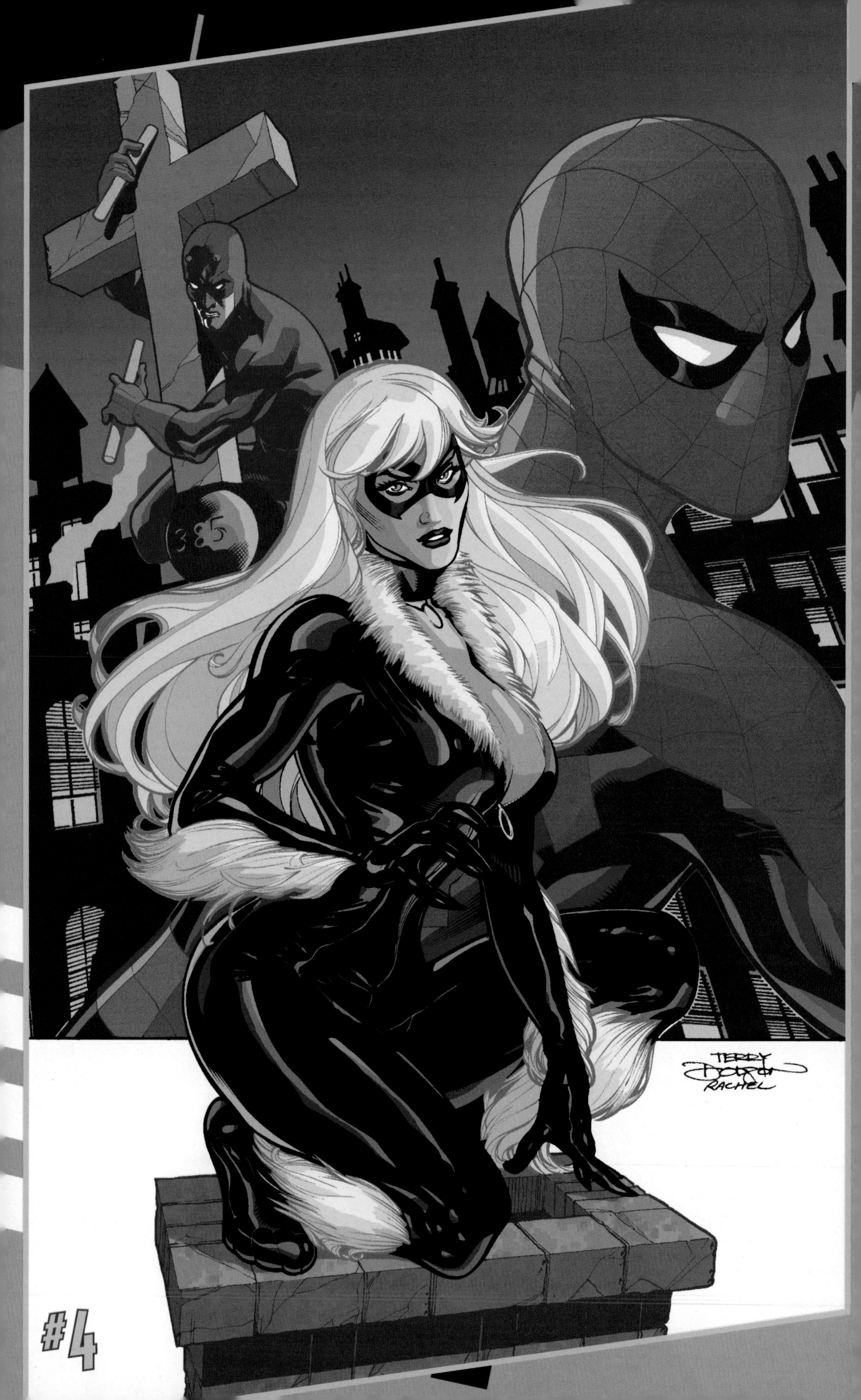
TERRY
DODSON
RACHEL

#4

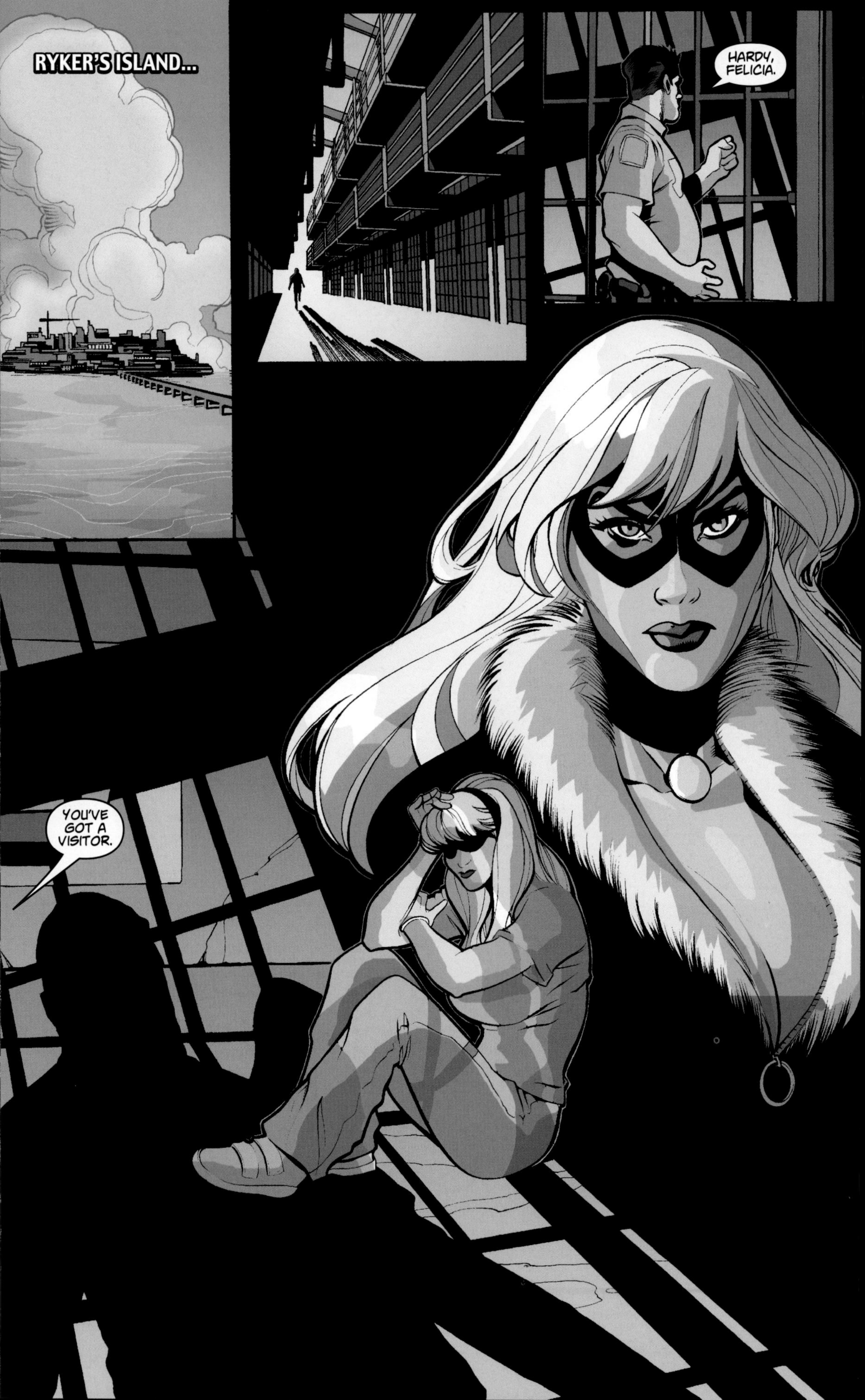
RYKER'S ISLAND...
HARDY, FELICIA.
YOU'VE GOT A VISITOR.

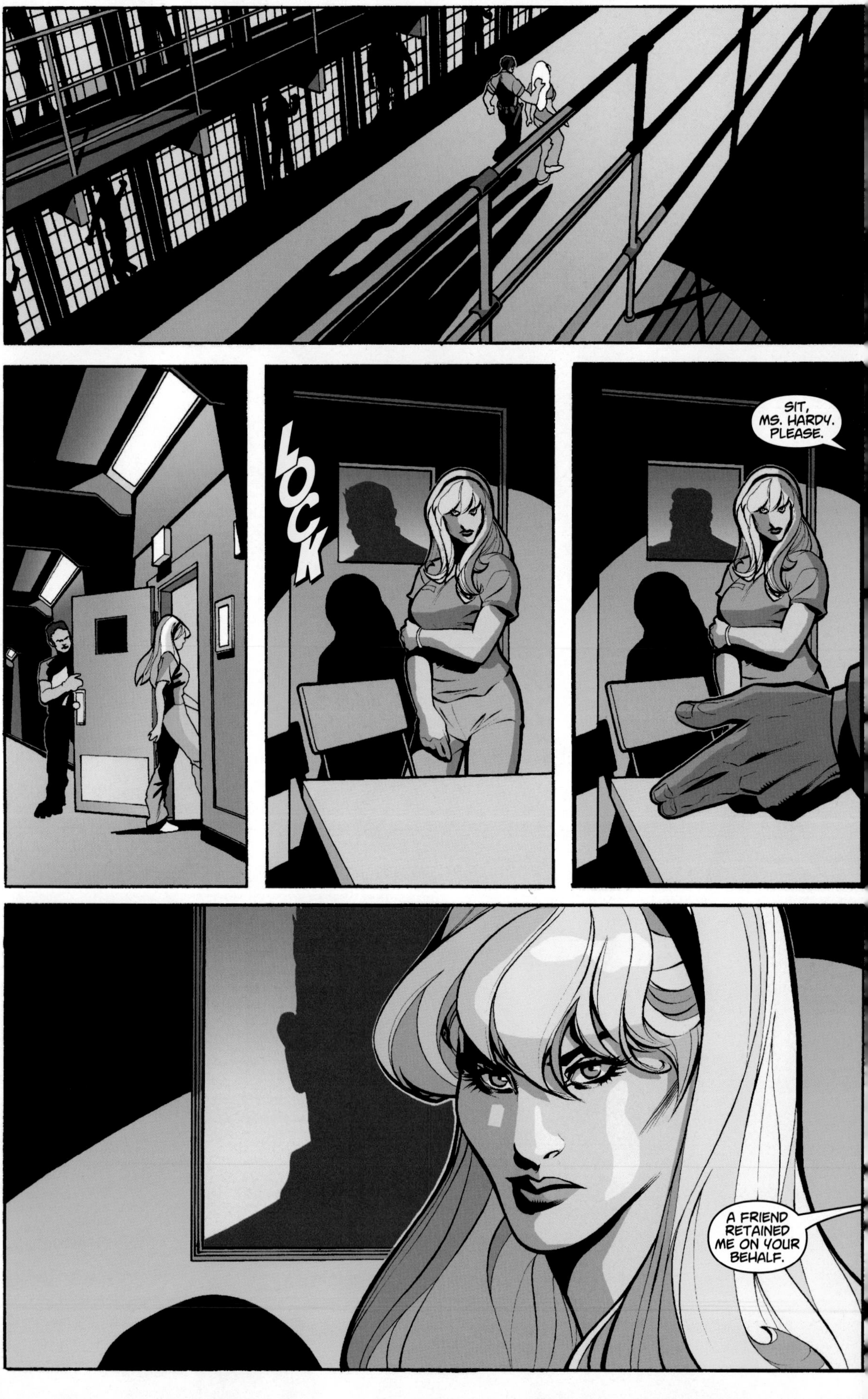
LOCK
SIT, MS. HARDY. PLEASE.
A FRIEND RETAINED ME ON YOUR BEHALF.

I'LL BE REPLACING THE COURT-APPOINTED WHO REPRESENTED YOU AT YOUR ARRAIGNMENT.

I'VE JUST SPOKEN TO THE PROSECUTOR.

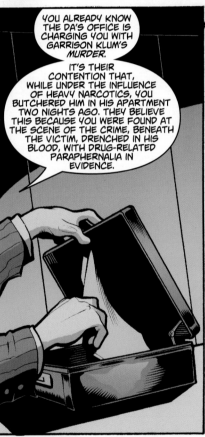

YOU ALREADY KNOW THE DA'S OFFICE IS CHARGING YOU WITH GARRISON KLUM'S *MURDER*.

IT'S THEIR CONTENTION THAT, WHILE UNDER THE INFLUENCE OF HEAVY NARCOTICS, YOU BUTCHERED HIM IN HIS APARTMENT TWO NIGHTS AGO. THEY BELIEVE THIS BECAUSE YOU WERE FOUND AT THE SCENE OF THE CRIME, BENEATH THE VICTIM, DRENCHED IN HIS BLOOD, WITH DRUG-RELATED PARAPHERNALIA IN EVIDENCE.

BUT THIS MORNING, THEY ADDED A COUNT OF *BURGLARY*. THEIR NEW THEORY IS THAT YOU KILLED KLUM DURING THE COMMISSION OF ANOTHER CRIME: ROBBERY.

BASED ON THAT, THEY'RE NOW CHARGING YOU WITH MURDER ONE.

THE MAYOR'S UP FOR RE-ELECTION, AND A CAPITAL CASE INVOLVING A COSTUME APPEALS TO HIS HONOR'S MORE *CONSERVATIVE* CONSTITUENTS.

I'LL BE SUBMITTING MY MOTION TO EXCLUDE YOUR PRIORS, AS THEY WERE EXPUNGED IN A DEAL YOU MADE WITH THE DA'S OFFICE A FEW YEARS BACK, WHEN YOU GAVE UP SOME OF YOUR UNDERWORLD CONTACTS.

WITHOUT YOUR PRIORS -- EVEN THOUGH YOU WERE WEARING YOUR BLACK CAT COSTUME -- THEY CAN'T MAKE THE ARGUMENT THAT YOU WERE BREAKING AND ENTERING INTO KLUM'S APARTMENT. WE CAN ARGUE THAT YOU WERE AN INVITED *GUEST*, WHO WAS SUDDENLY *FORCED* INTO A SELF-DEFENSE SITUATION.

I'M GONNA HAVE TO GET INTO SOME... *UNCOMFORTABLE* DETAILS NOW.

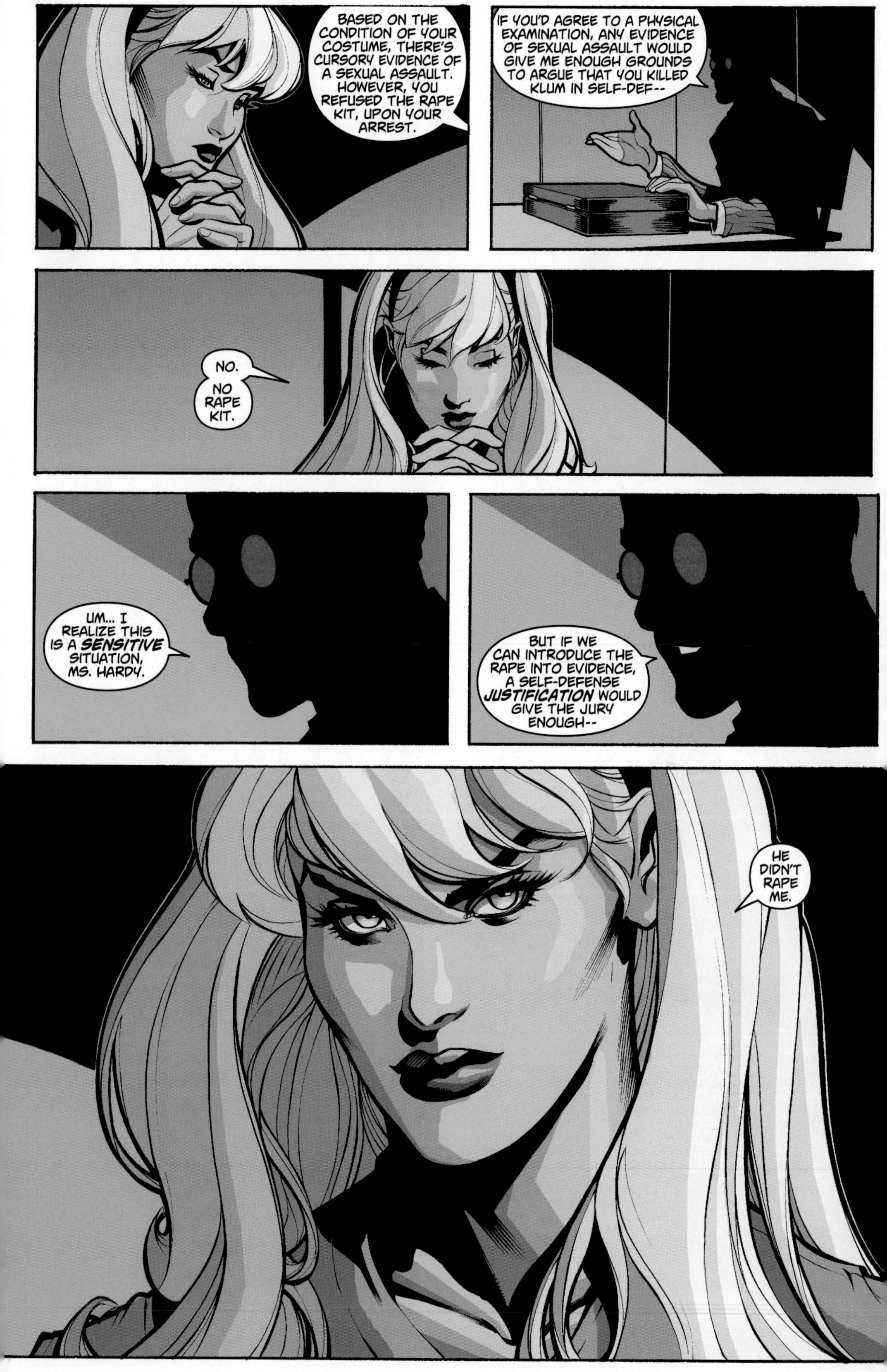

BASED ON THE CONDITION OF YOUR COSTUME, THERE'S CURSORY EVIDENCE OF A SEXUAL ASSAULT. HOWEVER, YOU REFUSED THE RAPE KIT, UPON YOUR ARREST.
IF YOU'D AGREE TO A PHYSICAL EXAMINATION, ANY EVIDENCE OF SEXUAL ASSAULT WOULD GIVE ME ENOUGH GROUNDS TO ARGUE THAT YOU KILLED KLUM IN SELF-DEF--
NO. NO RAPE KIT.
UM... I REALIZE THIS IS A SENSITIVE SITUATION, MS. HARDY.
BUT IF WE CAN INTRODUCE THE RAPE INTO EVIDENCE, A SELF-DEFENSE JUSTIFICATION WOULD GIVE THE JURY ENOUGH--
HE DIDN'T RAPE ME.

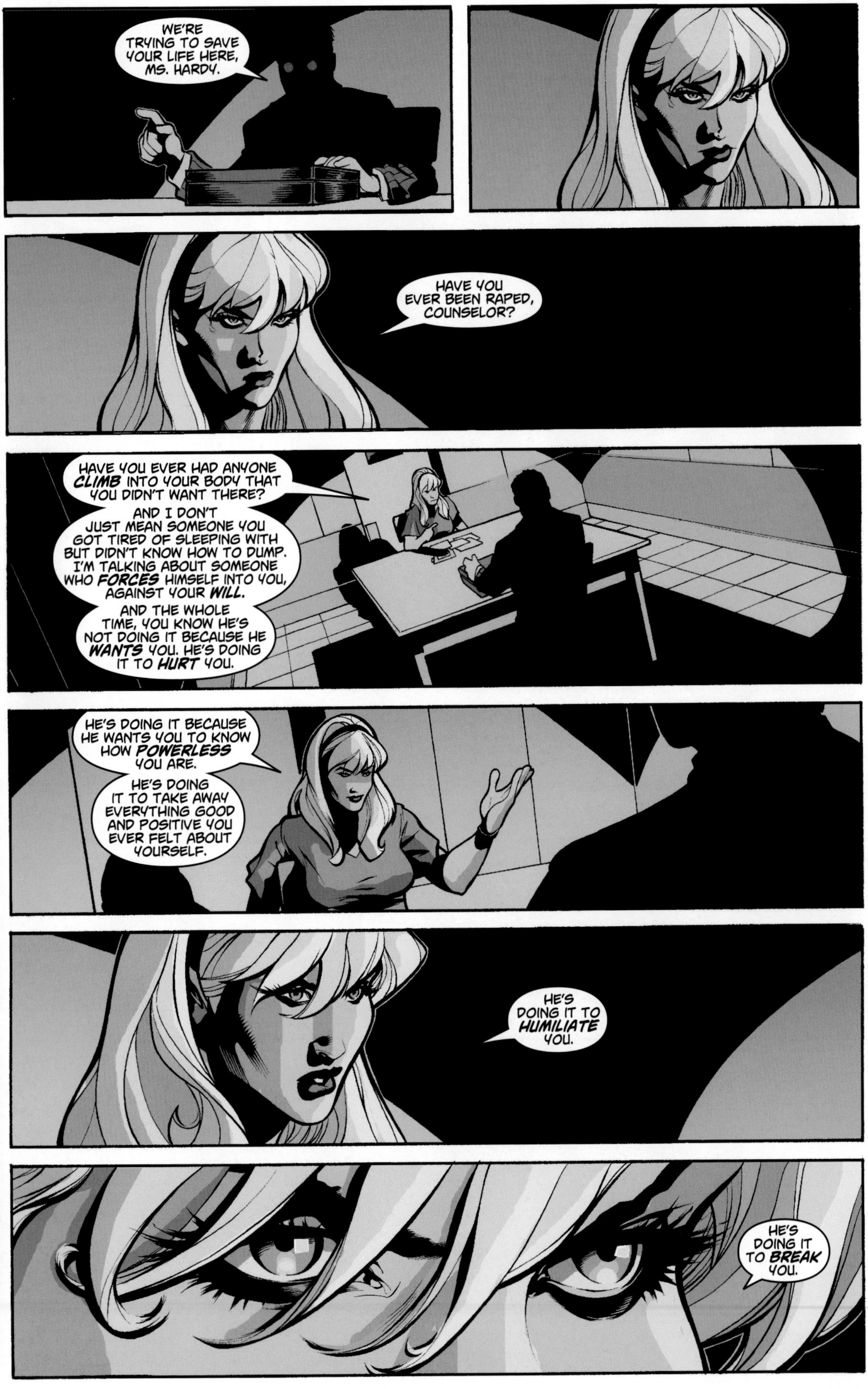
WE'RE TRYING TO SAVE YOUR LIFE HERE, MS. HARDY.
HAVE YOU EVER BEEN RAPED, COUNSELOR?
HAVE YOU EVER HAD ANYONE CLIMB INTO YOUR BODY THAT YOU DIDN'T WANT THERE?
AND I DON'T JUST MEAN SOMEONE YOU GOT TIRED OF SLEEPING WITH BUT DIDN'T KNOW HOW TO DUMP. I'M TALKING ABOUT SOMEONE WHO FORCES HIMSELF INTO YOU, AGAINST YOUR WILL.
AND THE WHOLE TIME, YOU KNOW HE'S NOT DOING IT BECAUSE HE WANTS YOU. HE'S DOING IT TO HURT YOU.
HE'S DOING IT BECAUSE HE WANTS YOU TO KNOW HOW POWERLESS YOU ARE.
HE'S DOING IT TO TAKE AWAY EVERYTHING GOOD AND POSITIVE YOU EVER FELT ABOUT YOURSELF.
HE'S DOING IT TO HUMILIATE YOU.
HE'S DOING IT TO BREAK YOU.

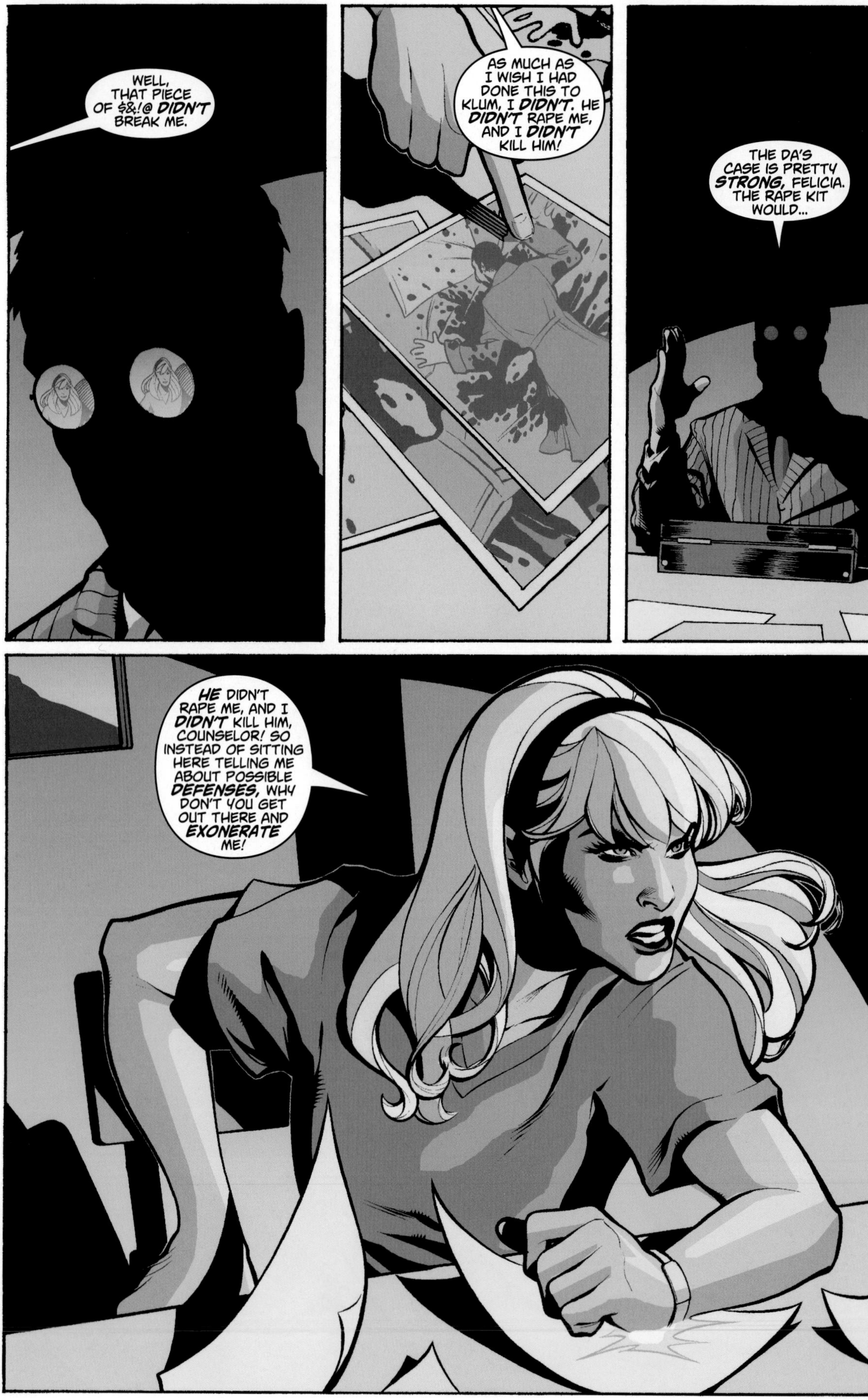
WELL, THAT PIECE OF $&!@ DIDN'T BREAK ME.
AS MUCH AS I WISH I HAD DONE THIS TO KLUM, I DIDN'T. HE DIDN'T RAPE ME, AND I DIDN'T KILL HIM!
THE DA'S CASE IS PRETTY STRONG, FELICIA. THE RAPE KIT WOULD...
HE DIDN'T RAPE ME, AND I DIDN'T KILL HIM, COUNSELOR! SO INSTEAD OF SITTING HERE TELLING ME ABOUT POSSIBLE DEFENSES, WHY DON'T YOU GET OUT THERE AND EXONERATE ME!

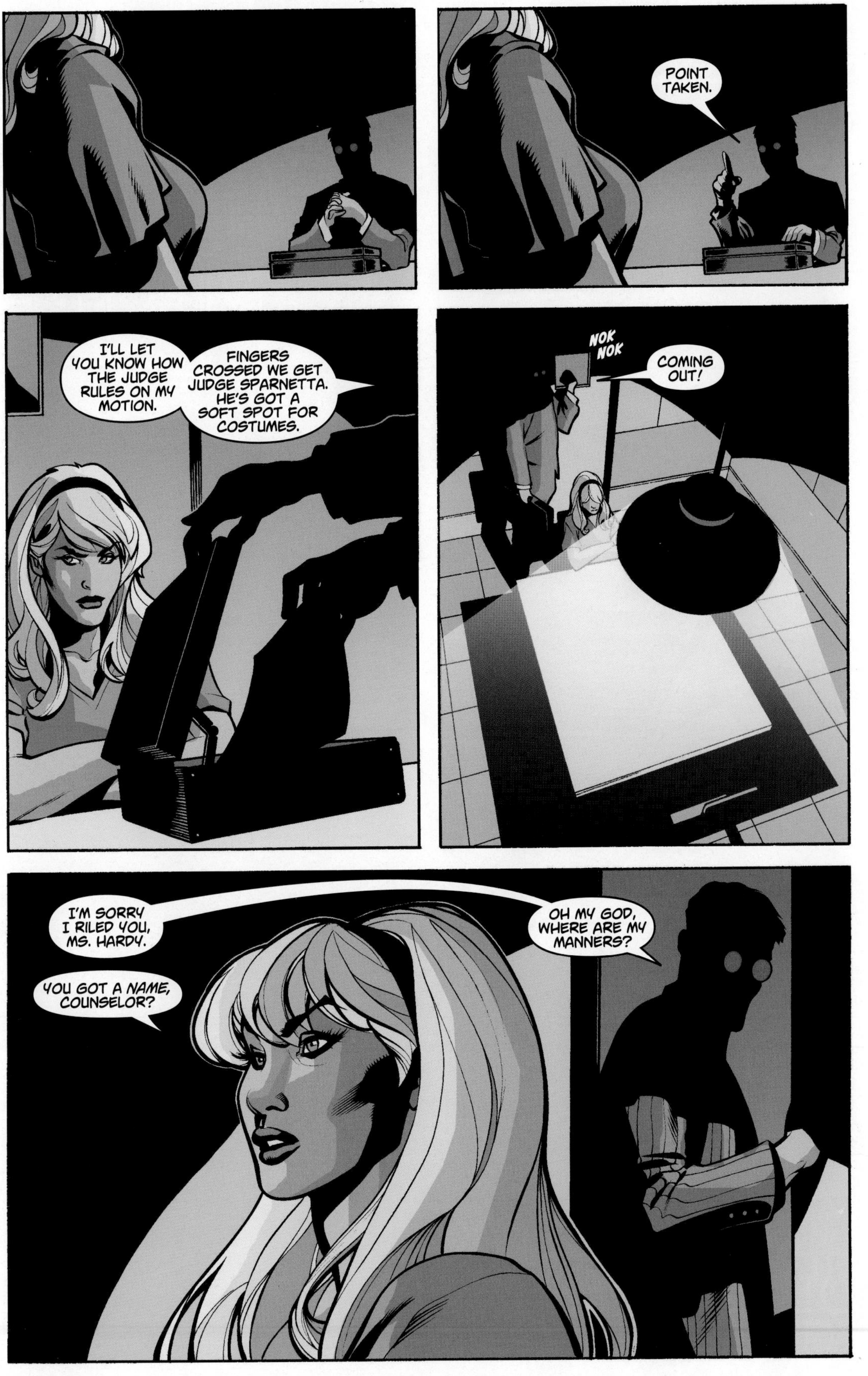
POINT TAKEN.
I'LL LET YOU KNOW HOW THE JUDGE RULES ON MY MOTION.
FINGERS CROSSED WE GET JUDGE SPARNETTA. HE'S GOT A SOFT SPOT FOR COSTUMES.
NOK NOK
COMING OUT!
I'M SORRY I RILED YOU, MS. HARDY.
OH MY GOD, WHERE ARE MY MANNERS?
YOU GOT A *NAME*, COUNSELOR?

MARVEL COMICS presents
A Book Three Years in the Making
(and hardly worth the wait)
The Amazing SPIDER-MAN and the BLACK CAT in
"The EVIL THAT MEN DO"
MY NAME'S MATT MURDOCK, MS. HARDY.
Part Four: A STUDY IN SCARLET

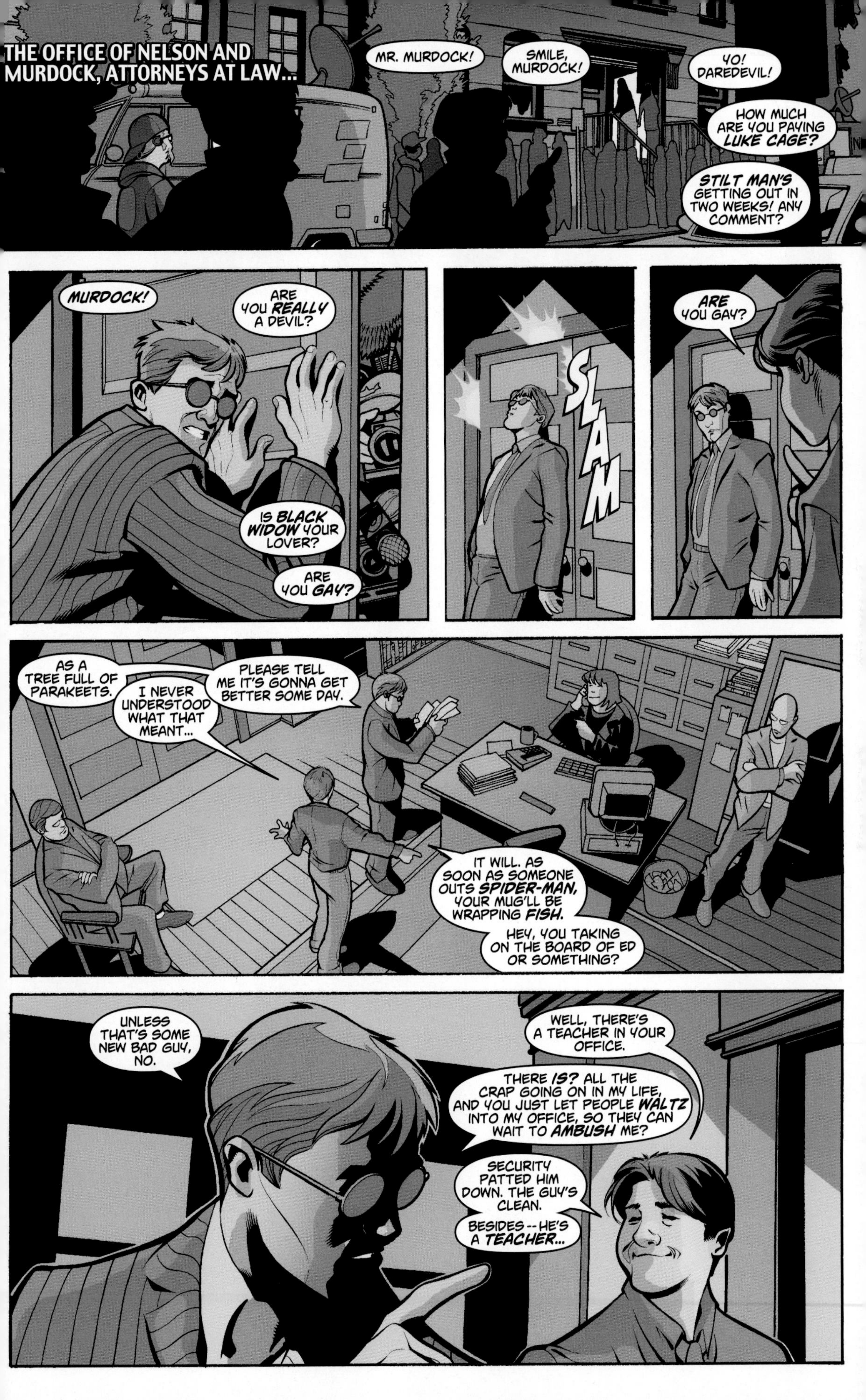
THE OFFICE OF NELSON AND MURDOCK, ATTORNEYS AT LAW...
MR. MURDOCK!
SMILE, MURDOCK!
YO! DAREDEVIL!
HOW MUCH ARE YOU PAYING LUKE CAGE?
STILT MAN'S GETTING OUT IN TWO WEEKS! ANY COMMENT?
MURDOCK!
ARE YOU REALLY A DEVIL?
IS BLACK WIDOW YOUR LOVER?
ARE YOU GAY?
SLAM
ARE YOU GAY?
PLEASE TELL ME IT'S GONNA GET BETTER SOME DAY.
AS A TREE FULL OF PARAKEETS.
I NEVER UNDERSTOOD WHAT THAT MEANT...
IT WILL. AS SOON AS SOMEONE OUTS SPIDER-MAN, YOUR MUG'LL BE WRAPPING FISH.
HEY, YOU TAKING ON THE BOARD OF ED OR SOMETHING?
UNLESS THAT'S SOME NEW BAD GUY, NO.
WELL, THERE'S A TEACHER IN YOUR OFFICE.
THERE IS? ALL THE CRAP GOING ON IN MY LIFE, AND YOU JUST LET PEOPLE WALTZ INTO MY OFFICE, SO THEY CAN WAIT TO AMBUSH ME?
SECURITY PATTED HIM DOWN. THE GUY'S CLEAN.
BESIDES -- HE'S A TEACHER...

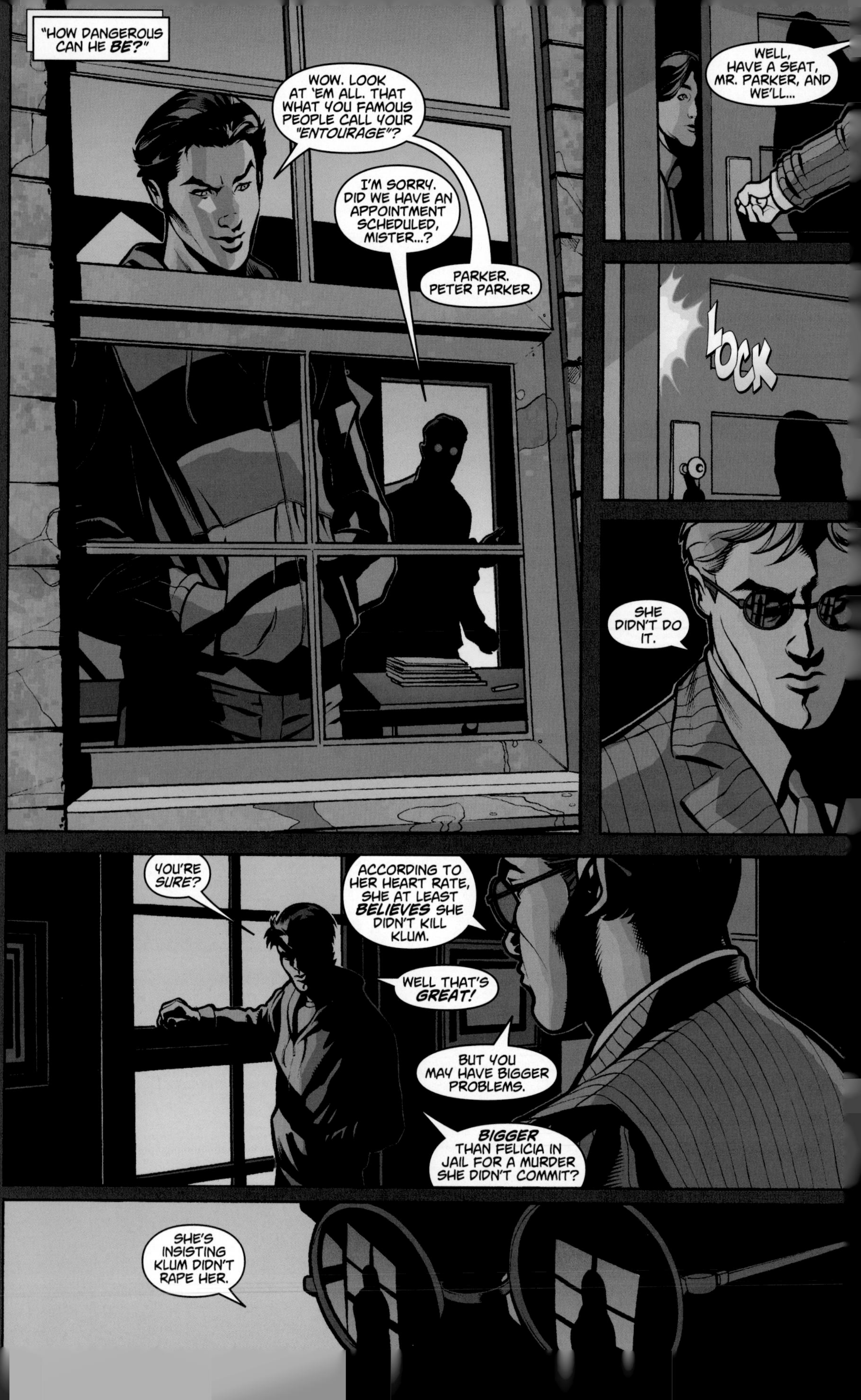
"HOW DANGEROUS CAN HE BE?"
WOW. LOOK AT 'EM ALL. THAT WHAT YOU FAMOUS PEOPLE CALL YOUR "ENTOURAGE"?
I'M SORRY. DID WE HAVE AN APPOINTMENT SCHEDULED, MISTER...?
PARKER. PETER PARKER.
WELL, HAVE A SEAT, MR. PARKER, AND WE'LL...
LOCK
SHE DIDN'T DO IT.
YOU'RE SURE?
ACCORDING TO HER HEART RATE, SHE AT LEAST BELIEVES SHE DIDN'T KILL KLUM.
WELL THAT'S GREAT!
BUT YOU MAY HAVE BIGGER PROBLEMS.
BIGGER THAN FELICIA IN JAIL FOR A MURDER SHE DIDN'T COMMIT?
SHE'S INSISTING KLUM DIDN'T RAPE HER.

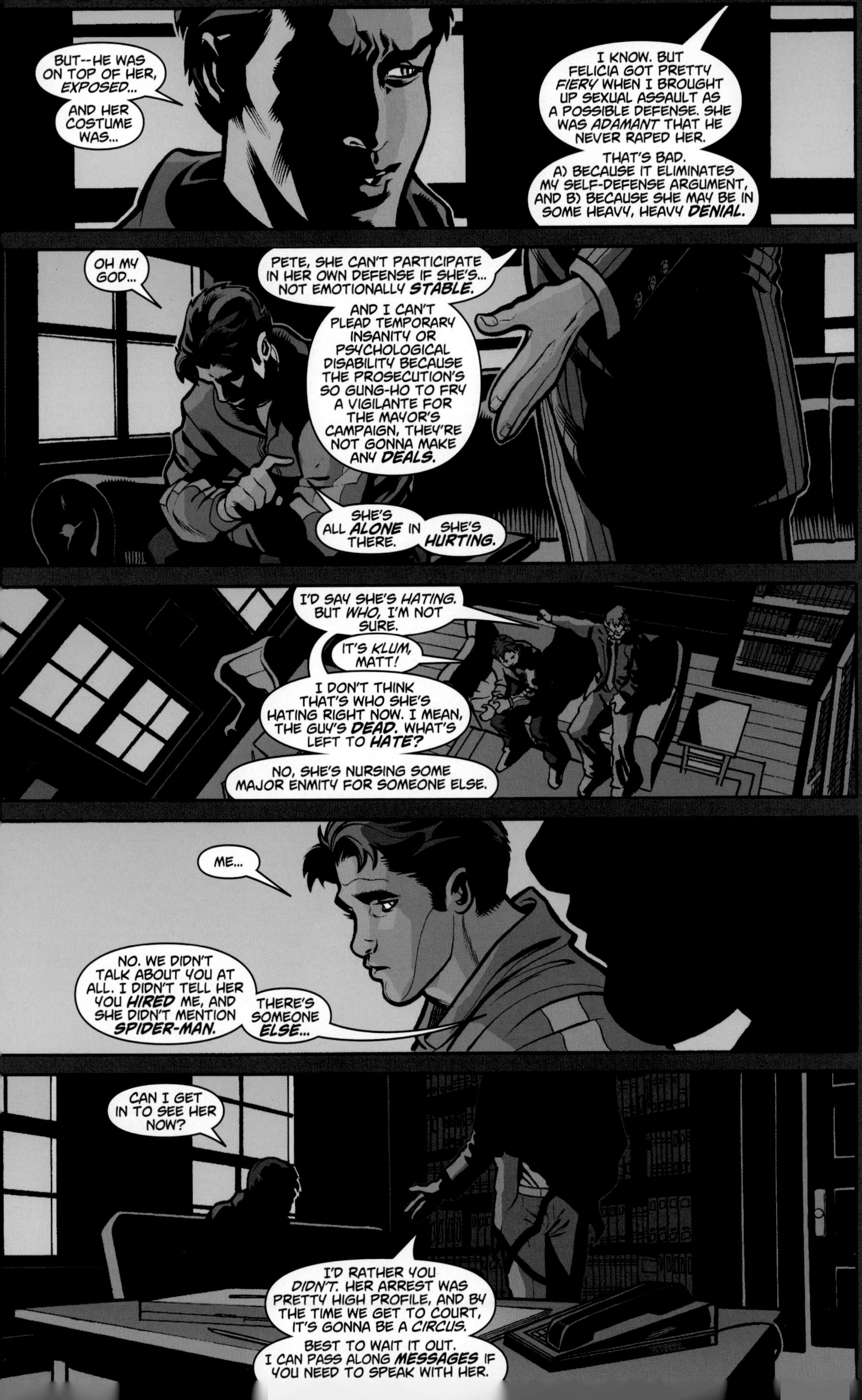
BUT--HE WAS ON TOP OF HER, EXPOSED...
AND HER COSTUME WAS...
I KNOW. BUT FELICIA GOT PRETTY FIERY WHEN I BROUGHT UP SEXUAL ASSAULT AS A POSSIBLE DEFENSE. SHE WAS ADAMANT THAT HE NEVER RAPED HER.
THAT'S BAD. A) BECAUSE IT ELIMINATES MY SELF-DEFENSE ARGUMENT, AND B) BECAUSE SHE MAY BE IN SOME HEAVY, HEAVY DENIAL.
OH MY GOD...
PETE, SHE CAN'T PARTICIPATE IN HER OWN DEFENSE IF SHE'S... NOT EMOTIONALLY STABLE.
AND I CAN'T PLEAD TEMPORARY INSANITY OR PSYCHOLOGICAL DISABILITY BECAUSE THE PROSECUTION'S SO GUNG-HO TO FRY A VIGILANTE FOR THE MAYOR'S CAMPAIGN, THEY'RE NOT GONNA MAKE ANY DEALS.
SHE'S ALL ALONE IN THERE.
SHE'S HURTING.
I'D SAY SHE'S HATING. BUT WHO, I'M NOT SURE.
IT'S KLUM, MATT!
I DON'T THINK THAT'S WHO SHE'S HATING RIGHT NOW. I MEAN, THE GUY'S DEAD. WHAT'S LEFT TO HATE?
NO, SHE'S NURSING SOME MAJOR ENMITY FOR SOMEONE ELSE.
ME...
NO. WE DIDN'T TALK ABOUT YOU AT ALL. I DIDN'T TELL HER YOU HIRED ME, AND SHE DIDN'T MENTION SPIDER-MAN.
THERE'S SOMEONE ELSE...
CAN I GET IN TO SEE HER NOW?
I'D RATHER YOU DIDN'T. HER ARREST WAS PRETTY HIGH PROFILE, AND BY THE TIME WE GET TO COURT, IT'S GONNA BE A CIRCUS.
BEST TO WAIT IT OUT. I CAN PASS ALONG MESSAGES IF YOU NEED TO SPEAK WITH HER.

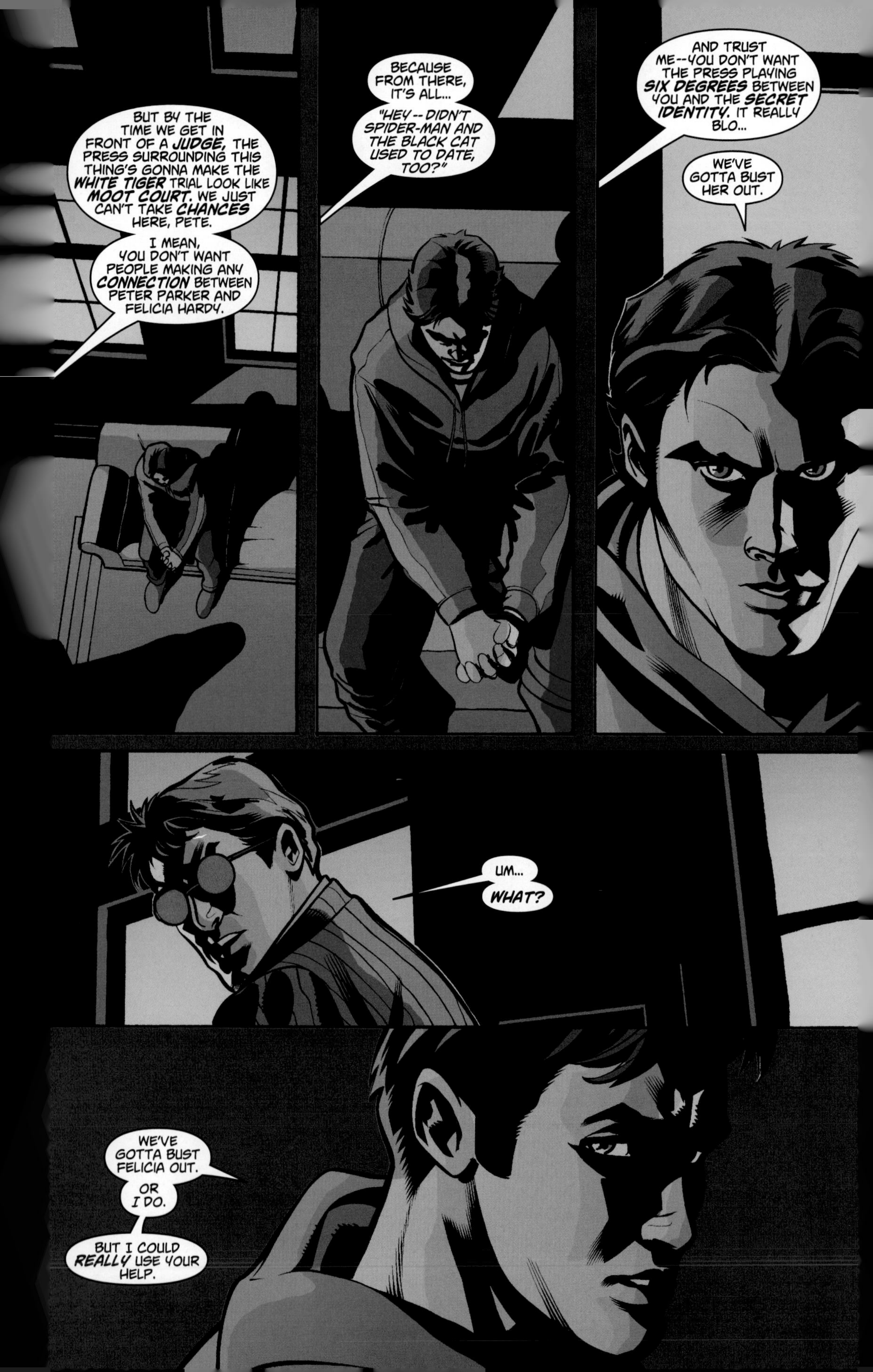
BUT BY THE TIME WE GET IN FRONT OF A JUDGE, THE PRESS SURROUNDING THIS THING'S GONNA MAKE THE WHITE TIGER TRIAL LOOK LIKE MOOT COURT. WE JUST CAN'T TAKE CHANCES HERE, PETE.
I MEAN, YOU DON'T WANT PEOPLE MAKING ANY CONNECTION BETWEEN PETER PARKER AND FELICIA HARDY.
BECAUSE FROM THERE, IT'S ALL...
"HEY -- DIDN'T SPIDER-MAN AND THE BLACK CAT USED TO DATE, TOO?"
AND TRUST ME--YOU DON'T WANT THE PRESS PLAYING SIX DEGREES BETWEEN YOU AND THE SECRET IDENTITY. IT REALLY BLO...
WE'VE GOTTA BUST HER OUT.
UM...
WHAT?
WE'VE GOTTA BUST FELICIA OUT.
OR I DO.
BUT I COULD REALLY USE YOUR HELP.

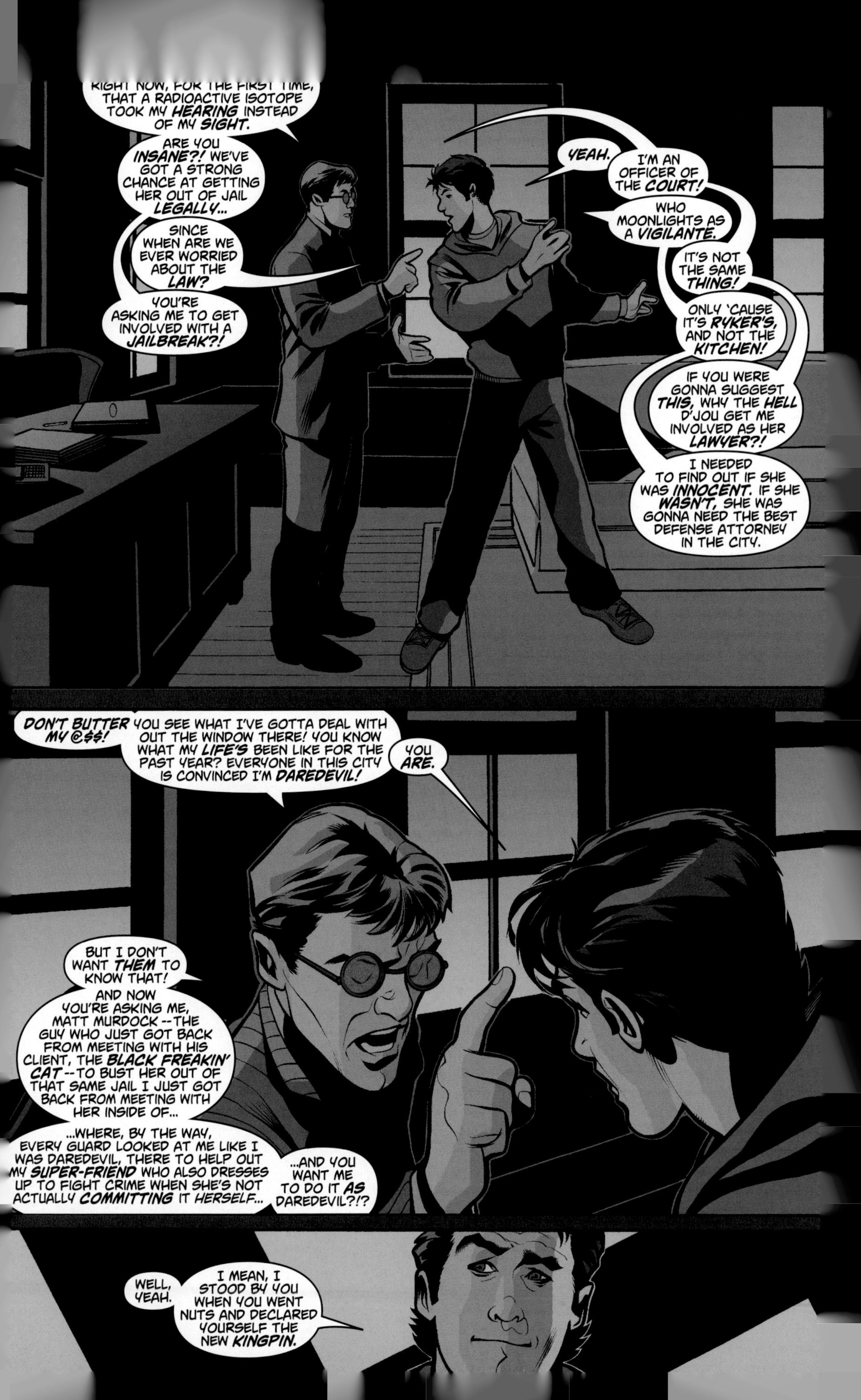
RIGHT NOW, FOR THE FIRST TIME, THAT A RADIOACTIVE ISOTOPE TOOK MY HEARING INSTEAD OF MY SIGHT.
ARE YOU INSANE?! WE'VE GOT A STRONG CHANCE AT GETTING HER OUT OF JAIL LEGALLY...
YEAH.
I'M AN OFFICER OF THE COURT!
WHO MOONLIGHTS AS A VIGILANTE.
SINCE WHEN ARE WE EVER WORRIED ABOUT THE LAW?
IT'S NOT THE SAME THING!
ONLY 'CAUSE IT'S RYKER'S, AND NOT THE KITCHEN!
YOU'RE ASKING ME TO GET INVOLVED WITH A JAILBREAK?!
IF YOU WERE GONNA SUGGEST THIS, WHY THE HELL D'JOU GET ME INVOLVED AS HER LAWYER?!
I NEEDED TO FIND OUT IF SHE WAS INNOCENT. IF SHE WASN'T, SHE WAS GONNA NEED THE BEST DEFENSE ATTORNEY IN THE CITY.
DON'T BUTTER MY @$$!
YOU SEE WHAT I'VE GOTTA DEAL WITH OUT THE WINDOW THERE! YOU KNOW WHAT MY LIFE'S BEEN LIKE FOR THE PAST YEAR? EVERYONE IN THIS CITY IS CONVINCED I'M DAREDEVIL!
YOU ARE.
BUT I DON'T WANT THEM TO KNOW THAT!
AND NOW YOU'RE ASKING ME, MATT MURDOCK --THE GUY WHO JUST GOT BACK FROM MEETING WITH HIS CLIENT, THE BLACK FREAKIN' CAT --TO BUST HER OUT OF THAT SAME JAIL I JUST GOT BACK FROM MEETING WITH HER INSIDE OF...
...WHERE, BY THE WAY, EVERY GUARD LOOKED AT ME LIKE I WAS DAREDEVIL, THERE TO HELP OUT MY SUPER-FRIEND WHO ALSO DRESSES UP TO FIGHT CRIME WHEN SHE'S NOT ACTUALLY COMMITTING IT HERSELF...
...AND YOU WANT ME TO DO IT AS DAREDEVIL?!?
WELL, YEAH.
I MEAN, I STOOD BY YOU WHEN YOU WENT NUTS AND DECLARED YOURSELF THE NEW KINGPIN.

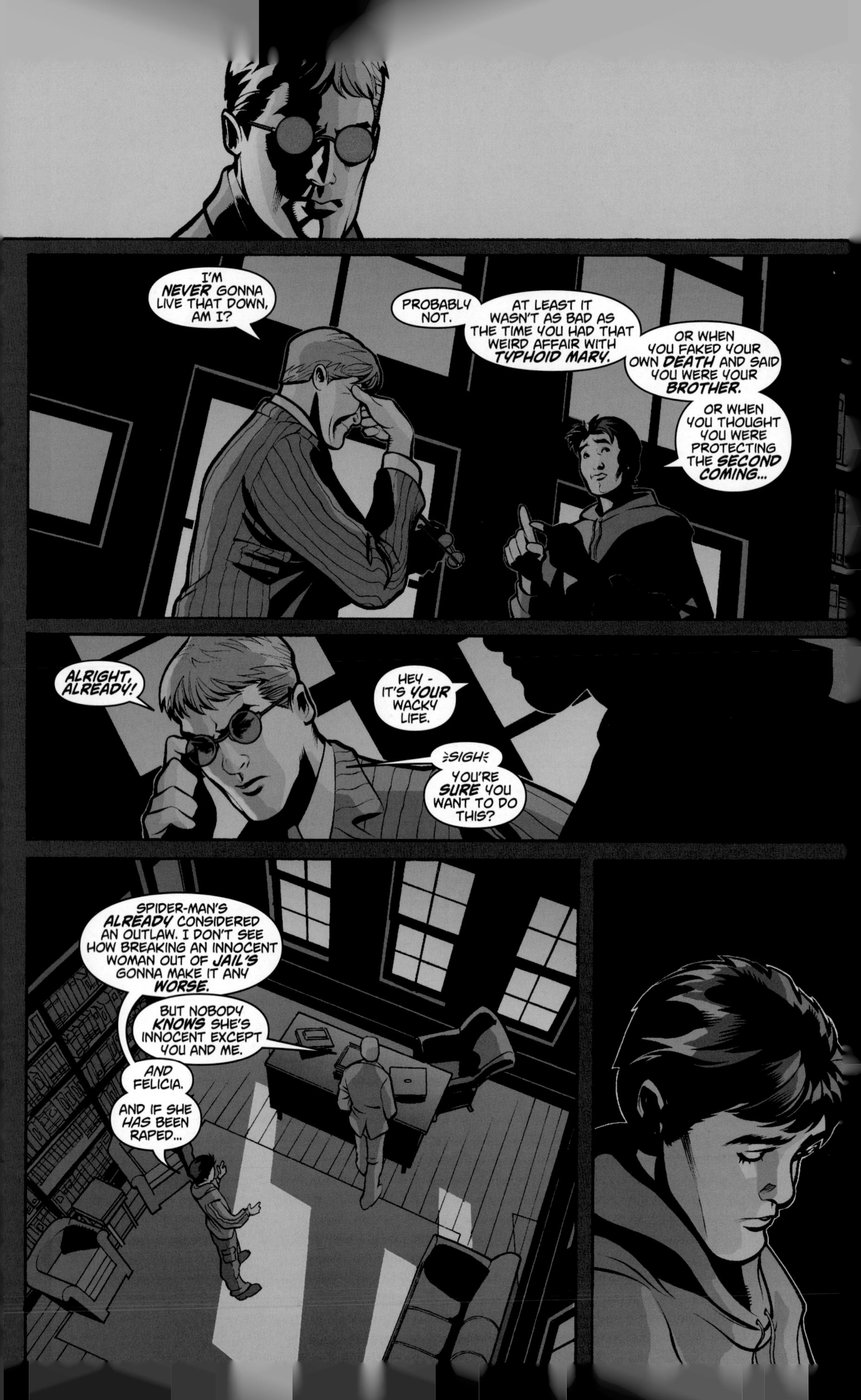
I'M NEVER GONNA LIVE THAT DOWN, AM I?
PROBABLY NOT.
AT LEAST IT WASN'T AS BAD AS THE TIME YOU HAD THAT WEIRD AFFAIR WITH TYPHOID MARY.
OR WHEN YOU FAKED YOUR OWN DEATH AND SAID YOU WERE YOUR BROTHER.
OR WHEN YOU THOUGHT YOU WERE PROTECTING THE SECOND COMING...
ALRIGHT, ALREADY!
HEY - IT'S YOUR WACKY LIFE.
SIGH
YOU'RE SURE YOU WANT TO DO THIS?
SPIDER-MAN'S ALREADY CONSIDERED AN OUTLAW. I DON'T SEE HOW BREAKING AN INNOCENT WOMAN OUT OF JAIL'S GONNA MAKE IT ANY WORSE.
BUT NOBODY KNOWS SHE'S INNOCENT EXCEPT YOU AND ME.
AND FELICIA.
AND IF SHE HAS BEEN RAPED...

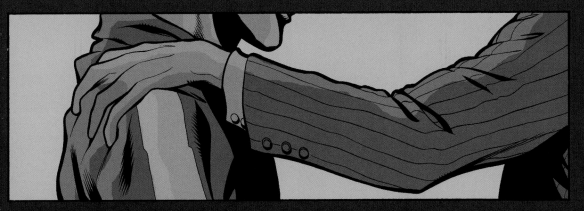

SHE'S AN INNOCENT IN NEED OF HELP, MATT. WHAT MAKES HER ANY *DIFFERENT* THAN THE OTHER PEOPLE WE SPEND ALL OUR TIME TRYING TO SAVE?

ALRIGHT, I'M IN.

THANKS, MATTY.

GOD, YOU DEBATE LIKE A *PRO.*

YOU SHOULD'VE BEEN A *LAWYER,* PETE.

NO *THANKS...*

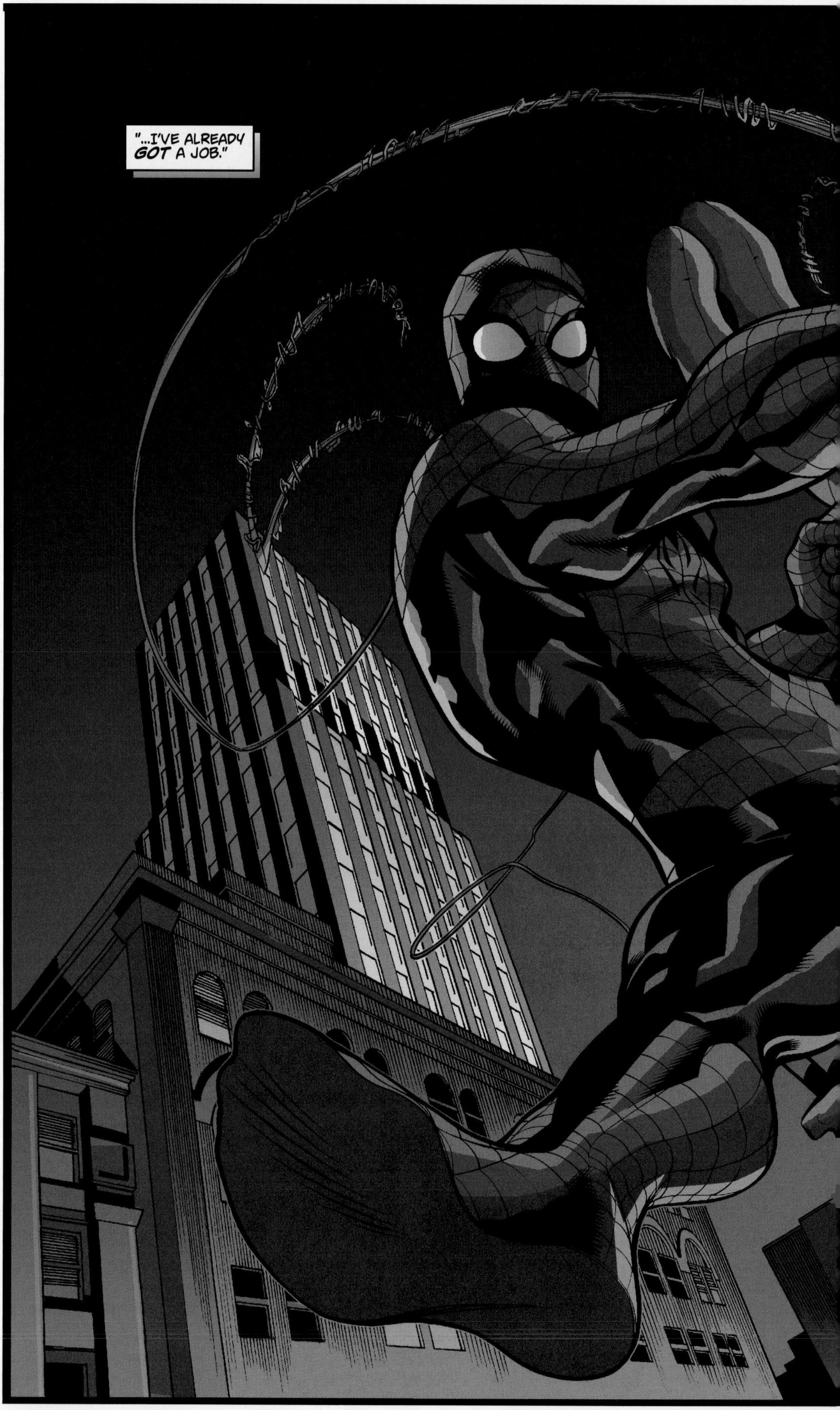
"...I'VE ALREADY GOT A JOB."

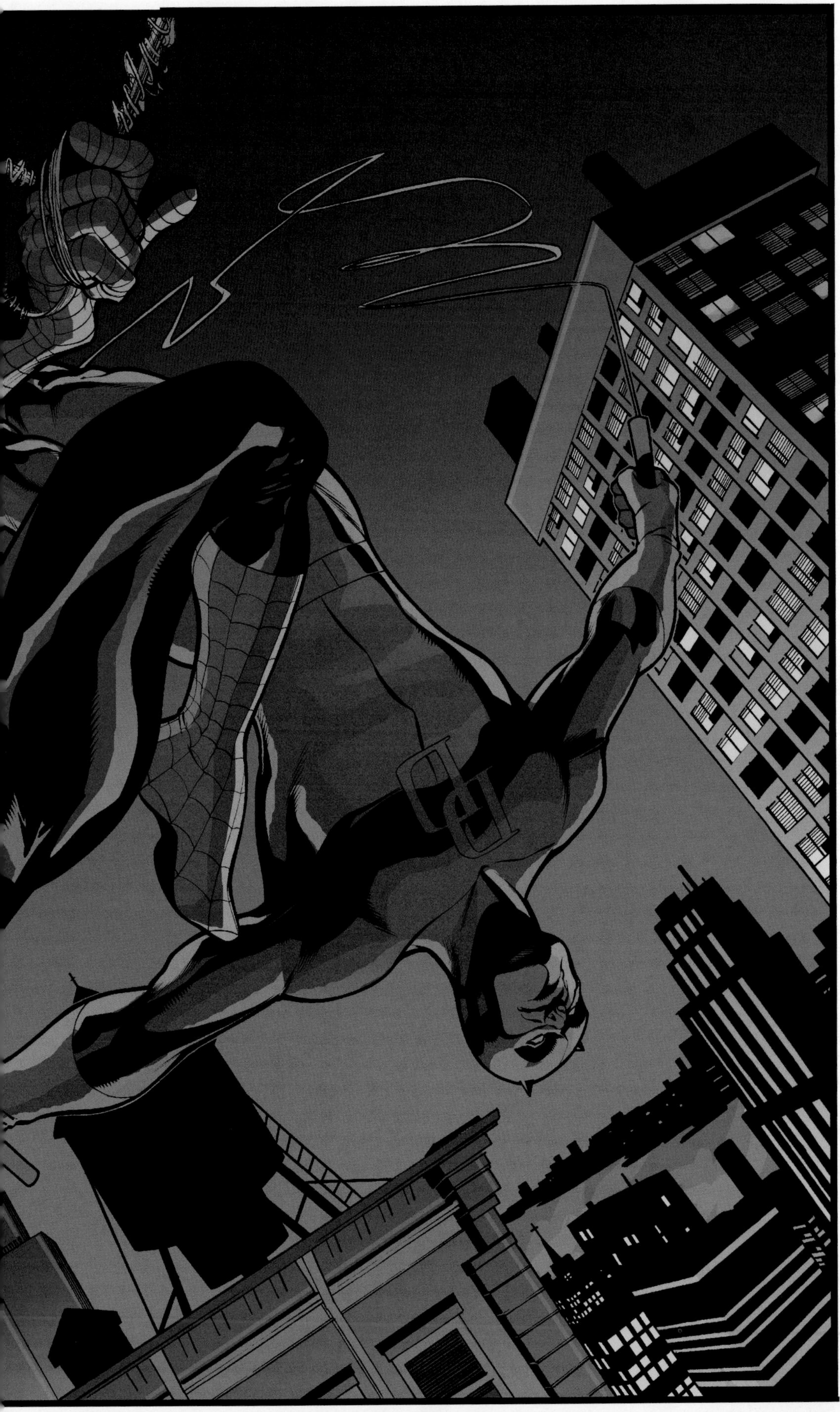

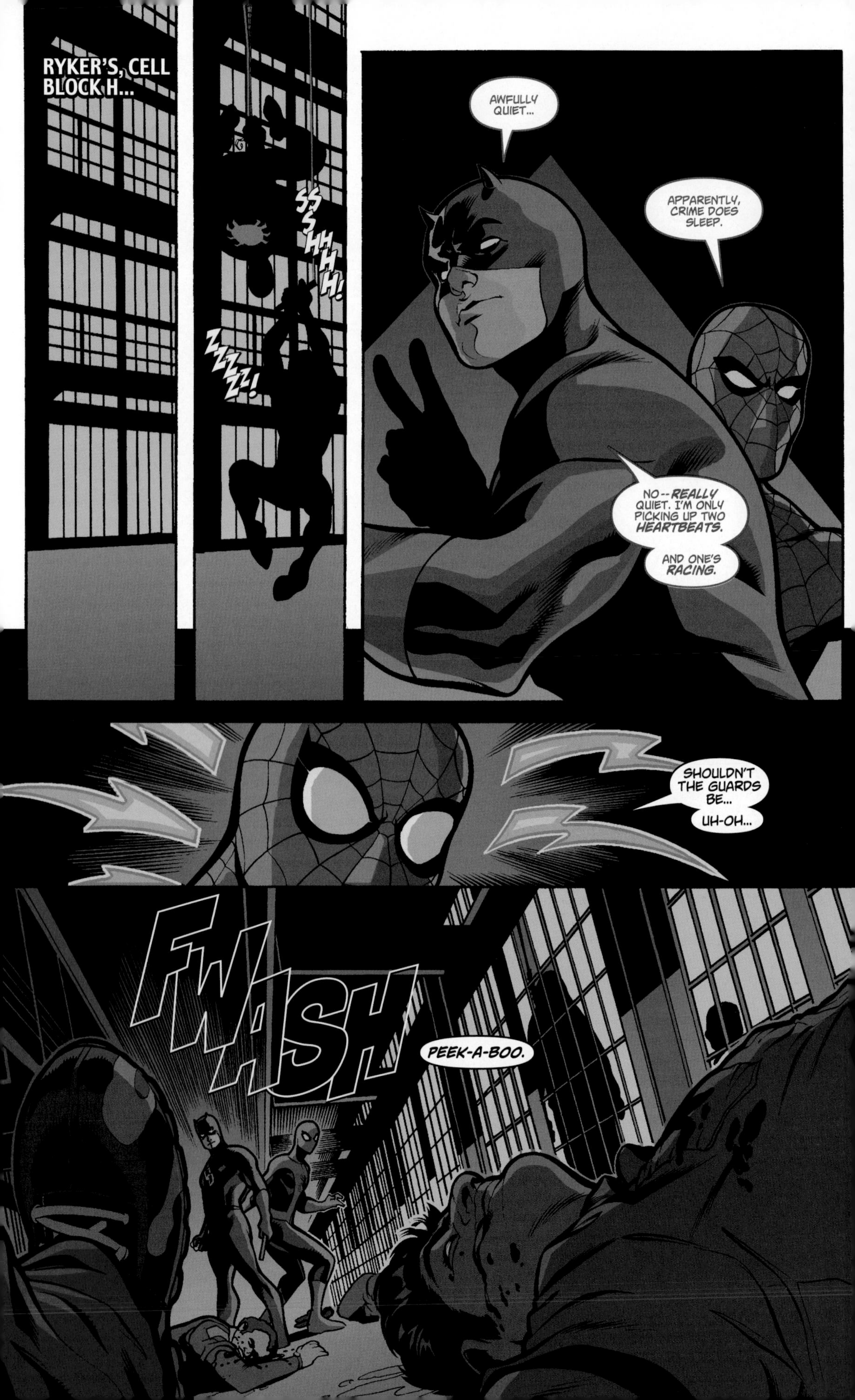
RYKER'S, CELL BLOCK H...
SSSHHHH!
ZZZZZZ!
AWFULLY QUIET...
APPARENTLY, CRIME DOES SLEEP.
NO--REALLY QUIET. I'M ONLY PICKING UP TWO HEARTBEATS.
AND ONE'S RACING.
SHOULDN'T THE GUARDS BE...
UH-OH...
FWASH
PEEK-A-BOO.

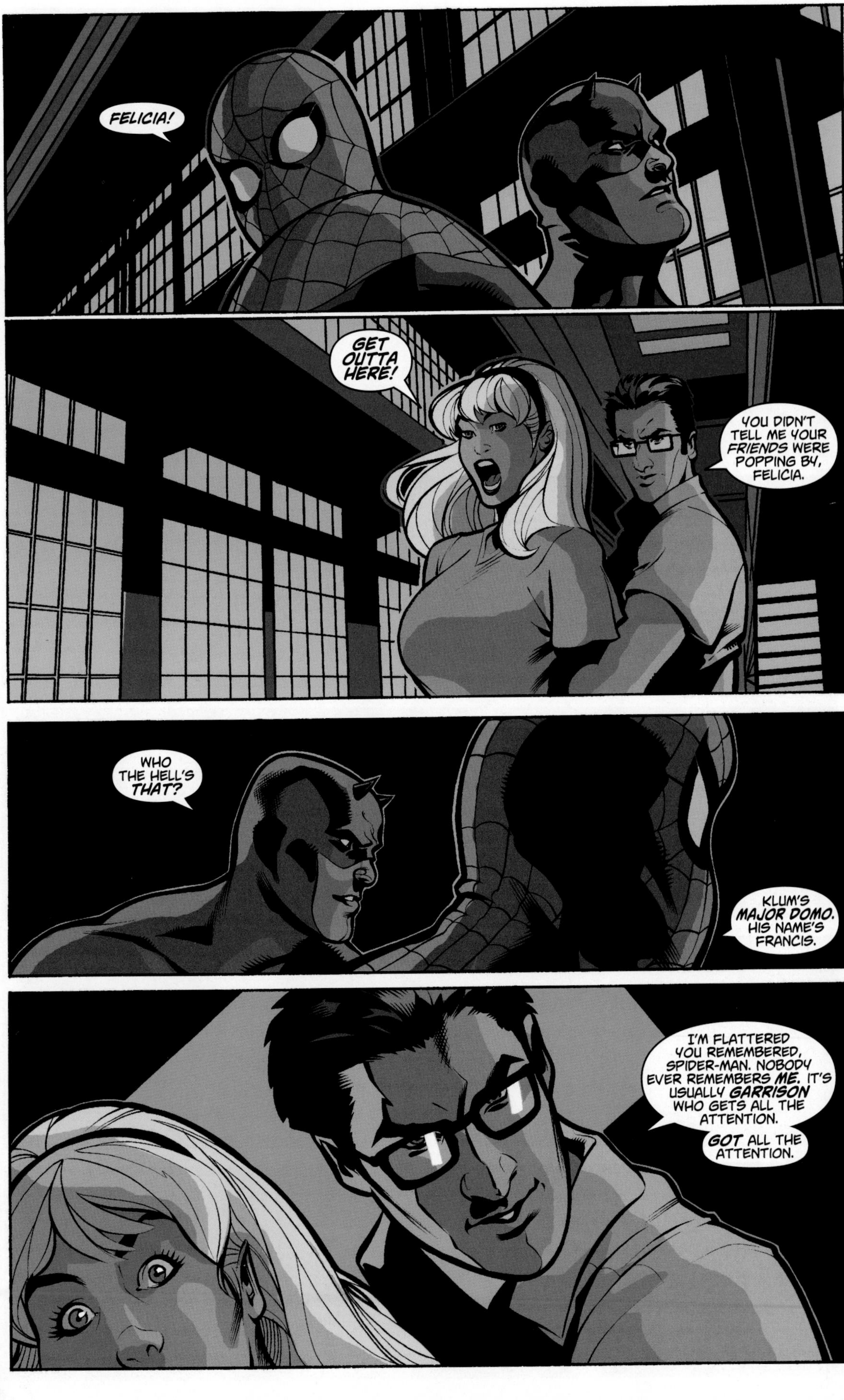
FELICIA!
GET OUTTA HERE!
YOU DIDN'T TELL ME YOUR FRIENDS WERE POPPING BY, FELICIA.
WHO THE HELL'S THAT?
KLUM'S MAJOR DOMO. HIS NAME'S FRANCIS.
I'M FLATTERED YOU REMEMBERED, SPIDER-MAN. NOBODY EVER REMEMBERS ME. IT'S USUALLY GARRISON WHO GETS ALL THE ATTENTION.
GOT ALL THE ATTENTION.

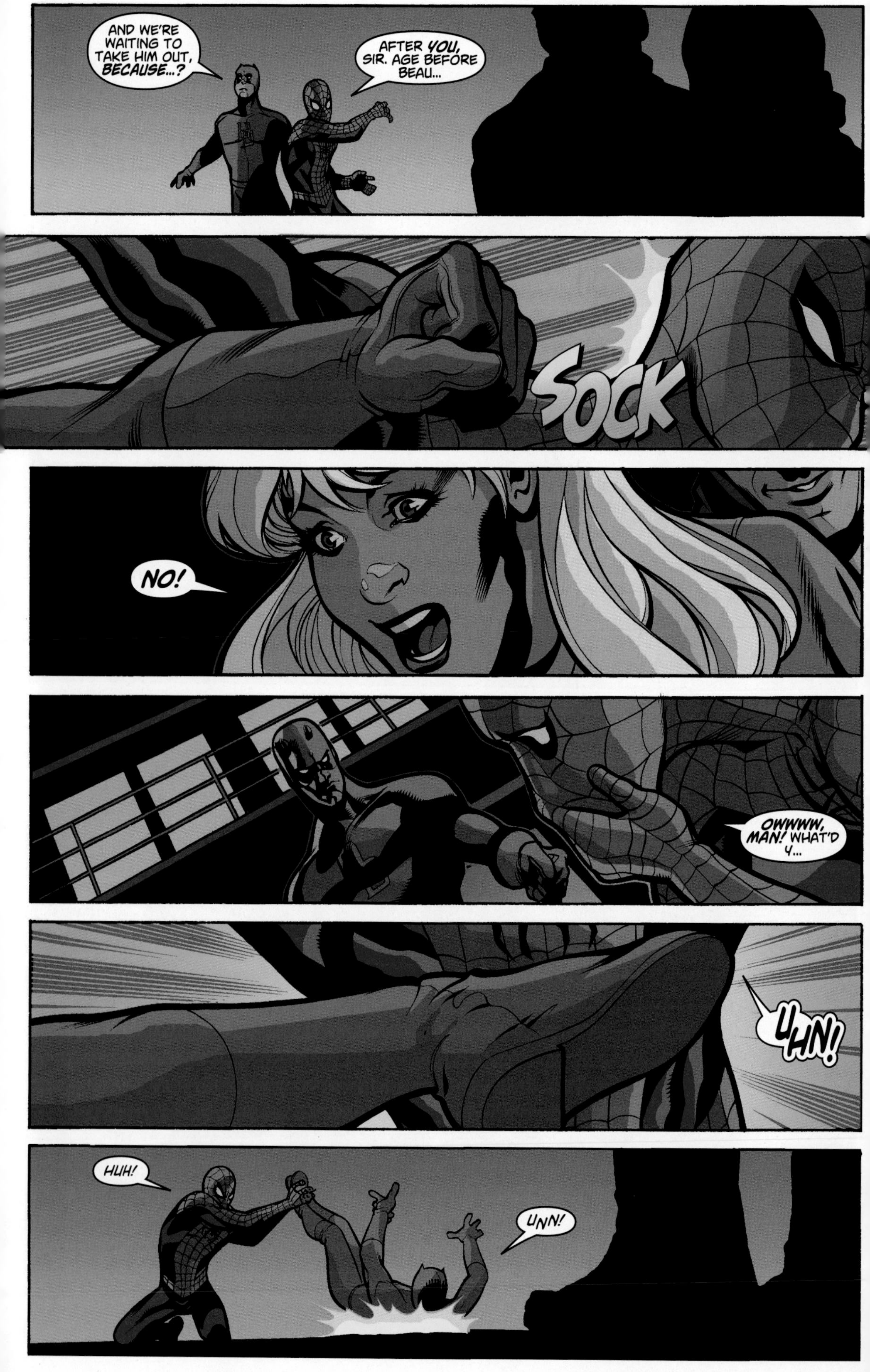
AND WE'RE WAITING TO TAKE HIM OUT, BECAUSE...?
AFTER YOU, SIR. AGE BEFORE BEAU...
SOCK
NO!
OWWWW, MAN! WHAT'D Y...
UHN!
HUH!
UNN!

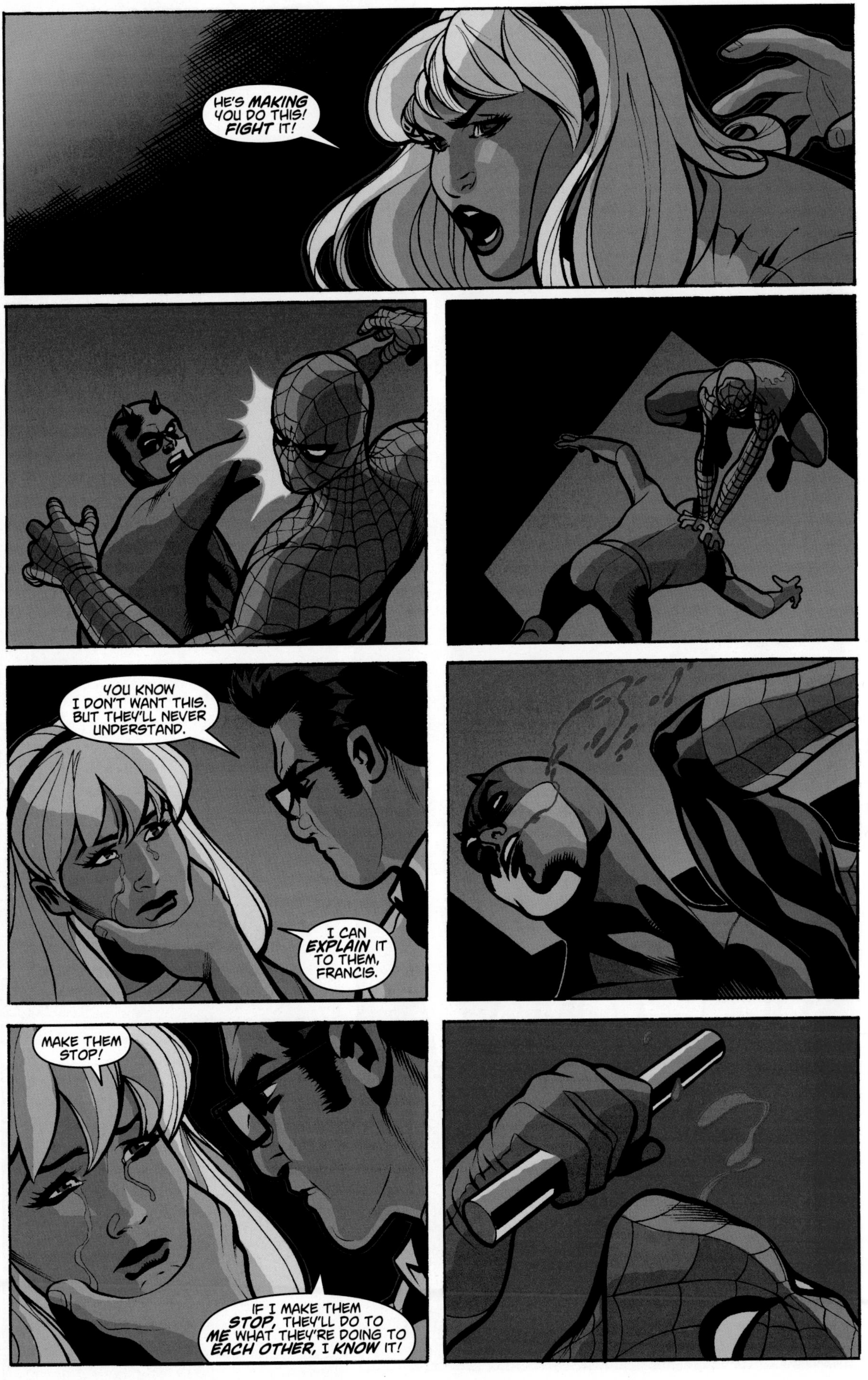
HE'S MAKING YOU DO THIS! FIGHT IT!
YOU KNOW I DON'T WANT THIS. BUT THEY'LL NEVER UNDERSTAND.
I CAN EXPLAIN IT TO THEM, FRANCIS.
MAKE THEM STOP!
IF I MAKE THEM STOP, THEY'LL DO TO ME WHAT THEY'RE DOING TO EACH OTHER, I KNOW IT!

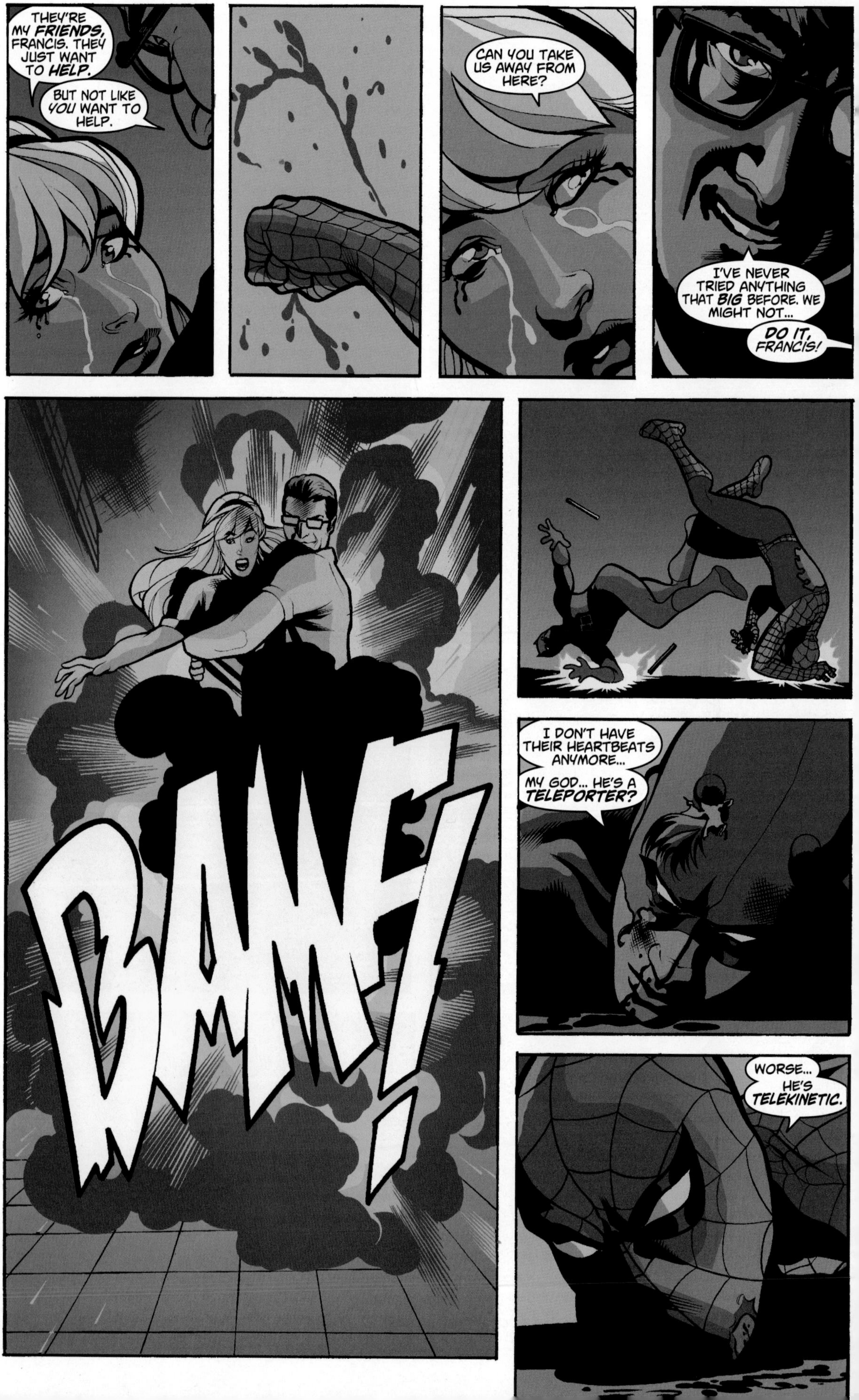
THEY'RE MY FRIENDS, FRANCIS. THEY JUST WANT TO HELP.
BUT NOT LIKE YOU WANT TO HELP.
CAN YOU TAKE US AWAY FROM HERE?
I'VE NEVER TRIED ANYTHING THAT BIG BEFORE. WE MIGHT NOT...
DO IT, FRANCIS!
BAMF!
I DON'T HAVE THEIR HEARTBEATS ANYMORE...
MY GOD... HE'S A TELEPORTER?
WORSE... HE'S TELEKINETIC.

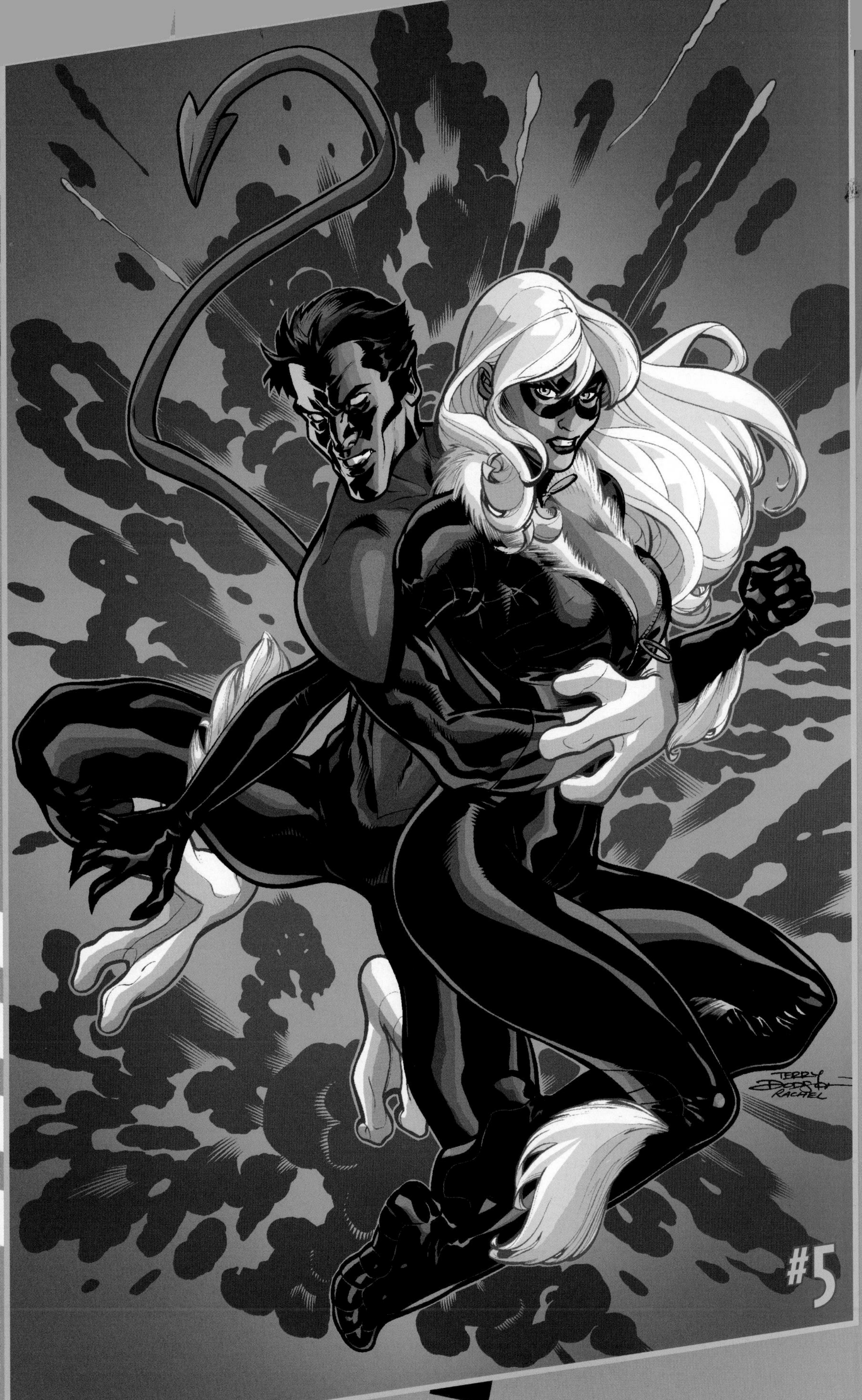
#5

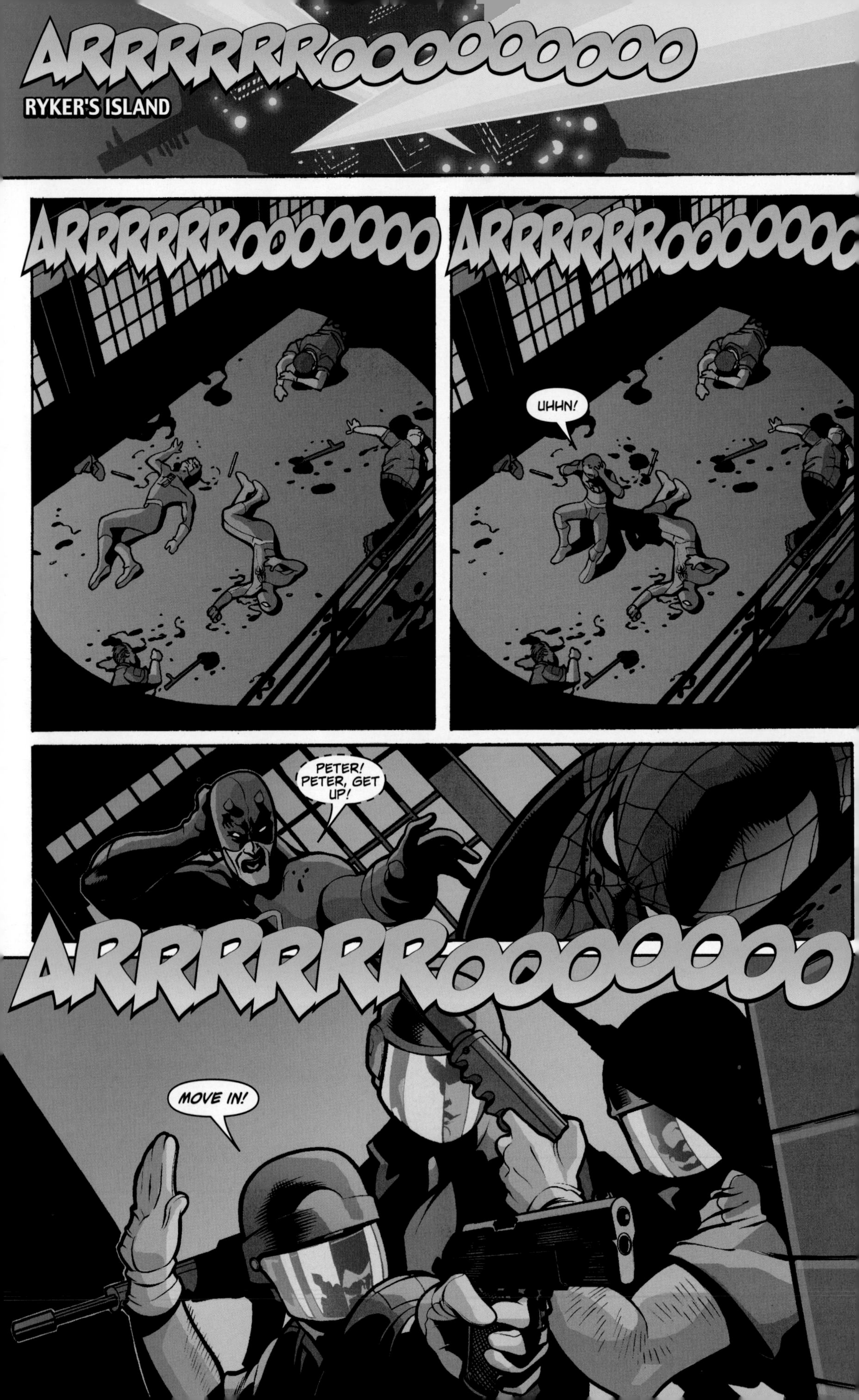
ARRRRRRoooooooooo
RYKER'S ISLAND
ARRRRRRooooooo
ARRRRRRooooooo
UHHN!
PETER! PETER, GET UP!
ARRRRRRoooooooo
MOVE IN!

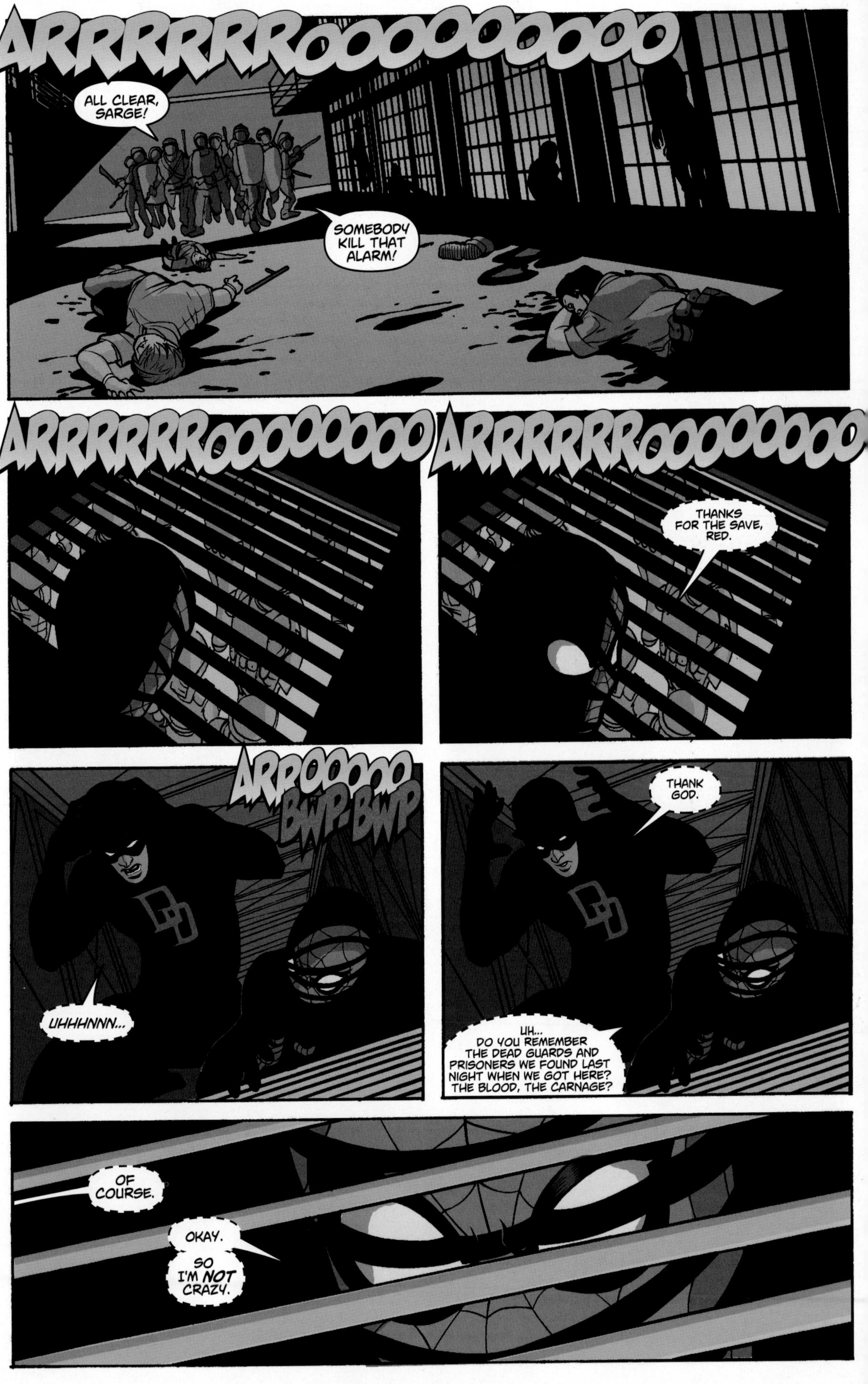
ARRRRRROOOOOOOOO
ALL CLEAR, SARGE!
SOMEBODY KILL THAT ALARM!
ARRRRRROOOOOOOO
ARRRRRROOOOOOOO
THANKS FOR THE SAVE, RED.
ARROOOOO
BWP BWP
UHHHNNN...
THANK GOD.
UH... DO YOU REMEMBER THE DEAD GUARDS AND PRISONERS WE FOUND LAST NIGHT WHEN WE GOT HERE? THE BLOOD, THE CARNAGE?
OF COURSE.
OKAY.
SO I'M NOT CRAZY.

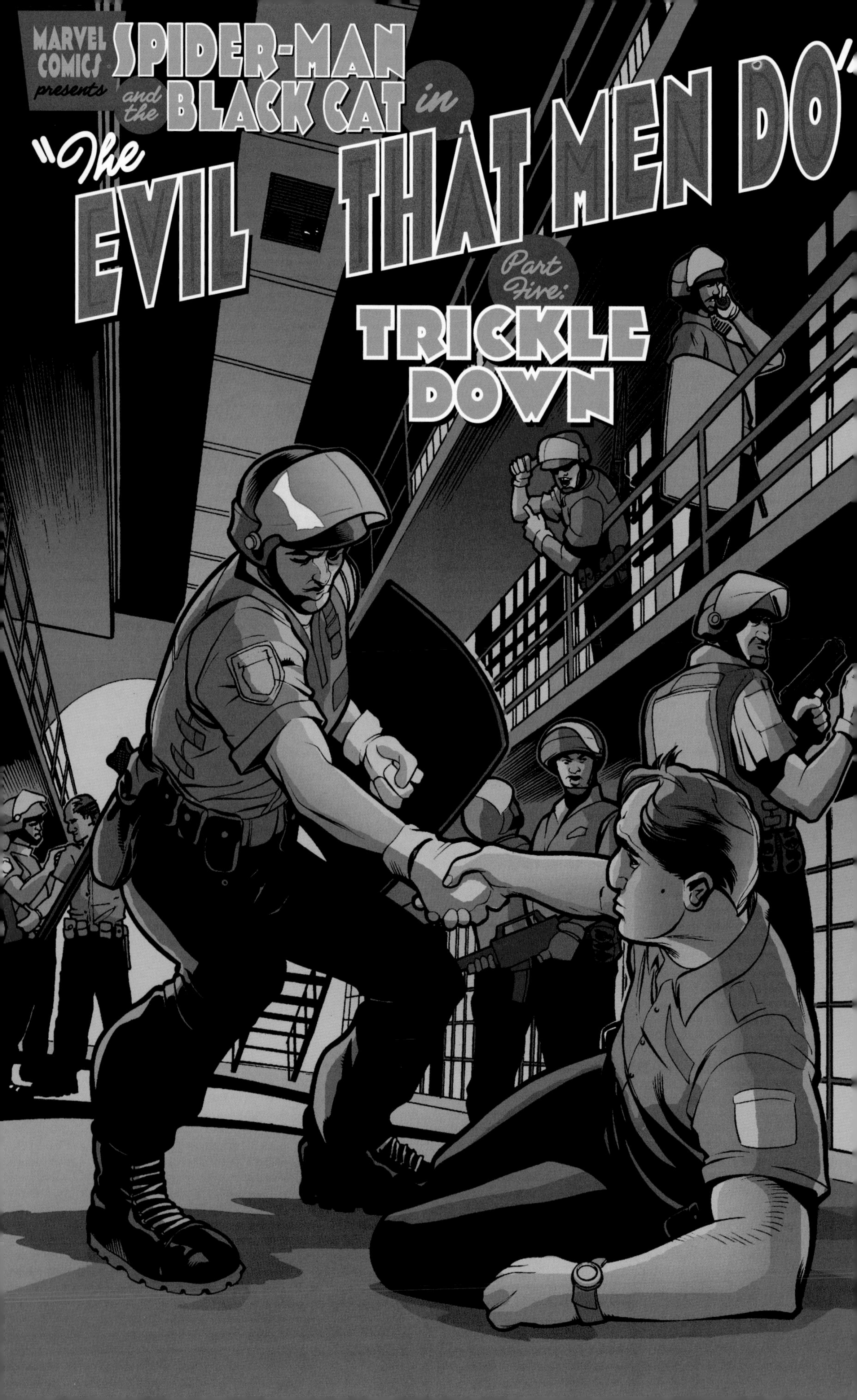
MARVEL COMICS presents
SPIDER-MAN and the BLACK CAT in
"The EVIL THAT MEN DO"
Part Five:
TRICKLE DOWN

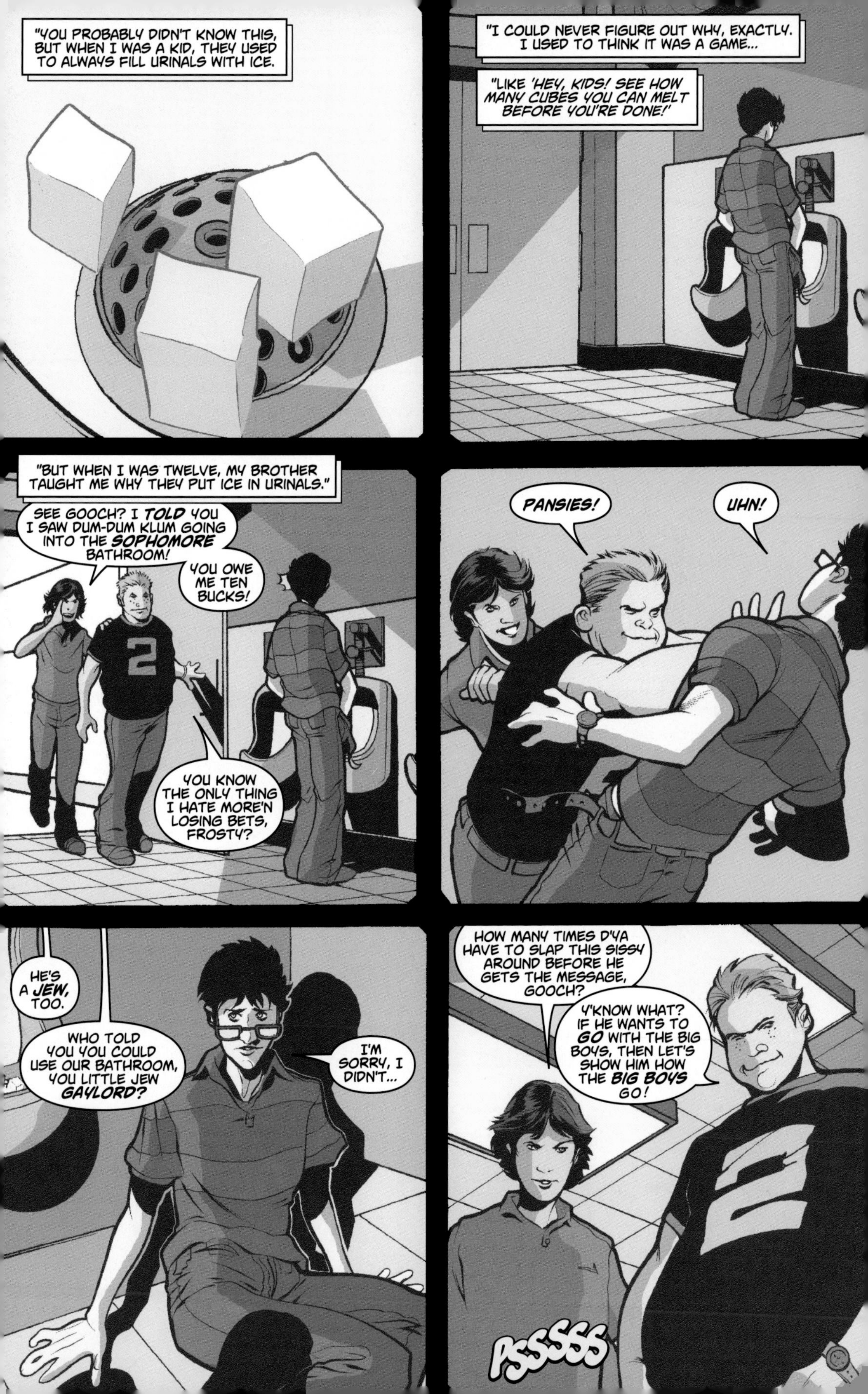
"YOU PROBABLY DIDN'T KNOW THIS, BUT WHEN I WAS A KID, THEY USED TO ALWAYS FILL URINALS WITH ICE.
"I COULD NEVER FIGURE OUT WHY, EXACTLY. I USED TO THINK IT WAS A GAME...
"LIKE 'HEY, KIDS! SEE HOW MANY CUBES YOU CAN MELT BEFORE YOU'RE DONE!'
"BUT WHEN I WAS TWELVE, MY BROTHER TAUGHT ME WHY THEY PUT ICE IN URINALS."
SEE GOOCH? I TOLD YOU I SAW DUM-DUM KLUM GOING INTO THE SOPHOMORE BATHROOM!
YOU OWE ME TEN BUCKS!
YOU KNOW THE ONLY THING I HATE MORE'N LOSING BETS, FROSTY?
PANSIES!
UHN!
HE'S A JEW, TOO.
WHO TOLD YOU YOU COULD USE OUR BATHROOM, YOU LITTLE JEW GAYLORD?
I'M SORRY, I DIDN'T...
HOW MANY TIMES D'YA HAVE TO SLAP THIS SISSY AROUND BEFORE HE GETS THE MESSAGE, GOOCH?
Y'KNOW WHAT? IF HE WANTS TO GO WITH THE BIG BOYS, THEN LET'S SHOW HIM HOW THE BIG BOYS GO!
PSSSSS

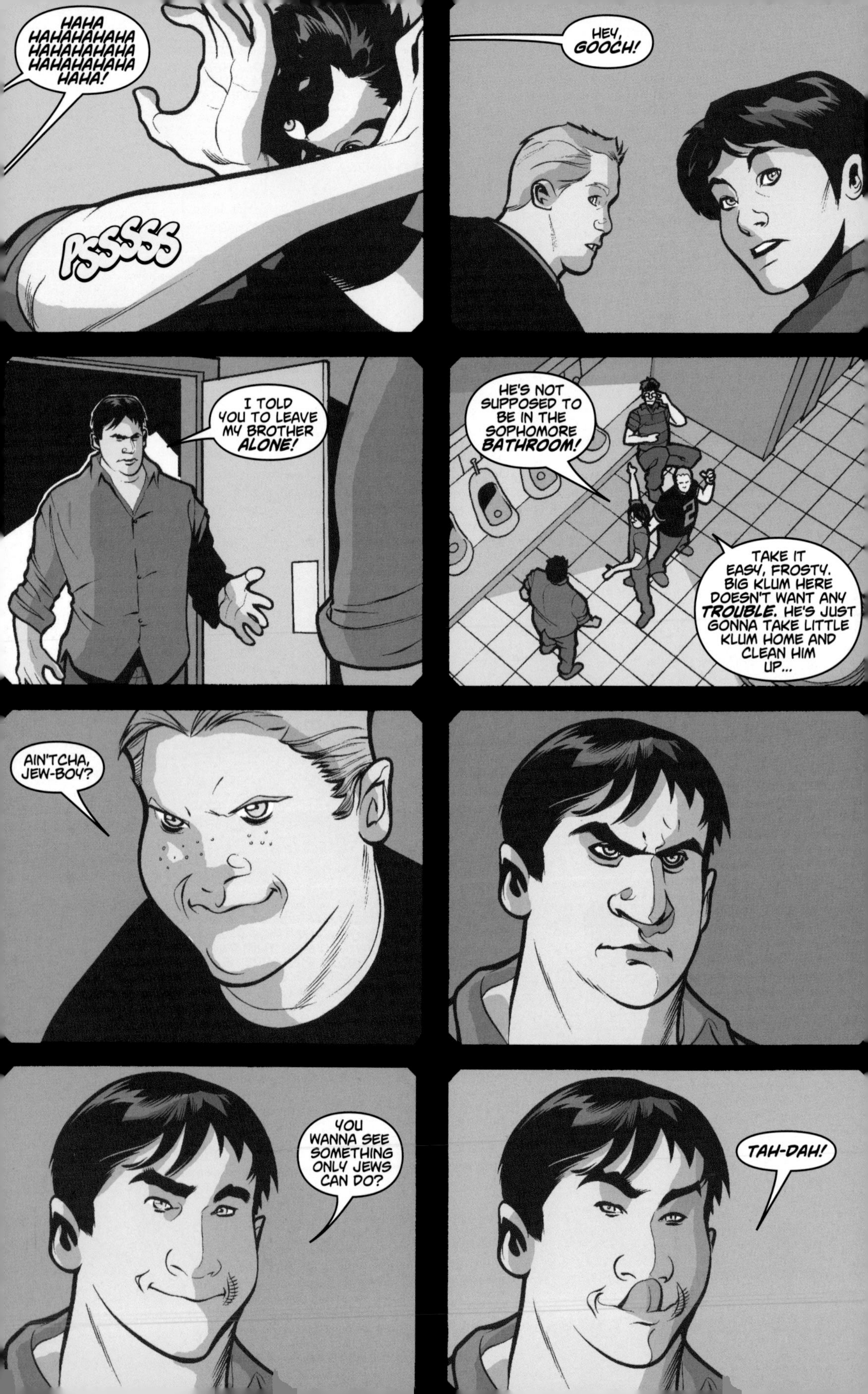
HAHA HAHAHAHAHA HAHAHAHAHA HAHAHAHAHA HAHA!
PSSSSS
HEY, GOOCH!
I TOLD YOU TO LEAVE MY BROTHER ALONE!
HE'S NOT SUPPOSED TO BE IN THE SOPHOMORE BATHROOM!
TAKE IT EASY, FROSTY. BIG KLUM HERE DOESN'T WANT ANY TROUBLE. HE'S JUST GONNA TAKE LITTLE KLUM HOME AND CLEAN HIM UP...
AIN'TCHA, JEW-BOY?
YOU WANNA SEE SOMETHING ONLY JEWS CAN DO?
TAH-DAH!

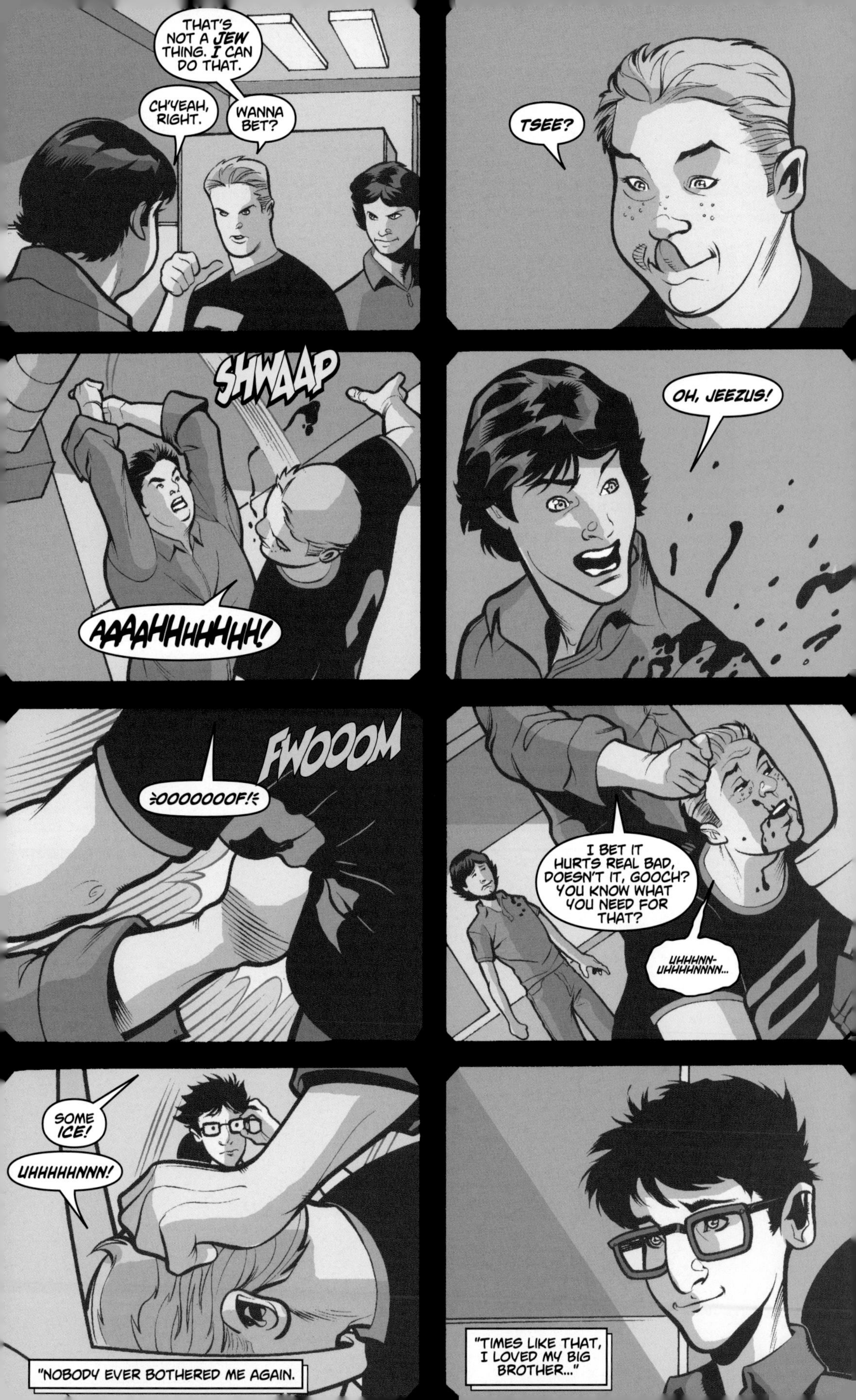
THAT'S NOT A JEW THING. I CAN DO THAT.
CH'YEAH, RIGHT.
WANNA BET?
TSEE?
SHWAAP
AAAAHHHHHHH!
OH, JEEZUS!
FWOOOM
OOOOOOOF!
I BET IT HURTS REAL BAD, DOESN'T IT, GOOCH? YOU KNOW WHAT YOU NEED FOR THAT?
UHHHNN- UHHHHNNNN...
SOME ICE!
UHHHHHNNN!
"NOBODY EVER BOTHERED ME AGAIN.
"TIMES LIKE THAT, I LOVED MY BIG BROTHER..."

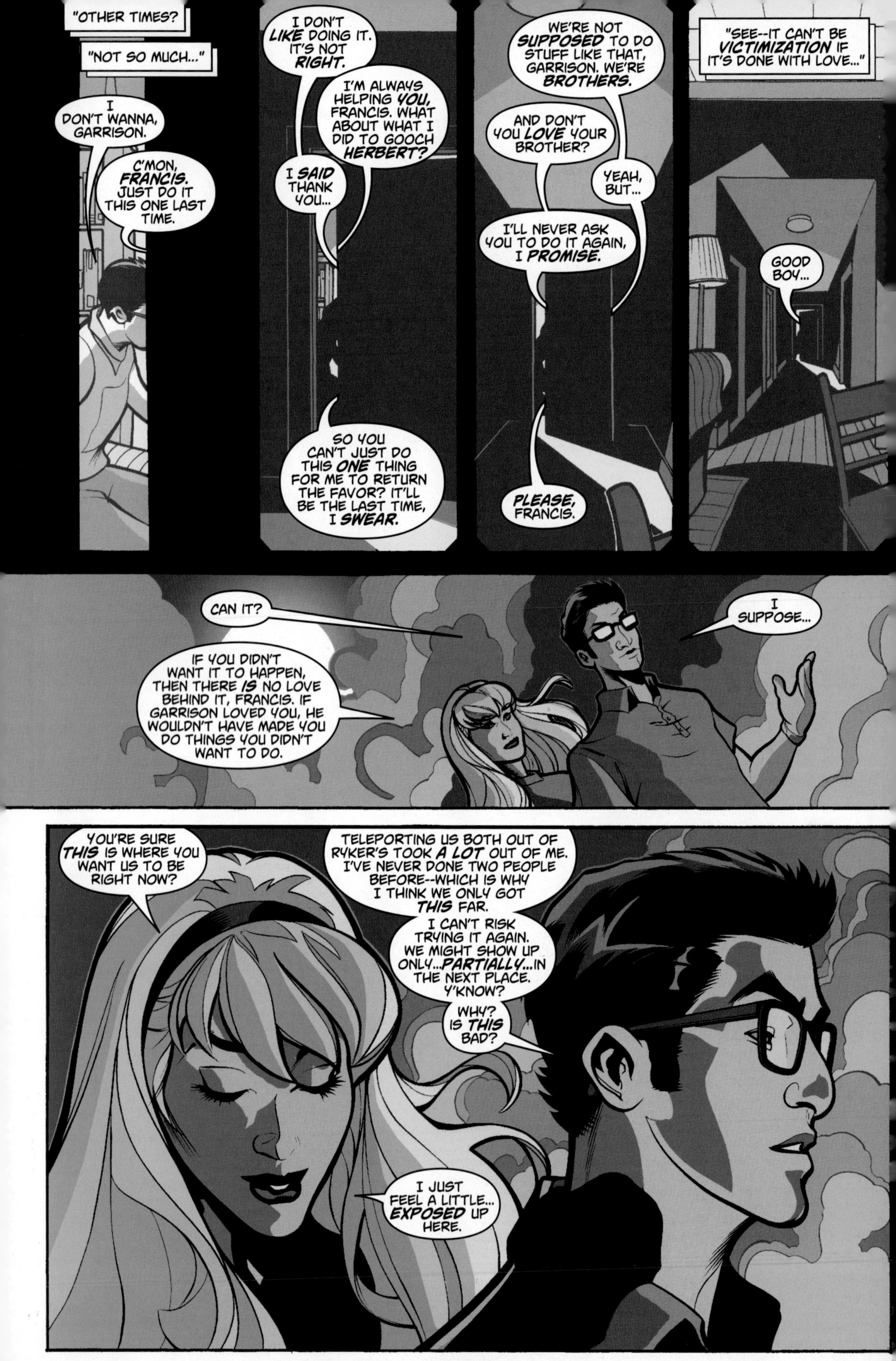
"OTHER TIMES?
"NOT SO MUCH..."
I DON'T WANNA, GARRISON.
C'MON, FRANCIS. JUST DO IT THIS ONE LAST TIME.
I DON'T LIKE DOING IT. IT'S NOT RIGHT.
I'M ALWAYS HELPING YOU, FRANCIS. WHAT ABOUT WHAT I DID TO GOOCH HERBERT?
I SAID THANK YOU...
SO YOU CAN'T JUST DO THIS ONE THING FOR ME TO RETURN THE FAVOR? IT'LL BE THE LAST TIME, I SWEAR.
WE'RE NOT SUPPOSED TO DO STUFF LIKE THAT, GARRISON. WE'RE BROTHERS.
AND DON'T YOU LOVE YOUR BROTHER?
YEAH, BUT...
I'LL NEVER ASK YOU TO DO IT AGAIN, I PROMISE.
PLEASE, FRANCIS.
"SEE--IT CAN'T BE VICTIMIZATION IF IT'S DONE WITH LOVE..."
GOOD BOY...
CAN IT?
IF YOU DIDN'T WANT IT TO HAPPEN, THEN THERE IS NO LOVE BEHIND IT, FRANCIS. IF GARRISON LOVED YOU, HE WOULDN'T HAVE MADE YOU DO THINGS YOU DIDN'T WANT TO DO.
I SUPPOSE...
YOU'RE SURE THIS IS WHERE YOU WANT US TO BE RIGHT NOW?
TELEPORTING US BOTH OUT OF RYKER'S TOOK A LOT OUT OF ME. I'VE NEVER DONE TWO PEOPLE BEFORE--WHICH IS WHY I THINK WE ONLY GOT THIS FAR.
I CAN'T RISK TRYING IT AGAIN. WE MIGHT SHOW UP ONLY...PARTIALLY...IN THE NEXT PLACE. Y'KNOW?
WHY? IS THIS BAD?
I JUST FEEL A LITTLE... EXPOSED UP HERE.

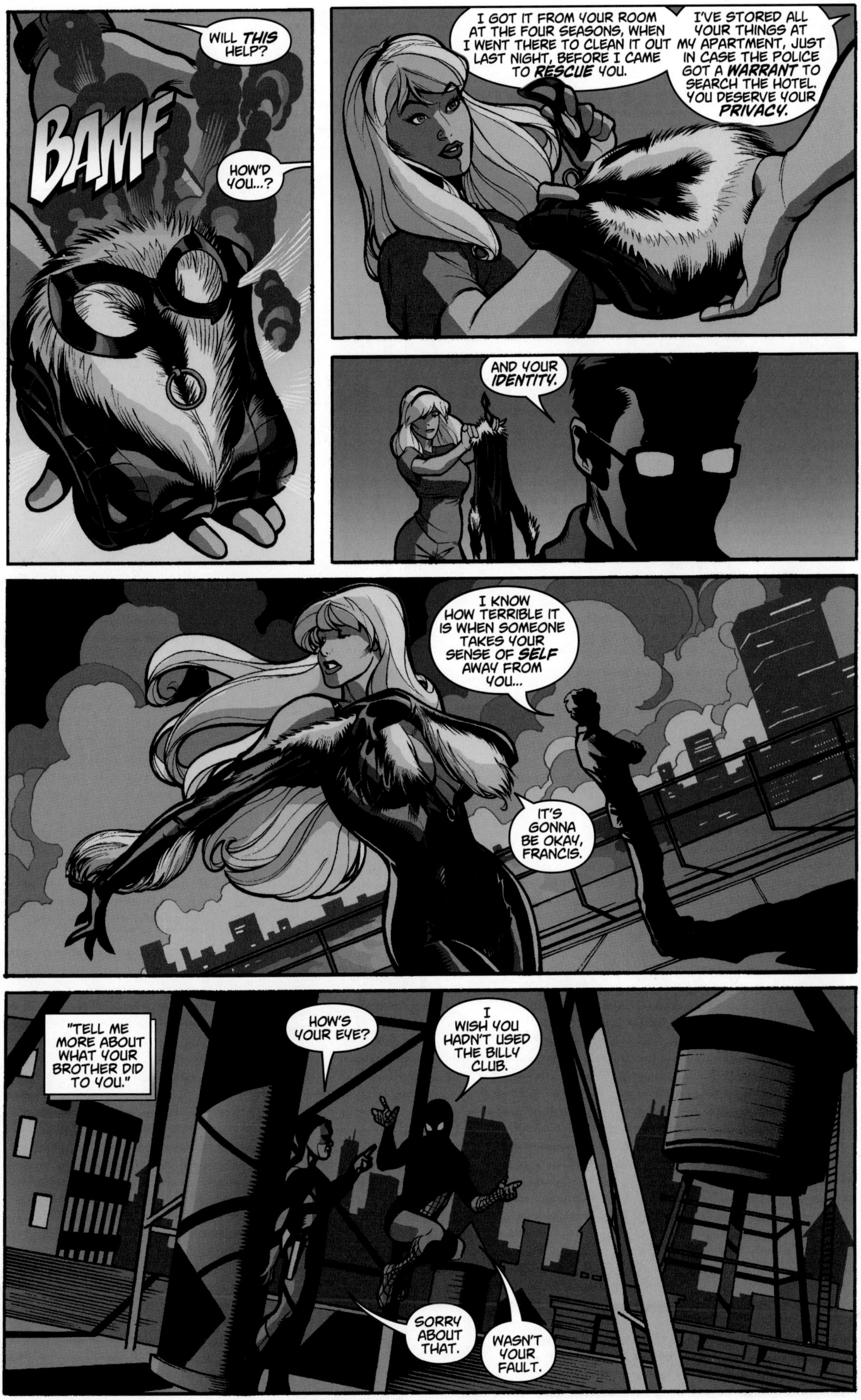
WILL THIS HELP?
BAMF
HOW'D YOU...?
I GOT IT FROM YOUR ROOM AT THE FOUR SEASONS, WHEN I WENT THERE TO CLEAN IT OUT LAST NIGHT, BEFORE I CAME TO RESCUE YOU.
I'VE STORED ALL YOUR THINGS AT MY APARTMENT, JUST IN CASE THE POLICE GOT A WARRANT TO SEARCH THE HOTEL. YOU DESERVE YOUR PRIVACY.
AND YOUR IDENTITY.
I KNOW HOW TERRIBLE IT IS WHEN SOMEONE TAKES YOUR SENSE OF SELF AWAY FROM YOU...
IT'S GONNA BE OKAY, FRANCIS.
"TELL ME MORE ABOUT WHAT YOUR BROTHER DID TO YOU."
HOW'S YOUR EYE?
I WISH YOU HADN'T USED THE BILLY CLUB.
SORRY ABOUT THAT.
WASN'T YOUR FAULT.

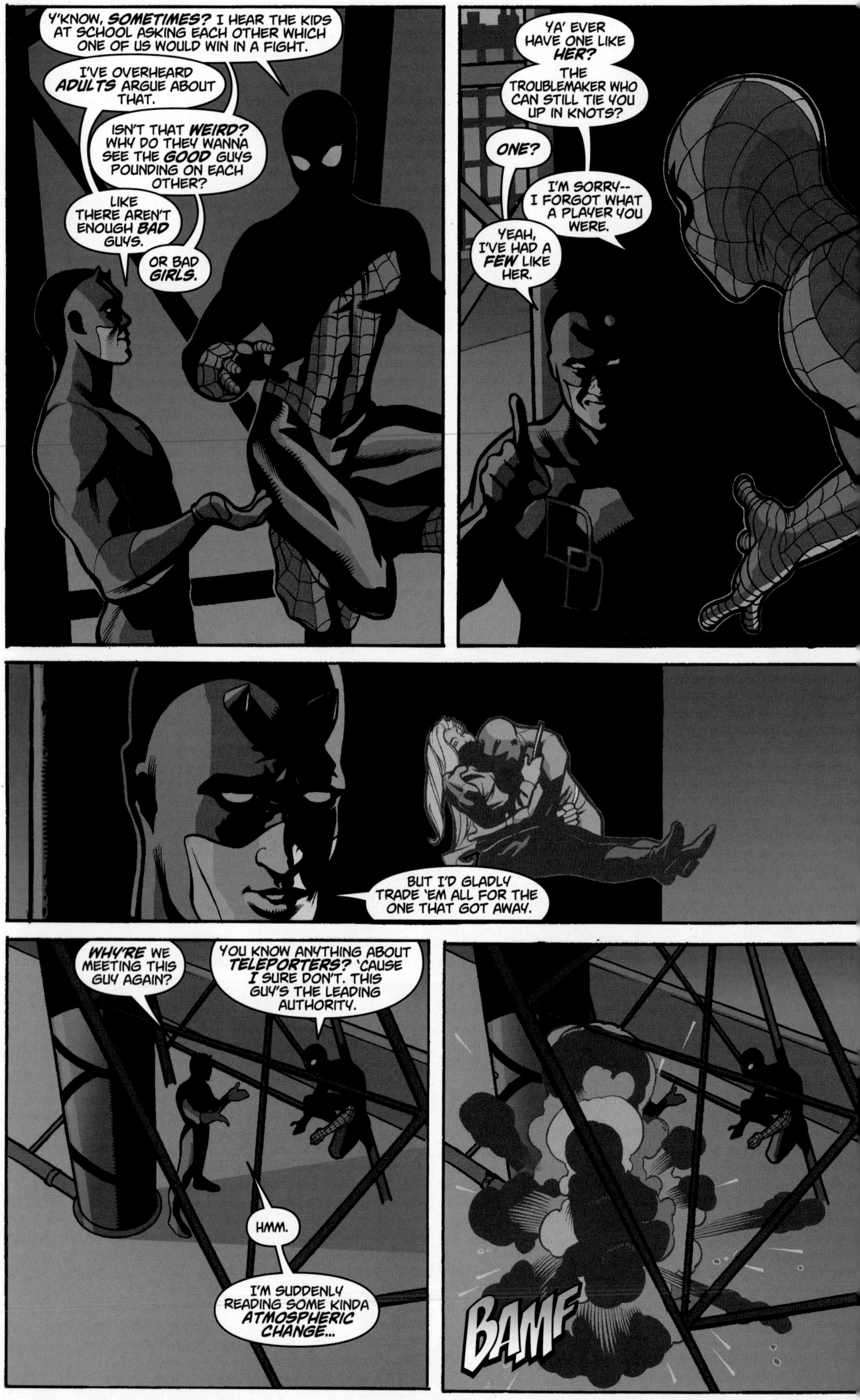
Y'KNOW, SOMETIMES? I HEAR THE KIDS AT SCHOOL ASKING EACH OTHER WHICH ONE OF US WOULD WIN IN A FIGHT.
I'VE OVERHEARD ADULTS ARGUE ABOUT THAT.
ISN'T THAT WEIRD? WHY DO THEY WANNA SEE THE GOOD GUYS POUNDING ON EACH OTHER?
LIKE THERE AREN'T ENOUGH BAD GUYS.
OR BAD GIRLS.
YA' EVER HAVE ONE LIKE HER?
THE TROUBLEMAKER WHO CAN STILL TIE YOU UP IN KNOTS?
ONE?
I'M SORRY-- I FORGOT WHAT A PLAYER YOU WERE.
YEAH, I'VE HAD A FEW LIKE HER.
BUT I'D GLADLY TRADE 'EM ALL FOR THE ONE THAT GOT AWAY.
WHY'RE WE MEETING THIS GUY AGAIN?
YOU KNOW ANYTHING ABOUT TELEPORTERS? 'CAUSE I SURE DON'T. THIS GUY'S THE LEADING AUTHORITY.
HMM.
I'M SUDDENLY READING SOME KINDA ATMOSPHERIC CHANGE...
BAMF

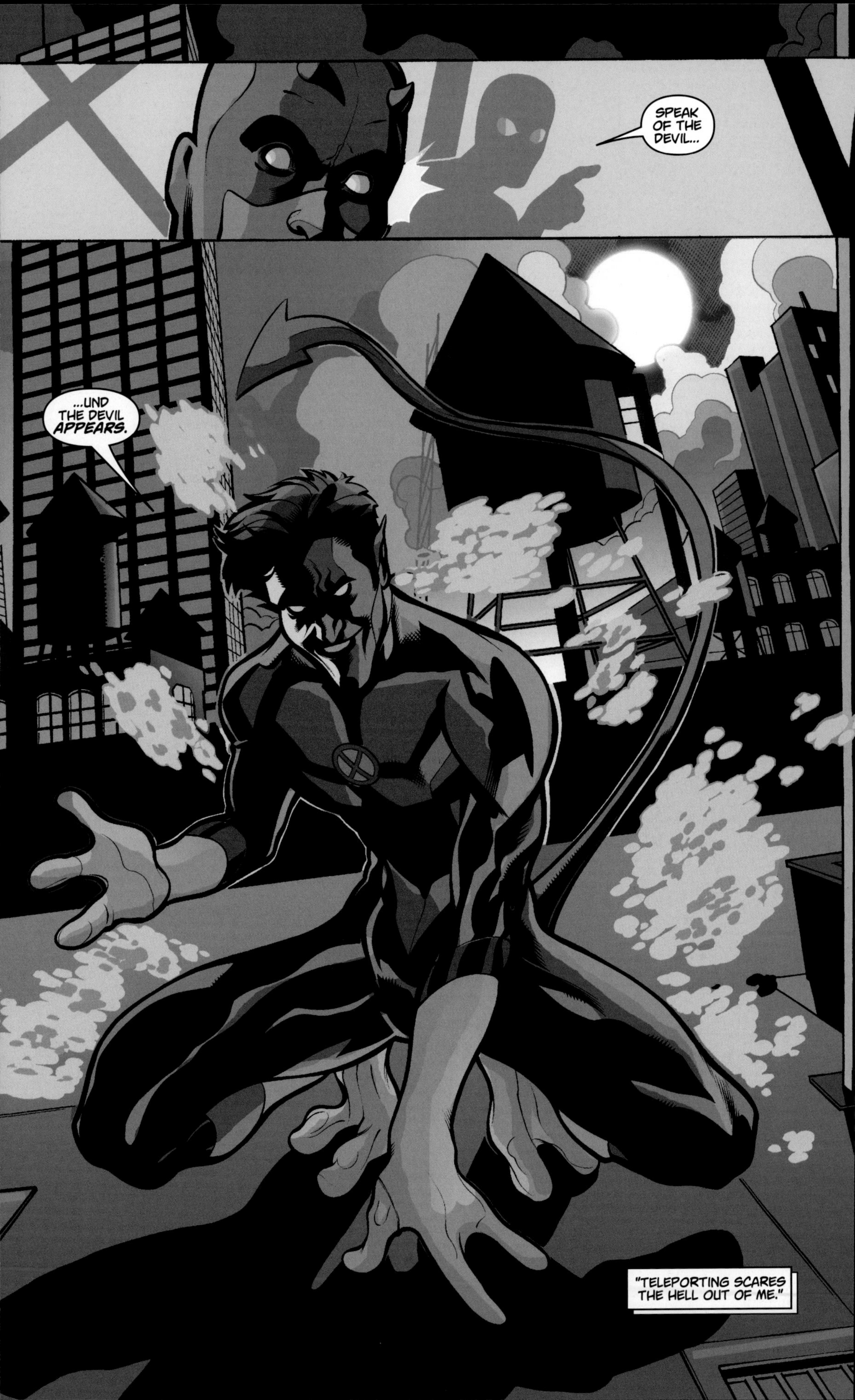
SPEAK OF THE DEVIL...
...UND THE DEVIL APPEARS.
"TELEPORTING SCARES THE HELL OUT OF ME."

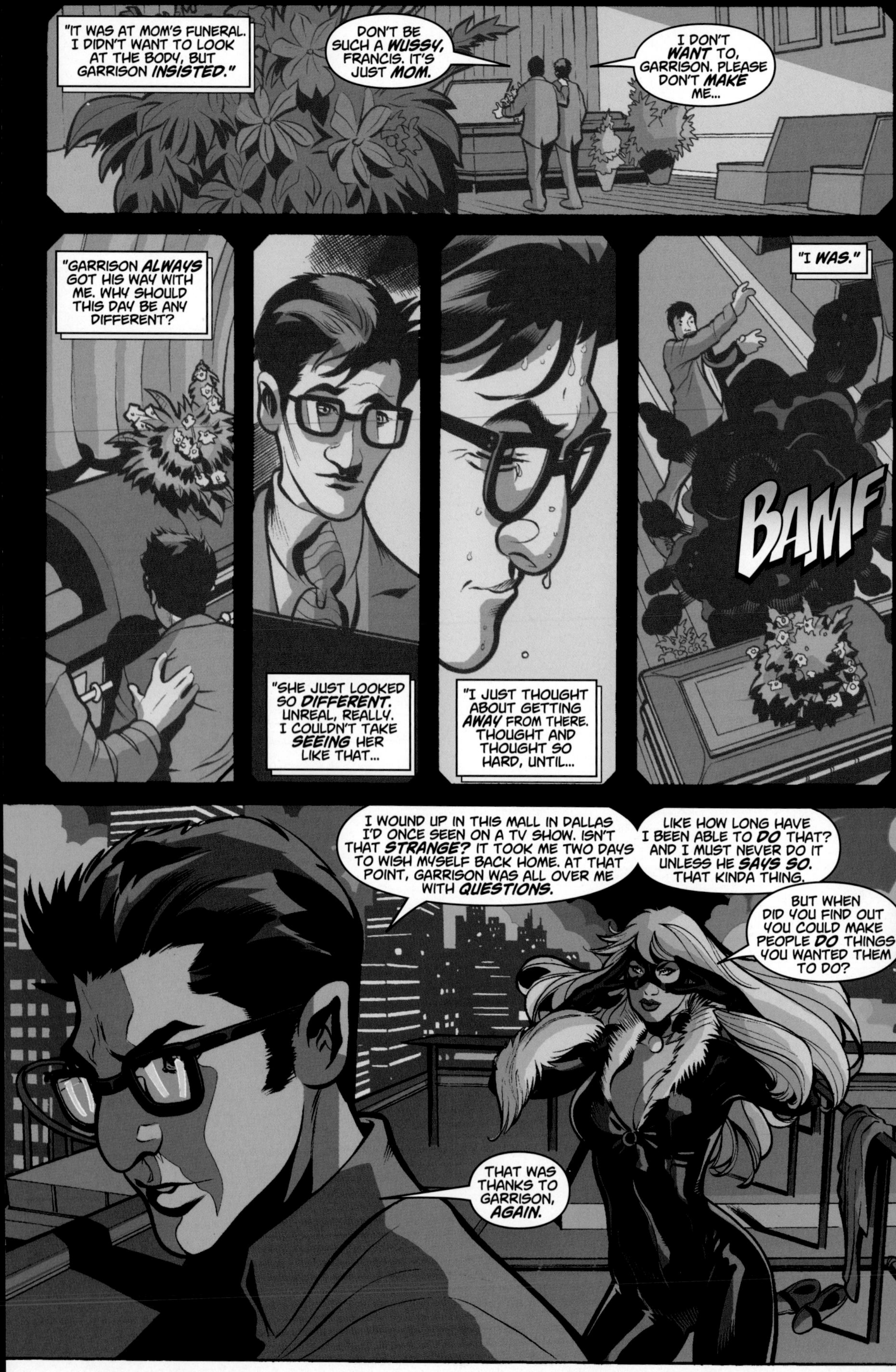
"IT WAS AT MOM'S FUNERAL. I DIDN'T WANT TO LOOK AT THE BODY, BUT GARRISON INSISTED."
DON'T BE SUCH A WUSSY, FRANCIS. IT'S JUST MOM.
I DON'T WANT TO, GARRISON. PLEASE DON'T MAKE ME...
"GARRISON ALWAYS GOT HIS WAY WITH ME. WHY SHOULD THIS DAY BE ANY DIFFERENT?
"SHE JUST LOOKED SO DIFFERENT. UNREAL, REALLY. I COULDN'T TAKE SEEING HER LIKE THAT...
"I JUST THOUGHT ABOUT GETTING AWAY FROM THERE. THOUGHT AND THOUGHT SO HARD, UNTIL...
"I WAS."
BAMF
I WOUND UP IN THIS MALL IN DALLAS I'D ONCE SEEN ON A TV SHOW. ISN'T THAT STRANGE? IT TOOK ME TWO DAYS TO WISH MYSELF BACK HOME. AT THAT POINT, GARRISON WAS ALL OVER ME WITH QUESTIONS.
LIKE HOW LONG HAVE I BEEN ABLE TO DO THAT? AND I MUST NEVER DO IT UNLESS HE SAYS SO. THAT KINDA THING.
BUT WHEN DID YOU FIND OUT YOU COULD MAKE PEOPLE DO THINGS YOU WANTED THEM TO DO?
THAT WAS THANKS TO GARRISON, AGAIN.

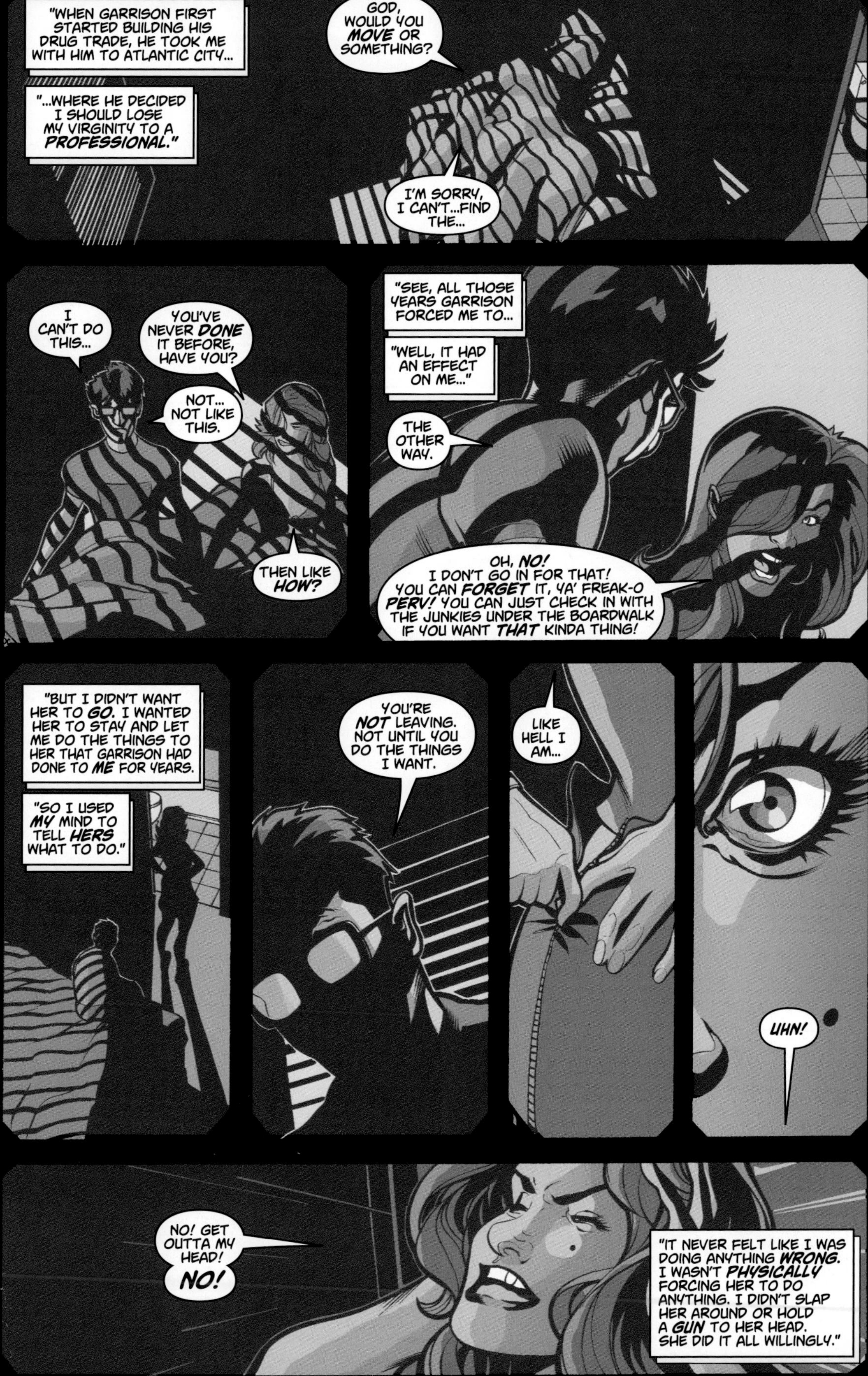
"WHEN GARRISON FIRST STARTED BUILDING HIS DRUG TRADE, HE TOOK ME WITH HIM TO ATLANTIC CITY...
"...WHERE HE DECIDED I SHOULD LOSE MY VIRGINITY TO A PROFESSIONAL."
GOD, WOULD YOU MOVE OR SOMETHING?
I'M SORRY, I CAN'T...FIND THE...
I CAN'T DO THIS...
YOU'VE NEVER DONE IT BEFORE, HAVE YOU?
NOT... NOT LIKE THIS.
THEN LIKE HOW?
"SEE, ALL THOSE YEARS GARRISON FORCED ME TO...
"WELL, IT HAD AN EFFECT ON ME..."
THE OTHER WAY.
OH, NO! I DON'T GO IN FOR THAT! YOU CAN FORGET IT, YA' FREAK-O PERV! YOU CAN JUST CHECK IN WITH THE JUNKIES UNDER THE BOARDWALK IF YOU WANT THAT KINDA THING!
"BUT I DIDN'T WANT HER TO GO. I WANTED HER TO STAY AND LET ME DO THE THINGS TO HER THAT GARRISON HAD DONE TO ME FOR YEARS.
"SO I USED MY MIND TO TELL HERS WHAT TO DO."
YOU'RE NOT LEAVING. NOT UNTIL YOU DO THE THINGS I WANT.
LIKE HELL I AM...
UHN!
NO! GET OUTTA MY HEAD! NO!
"IT NEVER FELT LIKE I WAS DOING ANYTHING WRONG. I WASN'T PHYSICALLY FORCING HER TO DO ANYTHING. I DIDN'T SLAP HER AROUND OR HOLD A GUN TO HER HEAD. SHE DID IT ALL WILLINGLY."

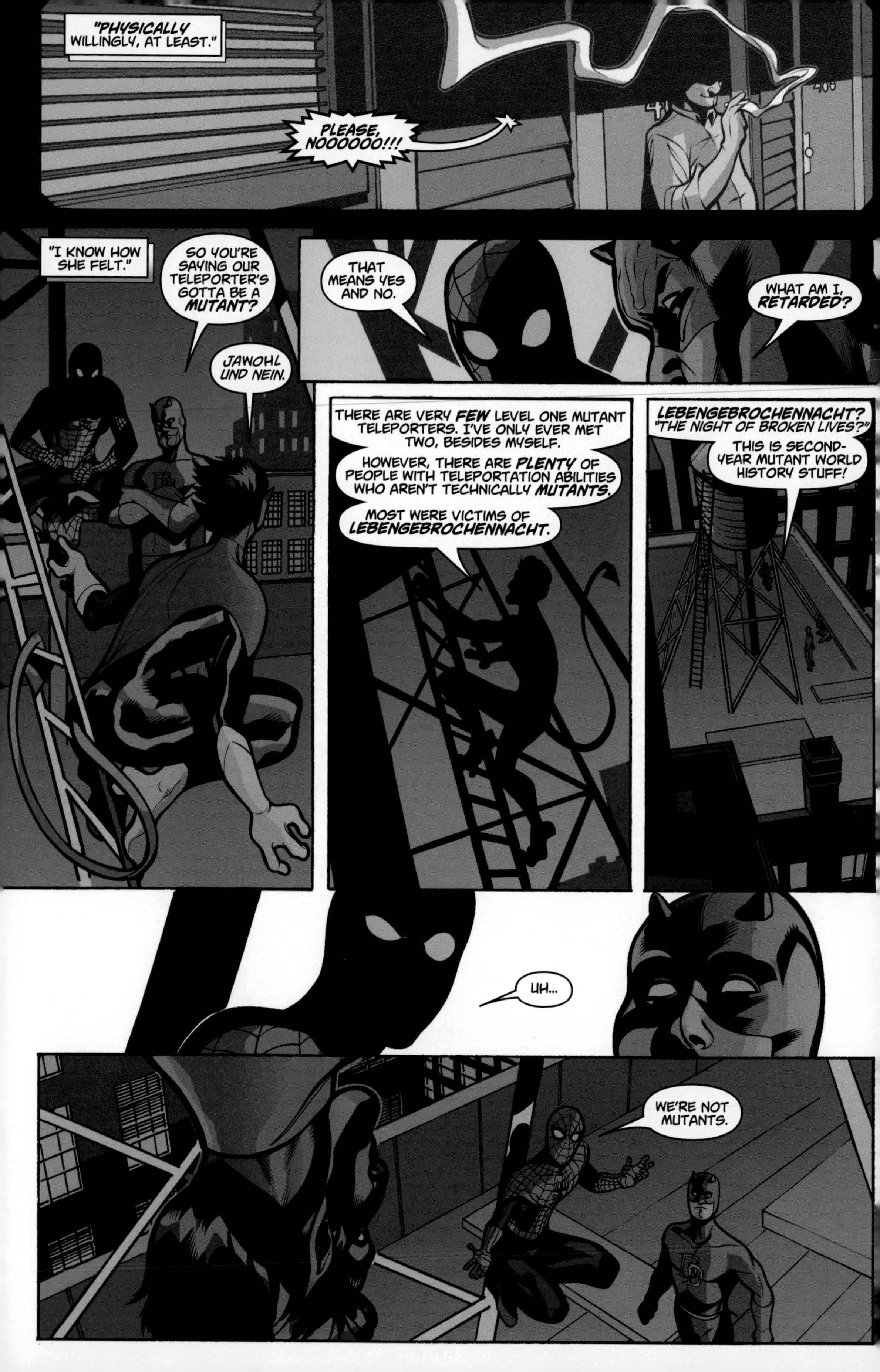
"PHYSICALLY WILLINGLY, AT LEAST."
PLEASE, NOOOOOO!!!
"I KNOW HOW SHE FELT."
SO YOU'RE SAYING OUR TELEPORTER'S GOTTA BE A MUTANT?
JAWOHL UND NEIN.
THAT MEANS YES AND NO.
WHAT AM I, RETARDED?
THERE ARE VERY FEW LEVEL ONE MUTANT TELEPORTERS. I'VE ONLY EVER MET TWO, BESIDES MYSELF.
HOWEVER, THERE ARE PLENTY OF PEOPLE WITH TELEPORTATION ABILITIES WHO AREN'T TECHNICALLY MUTANTS.
MOST WERE VICTIMS OF LEBENGEBROCHENNACHT.
LEBENGEBROCHENNACHT? "THE NIGHT OF BROKEN LIVES?"
THIS IS SECOND-YEAR MUTANT WORLD HISTORY STUFF!
UH...
WE'RE NOT MUTANTS.

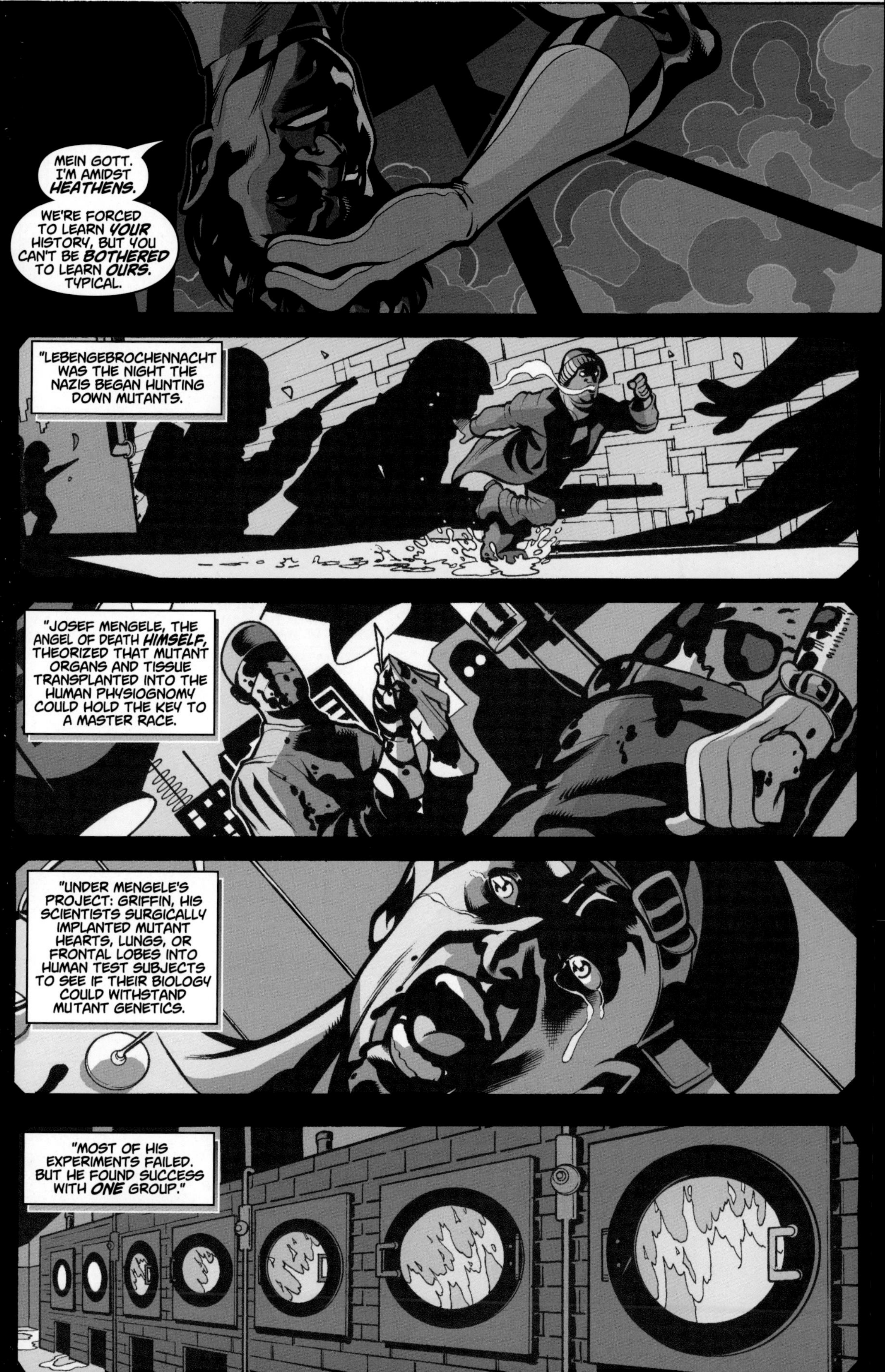
MEIN GOTT. I'M AMIDST HEATHENS.
WE'RE FORCED TO LEARN YOUR HISTORY, BUT YOU CAN'T BE BOTHERED TO LEARN OURS. TYPICAL.
"LEBENGEBROCHENNACHT WAS THE NIGHT THE NAZIS BEGAN HUNTING DOWN MUTANTS.
"JOSEF MENGELE, THE ANGEL OF DEATH HIMSELF, THEORIZED THAT MUTANT ORGANS AND TISSUE TRANSPLANTED INTO THE HUMAN PHYSIOGNOMY COULD HOLD THE KEY TO A MASTER RACE.
"UNDER MENGELE'S PROJECT: GRIFFIN, HIS SCIENTISTS SURGICALLY IMPLANTED MUTANT HEARTS, LUNGS, OR FRONTAL LOBES INTO HUMAN TEST SUBJECTS TO SEE IF THEIR BIOLOGY COULD WITHSTAND MUTANT GENETICS.
"MOST OF HIS EXPERIMENTS FAILED. BUT HE FOUND SUCCESS WITH ONE GROUP."

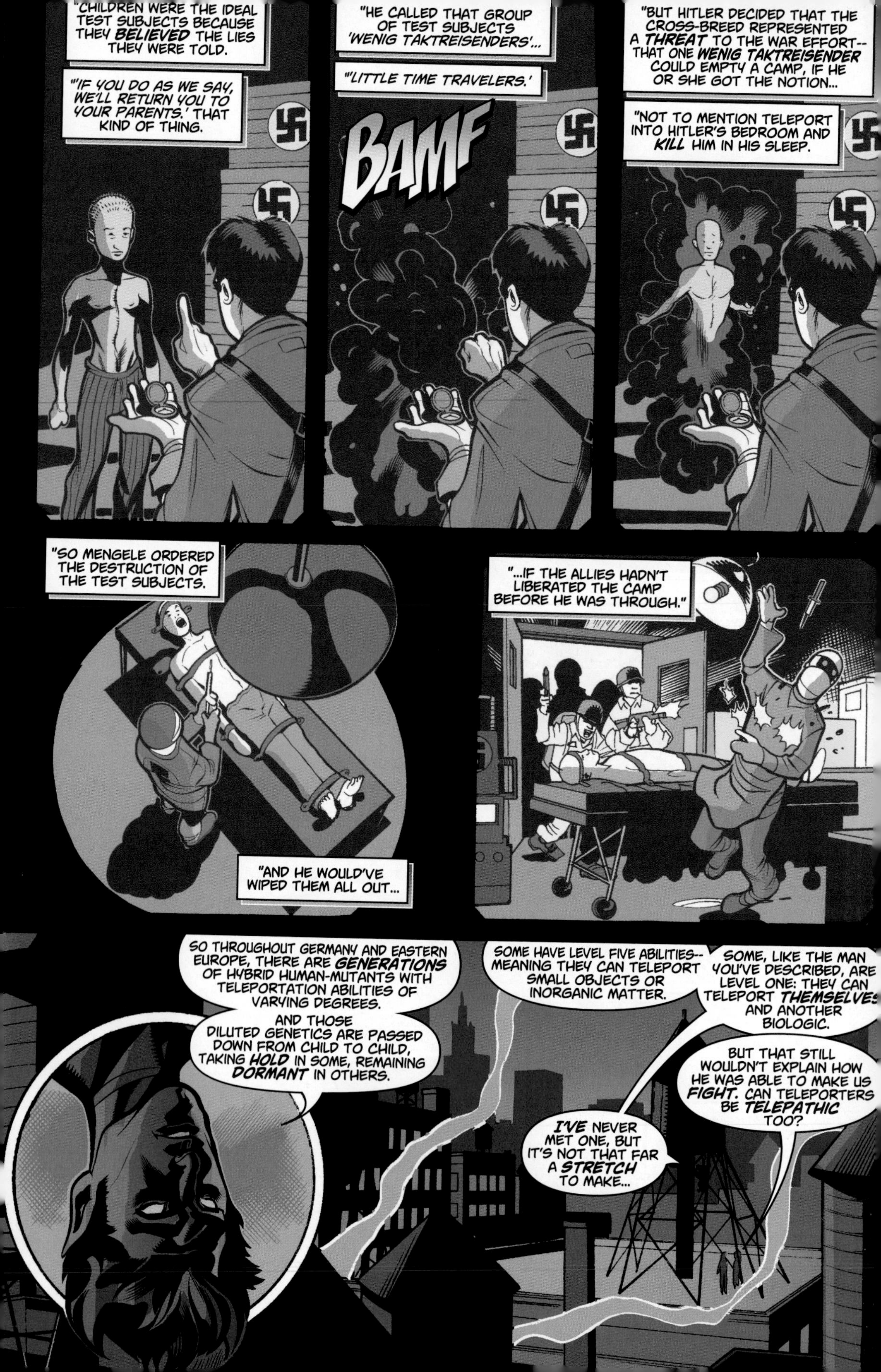

"CHILDREN WERE THE IDEAL TEST SUBJECTS BECAUSE THEY BELIEVED THE LIES THEY WERE TOLD.
"'IF YOU DO AS WE SAY, WE'LL RETURN YOU TO YOUR PARENTS.' THAT KIND OF THING.
"HE CALLED THAT GROUP OF TEST SUBJECTS 'WENIG TAKTREISENDERS'...
"'LITTLE TIME TRAVELERS.'
BAMF
"BUT HITLER DECIDED THAT THE CROSS-BREED REPRESENTED A THREAT TO THE WAR EFFORT--THAT ONE WENIG TAKTREISENDER COULD EMPTY A CAMP, IF HE OR SHE GOT THE NOTION...
"NOT TO MENTION TELEPORT INTO HITLER'S BEDROOM AND KILL HIM IN HIS SLEEP.
"SO MENGELE ORDERED THE DESTRUCTION OF THE TEST SUBJECTS.
"AND HE WOULD'VE WIPED THEM ALL OUT...
"...IF THE ALLIES HADN'T LIBERATED THE CAMP BEFORE HE WAS THROUGH."
SO THROUGHOUT GERMANY AND EASTERN EUROPE, THERE ARE GENERATIONS OF HYBRID HUMAN-MUTANTS WITH TELEPORTATION ABILITIES OF VARYING DEGREES.
AND THOSE DILUTED GENETICS ARE PASSED DOWN FROM CHILD TO CHILD, TAKING HOLD IN SOME, REMAINING DORMANT IN OTHERS.
SOME HAVE LEVEL FIVE ABILITIES--MEANING THEY CAN TELEPORT SMALL OBJECTS OR INORGANIC MATTER.
SOME, LIKE THE MAN YOU'VE DESCRIBED, ARE LEVEL ONE: THEY CAN TELEPORT THEMSELVES AND ANOTHER BIOLOGIC.
BUT THAT STILL WOULDN'T EXPLAIN HOW HE WAS ABLE TO MAKE US FIGHT. CAN TELEPORTERS BE TELEPATHIC TOO?
I'VE NEVER MET ONE, BUT IT'S NOT THAT FAR A STRETCH TO MAKE...

"WHAT IS TELEPATHY IF NOT THE TELEPORTATION OF *IDEAS* OR *SUGGESTIONS?*"

"WHEN I TOLD FRANCIS ABOUT WHAT I DID WITH THE PROSTITUTE, HE IMMEDIATELY RECONFIGURED HIS BUSINESS MODEL.

"THE PLAN WAS FOR ME TO USE MY *'PROMPT'* TO GET RICH AND FAMOUS PEOPLE TO TRY GARRISON'S HEROIN, AND THEN HE'D TELEPORT FIXES DIRECTLY INTO THEIR BLOODSTREAMS.

"ONCE THE WORD SPREAD THAT MR. BROWNSTONE COULD GET YOU DOSED WITH NO MESSY NEEDLES OR TRACK MARKS TO WORRY ABOUT, I HARDLY NEEDED TO DO MUCH *PROMPTING* ANYMORE.

"OUR CLIENT LIST READ LIKE A WHO'S-WHO OF MOVIE STARS, POLITICIANS, CELEBUTANTS AND THE CITY'S IDLE RICH.

"BY THE SIX-MONTH MARK, WE HAD ENOUGH MONEY TO BUY THE CLUB USED TO WORK OUT OF.

"BY THE END OF THE YEAR, WE BOUGHT OUR FIFTH BUILDING.

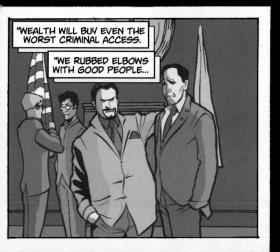

"WEALTH WILL BUY EVEN THE WORST CRIMINAL ACCESS.

"WE RUBBED ELBOWS WITH GOOD PEOPLE...

"AND *NOT* SO GOOD PEOPLE.

"BY YEAR FIVE, WE WERE A LEGITIMATE ORGANIZATION ON THE SURFACE. FEW KNEW WE WERE FUELED BY THE DRUG TRADE.

"TWO BROTHERS FROM A NOTHING FAMILY HAD CONQUERED THE GREATEST CITY IN THE WORLD. YOU WOULD'VE THOUGHT IT WAS CONQUEST *ENOUGH* FOR GARRISON...

"I'D LEARN IT *WASN'T*..."

ABSOLUTELY, YOUR HONOR... NOT A PROBLEM AT ALL...TEN TONIGHT... ENJOY YOUR RIDE, SIR.

THAT MAKES, WHAT? *THREE* CIRCUIT COURT JUDGES IN OUR POCKET?

OSCORP IS LOW-BALLING THAT OFFER FOR THE BUILDING ON THE WEST SIDE HIGHWAY.

NORMAN OSBORN CAN GO TO *HELL*. LIKE I *NEED* ANY MORE MONEY.

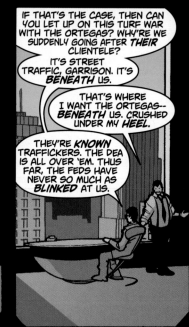

IF THAT'S THE CASE, THEN CAN YOU LET UP ON THIS TURF WAR WITH THE ORTEGAS? WHY'RE WE SUDDENLY GOING AFTER *THEIR* CLIENTELE?

IT'S STREET TRAFFIC, GARRISON. IT'S *BENEATH* US.

THAT'S WHERE I WANT THE ORTEGAS-- *BENEATH* US. CRUSHED UNDER MY *HEEL*.

THEY'RE *KNOWN* TRAFFICKERS. THE DEA IS ALL OVER 'EM. THUS FAR, THE FEDS HAVE NEVER SO MUCH AS *BLINKED* AT US.

IF WE GET INTO IT WITH THE ORTEGAS, WE'RE GONNA DRAW HEAT FROM THE *NARCS*, AND OPEN UP A *REALLY* MESSY CAN OF WORMS.

YOU SHOULD *RELAX*, FRANCIS. YOU WORRY TOO MUCH.

YOU DON'T WORRY *ENOUGH*. YOU'RE GETTING TOO CAVALIER.

WHAT'RE YOU *DOING*?

IT'S A LITTLE TOO *BRIGHT* IN HERE.

CLIK
WHIRRRRRRRR

"IT'D BEEN YEARS, BUT I KNEW WHAT HE WAS GOING TO SAY BEFORE HE EVEN SAID IT..."

I WANT YOU TO *DO* SOMETHING FOR ME, FRANCIS...

WHIRRRRRRRR

"HE DIDN'T EVEN *NEED* ME ANYMORE, LIKE HE DID WHEN I WAS A KID. HE WAS PUSHER TO THE STARS--HE COULD'VE HAD *ANYBODY*.

"BUT IT WAS NEVER ABOUT *SEX*. HE JUST WANTED TO REMIND ME WHO WAS IN *CHARGE*."

GARRISON... PLEASE DON'T...

SHHHHHH... THAT'S A *GOOD BOY*...

WHIRRRRRRRR *CLIK*

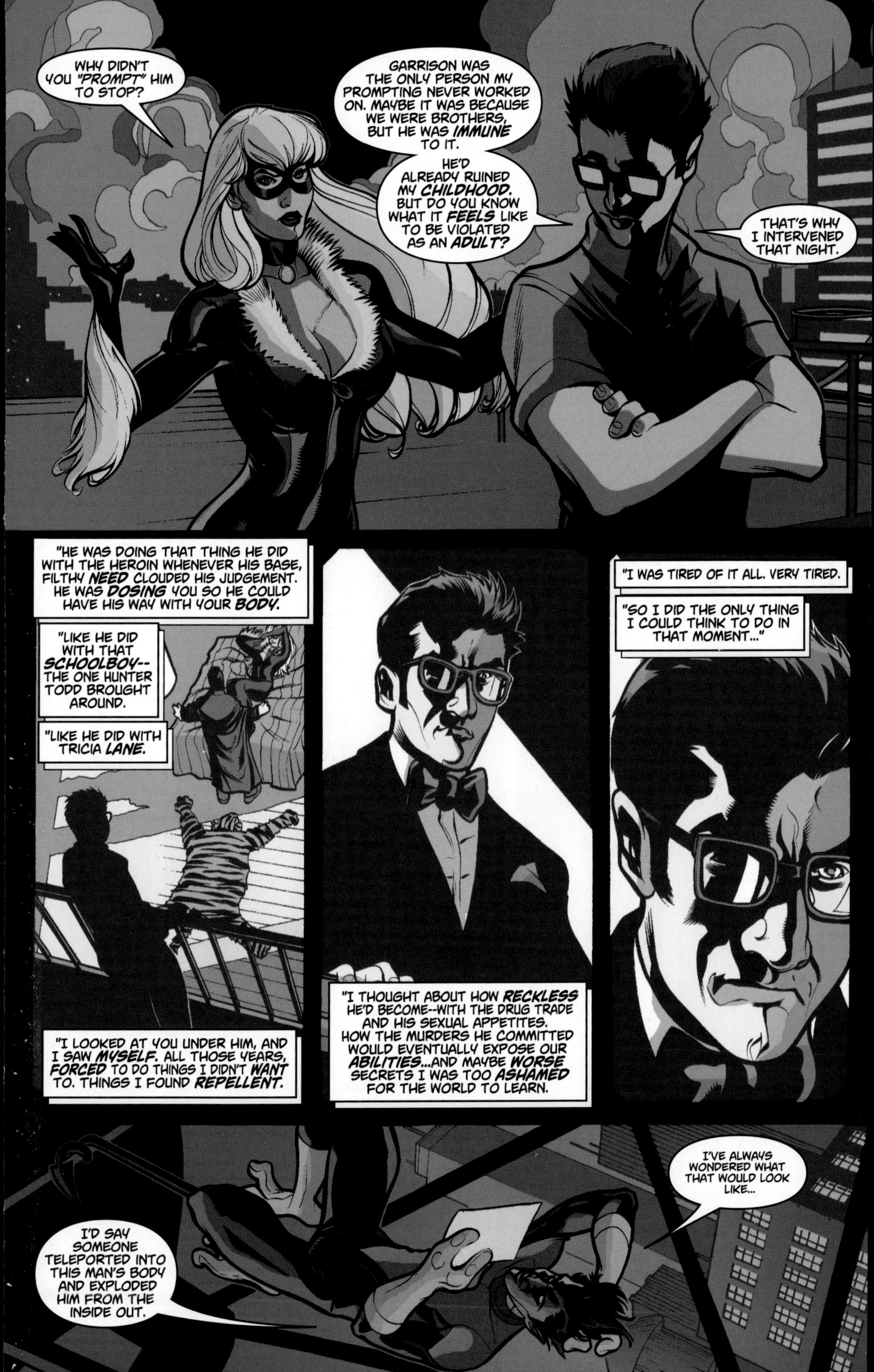
WHY DIDN'T YOU "PROMPT" HIM TO STOP?
GARRISON WAS THE ONLY PERSON MY PROMPTING NEVER WORKED ON. MAYBE IT WAS BECAUSE WE WERE BROTHERS, BUT HE WAS IMMUNE TO IT.
HE'D ALREADY RUINED MY CHILDHOOD. BUT DO YOU KNOW WHAT IT FEELS LIKE TO BE VIOLATED AS AN ADULT?
THAT'S WHY I INTERVENED THAT NIGHT.
"HE WAS DOING THAT THING HE DID WITH THE HEROIN WHENEVER HIS BASE, FILTHY NEED CLOUDED HIS JUDGEMENT. HE WAS DOSING YOU SO HE COULD HAVE HIS WAY WITH YOUR BODY.
"LIKE HE DID WITH THAT SCHOOLBOY-- THE ONE HUNTER TODD BROUGHT AROUND.
"LIKE HE DID WITH TRICIA LANE.
"I LOOKED AT YOU UNDER HIM, AND I SAW MYSELF. ALL THOSE YEARS, FORCED TO DO THINGS I DIDN'T WANT TO. THINGS I FOUND REPELLENT.
"I THOUGHT ABOUT HOW RECKLESS HE'D BECOME--WITH THE DRUG TRADE AND HIS SEXUAL APPETITES. HOW THE MURDERS HE COMMITTED WOULD EVENTUALLY EXPOSE OUR ABILITIES...AND MAYBE WORSE SECRETS I WAS TOO ASHAMED FOR THE WORLD TO LEARN.
"I WAS TIRED OF IT ALL. VERY TIRED.
"SO I DID THE ONLY THING I COULD THINK TO DO IN THAT MOMENT..."
I'VE ALWAYS WONDERED WHAT THAT WOULD LOOK LIKE...
I'D SAY SOMEONE TELEPORTED INTO THIS MAN'S BODY AND EXPLODED HIM FROM THE INSIDE OUT.

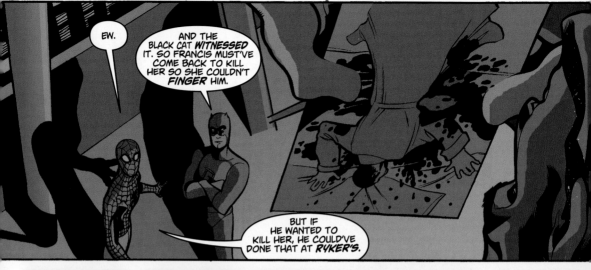

EW.

AND THE BLACK CAT *WITNESSED* IT. SO FRANCIS MUST'VE COME BACK TO KILL HER SO SHE COULDN'T *FINGER* HIM.

BUT IF HE WANTED TO KILL HER, HE COULD'VE DONE THAT AT *RYKER'S.*

RYKER'S?

THE *PRISON* RYKER'S?

YEAH-- RYKER'S ISLAND.

THIS FRAÜLEIN YOU SPEAK OF--SHE WAS *AT* RYKER'S ISLAND?

UNTIL SHE WAS *ABDUCTED* BY THE TELEPORTER LAST NIGHT.

MEIN GOTT...

AT THE XAVIER INSTITUTE, THERE IS A COMPUTER CALLED *CEREBRA*...

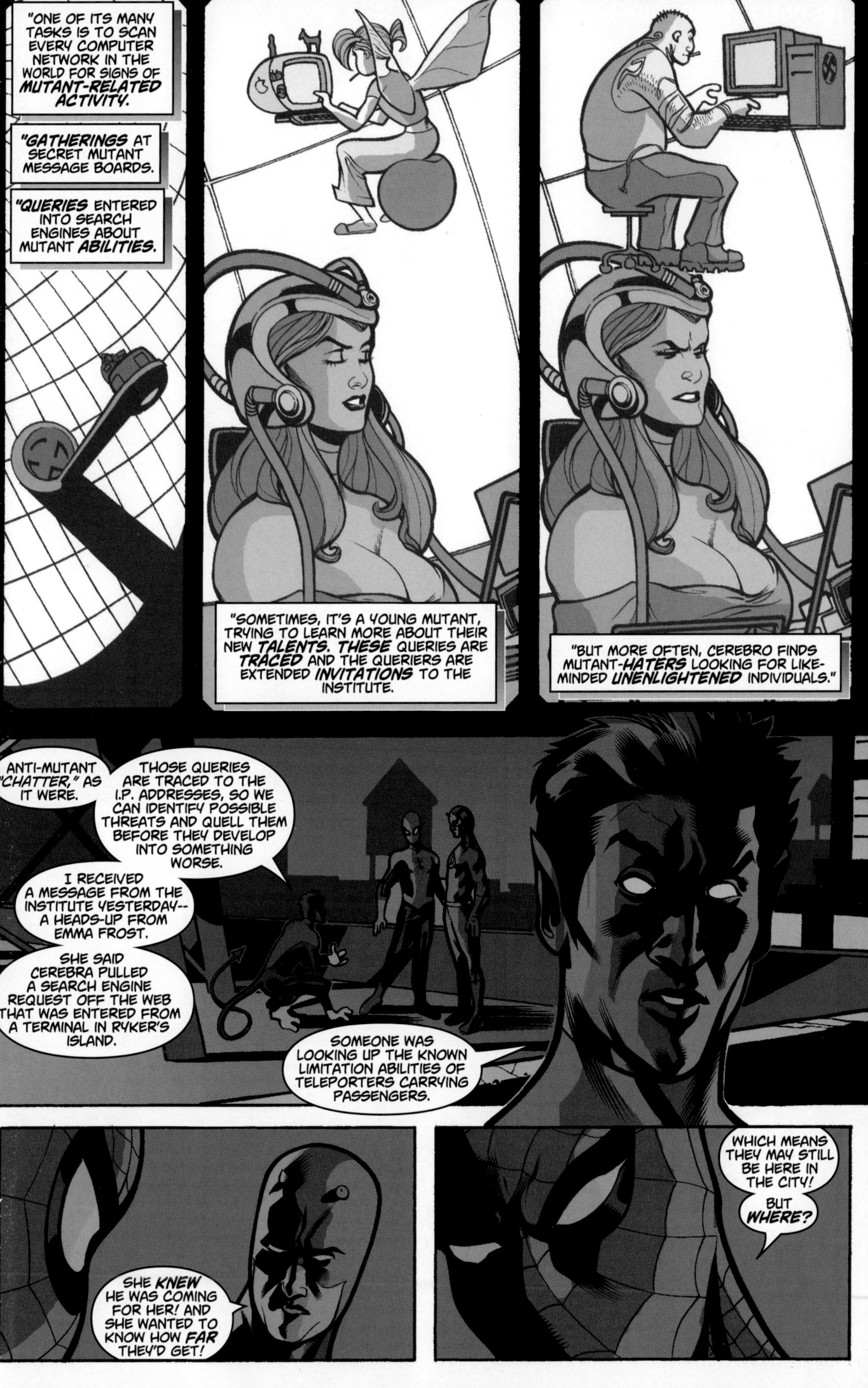
"ONE OF ITS MANY TASKS IS TO SCAN EVERY COMPUTER NETWORK IN THE WORLD FOR SIGNS OF MUTANT-RELATED ACTIVITY.
"GATHERINGS AT SECRET MUTANT MESSAGE BOARDS.
"QUERIES ENTERED INTO SEARCH ENGINES ABOUT MUTANT ABILITIES.
"SOMETIMES, IT'S A YOUNG MUTANT, TRYING TO LEARN MORE ABOUT THEIR NEW TALENTS. THESE QUERIES ARE TRACED AND THE QUERIERS ARE EXTENDED INVITATIONS TO THE INSTITUTE.
"BUT MORE OFTEN, CEREBRO FINDS MUTANT-HATERS LOOKING FOR LIKE-MINDED UNENLIGHTENED INDIVIDUALS."
ANTI-MUTANT "CHATTER," AS IT WERE.
THOSE QUERIES ARE TRACED TO THE I.P. ADDRESSES, SO WE CAN IDENTIFY POSSIBLE THREATS AND QUELL THEM BEFORE THEY DEVELOP INTO SOMETHING WORSE.
I RECEIVED A MESSAGE FROM THE INSTITUTE YESTERDAY-- A HEADS-UP FROM EMMA FROST.
SHE SAID CEREBRA PULLED A SEARCH ENGINE REQUEST OFF THE WEB THAT WAS ENTERED FROM A TERMINAL IN RYKER'S ISLAND.
SOMEONE WAS LOOKING UP THE KNOWN LIMITATION ABILITIES OF TELEPORTERS CARRYING PASSENGERS.
SHE KNEW HE WAS COMING FOR HER! AND SHE WANTED TO KNOW HOW FAR THEY'D GET!
WHICH MEANS THEY MAY STILL BE HERE IN THE CITY!
BUT WHERE?

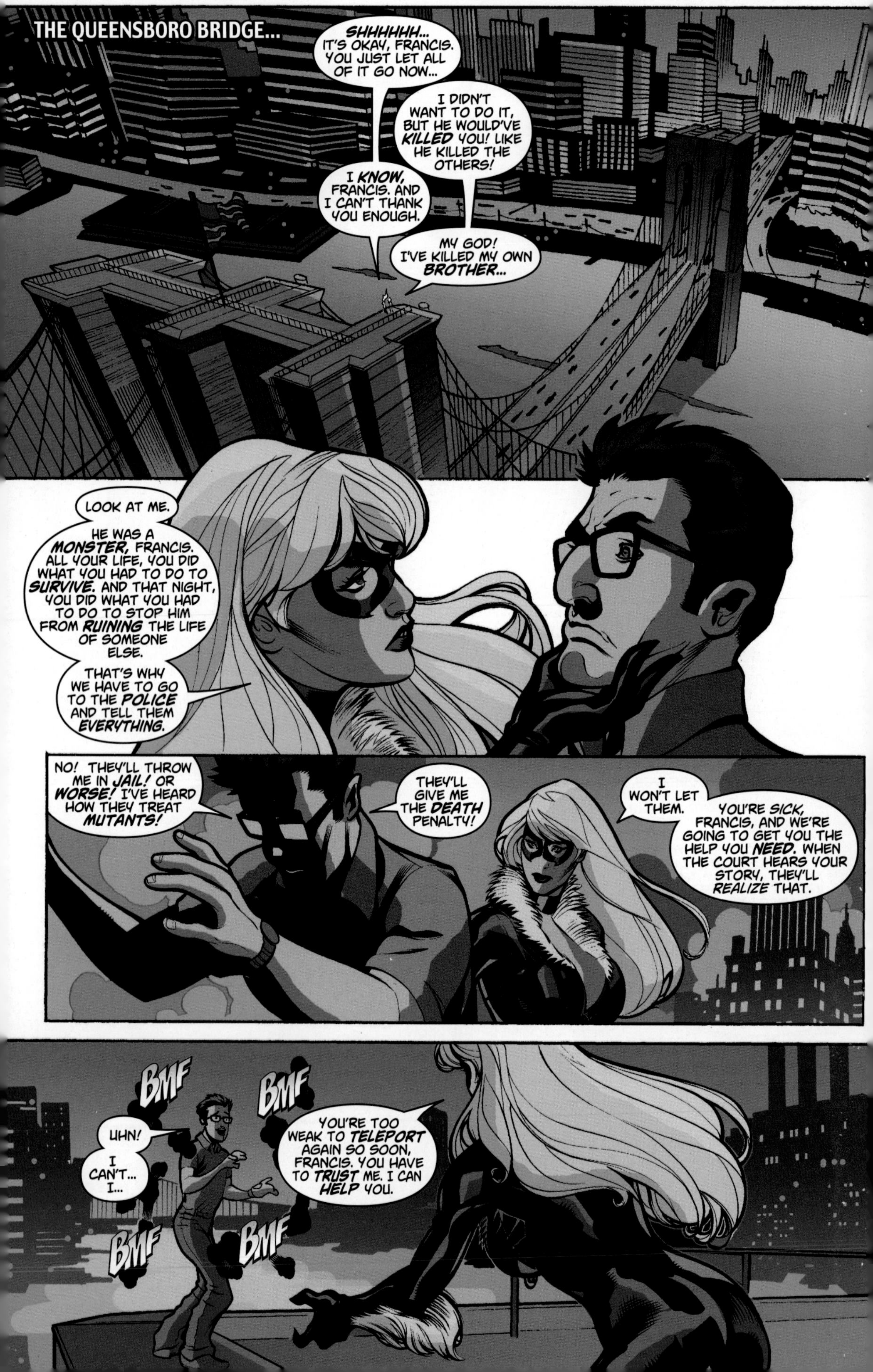
THE QUEENSBORO BRIDGE...
SHHHHHH... IT'S OKAY, FRANCIS. YOU JUST LET ALL OF IT GO NOW...
I DIDN'T WANT TO DO IT, BUT HE WOULD'VE KILLED YOU! LIKE HE KILLED THE OTHERS!
I KNOW, FRANCIS. AND I CAN'T THANK YOU ENOUGH.
MY GOD! I'VE KILLED MY OWN BROTHER...
LOOK AT ME.
HE WAS A MONSTER, FRANCIS. ALL YOUR LIFE, YOU DID WHAT YOU HAD TO DO TO SURVIVE. AND THAT NIGHT, YOU DID WHAT YOU HAD TO DO TO STOP HIM FROM RUINING THE LIFE OF SOMEONE ELSE.
THAT'S WHY WE HAVE TO GO TO THE POLICE AND TELL THEM EVERYTHING.
NO! THEY'LL THROW ME IN JAIL! OR WORSE! I'VE HEARD HOW THEY TREAT MUTANTS!
THEY'LL GIVE ME THE DEATH PENALTY!
I WON'T LET THEM.
YOU'RE SICK, FRANCIS, AND WE'RE GOING TO GET YOU THE HELP YOU NEED. WHEN THE COURT HEARS YOUR STORY, THEY'LL REALIZE THAT.
BMF
BMF
UHN!
I CAN'T... I...
YOU'RE TOO WEAK TO TELEPORT AGAIN SO SOON, FRANCIS. YOU HAVE TO TRUST ME. I CAN HELP YOU.
BMF
BMF

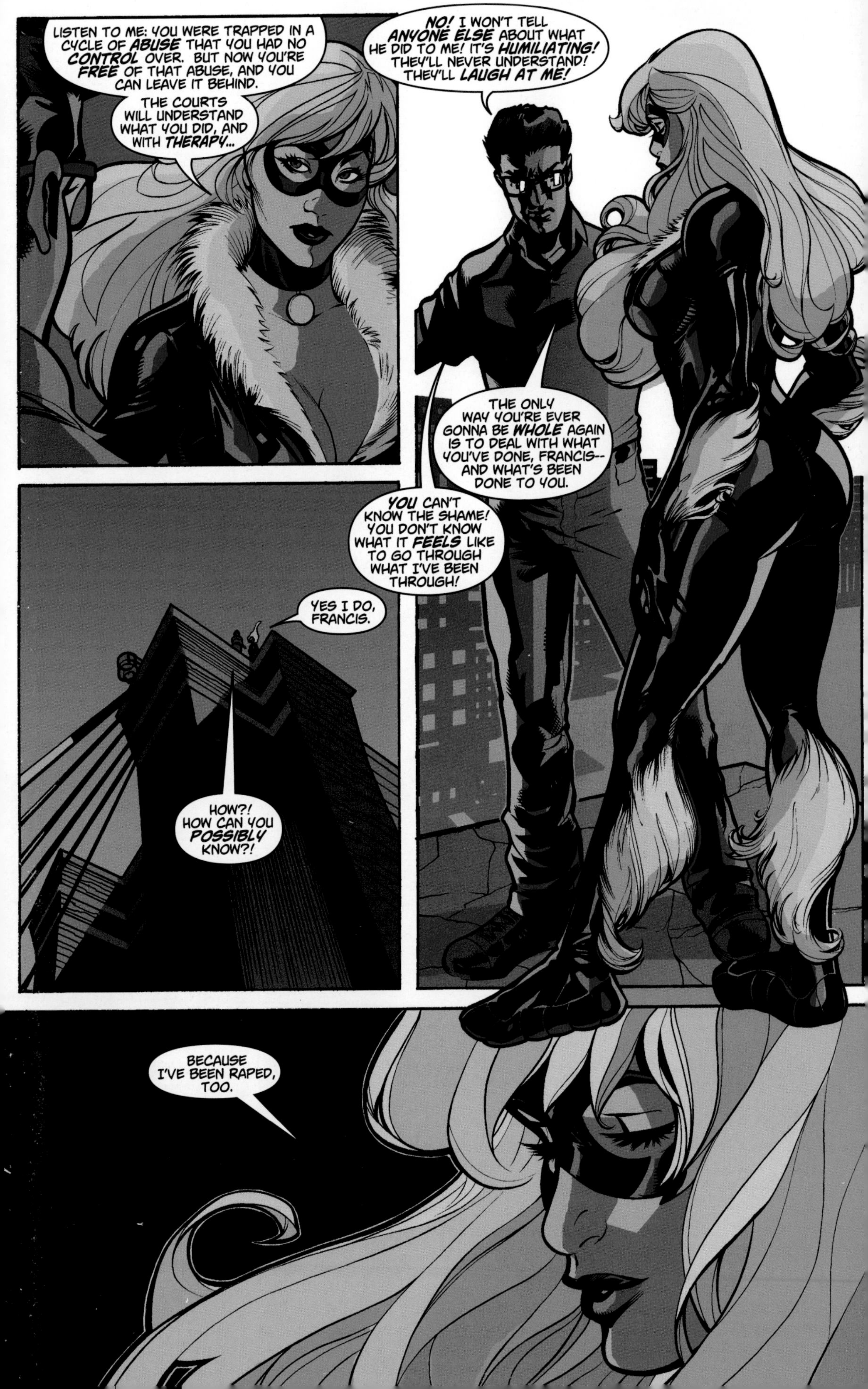
LISTEN TO ME: YOU WERE TRAPPED IN A CYCLE OF ABUSE THAT YOU HAD NO CONTROL OVER. BUT NOW YOU'RE FREE OF THAT ABUSE, AND YOU CAN LEAVE IT BEHIND.
THE COURTS WILL UNDERSTAND WHAT YOU DID, AND WITH THERAPY...
NO! I WON'T TELL ANYONE ELSE ABOUT WHAT HE DID TO ME! IT'S HUMILIATING! THEY'LL NEVER UNDERSTAND! THEY'LL LAUGH AT ME!
THE ONLY WAY YOU'RE EVER GONNA BE WHOLE AGAIN IS TO DEAL WITH WHAT YOU'VE DONE, FRANCIS-- AND WHAT'S BEEN DONE TO YOU.
YOU CAN'T KNOW THE SHAME! YOU DON'T KNOW WHAT IT FEELS LIKE TO GO THROUGH WHAT I'VE BEEN THROUGH!
YES I DO, FRANCIS.
HOW?! HOW CAN YOU POSSIBLY KNOW?!
BECAUSE I'VE BEEN RAPED, TOO.

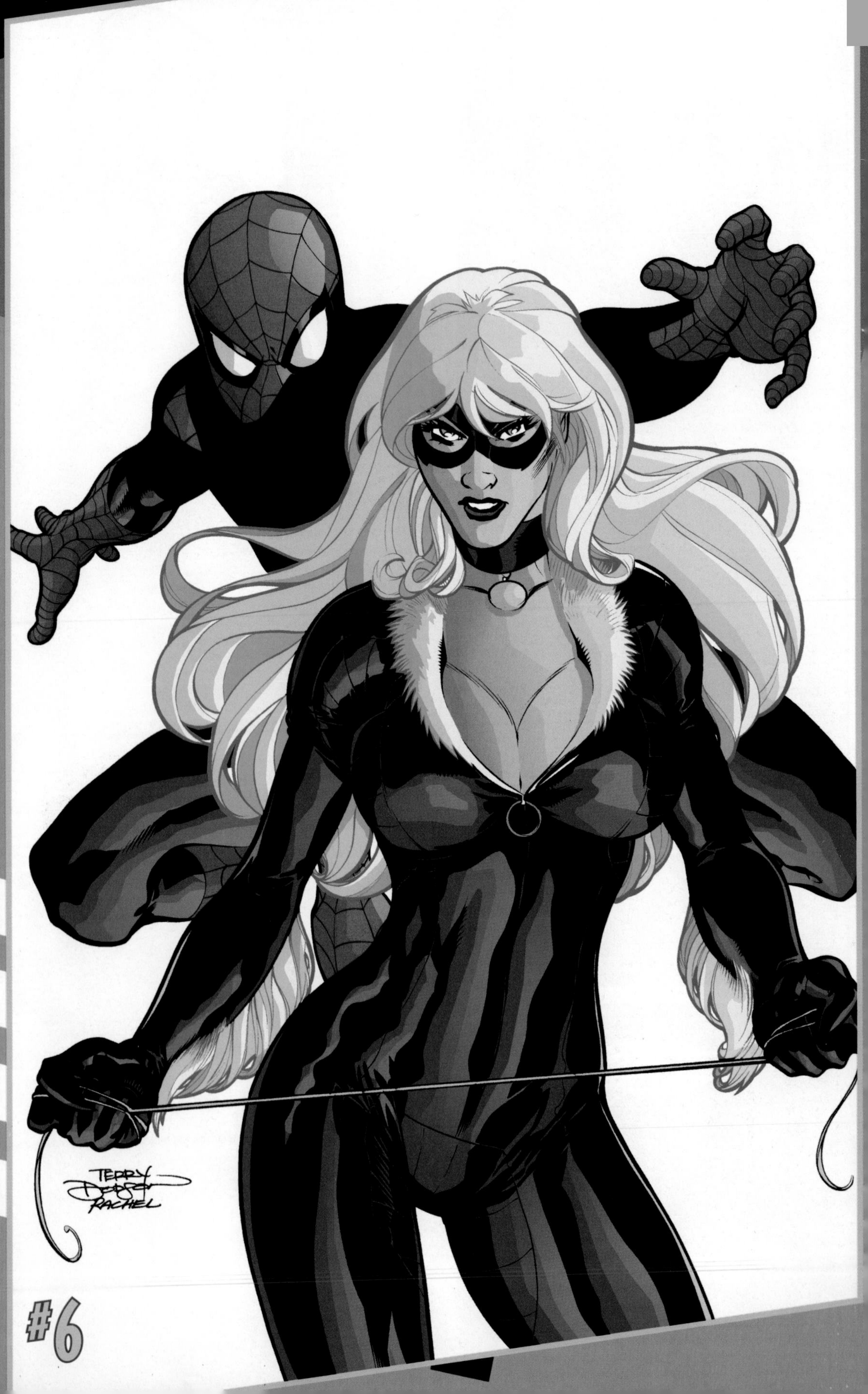
#6

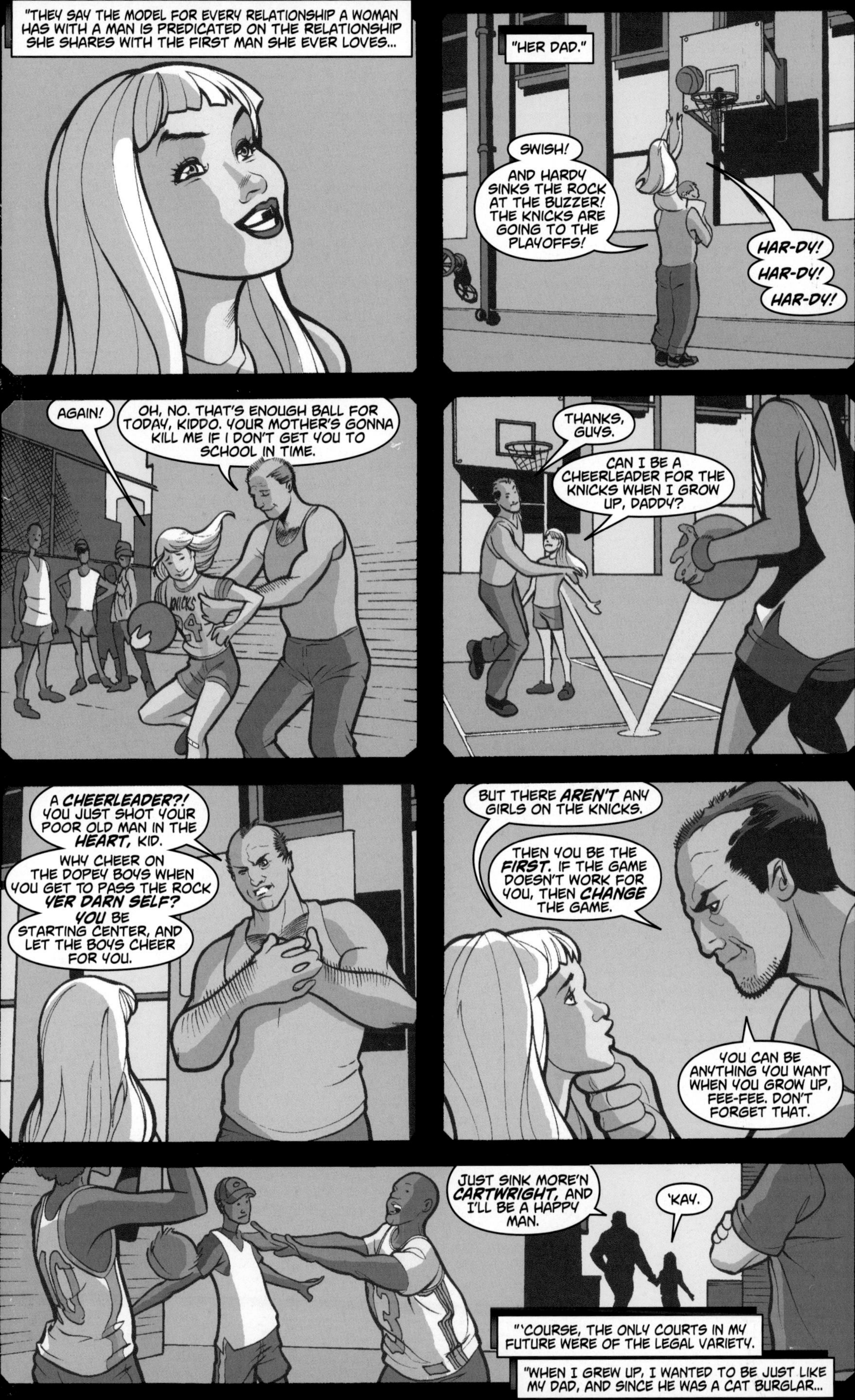
"THEY SAY THE MODEL FOR EVERY RELATIONSHIP A WOMAN HAS WITH A MAN IS PREDICATED ON THE RELATIONSHIP SHE SHARES WITH THE FIRST MAN SHE EVER LOVES...
"HER DAD."
SWISH!
AND HARDY SINKS THE ROCK AT THE BUZZER! THE KNICKS ARE GOING TO THE PLAYOFFS!
HAR-DY!
HAR-DY!
HAR-DY!
AGAIN!
OH, NO. THAT'S ENOUGH BALL FOR TODAY, KIDDO. YOUR MOTHER'S GONNA KILL ME IF I DON'T GET YOU TO SCHOOL IN TIME.
KNICKS
THANKS, GUYS.
CAN I BE A CHEERLEADER FOR THE KNICKS WHEN I GROW UP, DADDY?
A CHEERLEADER?! YOU JUST SHOT YOUR POOR OLD MAN IN THE HEART, KID.
WHY CHEER ON THE DOPEY BOYS WHEN YOU GET TO PASS THE ROCK YER DARN SELF? YOU BE STARTING CENTER, AND LET THE BOYS CHEER FOR YOU.
BUT THERE AREN'T ANY GIRLS ON THE KNICKS.
THEN YOU BE THE FIRST. IF THE GAME DOESN'T WORK FOR YOU, THEN CHANGE THE GAME.
YOU CAN BE ANYTHING YOU WANT WHEN YOU GROW UP, FEE-FEE. DON'T FORGET THAT.
JUST SINK MORE'N CARTWRIGHT, AND I'LL BE A HAPPY MAN.
'KAY.
"'COURSE, THE ONLY COURTS IN MY FUTURE WERE OF THE LEGAL VARIETY.
"WHEN I GREW UP, I WANTED TO BE JUST LIKE MY DAD, AND SINCE HE WAS A CAT BURGLAR...

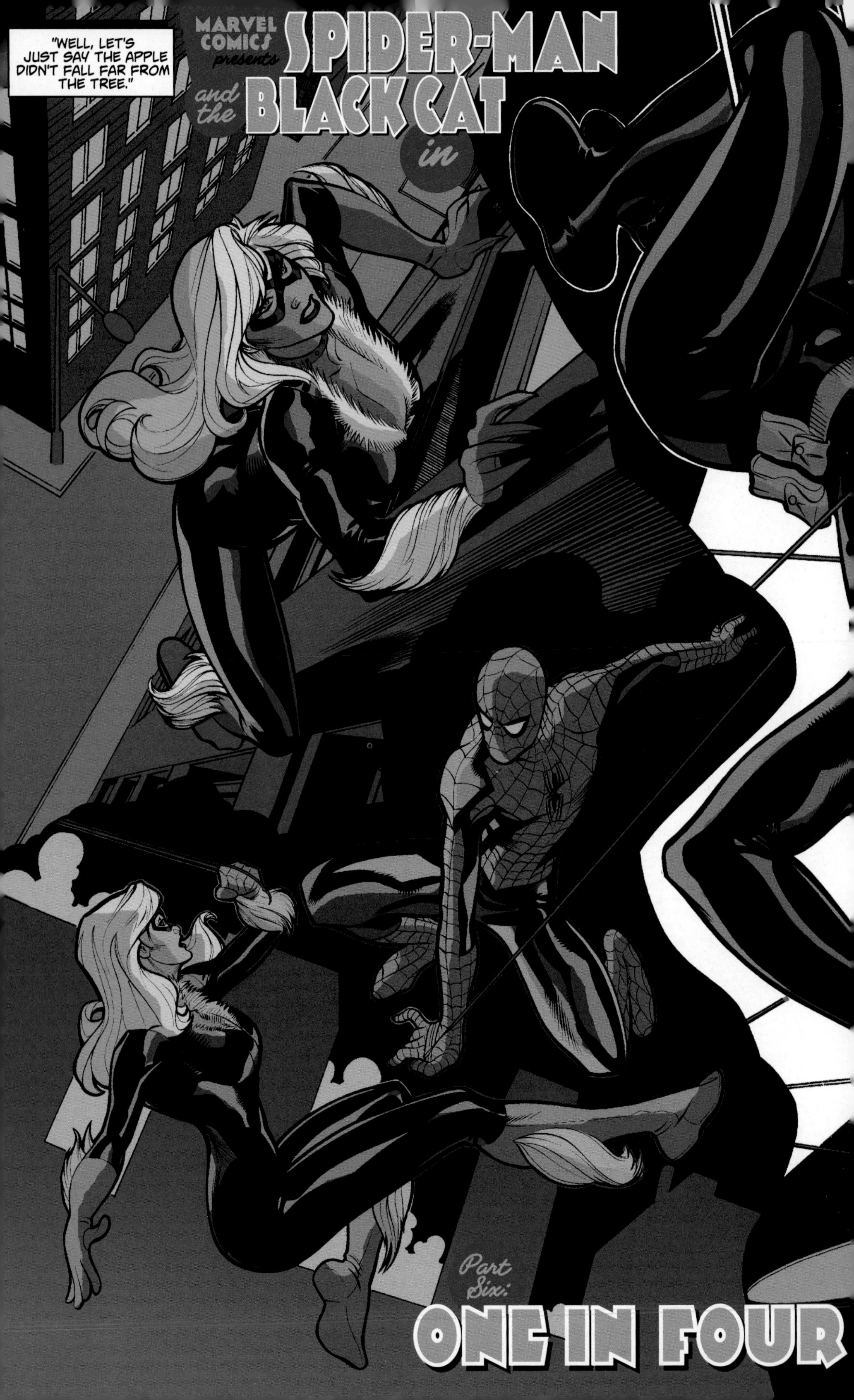
"WELL, LET'S JUST SAY THE APPLE DIDN'T FALL FAR FROM THE TREE."
MARVEL COMICS presents SPIDER-MAN and the BLACK CAT in
Part Six:
ONE IN FOUR

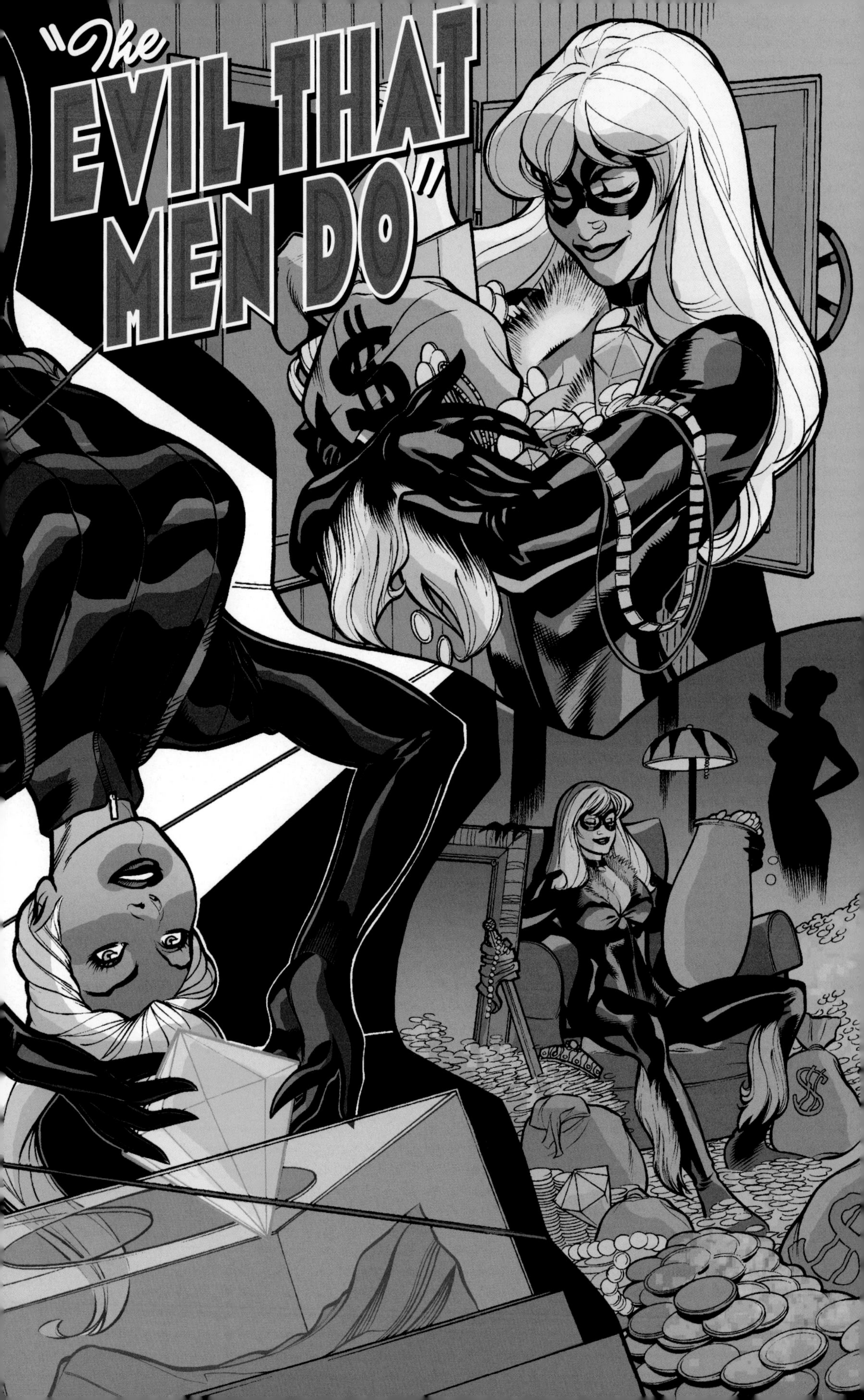
"The EVIL THAT MEN DO"

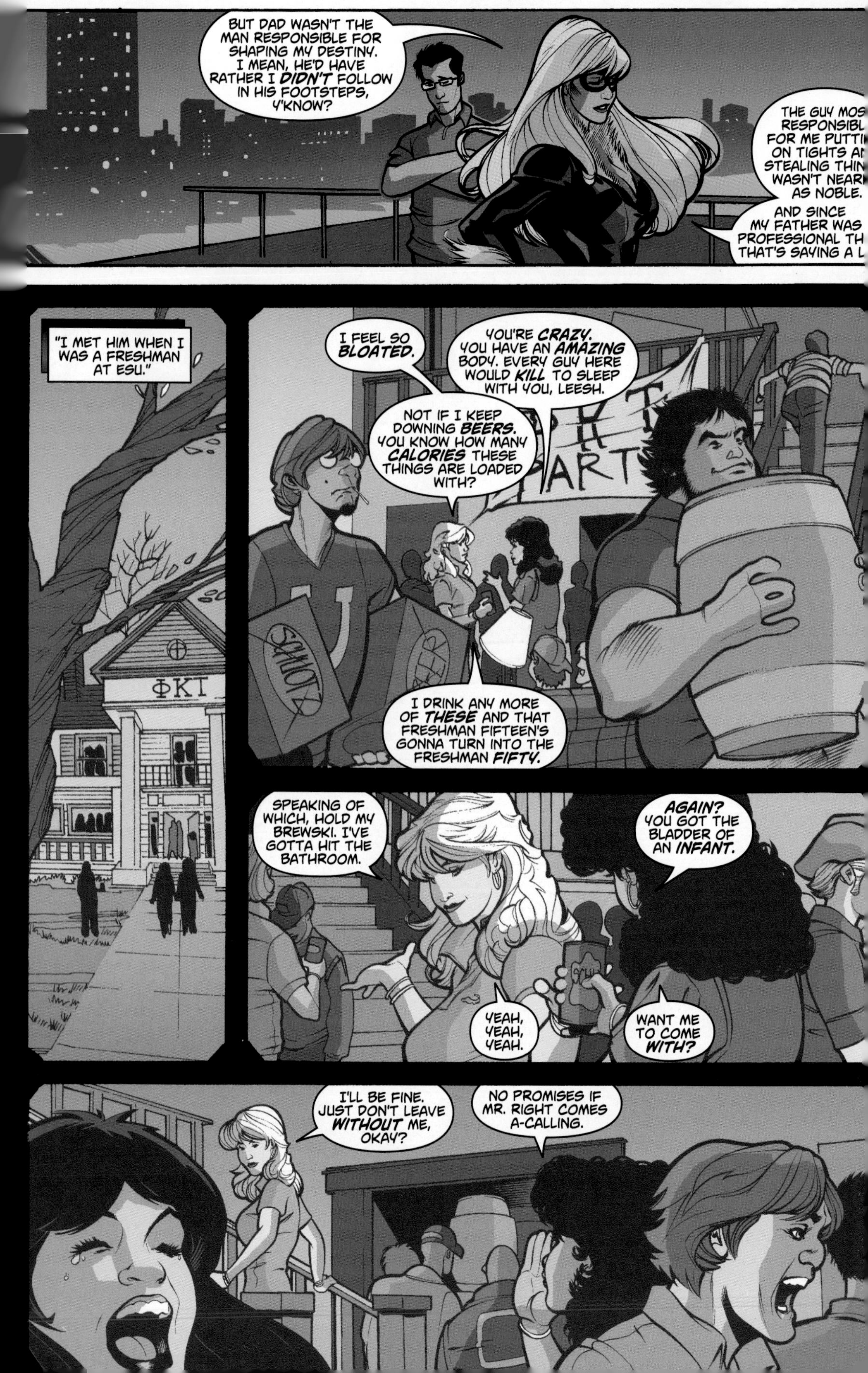
BUT DAD WASN'T THE MAN RESPONSIBLE FOR SHAPING MY DESTINY. I MEAN, HE'D HAVE RATHER I DIDN'T FOLLOW IN HIS FOOTSTEPS, Y'KNOW?
THE GUY MOS RESPONSIBL FOR ME PUTTI ON TIGHTS A STEALING THIN WASN'T NEAR AS NOBLE.
AND SINCE MY FATHER WAS PROFESSIONAL TH THAT'S SAYING A L
"I MET HIM WHEN I WAS A FRESHMAN AT ESU."
ΦKT
I FEEL SO BLOATED.
YOU'RE CRAZY. YOU HAVE AN AMAZING BODY. EVERY GUY HERE WOULD KILL TO SLEEP WITH YOU, LEESH.
NOT IF I KEEP DOWNING BEERS. YOU KNOW HOW MANY CALORIES THESE THINGS ARE LOADED WITH?
I DRINK ANY MORE OF THESE AND THAT FRESHMAN FIFTEEN'S GONNA TURN INTO THE FRESHMAN FIFTY.
SPEAKING OF WHICH, HOLD MY BREWSKI. I'VE GOTTA HIT THE BATHROOM.
AGAIN? YOU GOT THE BLADDER OF AN INFANT.
YEAH, YEAH, YEAH.
WANT ME TO COME WITH?
I'LL BE FINE. JUST DON'T LEAVE WITHOUT ME, OKAY?
NO PROMISES IF MR. RIGHT COMES A-CALLING.

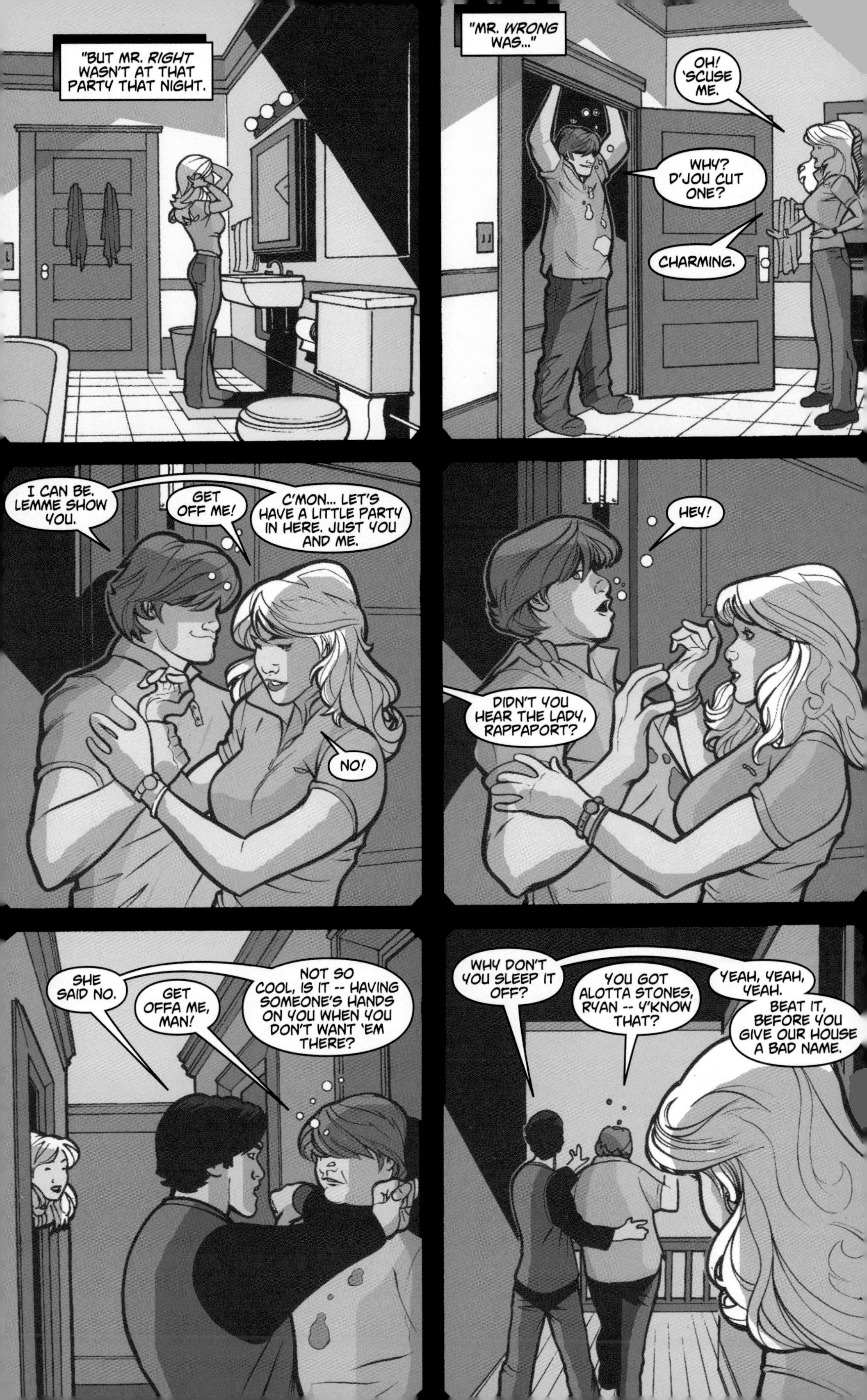
"BUT MR. RIGHT WASN'T AT THAT PARTY THAT NIGHT.
"MR. WRONG WAS..."
OH! 'SCUSE ME.
WHY? D'JOU CUT ONE?
CHARMING.
I CAN BE. LEMME SHOW YOU.
GET OFF ME!
C'MON... LET'S HAVE A LITTLE PARTY IN HERE. JUST YOU AND ME.
NO!
HEY!
DIDN'T YOU HEAR THE LADY, RAPPAPORT?
SHE SAID NO.
GET OFFA ME, MAN!
NOT SO COOL, IS IT -- HAVING SOMEONE'S HANDS ON YOU WHEN YOU DON'T WANT 'EM THERE?
WHY DON'T YOU SLEEP IT OFF?
YOU GOT ALOTTA STONES, RYAN -- Y'KNOW THAT?
YEAH, YEAH, YEAH.
BEAT IT, BEFORE YOU GIVE OUR HOUSE A BAD NAME.

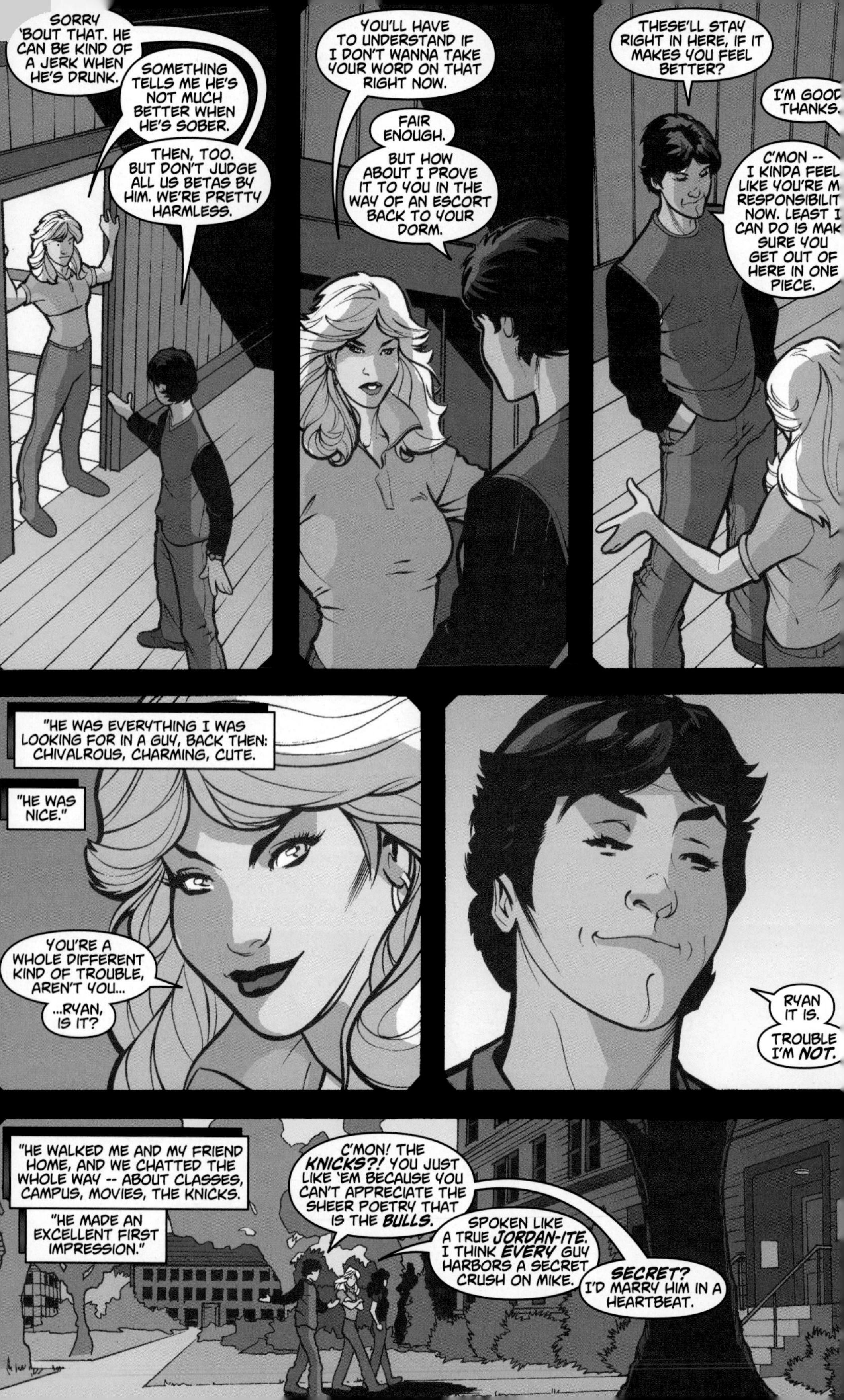
SORRY 'BOUT THAT. HE CAN BE KIND OF A JERK WHEN HE'S DRUNK.
SOMETHING TELLS ME HE'S NOT MUCH BETTER WHEN HE'S SOBER.
THEN, TOO. BUT DON'T JUDGE ALL US BETAS BY HIM. WE'RE PRETTY HARMLESS.
YOU'LL HAVE TO UNDERSTAND IF I DON'T WANNA TAKE YOUR WORD ON THAT RIGHT NOW.
FAIR ENOUGH.
BUT HOW ABOUT I PROVE IT TO YOU IN THE WAY OF AN ESCORT BACK TO YOUR DORM.
THESE'LL STAY RIGHT IN HERE, IF IT MAKES YOU FEEL BETTER?
I'M GOOD THANKS.
C'MON -- I KINDA FEEL LIKE YOU'RE M RESPONSIBILIT NOW. LEAST I CAN DO IS MAK SURE YOU GET OUT OF HERE IN ONE PIECE.
"HE WAS EVERYTHING I WAS LOOKING FOR IN A GUY, BACK THEN: CHIVALROUS, CHARMING, CUTE.
"HE WAS NICE."
YOU'RE A WHOLE DIFFERENT KIND OF TROUBLE, AREN'T YOU...
...RYAN, IS IT?
RYAN IT IS.
TROUBLE I'M NOT.
"HE WALKED ME AND MY FRIEND HOME, AND WE CHATTED THE WHOLE WAY -- ABOUT CLASSES, CAMPUS, MOVIES, THE KNICKS.
"HE MADE AN EXCELLENT FIRST IMPRESSION."
C'MON! THE KNICKS?! YOU JUST LIKE 'EM BECAUSE YOU CAN'T APPRECIATE THE SHEER POETRY THAT IS THE BULLS.
SPOKEN LIKE A TRUE JORDAN-ITE. I THINK EVERY GUY HARBORS A SECRET CRUSH ON MIKE.
SECRET? I'D MARRY HIM IN A HEARTBEAT.

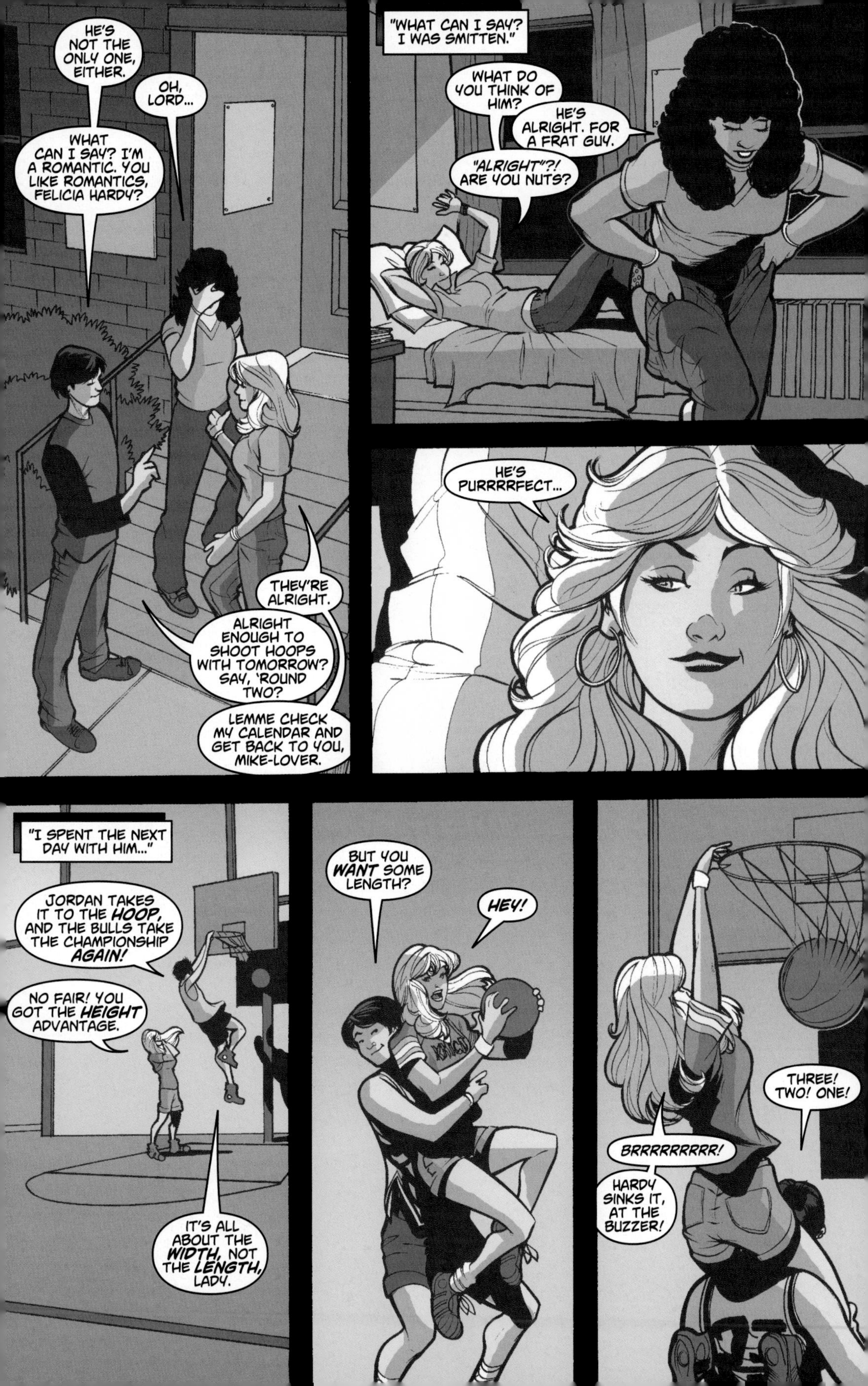
HE'S NOT THE ONLY ONE, EITHER.
OH, LORD...
WHAT CAN I SAY? I'M A ROMANTIC. YOU LIKE ROMANTICS, FELICIA HARDY?
THEY'RE ALRIGHT.
ALRIGHT ENOUGH TO SHOOT HOOPS WITH TOMORROW? SAY, 'ROUND TWO?
LEMME CHECK MY CALENDAR AND GET BACK TO YOU, MIKE-LOVER.
"WHAT CAN I SAY? I WAS SMITTEN."
WHAT DO YOU THINK OF HIM?
HE'S ALRIGHT. FOR A FRAT GUY.
"ALRIGHT"?! ARE YOU NUTS?
HE'S PURRRRFECT...
"I SPENT THE NEXT DAY WITH HIM..."
JORDAN TAKES IT TO THE HOOP, AND THE BULLS TAKE THE CHAMPIONSHIP AGAIN!
NO FAIR! YOU GOT THE HEIGHT ADVANTAGE.
IT'S ALL ABOUT THE WIDTH, NOT THE LENGTH, LADY.
BUT YOU WANT SOME LENGTH?
HEY!
THREE! TWO! ONE!
BRRRRRRRRR!
HARDY SINKS IT, AT THE BUZZER!

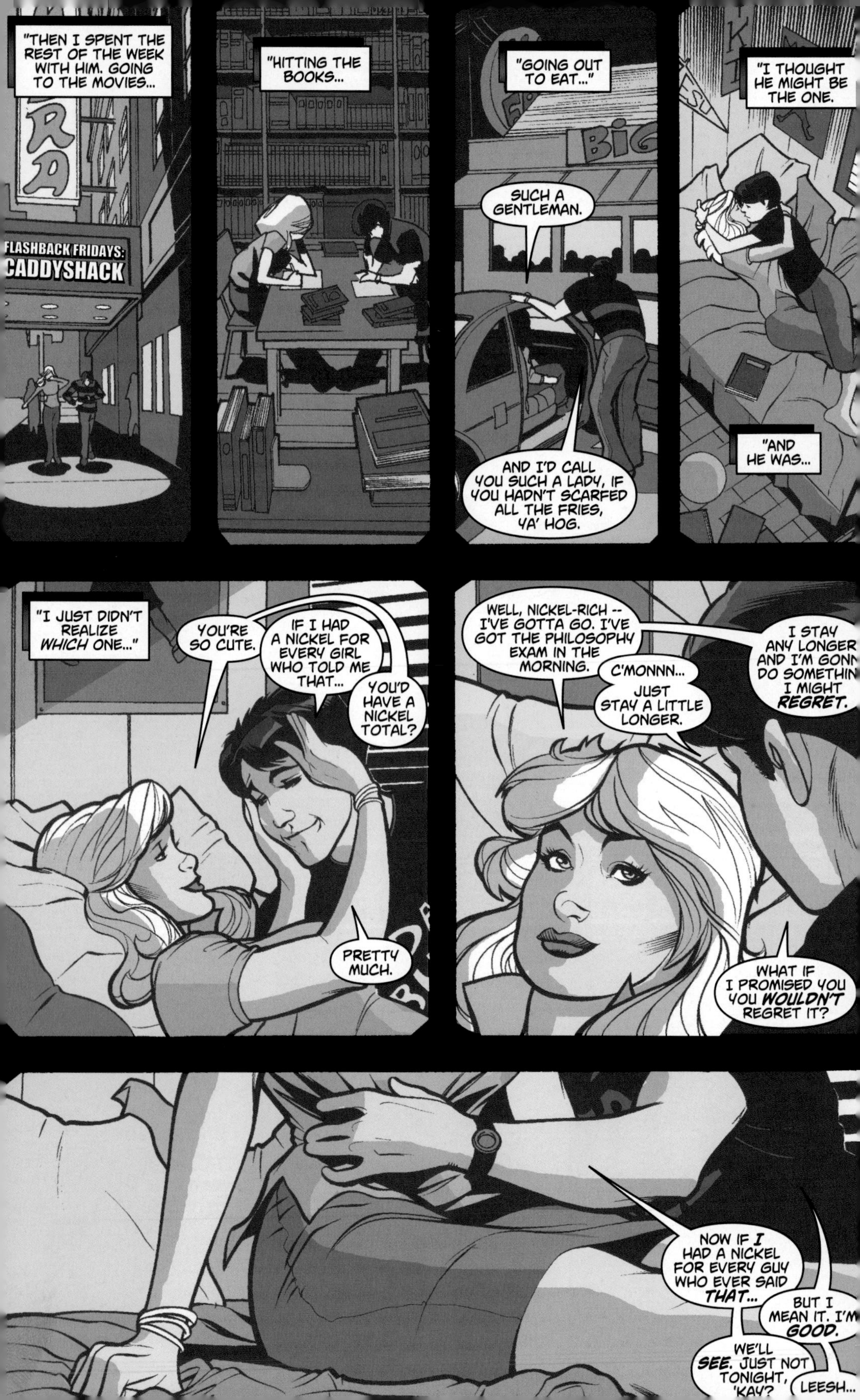
"THEN I SPENT THE REST OF THE WEEK WITH HIM. GOING TO THE MOVIES...
FLASHBACK FRIDAYS: CADDYSHACK
"HITTING THE BOOKS...
"GOING OUT TO EAT..."
SUCH A GENTLEMAN.
AND I'D CALL YOU SUCH A LADY, IF YOU HADN'T SCARFED ALL THE FRIES, YA' HOG.
"I THOUGHT HE MIGHT BE THE ONE.
"AND HE WAS...
"I JUST DIDN'T REALIZE WHICH ONE..."
YOU'RE SO CUTE.
IF I HAD A NICKEL FOR EVERY GIRL WHO TOLD ME THAT...
YOU'D HAVE A NICKEL TOTAL?
PRETTY MUCH.
WELL, NICKEL-RICH -- I'VE GOTTA GO. I'VE GOT THE PHILOSOPHY EXAM IN THE MORNING.
C'MONNN... JUST STAY A LITTLE LONGER.
I STAY ANY LONGER AND I'M GONN DO SOMETHIN I MIGHT REGRET.
WHAT IF I PROMISED YOU YOU WOULDN'T REGRET IT?
NOW IF I HAD A NICKEL FOR EVERY GUY WHO EVER SAID THAT...
BUT I MEAN IT. I'M GOOD.
WE'LL SEE. JUST NOT TONIGHT, 'KAY?
LEESH...

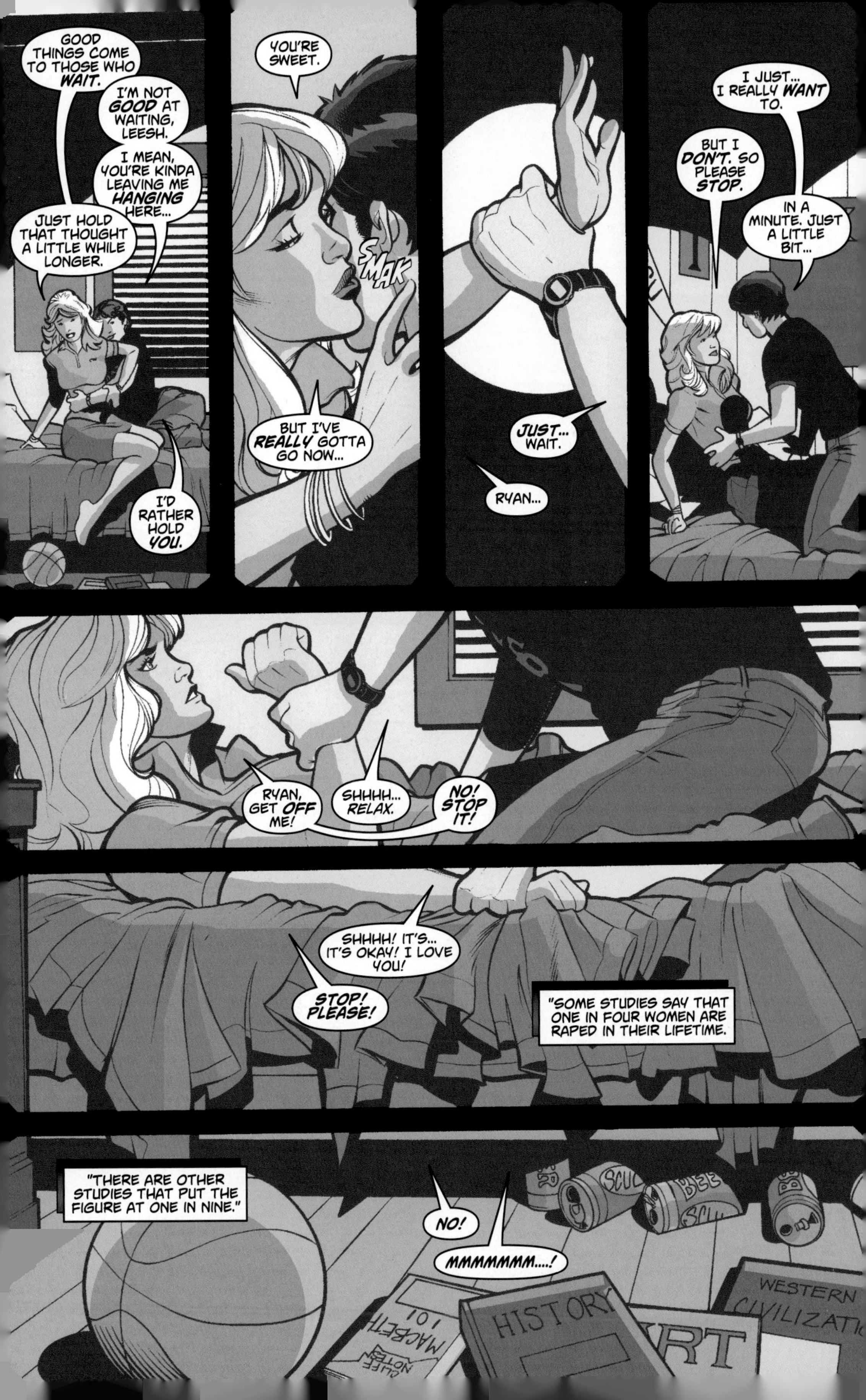
GOOD THINGS COME TO THOSE WHO *WAIT*.
I'M NOT *GOOD* AT WAITING, LEESH.
I MEAN, YOU'RE KINDA LEAVING ME *HANGING* HERE...
JUST HOLD THAT THOUGHT A LITTLE WHILE LONGER.
I'D RATHER HOLD *YOU*.
YOU'RE SWEET.
SMAK
BUT I'VE *REALLY* GOTTA GO NOW...
JUST... WAIT.
RYAN...
I JUST... I REALLY *WANT* TO.
BUT I *DON'T*. SO PLEASE *STOP*.
IN A MINUTE. JUST A LITTLE BIT...
RYAN, GET *OFF* ME!
SHHHH... RELAX.
NO! STOP IT!
SHHHH! IT'S... IT'S OKAY! I LOVE YOU!
STOP! PLEASE!
"SOME STUDIES SAY THAT ONE IN FOUR WOMEN ARE RAPED IN THEIR LIFETIME.
"THERE ARE OTHER STUDIES THAT PUT THE FIGURE AT ONE IN NINE."
NO!
MMMMMMM....!
MACBETH
101
HISTORY

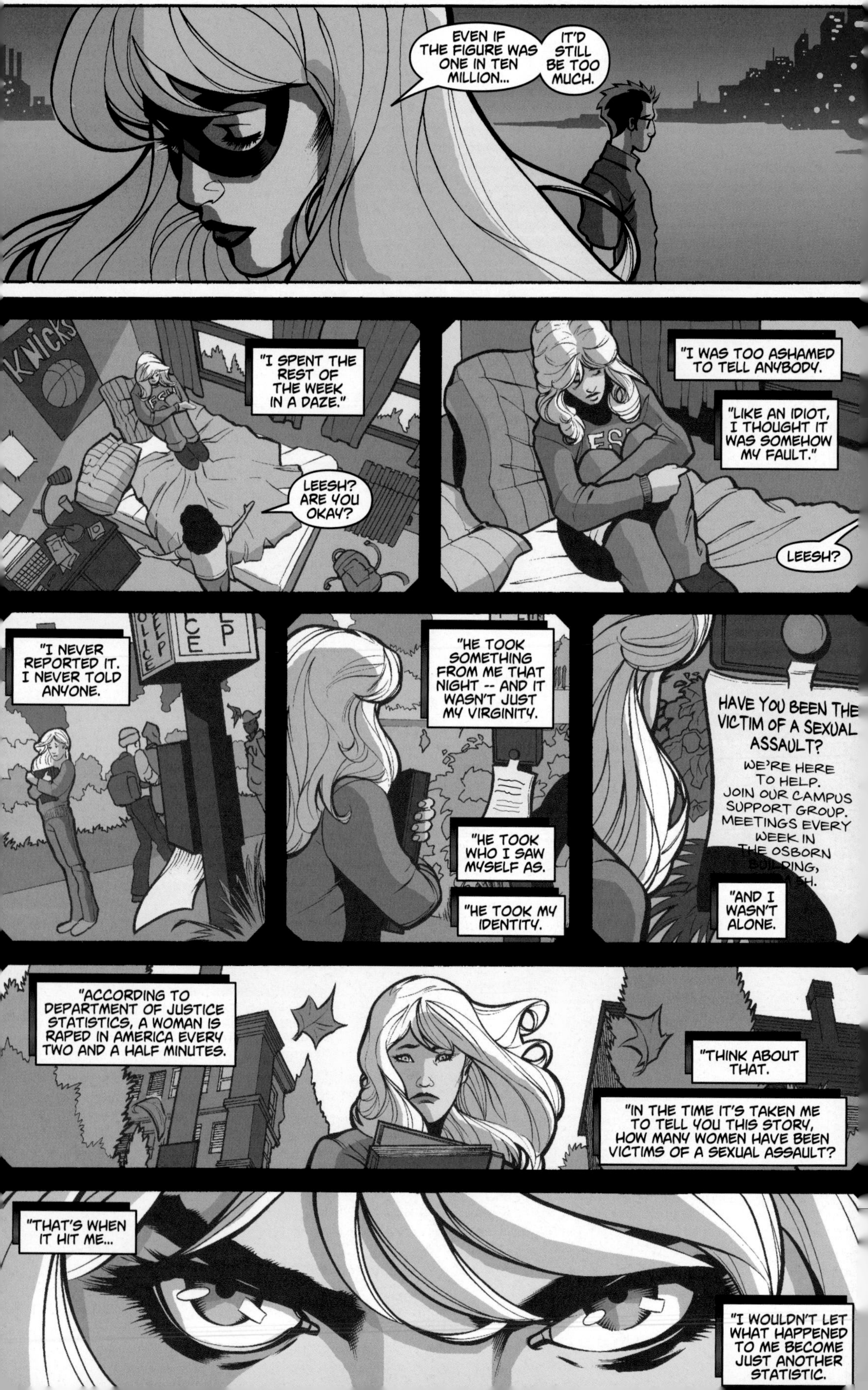

EVEN IF THE FIGURE WAS ONE IN TEN MILLION...
IT'D STILL BE TOO MUCH.
KNICKS
"I SPENT THE REST OF THE WEEK IN A DAZE."
LEESH? ARE YOU OKAY?
"I WAS TOO ASHAMED TO TELL ANYBODY.
"LIKE AN IDIOT, I THOUGHT IT WAS SOMEHOW MY FAULT."
LEESH?
"I NEVER REPORTED IT. I NEVER TOLD ANYONE.
"HE TOOK SOMETHING FROM ME THAT NIGHT -- AND IT WASN'T JUST MY VIRGINITY.
"HE TOOK WHO I SAW MYSELF AS.
"HE TOOK MY IDENTITY.
HAVE YOU BEEN THE VICTIM OF A SEXUAL ASSAULT?
WE'RE HERE TO HELP. JOIN OUR CAMPUS SUPPORT GROUP. MEETINGS EVERY WEEK IN THE OSBORN BUILDING,
"AND I WASN'T ALONE.
"ACCORDING TO DEPARTMENT OF JUSTICE STATISTICS, A WOMAN IS RAPED IN AMERICA EVERY TWO AND A HALF MINUTES.
"THINK ABOUT THAT.
"IN THE TIME IT'S TAKEN ME TO TELL YOU THIS STORY, HOW MANY WOMEN HAVE BEEN VICTIMS OF A SEXUAL ASSAULT?
"THAT'S WHEN IT HIT ME...
"I WOULDN'T LET WHAT HAPPENED TO ME BECOME JUST ANOTHER STATISTIC.

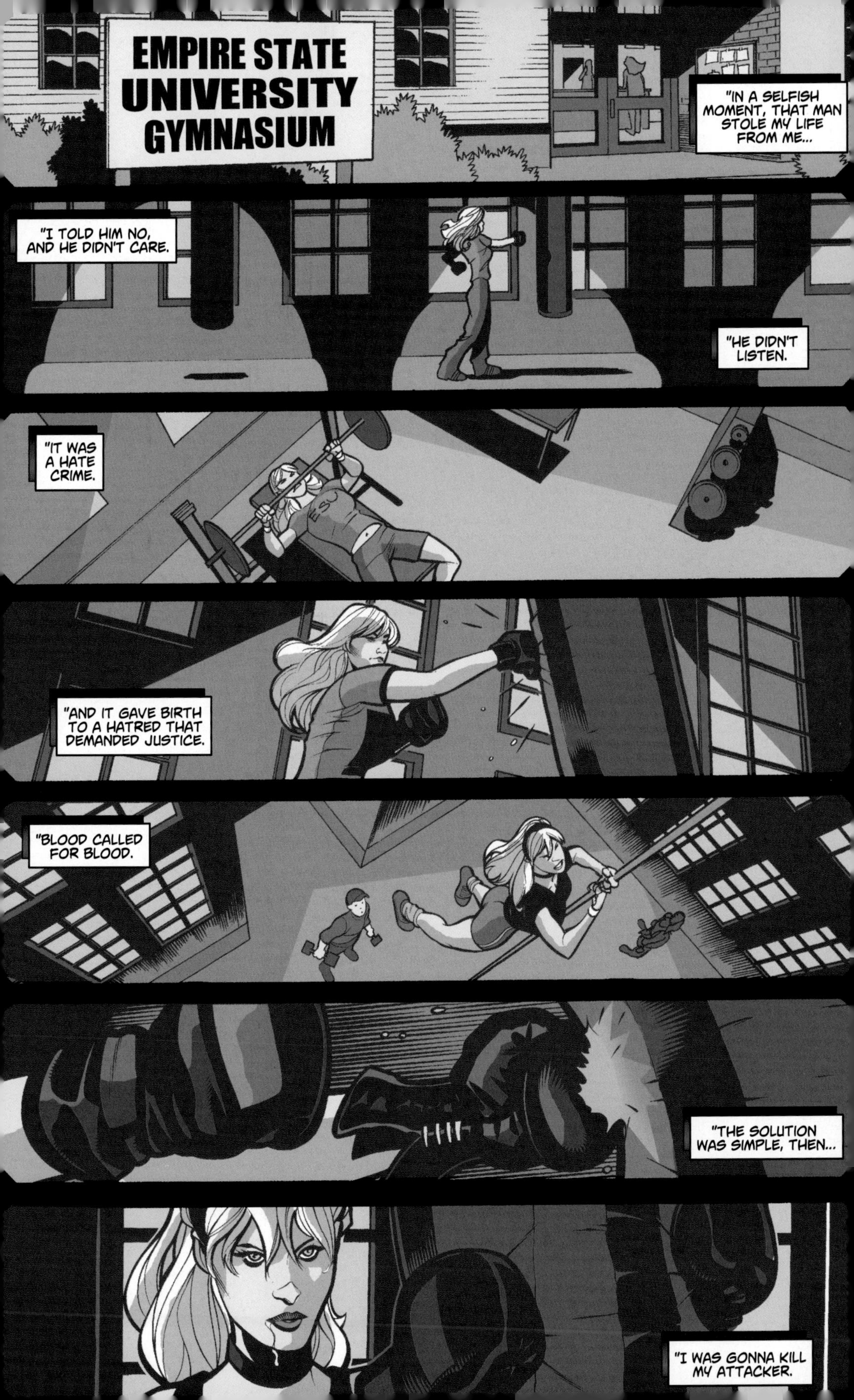
EMPIRE STATE UNIVERSITY GYMNASIUM
"IN A SELFISH MOMENT, THAT MAN STOLE MY LIFE FROM ME...
"I TOLD HIM NO, AND HE DIDN'T CARE.
"HE DIDN'T LISTEN.
"IT WAS A HATE CRIME.
"AND IT GAVE BIRTH TO A HATRED THAT DEMANDED JUSTICE.
"BLOOD CALLED FOR BLOOD.
"THE SOLUTION WAS SIMPLE, THEN...
"I WAS GONNA KILL MY ATTACKER.

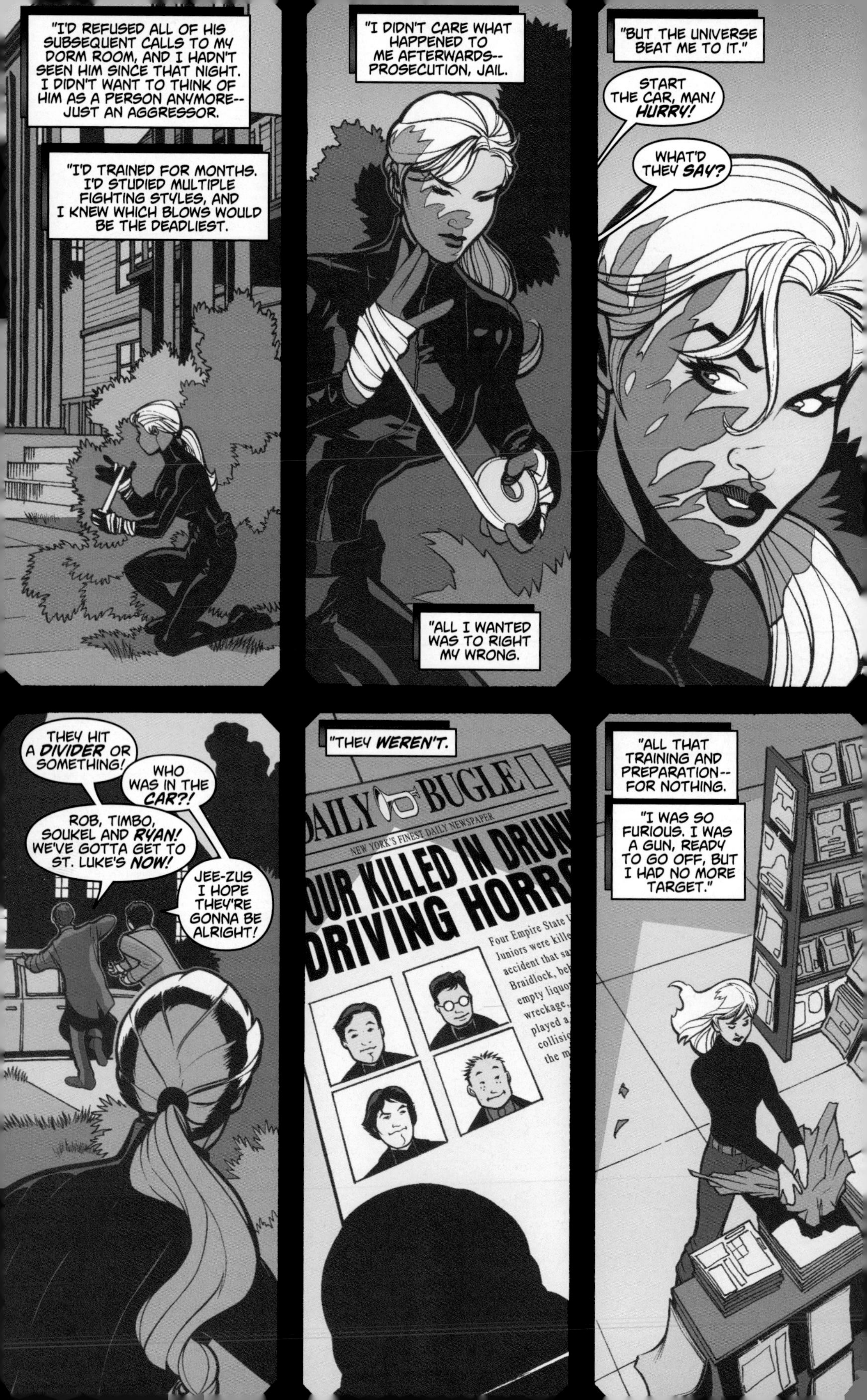
"I'D REFUSED ALL OF HIS SUBSEQUENT CALLS TO MY DORM ROOM, AND I HADN'T SEEN HIM SINCE THAT NIGHT. I DIDN'T WANT TO THINK OF HIM AS A PERSON ANYMORE-- JUST AN AGGRESSOR.
"I'D TRAINED FOR MONTHS. I'D STUDIED MULTIPLE FIGHTING STYLES, AND I KNEW WHICH BLOWS WOULD BE THE DEADLIEST.
"I DIDN'T CARE WHAT HAPPENED TO ME AFTERWARDS-- PROSECUTION, JAIL.
"ALL I WANTED WAS TO RIGHT MY WRONG.
"BUT THE UNIVERSE BEAT ME TO IT."
START THE CAR, MAN! HURRY!
WHAT'D THEY SAY?
THEY HIT A DIVIDER OR SOMETHING!
WHO WAS IN THE CAR?!
ROB, TIMBO, SOUKEL AND RYAN! WE'VE GOTTA GET TO ST. LUKE'S NOW!
JEE-ZUS I HOPE THEY'RE GONNA BE ALRIGHT!
"THEY WEREN'T.
DAILY BUGLE
NEW YORK'S FINEST DAILY NEWSPAPER
OUR KILLED IN DRUN
DRIVING HORR
Four Empire State
Juniors were kille
accident that sa
Braidlock, beh
empty liquo
wreckage,
played a
collisi
the m
"ALL THAT TRAINING AND PREPARATION-- FOR NOTHING.
"I WAS SO FURIOUS. I WAS A GUN, READY TO GO OFF, BUT I HAD NO MORE TARGET."

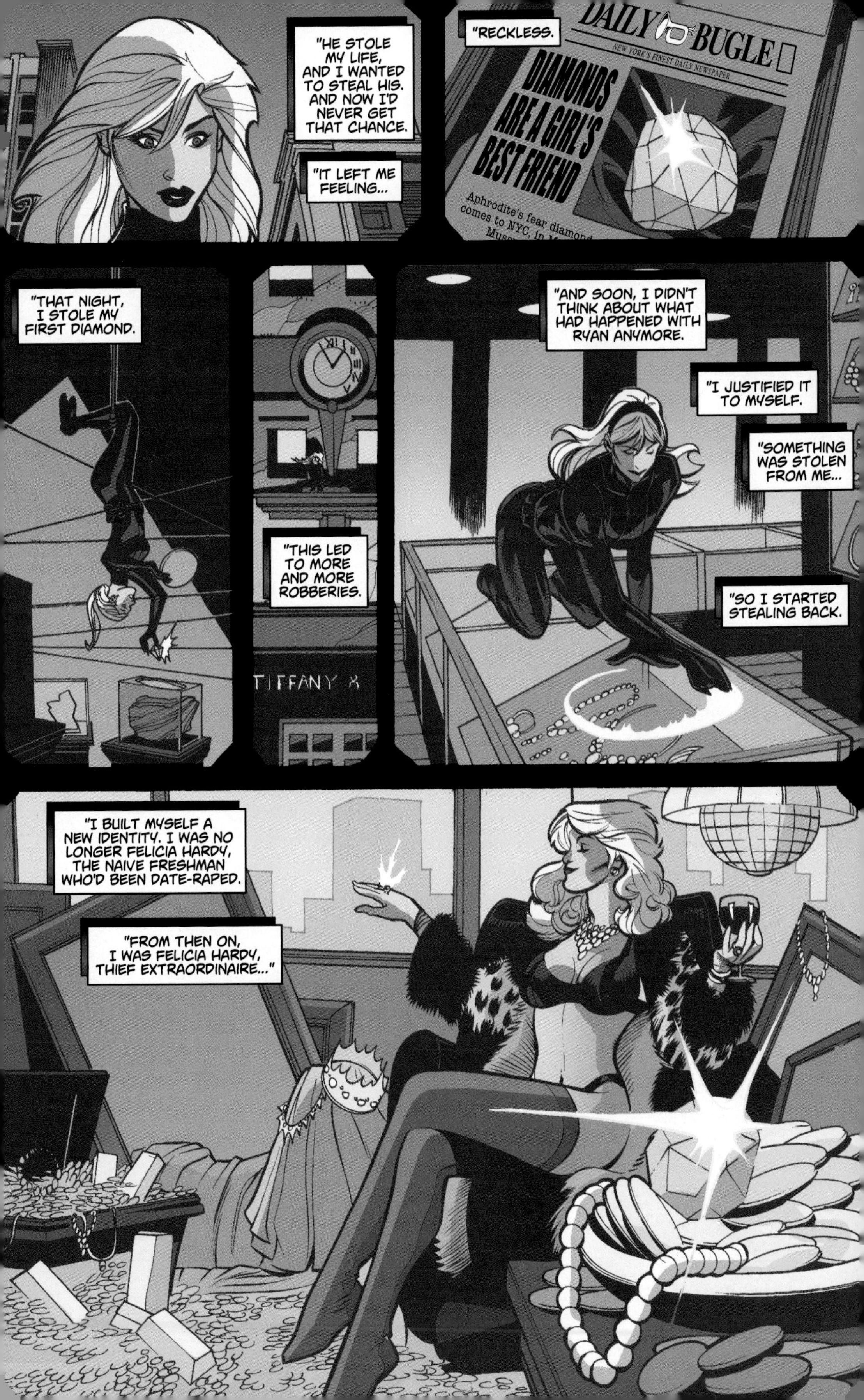
"HE STOLE MY LIFE, AND I WANTED TO STEAL HIS. AND NOW I'D NEVER GET THAT CHANCE.
"IT LEFT ME FEELING...
"RECKLESS.
DAILY BUGLE
NEW YORK'S FINEST DAILY NEWSPAPER
DIAMONDS ARE A GIRL'S BEST FRIEND
Aphrodite's fear diamond comes to NYC, in
"THAT NIGHT, I STOLE MY FIRST DIAMOND.
"THIS LED TO MORE AND MORE ROBBERIES.
TIFFANY &
"AND SOON, I DIDN'T THINK ABOUT WHAT HAD HAPPENED WITH RYAN ANYMORE.
"I JUSTIFIED IT TO MYSELF.
"SOMETHING WAS STOLEN FROM ME...
"SO I STARTED STEALING BACK.
"I BUILT MYSELF A NEW IDENTITY. I WAS NO LONGER FELICIA HARDY, THE NAIVE FRESHMAN WHO'D BEEN DATE-RAPED.
"FROM THEN ON, I WAS FELICIA HARDY, THIEF EXTRAORDINAIRE..."

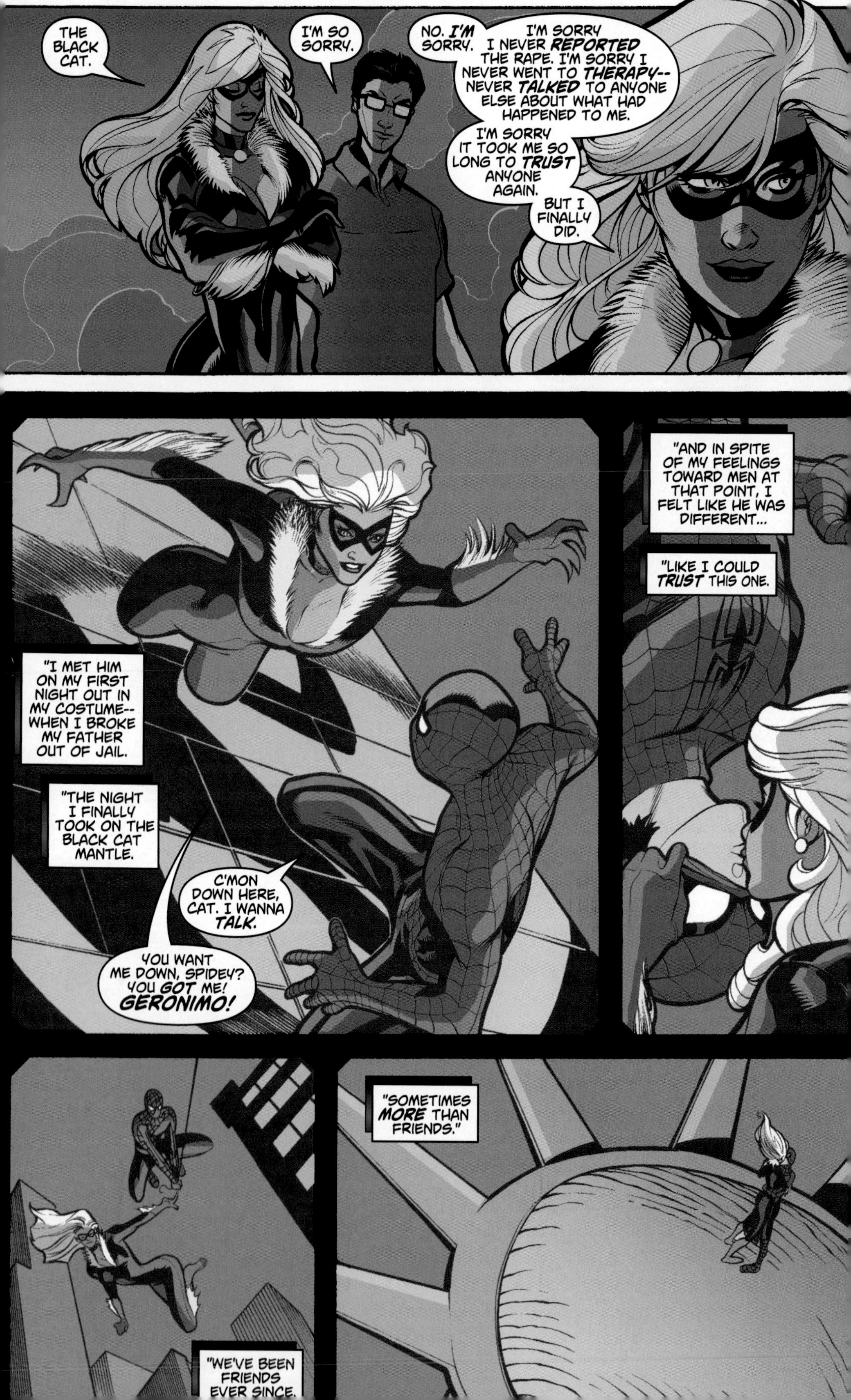
THE BLACK CAT.
I'M SO SORRY.
NO. *I'M* SORRY.
I'M SORRY I NEVER **REPORTED** THE RAPE. I'M SORRY I NEVER WENT TO **THERAPY**-- NEVER **TALKED** TO ANYONE ELSE ABOUT WHAT HAD HAPPENED TO ME.
I'M SORRY IT TOOK ME SO LONG TO **TRUST** ANYONE AGAIN.
BUT I FINALLY DID.
"I MET HIM ON MY FIRST NIGHT OUT IN MY COSTUME-- WHEN I BROKE MY FATHER OUT OF JAIL.
"THE NIGHT I FINALLY TOOK ON THE BLACK CAT MANTLE.
C'MON DOWN HERE, CAT. I WANNA **TALK**.
YOU WANT ME DOWN, SPIDEY? YOU **GOT** ME! **GERONIMO!**
"AND IN SPITE OF MY FEELINGS TOWARD MEN AT THAT POINT, I FELT LIKE HE WAS DIFFERENT...
"LIKE I COULD **TRUST** THIS ONE.
"WE'VE BEEN FRIENDS EVER SINCE.
"SOMETIMES **MORE** THAN FRIENDS."

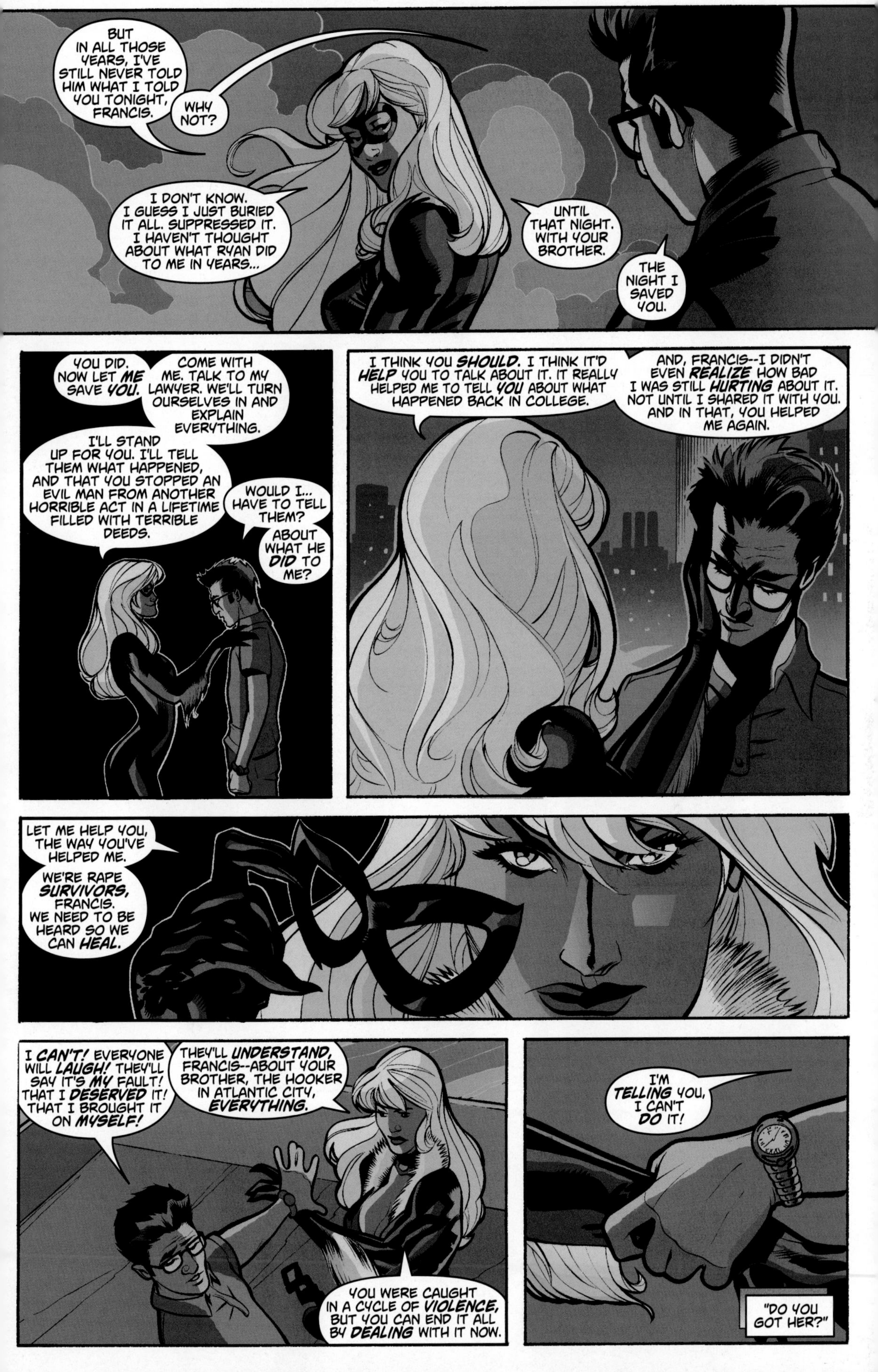

BUT IN ALL THOSE YEARS, I'VE STILL NEVER TOLD HIM WHAT I TOLD YOU TONIGHT, FRANCIS.
WHY NOT?
I DON'T KNOW. I GUESS I JUST BURIED IT ALL. SUPPRESSED IT. I HAVEN'T THOUGHT ABOUT WHAT RYAN DID TO ME IN YEARS...
UNTIL THAT NIGHT. WITH YOUR BROTHER.
THE NIGHT I SAVED YOU.
YOU DID. NOW LET ME SAVE YOU.
COME WITH ME. TALK TO MY LAWYER. WE'LL TURN OURSELVES IN AND EXPLAIN EVERYTHING.
I'LL STAND UP FOR YOU. I'LL TELL THEM WHAT HAPPENED, AND THAT YOU STOPPED AN EVIL MAN FROM ANOTHER HORRIBLE ACT IN A LIFETIME FILLED WITH TERRIBLE DEEDS.
WOULD I... HAVE TO TELL THEM?
ABOUT WHAT HE DID TO ME?
I THINK YOU SHOULD. I THINK IT'D HELP YOU TO TALK ABOUT IT. IT REALLY HELPED ME TO TELL YOU ABOUT WHAT HAPPENED BACK IN COLLEGE.
AND, FRANCIS--I DIDN'T EVEN REALIZE HOW BAD I WAS STILL HURTING ABOUT IT. NOT UNTIL I SHARED IT WITH YOU. AND IN THAT, YOU HELPED ME AGAIN.
LET ME HELP YOU, THE WAY YOU'VE HELPED ME.
WE'RE RAPE SURVIVORS, FRANCIS. WE NEED TO BE HEARD SO WE CAN HEAL.
I CAN'T! EVERYONE WILL LAUGH! THEY'LL SAY IT'S MY FAULT! THAT I DESERVED IT! THAT I BROUGHT IT ON MYSELF!
THEY'LL UNDERSTAND, FRANCIS--ABOUT YOUR BROTHER, THE HOOKER IN ATLANTIC CITY, EVERYTHING.
YOU WERE CAUGHT IN A CYCLE OF VIOLENCE, BUT YOU CAN END IT ALL BY DEALING WITH IT NOW.
I'M TELLING YOU, I CAN'T DO IT!
"DO YOU GOT HER?"

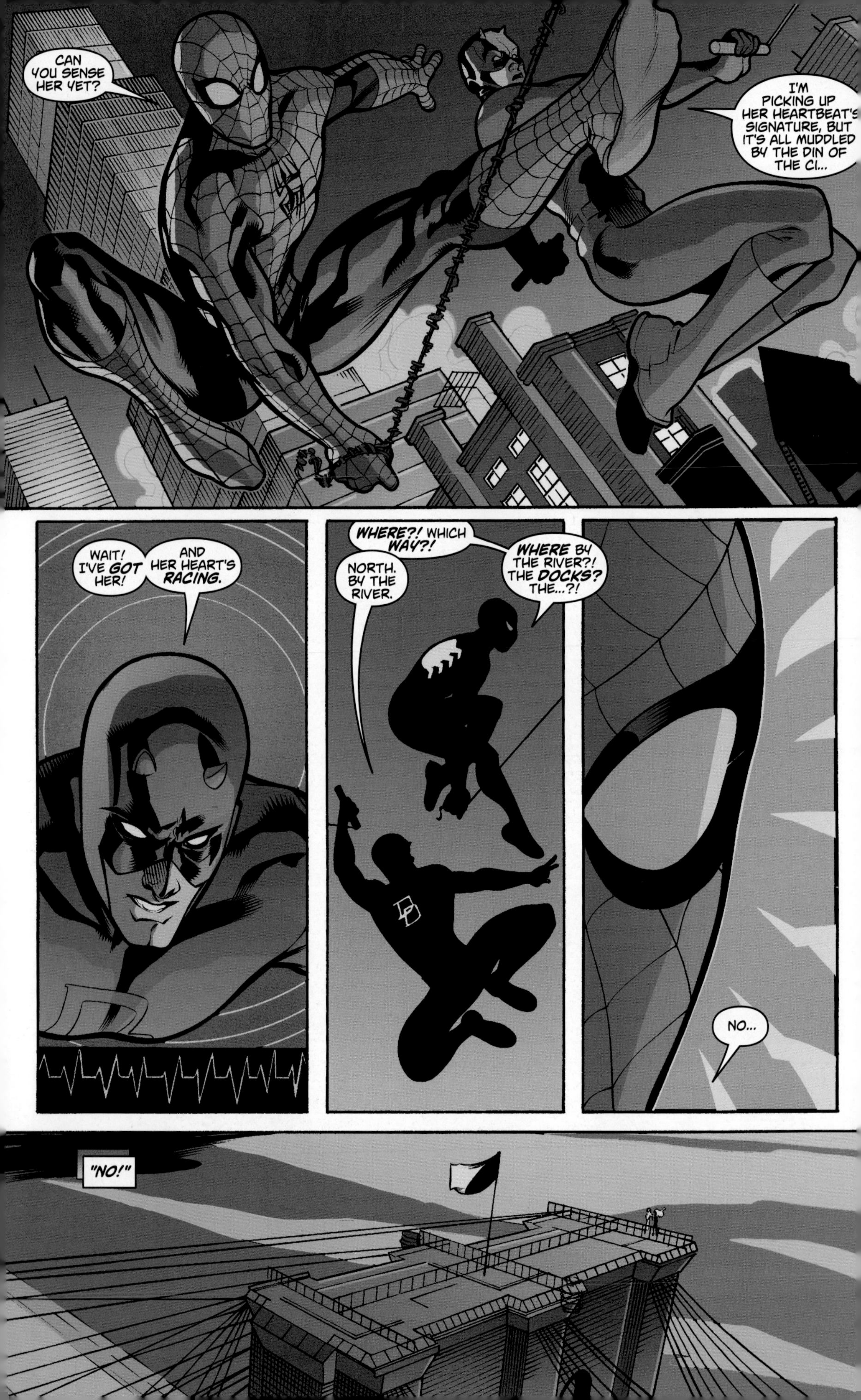
CAN YOU SENSE HER YET?
I'M PICKING UP HER HEARTBEAT'S SIGNATURE, BUT IT'S ALL MUDDLED BY THE DIN OF THE CI...
WAIT! I'VE GOT HER!
AND HER HEART'S RACING.
WHERE?! WHICH WAY?!
NORTH. BY THE RIVER.
WHERE BY THE RIVER?! THE DOCKS? THE...?!
NO...
"NO!"

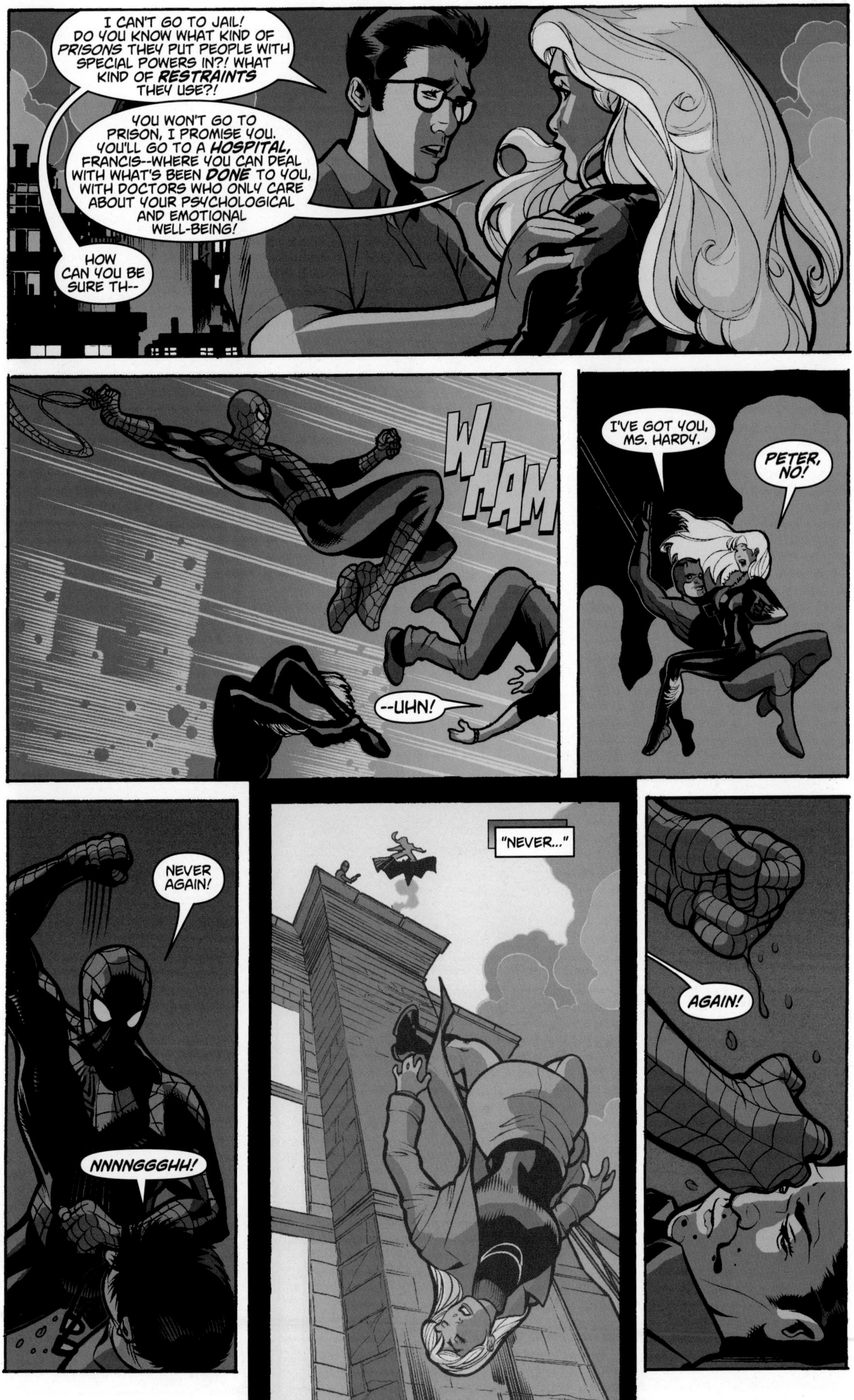
I CAN'T GO TO JAIL! DO YOU KNOW WHAT KIND OF PRISONS THEY PUT PEOPLE WITH SPECIAL POWERS IN?! WHAT KIND OF RESTRAINTS THEY USE?!
YOU WON'T GO TO PRISON, I PROMISE YOU. YOU'LL GO TO A HOSPITAL, FRANCIS--WHERE YOU CAN DEAL WITH WHAT'S BEEN DONE TO YOU, WITH DOCTORS WHO ONLY CARE ABOUT YOUR PSYCHOLOGICAL AND EMOTIONAL WELL-BEING!
HOW CAN YOU BE SURE TH--
WHAM
--UHN!
I'VE GOT YOU, MS. HARDY.
PETER, NO!
NEVER AGAIN!
NNNNGGGHH!
"NEVER..."
AGAIN!

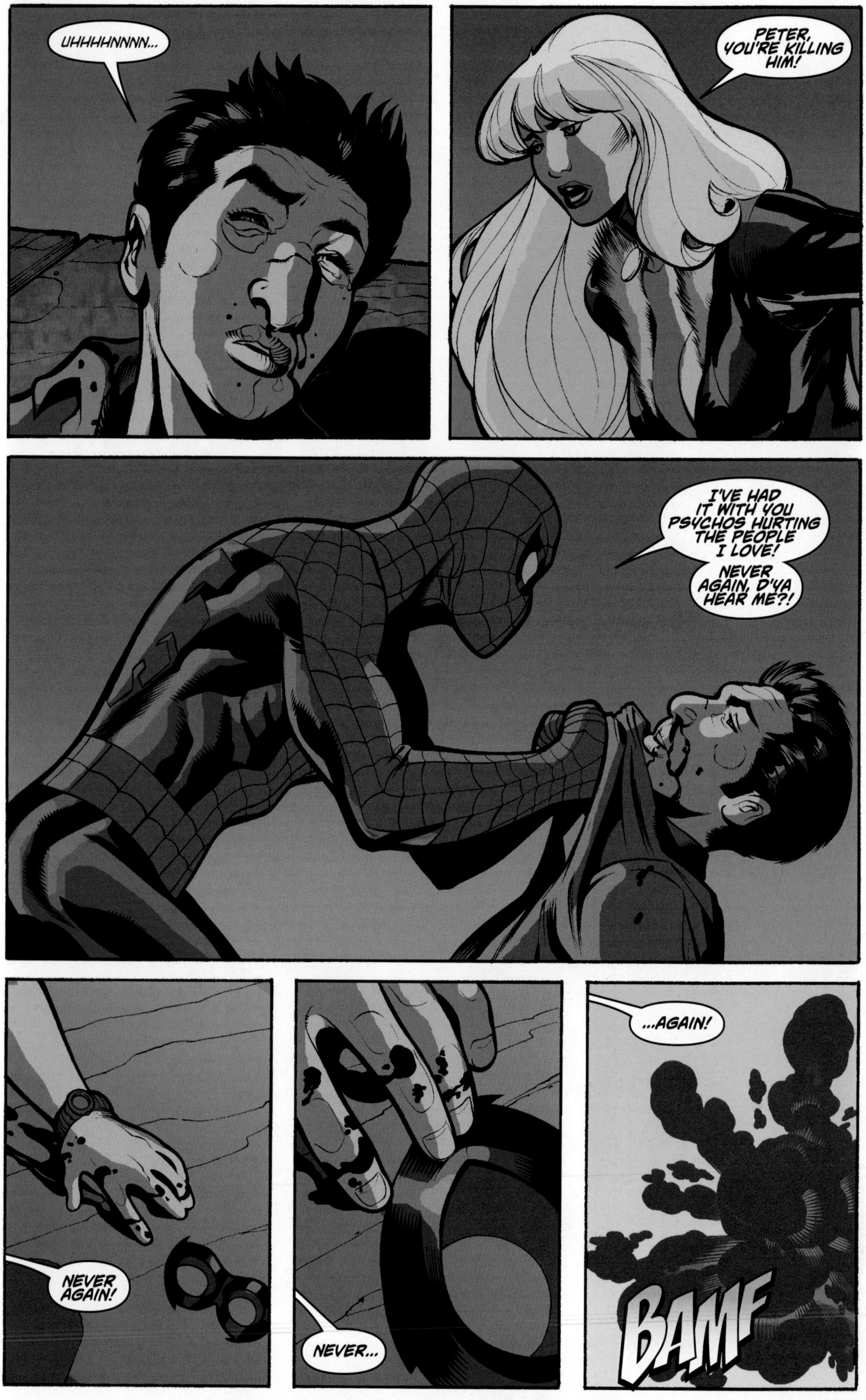
UHHHHNNNN...
PETER, YOU'RE KILLING HIM!
I'VE HAD IT WITH YOU PSYCHOS HURTING THE PEOPLE I LOVE!
NEVER AGAIN, D'YA HEAR ME?!
NEVER AGAIN!
NEVER...
...AGAIN!
BAMF

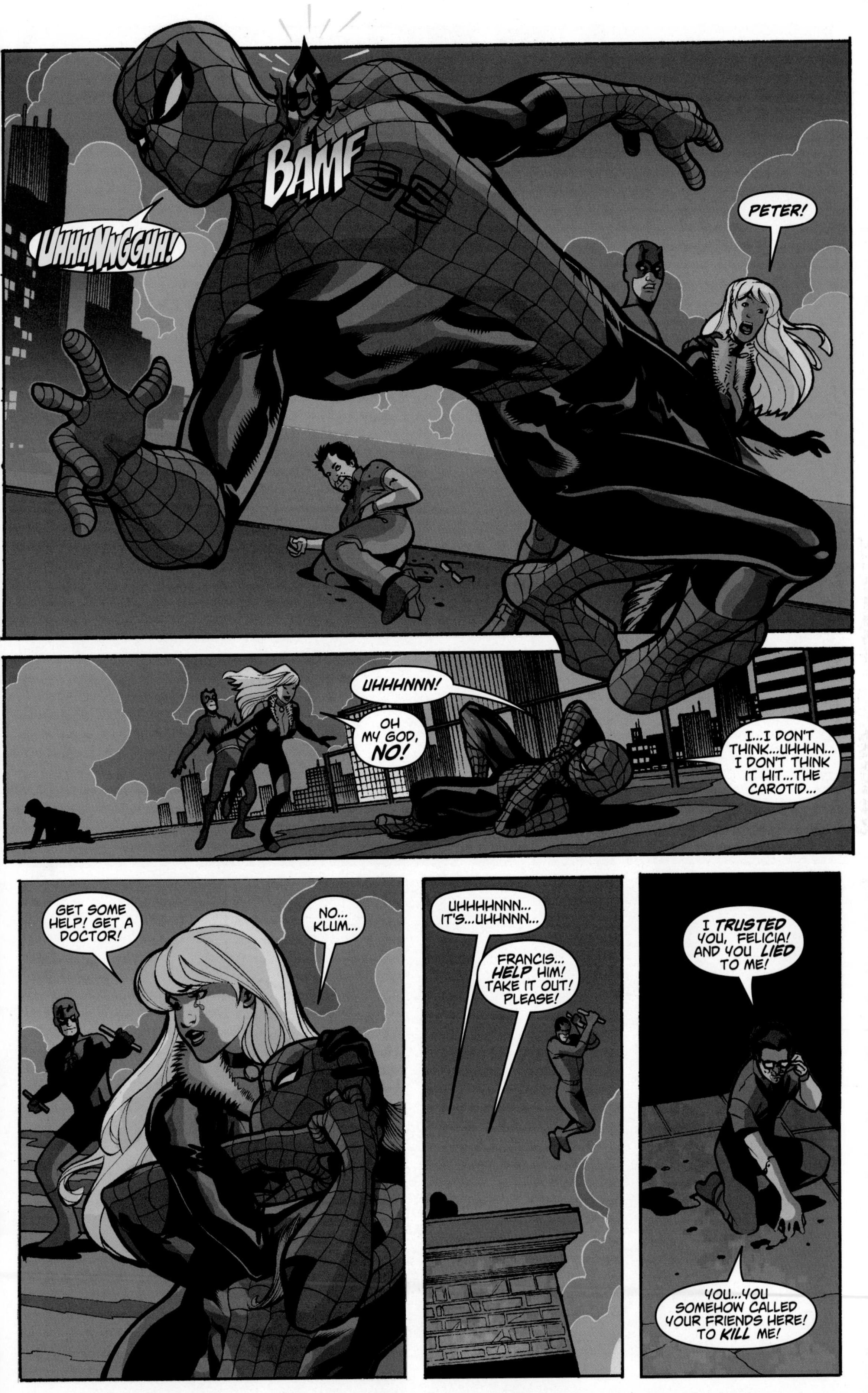
BAMF
UHHHNNGGHH!
PETER!
UHHHNNN!
OH MY GOD, NO!
I...I DON'T THINK...UHHHN... I DON'T THINK IT HIT...THE CAROTID...
GET SOME HELP! GET A DOCTOR!
NO... KLUM...
UHHHHNNN... IT'S...UHHNNN...
FRANCIS... HELP HIM! TAKE IT OUT! PLEASE!
I TRUSTED YOU, FELICIA! AND YOU LIED TO ME!
YOU...YOU SOMEHOW CALLED YOUR FRIENDS HERE! TO KILL ME!

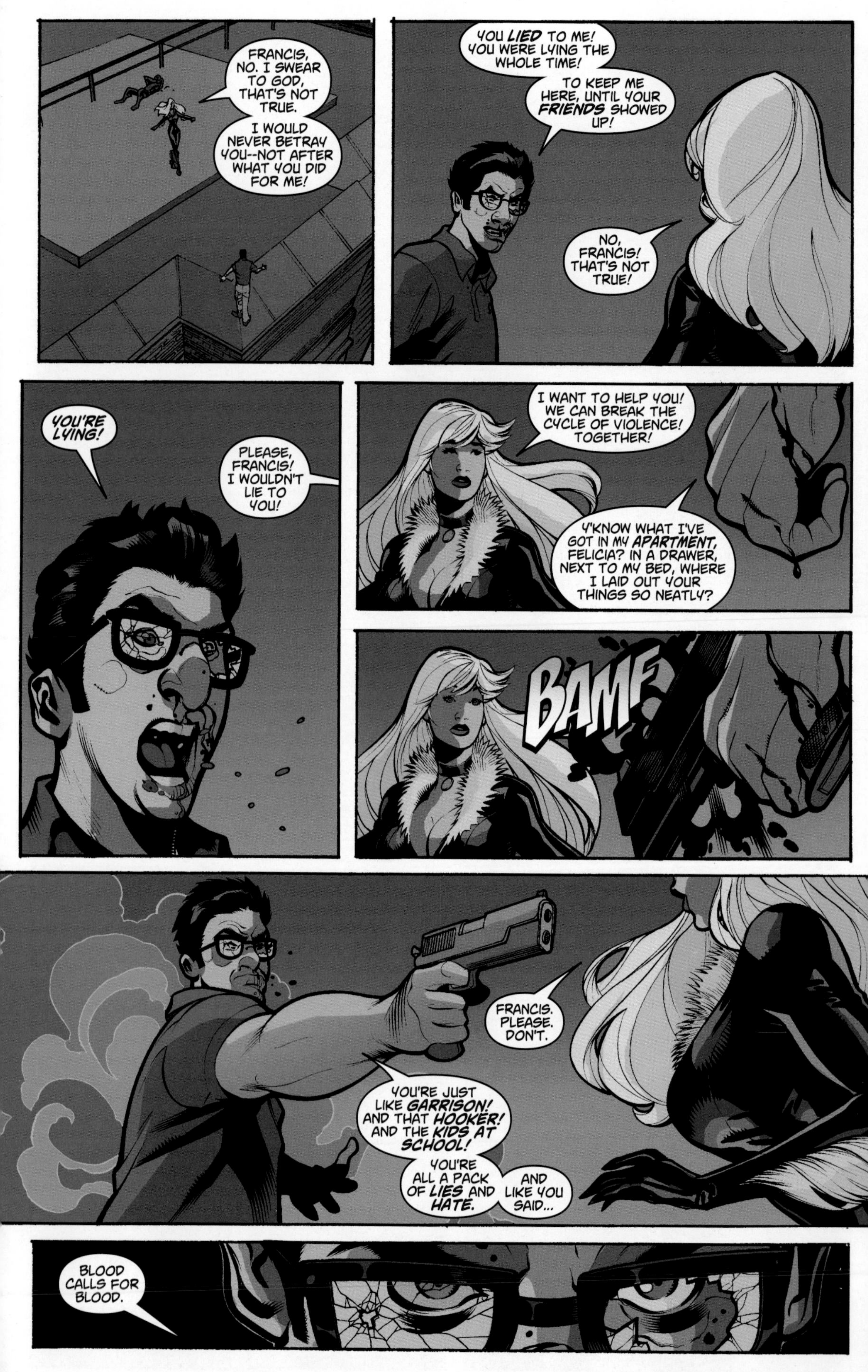
FRANCIS, NO. I SWEAR TO GOD, THAT'S NOT TRUE.
I WOULD NEVER BETRAY YOU--NOT AFTER WHAT YOU DID FOR ME!
YOU LIED TO ME! YOU WERE LYING THE WHOLE TIME!
TO KEEP ME HERE, UNTIL YOUR FRIENDS SHOWED UP!
NO, FRANCIS! THAT'S NOT TRUE!
YOU'RE LYING!
PLEASE, FRANCIS! I WOULDN'T LIE TO YOU!
I WANT TO HELP YOU! WE CAN BREAK THE CYCLE OF VIOLENCE! TOGETHER!
Y'KNOW WHAT I'VE GOT IN MY APARTMENT, FELICIA? IN A DRAWER, NEXT TO MY BED, WHERE I LAID OUT YOUR THINGS SO NEATLY?
BAMF
FRANCIS. PLEASE. DON'T.
YOU'RE JUST LIKE GARRISON! AND THAT HOOKER! AND THE KIDS AT SCHOOL!
YOU'RE ALL A PACK OF LIES AND HATE.
AND LIKE YOU SAID...
BLOOD CALLS FOR BLOOD.

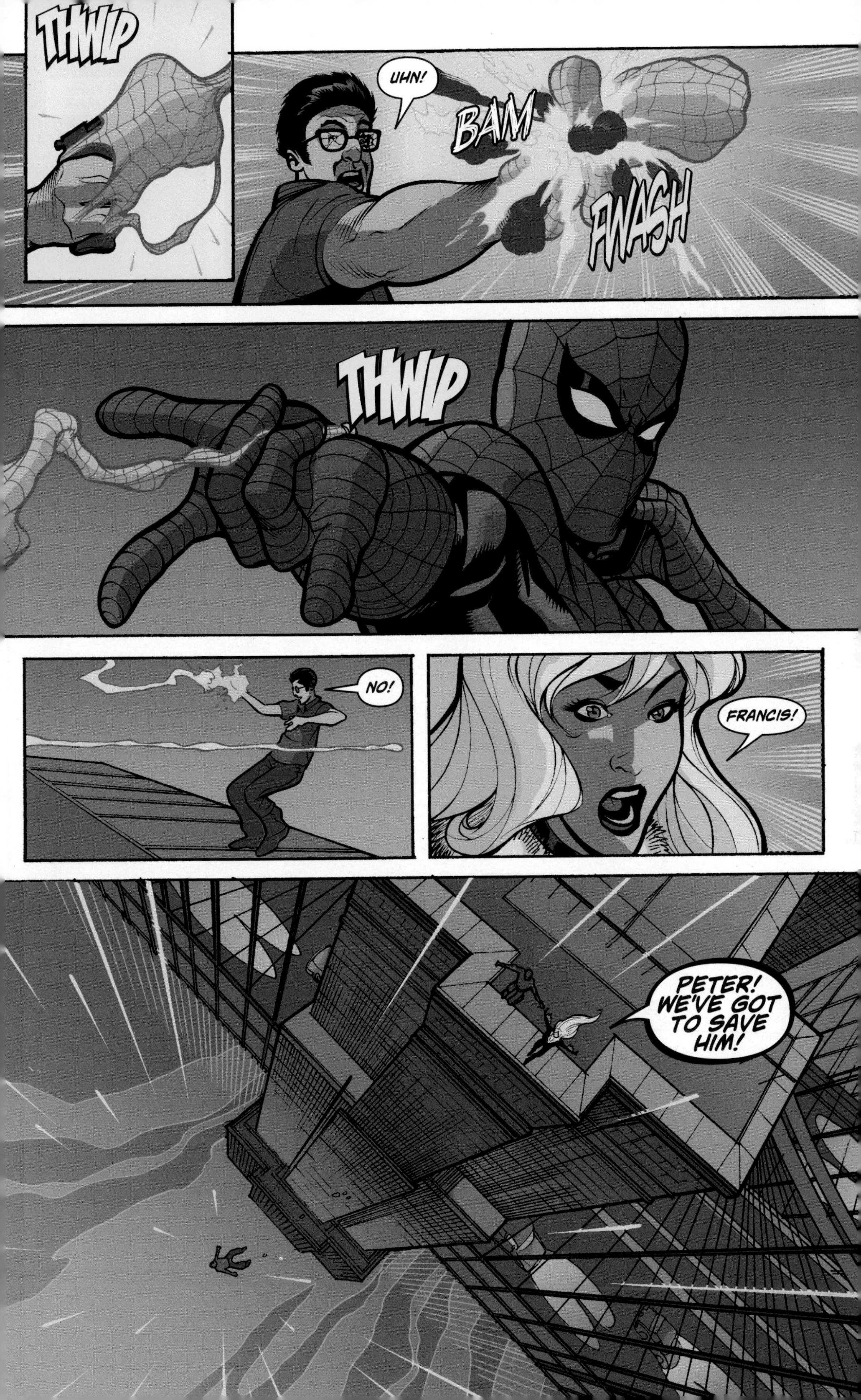
THWIP
UHN!
BAM
FWASH
THWIP
NO!
FRANCIS!
PETER! WE'VE GOT TO SAVE HIM!

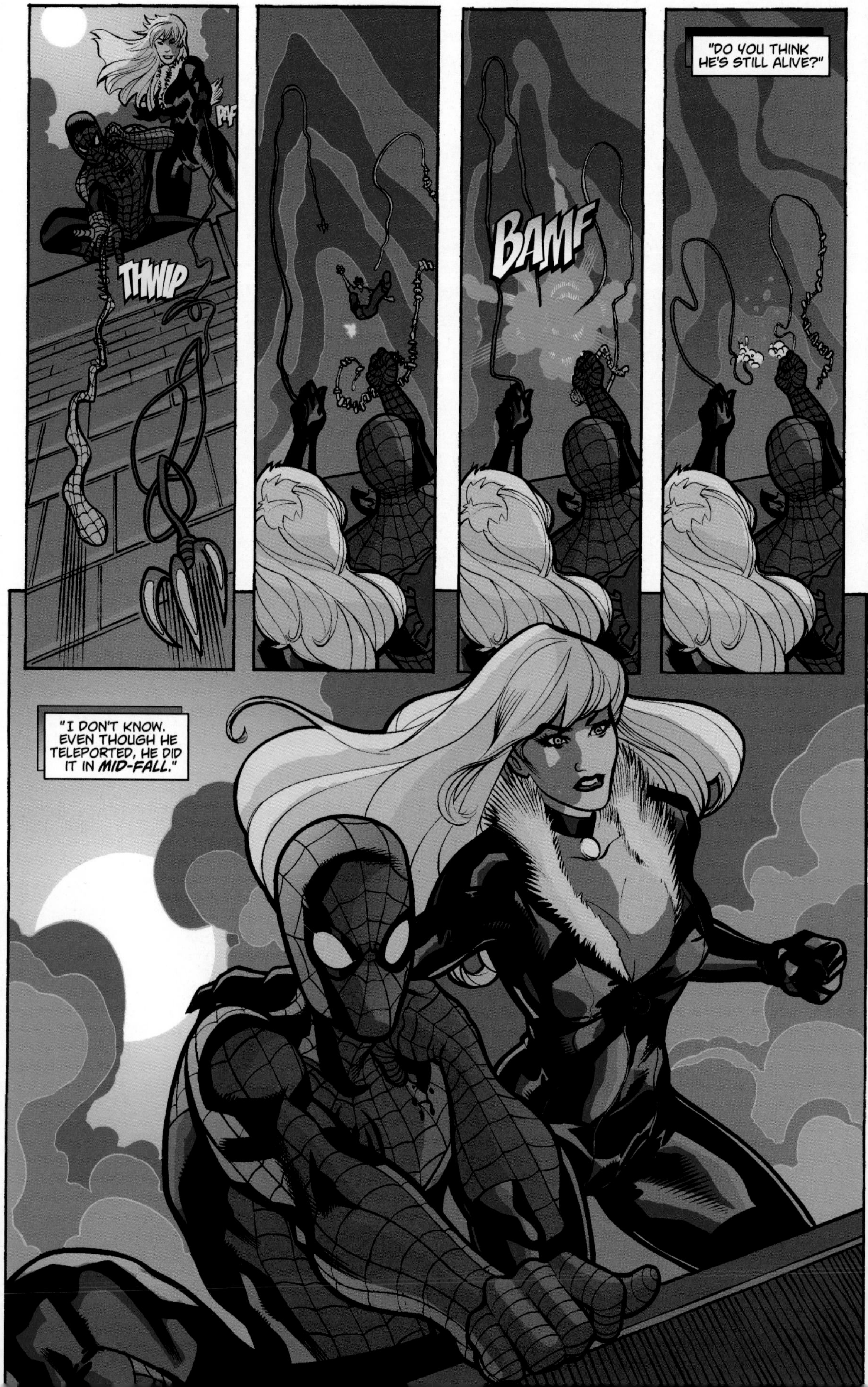
PAF
THWIP
BAMF
"DO YOU THINK HE'S STILL ALIVE?"
"I DON'T KNOW. EVEN THOUGH HE TELEPORTED, HE DID IT IN MID-FALL."

WHEREVER HE WOUND UP, HE STILL HAD TO *LAND*, Y'KNOW?

HE MAY HAVE GOTTEN OFF LIGHT IF HE *DID* DIE. AT LEAST HE DOESN'T HAVE TO LIVE THE REST OF *HIS* LIFE AS A FUGITIVE FROM THE LAW.

WE'LL GET YOU CLEARED, LEESH. IT MAY TAKE TIME, AND YOU'RE GONNA HAVE TO LAY LOW, BUT SOONER OR LATER, WE'LL GET YOU OUT FROM UNDER THE MURDER CHARGE.

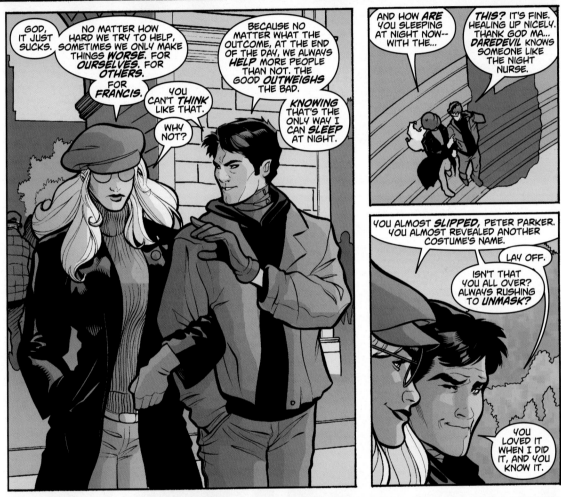

GOD, IT JUST *SUCKS*.

NO MATTER HOW HARD WE TRY TO HELP, SOMETIMES WE ONLY MAKE THINGS *WORSE*. FOR *OURSELVES*. FOR *OTHERS*. FOR *FRANCIS*.

BECAUSE NO MATTER WHAT THE OUTCOME, AT THE END OF THE DAY, WE ALWAYS *HELP* MORE PEOPLE THAN NOT. THE GOOD *OUTWEIGHS* THE BAD.

YOU CAN'T *THINK* LIKE THAT.

WHY NOT?

KNOWING THAT'S THE ONLY WAY I CAN *SLEEP* AT NIGHT.

AND HOW *ARE* YOU SLEEPING AT NIGHT NOW-- WITH THE...

THIS? IT'S FINE. HEALING UP NICELY. THANK GOD MA... *DAREDEVIL* KNOWS SOMEONE LIKE THE NIGHT NURSE.

YOU ALMOST *SLIPPED*, PETER PARKER. YOU ALMOST REVEALED ANOTHER COSTUME'S NAME.

LAY OFF.

ISN'T THAT YOU ALL OVER? ALWAYS RUSHING TO *UNMASK?*

YOU *LOVED* IT WHEN I DID IT, AND YOU KNOW IT.

I *DID*, ACTUALLY.

S'NOT WHAT YOU SAID *THEN*.

I WAS A *KID* THEN, PETER. I'VE GROWN UP A *LOT* SINCE THEN.

YOU TELLING ME WHO YOU WERE... EVEN THOUGH I DIDN'T SHOW IT AT THE TIME...

IT MEANT THE *WORLD* TO ME.

YOU *HELPED* ME.

HELPED YOU *HOW?*

YOU HELPED ME TO *TRUST* AGAIN.

REALLY? *NOW* YOU TELL ME--WHEN I'M ALL *MARRIED* AND STUFF.

AND WHAT DO YOU MEAN "TRUST AGAIN?"

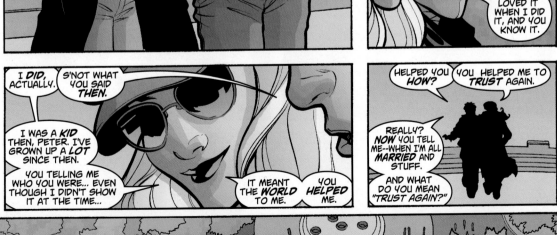

PETER, I THINK IT'S TIME I TOLD YOU SOMETHING.

SOMETHING THAT HAPPENED TO ME WHEN I WAS IN COLLEGE...

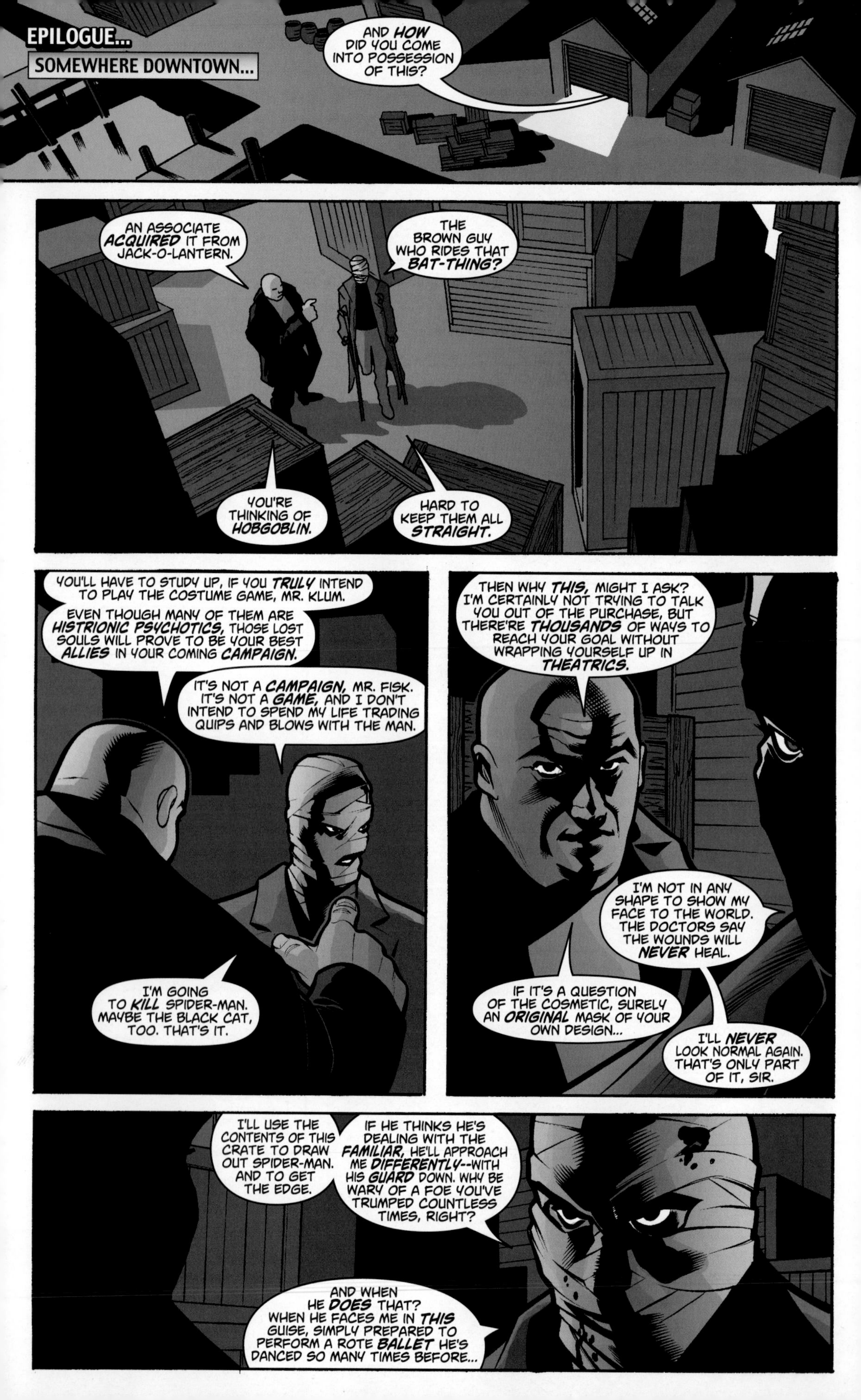
EPILOGUE...
SOMEWHERE DOWNTOWN...
AND HOW DID YOU COME INTO POSSESSION OF THIS?
AN ASSOCIATE ACQUIRED IT FROM JACK-O-LANTERN.
THE BROWN GUY WHO RIDES THAT BAT-THING?
YOU'RE THINKING OF HOBGOBLIN.
HARD TO KEEP THEM ALL STRAIGHT.
YOU'LL HAVE TO STUDY UP, IF YOU TRULY INTEND TO PLAY THE COSTUME GAME, MR. KLUM.
EVEN THOUGH MANY OF THEM ARE HISTRIONIC PSYCHOTICS, THOSE LOST SOULS WILL PROVE TO BE YOUR BEST ALLIES IN YOUR COMING CAMPAIGN.
IT'S NOT A CAMPAIGN, MR. FISK. IT'S NOT A GAME, AND I DON'T INTEND TO SPEND MY LIFE TRADING QUIPS AND BLOWS WITH THE MAN.
I'M GOING TO KILL SPIDER-MAN. MAYBE THE BLACK CAT, TOO. THAT'S IT.
THEN WHY THIS, MIGHT I ASK? I'M CERTAINLY NOT TRYING TO TALK YOU OUT OF THE PURCHASE, BUT THERE'RE THOUSANDS OF WAYS TO REACH YOUR GOAL WITHOUT WRAPPING YOURSELF UP IN THEATRICS.
I'M NOT IN ANY SHAPE TO SHOW MY FACE TO THE WORLD. THE DOCTORS SAY THE WOUNDS WILL NEVER HEAL.
IF IT'S A QUESTION OF THE COSMETIC, SURELY AN ORIGINAL MASK OF YOUR OWN DESIGN...
I'LL NEVER LOOK NORMAL AGAIN. THAT'S ONLY PART OF IT, SIR.
I'LL USE THE CONTENTS OF THIS CRATE TO DRAW OUT SPIDER-MAN. AND TO GET THE EDGE.
IF HE THINKS HE'S DEALING WITH THE FAMILIAR, HE'LL APPROACH ME DIFFERENTLY--WITH HIS GUARD DOWN. WHY BE WARY OF A FOE YOU'VE TRUMPED COUNTLESS TIMES, RIGHT?
AND WHEN HE DOES THAT? WHEN HE FACES ME IN THIS GUISE, SIMPLY PREPARED TO PERFORM A ROTE BALLET HE'S DANCED SO MANY TIMES BEFORE...

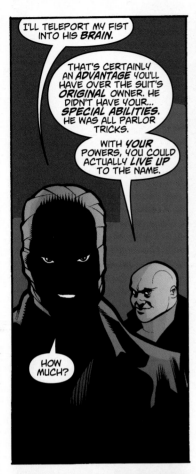

I'LL TELEPORT MY FIST INTO HIS *BRAIN*.

THAT'S CERTAINLY AN *ADVANTAGE* YOU'LL HAVE OVER THE SUIT'S *ORIGINAL* OWNER. HE DIDN'T HAVE YOUR... *SPECIAL ABILITIES*. HE WAS ALL PARLOR TRICKS.

WITH *YOUR* POWERS, YOU COULD ACTUALLY *LIVE UP* TO THE NAME.

HOW MUCH?

AH--THE UNCOMFORTABLE DISCUSSION OF *MONEY*.

TEN MILLION.

SEEMS KINDA *HIGH* FOR A SUIT THAT'S BEEN SITTING IN *MOTHBALLS* FOR AWHILE.

YOU'RE NOT JUST BUYING THE *SUIT*, SIR. YOU'RE BUYING ALL THE *ACCOUTREMENTS* THE DESIGNER OF THIS IDENTITY CREATED AS WELL. HIS CONTRAPTIONS, WHICH--WHILE ADMITTEDLY RATHER CHILDISH--*DO* EXTEND THE MYSTIQUE HE AFFORDED HIMSELF...JUST PRIOR TO HIS ROUTINE *THRASHINGS* AT THE HANDS OF SPIDER-MAN.

A FATE I'M *SURE* YOU'LL NOT SHARE.

AND ASIDE FROM THE *HISTORY* AND THE *ANONYMITY* THE SUIT PROVIDES, DON'T FORGET THAT YOU'RE ALSO BUYING THIS *ENTIRE WAREHOUSE*.

IT'S A *TURNKEY OPERATION*, MR. KLUM. YOU HAND ME A BRIEFCASE, AND I HAND YOU THE KEYS TO A *KINGDOM*--ONE YOU COULD RESCUE FROM *RIDICULE*.

AND TEN MILLION CERTAINLY PUTS YOU WELL ON YOUR WAY TO REBUILDING *YOUR* EMPIRE, DOESN'T IT, MR. FISK?

THERE'S THAT, YES.

MAKE IT EIGHT, AND WHEN I'M DONE KILLING THE *ARACH-KNIGHT*, I'LL DO AWAY WITH *DAREDEVIL* FOR YOU AS WELL.

A KIND OFFER, TO BE SURE.

BUT THERE ARE SOME THINGS A MAN HAS TO DO FOR *HIMSELF*, SIR.

I'M AFRAID IT'S TEN MILLION OR *NOTHING*.

SUCH A *SMALL* PRICE TO PAY FOR REVENGE ON YOUR *BROTHER'S* KILLERS, NO?

Hm.

SO... DO WE HAVE A *DEAL*?

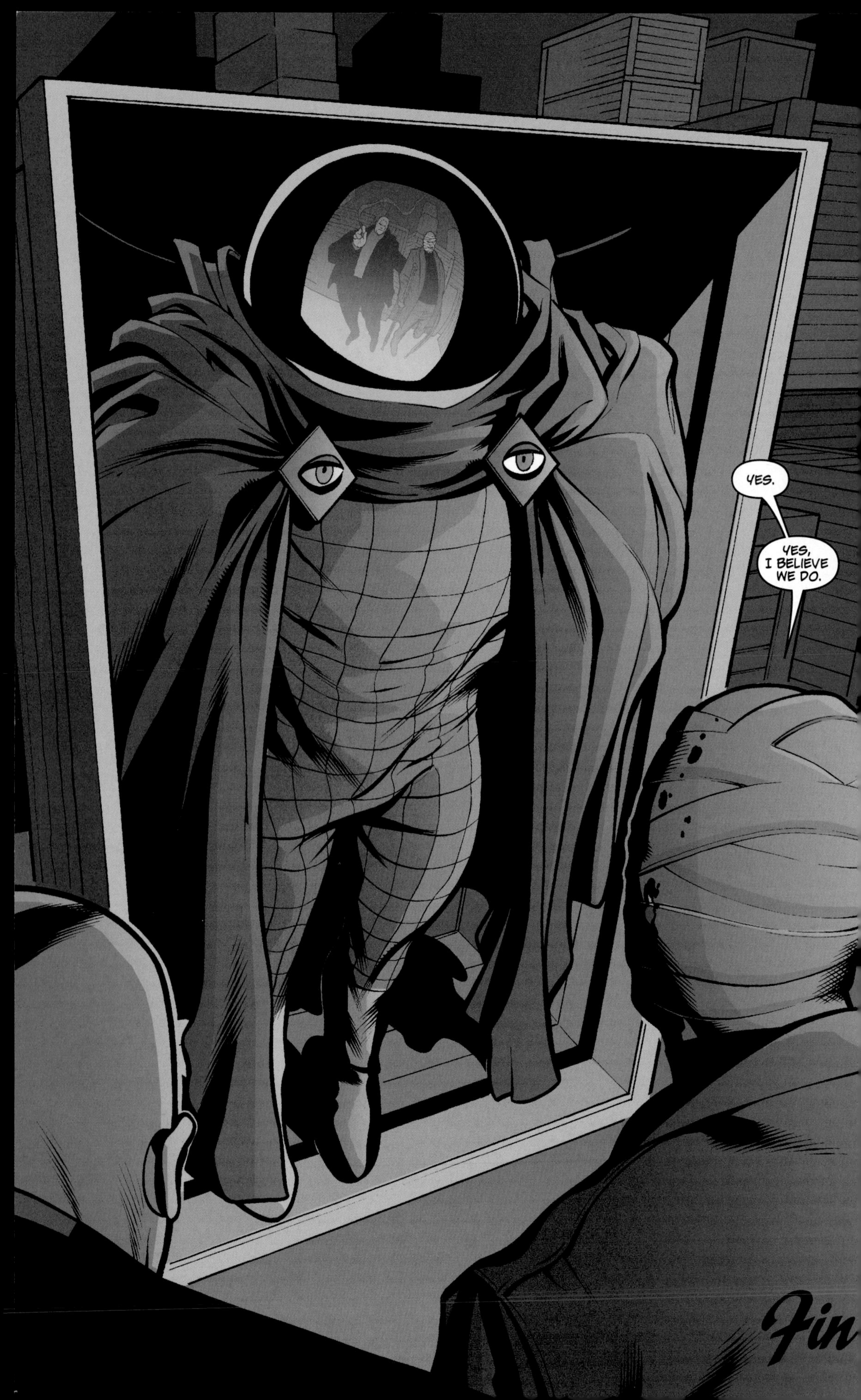
YES.
YES, I BELIEVE WE DO.
Fin

ISSUE #6 SCRIPT BY KEVIN SMITH
WITH SKETCHES BY TERRY DODSON

PAGE ONE

Panel One:

An image of a happy, smiling, beautiful six year old Felicia Hardy.

BLACK CAT VO
They say the model for every relationship a woman has with a man is predicated on the relationship she shares with the first man she ever loves...

Panel Two:

EXT NYC BASKETBALL COURT - DAY

Wider on that image now: young Felicia rides the shoulders of WALTER HARDY, her father. She's putting a basketball in a hoop. A picture of joy.

BLACK CAT VO
Her Dad.

WALTER
Swish!

(balloon two)
And Hardy sinks the rock at the buzzer! The Knicks are going to the playoffs!

FELICIA
HAR-DY! HAR-DY! HAR-DY!

Panel Three:

Other ballers are moving onto the court now, waiting for the ball, as Walter lifts Felicia off his shoulders.

FELICIA
Again!

WALTER
Oh, no. That's enough ball for today, kiddo. Your mother's gonna kill me if I don't get you to school in time.

Panel Four:

Felicia by his side, Walter bounces the ball back to the waiting, smiling players.

WALTER
Thanks, guys.

FELICIA
Can I be a cheerleader for the Knicks when I grow up, Daddy?

Panel Five:

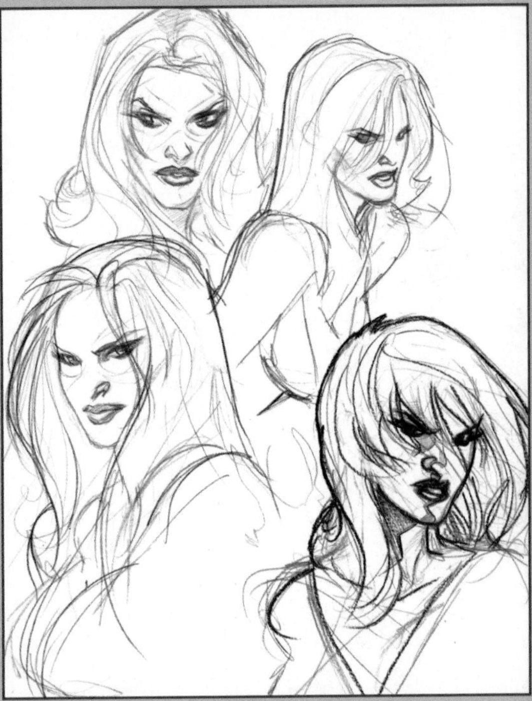

Walter acts as if he's been shot in the heart. Felicia smiles.

WALTER
A cheerleader?! You just shot your poor old man in the heart, kid.

(balloon two)
Why cheer on the dopey boys when you get to pass the rock yer darn self? You be starting center, and let the boys cheer for you.

Panel Six:

Walter has his hand under Felcia's chin, lifting her face to look at him.

FELICIA
But there are no girls on the Knicks.

WALTER
Then you be the first. If the game doesn't work for you, then change the game.

(balloon two)
You can be anything you want when you grow up, Fee-Fee. Don't forget that.

Panel Seven:

A wide on the court. In the foreground, the ballers are playing. In the background, Walter and Felicia, their backs to us, are leaving the court. Felicia carries a backpack.

WALTER
Just sink more'n Cartwright, and I'll be a happy man.

FELICIA
'Kay.

BLACK CAT VO
'Course, the only courts in my future were of the legal variety.

BLACK CAT VO
When I grew up, I wanted to be just like my Dad. And since he was a cat burglar...

PAGE TWO AND THREE

SPLASH PAGES/TITLE PAGE

A montage of The Black Cat in action:

- Climbing up the side of a building

- Holding fist-fulls of jewels she's extracted from a safe

- As Felicia Hardy, enjoying her wealth

- Facing off with Spider-Man

- The largest image in the center of the splash portrays

Felicia (NOT THE BLACK CAT, BUT FELICIA) hanging upside down from a cable in an incredibly limber and extremely sexy pose over a laser-beam-alarm protected museum display case, reaching for the massive diamond contained therein.

BLACK CAT VO
Well, let's just say the apple didn't fall far from the tree.

BILLING BLOCK
-Marvel Comics Presents,
-Spider-Man and
the Black Cat in
-The Evil That Men Do
-Part Six: One-in-Four
-Written By Kev
-Drawn and Colored by
Terry and Rachel
-Edited by Axel

PAGE FOUR

Panel One:

EXT QUEENSBORO BRIDGE - NIGHT

The Black Cat talks with Francis.

BLACK CAT
But Dad wasn't the man responsible for shaping my destiny. I mean, he'd have rather I didn't follow in his footsteps, y'know?

(balloon two)
The guy most responsible for me putting on tights and stealing things wasn't nearly as noble.

(balloon three)
And since my Father was a professional thief, that's saying a lot.

Panel Two:

EXT COLLEGE CAMPUS FRAT HOUSE - NIGHT

An establishing shot. There's a party in progress, which has spilled out onto the lawn. Drinking, music, etc.

BLACK CAT VO
I met him when I was a freshman at ESU.

Panel Three:

INT COLLEGE CAMPUS FRAT HOUSE - NIGHT

An eighteen year old Felicia nurses a beer, hanging out with another girlfriend. They're in the midst of the party, surrounded by other revelers. She's still in great shape, but not the defined, amazing shape of the Black Cat we know.

FELICIA
I feel so bloated.

GIRL
You're crazy. You have an amazing body. Every guy here would kill to sleep with you, Leesh.

FELICIA
Not if I keep downing beers. You know how many calories these things are loaded with?

(balloon two)
I drink anymore of these and that freshman fifteen's gonna turn into the freshman fifty.

Panel Four:

Felicia hands her beer off to her friend.

FELICIA
Speaking of which, hold my brewski. I've gotta hit the bathroom.

GIRL
Again? You got the bladder of an infant.

FELICIA
Yeah, yeah, yeah.

GIRL
Want me to come with?

Panel Five:

Felicia heads toward a staircase, moving through the crowd, calling back to her friend.

FELICIA
I'll be fine. Just don't leave without me, okay?

GIRL
No promises if Mr. Right comes a-calling.

PAGE FIVE

Panel One:

INT FRAT HOUSE BATHROOM - NIGHT

Felicia in the bathroom, post-leak, looking in the mirror, fixing her hair.

BLACK CAT VO
But Mr. Right wasn't at that party that night.

Panel Two:

Felicia opens the bathroom door to leave, and a drunken, heavy-set FRAT GUY is leaning in the doorway, hands against the top of the doorjam.

BLACK CAT VO
Mr. Wrong was...

FELICIA
Oh! 'Scuse me.

FRAT GUY
Why? D'jou fart?

FELICIA
Charming.

Panel Three:

Felicia tries to move past the guy, but he has his arms on her, pushing her back into the bathroom. Felicia looks a little scared.

FRAT GUY
I can be. Lemme' show you.

FELICIA
Get off me!

FRAT GUY
C'mon... let's have a little party in here. Just you and me.

FELICIA
No!

Panel Four:

Suddenly, another guy's arms yank the Frat Guy backwards, into the hallway. Felicia is surprised.

FRAT GUY
Hey!

OFF-PANEL GUY
Didn't you hear the lady, Rappaport?

Panel Five:

EXT FRAT HOUSE HALLWAY - NIGHT

A good-looking GUY has the Frat Guy pinned against the wall, his forearm under the Frat Guy's chin. Felicia looks on from the bathroom door.

GUY
She said no.

FRAT GUY
Get offa me, man!

GUY
Not so cool, is it -- having someone's hands on you when you don't want 'em there?

Panel Six:

The Guy shoves the fat Frat Guy down the hallway, as Felicia watches.

GUY
Why don't you sleep it off?

FRAT GUY
You got alotta stones, Ryan -- y'know that?

GUY
Yeah, yeah, yeah.

(balloon two)
Beat it, before you give our house a bad name.

Page Six

Panel One:

The handsome Guy extends his hand to Felicia.

GUY
Sorry 'bout that. He can be kind of an ██ when he's drunk.

FELICIA
Something tells me he's not much better when he's sober.

GUY
Then, too. But don't judge all us Beta's by him. We're pretty harmless.

Panel Two:

Felicia doesn't take his hand, but steps out into the hallway beside him.

FELICIA
You'll have to understand if I don't wanna take your word on that right now.

GUY
Fair enough.

(balloon two)
But how about I prove it to you in the way of an escort back to your dorm.

Panel Three:

The Guy shoves his hands in his pockets. Felicia's smiling.

GUY
These'll stay right in here, if it makes you feel better?

FELICIA
I'm good, thanks.

GUY
C'mon -- I kinda feel like you're my responsibility now. Least I can do is make sure you get out of here in one piece.

Panel Four:

On Felicia, smiling.

BLACK CAT VO
He was everything I was looking for a in guy, back then: chivalrous, charming, cute.

BLACK CAT VO 2
He was nice.

FELICIA
You're a whole different kind of trouble, aren't you -- Ryan, is it?

Panel Five:

On Ryan, the picture of college cool.

RYAN
Ryan it is.

(balloon two)
Trouble I'm not.

Panel Six:

EXT GIRL'S DORM - NIGHT

Ryan walks Felicia and her friend up to their building.

BLACK CAT VO
He walked me and my friend home, and we chatted the whole way -- about classes, campus, movies, the Knicks.

BLACK CAT VO 2
He made an excellent first impression.

RYAN
C'mon! The Knicks?! You just like 'em because you can't appreciate the sheer poetry that is the Bulls.

FELICIA
Spoken like a true Jordan-ite. I think every guy harbors a secret crush on Mike.

RYAN
Secret? I'd marry him in heartbeat.

PAGE SEVEN

Panel One:

At the door to the building, Ryan smiles at Felicia. Felicia smiles back. Felicia's friend rolls her eyes.

RYAN
He's not the only one, either.

GIRL
Oh, Lord...

RYAN
What can I say? I'm a romantic. You like romantics, Felicia Hardy?

FELICIA
They're alright.

RYAN
Alright enough to shoot hoops with tomorrow? Say, 'round two?

FELICIA
Lemme check my calendar and get back to you, Mike-Lover.

Panel Two:

INT DORM ROOM - NIGHT
Felicia collapses on her bed while her friend takes off her (own) pants.

BLACK CAT VO
What can I say? I was smitten.

FELICIA
What do you think of him?

GIRL
He's alright, for a frat guy.

FELICIA
"Alright"?! Are you nuts?

Panel Three:

Looking down on Felicia, who's laying face up on the bed, looking up, dreamily.

FELICIA
He's purrrrfect...

Panel Four:

EXT CAMPUS COURT - DAY

Ryan's dunking the ball, hanging from the rim. Felicia's laughing.

BLACK CAT VO
I spent the next day with him...

RYAN
Jordan takes it to the hoop, and the Bulls take the championship again!

FELICIA
No fair! You got the height advantage.

RYAN
It's all about the width, not the length, lady.

Panel Five:

Ryan picks Felicia up from behind. Her legs are flailing in the air. She's laughing.

RYAN
But you want some length?

FELICIA
Hey!

Panel Six:

Felicia's now sitting atop Ryan's shoulders, dunking the basketball, just as she had years ago with her Dad.

RYAN
Three! Two! One!

FELICIA
BRRRRRRRRRRRRRRRR!

(balloon two)
Hardy sinks it, at the buzzer!

PAGE EIGHT

Panel One:

EXT MOVIE THEATER - NIGHT

Felicia and Ryan, not arm-in-arm or anything, exit the movie theater, laughing. The marquee reads "Flashback Fridays: Caddyshack".

BLACK CAT VO
Then I spend the rest of the week with him. Going to the movies...

Panel Two:

INT LIBRARY - DAY

Ryan and Felicia sit across from one another. Both are buried in books, smiling, as they play footsie under the desk, not making eye contact, paperwork sprawled out in front of them.

BLACK CAT VO
Hitting the books...

Panel Three:

EXT RESTAURANT - NIGHT

Ryan holds the car door open for Felicia, as they leave a diner, flirting.

BLACK CAT VO
Going out to eat...

FELICIA
Such a gentleman.

RYAN
And I'd call you such a lady, if you hadn't scarfed all the fries, ya' fry-hog.

Panel Four:

INT RYAN'S ROOM - NIGHT

Ryan and Felicia make out on the bed, fully clothed. She's wearing a skirt.

BLACK CAT VO
I thought he might be the one. And he was...

Panel Five:

Ryan, to the side of Felicia, over her, with Felicia on her back. She plays with his hair. He's looking down at her.

BLACK CAT VO
I just didn't realize which one...

FELICIA
You're so cute.

RYAN
If I had a nickel for every girl who told me that...

FELICIA
You'd have a nickel total?

RYAN
Pretty much.

Panel Six:

More of the same, different angle.

FELICIA
I've gotta go, Nickel-rich. I've got the Philosophy exam in the morning.

RYAN
C'mon. Just stay a little longer.

FELICIA
I stay any longer, and I'm gonna do something I might regret.

RYAN
What if I promised you you wouldn't regret it?

Panel Seven:

Felicia starts to sit up, Ryan's still got his hands on her.

FELICIA
Now if I had a nickel for every guy who ever said that.

RYAN
But I mean it. I'm good.

FELICIA
We'll see. Just not tonight.

RYAN
C'mon.

PAGE NINE

Panel One:

Felicia's still trying to get up, but Ryan's still got his hands on her. She's looking mildly concerned now. He's looking desperate.

FELICIA
Good things come to those who wait.

RYAN
I'm not good at waiting, Leesh.

(balloon two)
I mean, you're kinda leaving me hanging here.

FELICIA
Just hold that thought a little while longer.

RYAN
I'd rather hold you.

Panel Two:

Felicia kisses him quickly.

FELICIA
You're sweet.

SFX
Smak.

FELICIA
But I've really gotta go now...

Panel Three:
Ryan pulls/pushes her back down onto the bed now.

RYAN
Just... wait.

FELICIA
Ryan...

Panel Four:

Felicia's back down on the bed, now looking really worried. Ryan's over her again, oblivious.

RYAN
I just... I really want to.

FELICIA
But I don't. So please stop.

RYAN
In a minute. Just a little bit...

Panel Five:

Ryan's now atop her. We start our push in, obscuring what he's doing with his hands, as he reaches below frame.

FELICIA
Ryan, get off me!

RYAN
I will. Shhhh... relax.

FELICIA
NO! STOP IT!

Panel Six:

Pushing closer. We're over his back, onto a terrified Felicia. Ryan's free hand is covering her mouth now.

RYAN
Shhhh! It's... it's okay!
I love you!

FELICIA
MMMMMM! MMMM!!!!

BLACK CAT VO
Some studies say that one in four women are raped in their lifetime.

BLACK CAT VO 2
There are other studies that put the figure at one in nine.

Panel Seven:

Even tighter on Felicia's face, Ryan's hand covering her mouth. She's now gone wide-eyed.

RYAN
Uhn...!

FELICIA
MMMMMMMMMMMMM....!!!!

PAGE TEN

EXT QUEENSBORO BRIDGE - NIGHT

Panel One:

Close on the Black Cat, eyes cast downward. Francis is behind her, in the far background.

BLACK CAT
Even if the figure was one in ten million...

(balloon two)
It'd still be too much.

Panel Two:

INT DORM ROOM - DAY

Felicia in her room, curled up on her bed, seated, holding her knees, looking shell-shocked. Her roommate's trying to talk to her.

BLACK CAT VO
I spent the rest of the week in a daze.

GIRL
Leesh? Are you okay?

Panel Three:

Closer on Felicia, same position. The Girl's off-panel.

BLACK CAT VO
I was too ashamed to tell anybody.

BLACK CAT VO 2
Like an idiot, I thought it was my fault, somehow.

GIRL
Leesh?

Panel Four:

EXT CAMPUS - DAY

Felicia holds her books against her chest, very guarded. She stares at a blue-light call box -- what they call "Rape Boxes" on college campuses. There's a notice taped to it.

BLACK CAT VO
I never reported it. I never told anyone.

Panel Five:

Felicia gets closer to read the notice.

BLACK CAT VO
He took something from me that night -- and it wasn't just my virginity.

BLACK CAT VO 2
He took my identity -- who I saw myself as.

Panel Six:

Over Felicia, onto the notice, which reads "Have you been the victim of a sexual assault?" Then, in smaller lettering "We're here to help. Join our campus support group. Meetings every week in the Osbourne Building, Room 5H."

BLACK CAT VO
And I wasn't alone.

Panel Seven:

Close on Felicia's face, tears welling up in her eyes.

BLACK CAT VO
According to Department of Justice statistics, a woman is raped in America every two and a half minutes.

BLACK CAT VO 2
Think about that.

BLACK CAT VO 3
In the time it's taken me to tell you this story, how many women have been victims of a sexual assault?

Panel Eight:

Same composition, but now Felicia's enraged.

BLACK CAT VO
That's when it hit me...

BLACK CAT VO 2
I wouldn't let what happened to me become just another statistic.

PAGE ELEVEN

Panel One:

INT GYM - DAY

Felicia is at the sign up desk, filling out paperwork.

BLACK CAT VO
In a selfish moment, that man stole my life from me...

Panel Two:

In a wide, Felicia works the heavy bag.

Over the progression of these images, you can show time passage through the windows in the gym: seasonal changes, like snow, rain, fall, bright day, dark night.

BLACK CAT VO
I told him no, and he didn't care. He wouldn't listen.

Panel Three:

Felicia benches weights, wearing a different outfit.

BLACK CAT VO
It was a hate crime.

Panel Four:

Back to the heavy bag set-up, pushing in on the same scene. The punches come faster. She's in a different outfit.

BLACK CAT VO
And it gave birth to a hatred that demanded justice.

Panel Five:

Felicia climbs a rope in the gym. We're looking down at her, face filled with determination, sweaty. She wears a different outfit.

BLACK CAT VO
Blood called for blood.

Panel Six:

Even closer on a differently dressed Felicia bludgeoning the heavy bag.

BLACK CAT VO
The solution was simple, then...

Panel Seven:

Felicia stops hitting the bag. She's a dead-eyed, sweaty mess.

BLACK CAT VO
I was gonna kill my attacker.

PAGE TWELVE

Panel One:

EXT FRAT HOUSE - NIGHT

Felicia, dressed in black, waits in the bushes outside Ryan's frat house. She wears an almost prototypical version of the Black Cat outfit, minus the fur, claws, heels, and mask. Her hair's pulled back in a long ponytail.

BLACK CAT VO
I'd refused all of his subsequent calls to my dorm room, and I hadn't seen him since that night. I didn't want to think of him as a person anymore -- just an aggressor.

Panel Two:

Closer on Felicia now, wrapping her hands with tape, like a fighter.

BLACK CAT VO
I'd trained for months. I'd studied multiple fighting styles, and I knew which blows would be the deadliest.

BLACK CAT VO 2
I didn't care what happened to me afterwards -- prosecution, jail. All I wanted was to right my wrong.

Panel Three:

Closer on Felicia, reacting to something off-panel.

BLACK CAT VO
But the universe beat me to it.

OFF-PANEL GUY
Start the car, man! Hurry!

OFF-PANEL GUY 2
What'd they say?

Panel Four:

Over the bush-hiding Felicia, onto a pair of Frat brothers, rushing out of the house, toward a parked car.

OFF-PANEL GUY
They hit a divider or something!

OFF-PANEL GUY 2
Who was in the car?!

OFF-PANEL GUY
Rob, Timbo, Soukel and Ryan! We've gotta get to St. Luke's now!

OFF-PANEL GUY 2
Jesus, I hope they're gonna be alright!

Panel Five:

EXT NEWSSTAND - DAY

Close on a newspaper headline, on page four of The Daily Bugle:
"FOUR KILLED IN DRUNK DRIVING HORROR." There are four high school grad pics of the four dead guys, including one of a younger-looking Ryan. The smaller text reads "Four Empire State University Juniors were killed in a horrific

car accident that saw the driver, Ryan Braidlock, beheaded. Police found empty liquor bottles amidst the wreckage, indicating alcohol played a factor in the head-on collision with a cement guardrail at the Midtown Tunnel.

BLACK CAT VO
They weren't.

Panel Six:

At a corner newsstand, Felicia throws the paper down angrily, atop a stack of Bugles, amidst a slew of other periodicals.

BLACK CAT VO
All that training and preparation -- for nothing.

BLACK CAT VO 2
I was so furious. I was a gun, ready to go off, but I had no more target.

PAGE THIRTEEN

Panel One:

Closer on Felicia, looking down now, noticing something off-panel.

BLACK CAT VO
He stole my life, and I wanted to steal his. And now I'd never get that chance.

BLACK CAT VO 2
It left me feeling...

Panel Two:

FELICIA'S POV: The front page of the Bugle screams "DIAMONDS ARE A GIRL'S BEST FRIEND!" There's an image of a massive diamond, on display in a museum. The sub-headline reads "Aphrodite's Tear Diamond comes to NYC, in Midtown Museum show."

BLACK CAT VO
Reckless.

Panel Three:

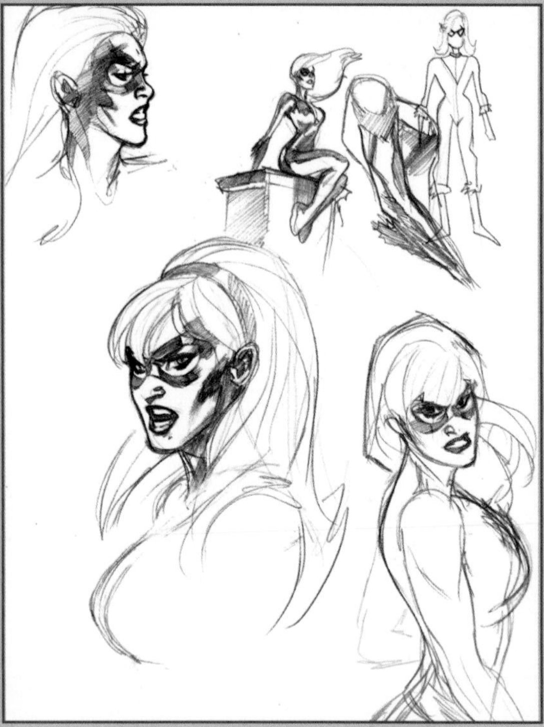

INT MUSEUM - NIGHT

From the opening splash page: Felicia hanging upside down from a cable in an incredibly limber and extremely sexy pose over a laser-beam-alarm protected museum display case, reaching for the massive diamond contained therein.

BLACK CAT VO
That night, I stole my first diamond.

Panel Four:

EXT TIFFANY'S - NIGHT

An establishing shot of the world famous jewelry store on Fifth Ave. Atop the building, we can make out the shape of Felicia.

BLACK CAT VO
That led to more and more robberies.

Panel Five:

INT TIFFANY'S - NIGHT

Felicia crawls across one of the counter-top glass cases on all fours, cutting into the glass.

BLACK CAT VO
And soon, I didn't think about what had happened anymore.

BLACK CAT VO 2
I justified it to myself.

BLACK CAT VO 3
Something was stolen from me...

Panel Six:

INT FELICIA'S NEW APARTMENT - NIGHT

Felicia, surrounded by stolen goods: jewels, paintings, statues, furs. She's in her bra and panties, wearing a diamond necklace and tiara, admiring a massive diamond ring on the finger of her hand that holds a glass of red wine.

BLACK CAT VO
So I started stealing back.

BLACK CAT VO 2
I built myself a new identity. I was no longer Felicia Hardy, the naive freshman who'd been daterapeed.

BLACK CAT VO 3
From then on, I was Felicia Hardy, thief extraordinaire...

PAGE FOURTEEN

EXT QUEENSBORO BRIDGE - NIGHT

Panel One:

A waist-up of Felicia, atop the bridge. Francis stands beside her, a hand on her shoulder.

BLACK CAT
The Black Cat.

FRANCIS
I'm so sorry.

BLACK CAT
No. I'm sorry.

(balloon two)
I'm sorry I never reported the rape. I'm sorry I never went to therapy - never talked to anyone else about what had happened to me.

Panel Two:

Closer on the Black Cat.

BLACK CAT
I'm sorry it took me so long to trust anyone again.

(balloon two)
But I finally did.

Panel Three:

Terry's rendition of THE FIRST MEETING (WITH DIALOGUE) between Spider-Man and the Black Cat, from issue 194 of "Amazing Spider-Man".

BLACK CAT VO
I met him on my first night out in my costume -- when I broke my Father out of jail.

BLACK CAT VO 2
The night I finally took on the Black Cat mantle.

Panel Four:

Terry's rendition of their first kiss (she pulls his mask up, Spidey-movie style), from that same issue.

BLACK CAT VO
And in spite of my feelings toward men at that point, I felt like he was different...

BLACK CAT VO 2
Like I could trust this one.

And, Axel? You've GOTTA include the old-style "Amazing Spider-Man, Ish 194 - Ed." box at the bottom of both of those panels.

Panel Five:

EXT NY SKYLINE - NIGHT
Spider-Man and the Black Cat swing through the city.

BLACK CAT VO
We've been friends ever since.

Panel Six:

EXT STATUE OF LIBERTY - NIGHT

Spider-Man and the Black Cat make out atop the crown of the Statue of Liberty.

BLACK CAT VO
Sometimes more than friends.

PAGE FIFTEEN

Panel One:

EXT QUEENSBORO BRIDGE - NIGHT

Felicia talks to Francis.

BLACK CAT
But in all those years, I've still never told him what I told you tonight, Francis.

FRANCIS
Why not?

BLACK CAT
I don't know. I guess I just buried it all. Suppressed it. I haven't thought about what Ryan did to me in years...

(balloon two)
Until that night. With your brother.

FRANCIS
The night I saved you.

Panel Two:

Felicia's holding Francis tenderly now, her hands on his shoulders.

BLACK CAT
You did. Now let me save you.

(balloon two)
Come with me. Talk to my lawyer. We'll turn ourselves in and explain everything.

(balloon three)
I'll stand up for you. I'll tell them what happened, and that you stopped an evil man from another horrible act in a lifetime filled with horrible deeds.

FRANCIS
Would I... have to tell them?

(balloon two)
About what he did to me?

Panel Three:

Felicia touches his face, tenderly.

BLACK CAT
I think you should. I think it'd help you to talk about it. It really helped me to tell you about what happened back in college.

(balloon two)
And, Francis -- I didn't even realize how bad I was still hurting about it. Not until I shared it with you. And in that, you helped me again.

Panel Four:

Felicia removes her Black Cat mask, still touching Francis' face.

BLACK CAT
Let me help you, the way you've helped me. We're rape survivors, Francis. We need to be heard so we can heal.

Panel Five:

Francis is crying, pushing her hands away from him -- not violently or angrily; just kinda in denial.

FRANCIS
I can't! Everyone will laugh! They'll say it's my fault! That I deserved it! That I brought it on myself!

BLACK CAT
They'll understand, Francis -- about your brother, the hooker in Atlantic City, everything.

(balloon two)
You were caught in a cycle of violence, but you can end it all by dealing with it now.

Panel Six:

Francis grabs the Black Cat firmly by the arms. Again, not offensively or in attack-mode; more out of emotional frustration.

FRANCIS
I'm telling you, I can't do it!

PAGE SIXTEEN

Panel One:

Daredevil and Spider-Man swing through the night air, searching. Daredevil's "listening" to their surroundings.

SPIDER-MAN
Do you got her yet?

DAREDEVIL
I'm picking up her heartbeat's signature, but it's all muddled by the din of the ci...

Panel Two:

Closer on DD, with that radar sense (represented by the circles around his head) in action. Along the bottom of the frame, there's a heartbeat, represented as if on a heart monitor. It's active.

DAREDEVIL
Wait! I've got her!

(balloon two)
And her heart's racing.

Panel Three:

Spider-Man and Daredevil, swinging.

SPIDER-MAN
Where?! Which way?!

DAREDEVIL
North. By the river.

SPIDER-MAN
Where by the river?! The docks? The...?!

Panel Four:

Close on Spider-Man, "reacting" in horror (those wide-eyes) to something off-panel. His spider sense is tingling.

SPIDER-MAN
No...

Panel Five

Spider-Man's POV: the unmasked Black Cat, in the clutches of a mad-man, atop an all too familiar and haunting bridge, dangerously close to the edge.

SPIDER-MAN VO
NO!

PAGE SEVENTEEN

EXT QUEENSBORO BRIDGE - NIGHT

Panel One:

Francis still holds the Black Cat, though this close, it doesn't seem as threatening or menacing.

FRANCIS
I can't go to jail! Do you know what kind of prisons they put people with special powers in?! What kind of restraints they use?!

BLACK CAT
You won't go to prison, I promise you. You'll go to a hospital, Francis -- where you can deal with what's been done to you, with doctors who only care about your psychological and emotional well being!

FRANCIS
How can you be sure th...

Panel Two:

Suddenly, Francis is struck from behind my a diving Spider-Man, knocking Black Cat free from his tame grasp. Francis buckles forward, like a hinge, almost bending in two.

SFX
SLAM!

FRANCIS
UHN!

Panel Three:

Daredevil "catches" the Black Cat.

DAREDEVIL
I've got you, Ms. Hardy.

BLACK CAT
PETER, NO!

Panel Four:

Spider-Man's atop Francis, beating the shit out of him.

> **SFX**
> KRAK!

> **FRANCIS**
> NNNNGGGHH!

> **SPIDER-MAN**
> Never again!

Panel Five:

A FLASHBACK in sepia of the GREEN GOBLIN throwing Gwen Stacey off the same bridge.

> **SPIDER-MAN VO**
> Never...

Panel Six:

Spider-Man continues to beat the grounded Francis, who's terrified and bloody.

> **SFX**
> BASH!

> **SPIDER-MAN**
> AGAIN!

PAGE EIGHTEEN

Panel One:

Close on the bloodied, dazed, terrified Francis.

> **FRANCIS**
> Uhhhhnnnn...

Panel Two:

Close on the Black Cat, restrained by Daredevil arms, wide-eyed, screaming at the off-panel mess.

> **BLACK CAT**
> PETER, YOU'RE KILLING HIM!

Panel Three:

Spider-Man holds Francis by his collar, lifting his head off the bridge-top floor. Francis is almost a meat puppet in his hands, bloodied and bruised. Spider-Man screams into his face.

> **SPIDER-MAN**
> I'VE HAD IT WITH YOU PSYCHOS HURTING THE PEOPLE I LOVE!

> (balloon two)
> NEVER AGAIN, D'YA HEAR ME?!

Panel Four:

Close on Francis' broken and bloody hand, struggling to reach the Black Cat's mask on the bridge-top floor.

> **SPIDER-MAN OP**
> NEVER AGAIN!

Panel Five:

Even closer on the tip of Francis' finger, as it reaches the mask.

> **SPIDER-MAN OP**
> NEVER...

Panel Six:

Suddenly, the mask is gone, in a puff of...

> **SPIDER-MAN OP**
> AGAIN!

> **SFX**
> BAMF!

PAGE NINETEEN

Panel One:

Big panel: Spider-Man seizes and arches his back, as if struck by something. The Black Cat mask has teleported into his neck, with a cloud of smoke and the requisite...

> **SFX**
> BAMF!

SPIDER-MAN
UNGHHHHNNNNGGHHHHH!!!

In the background, Daredevil and the Black Cat react, wide-eyed. The Black Cat screams...

BLACK CAT
PETER!

Panel Two:

The Black Cat struggles from the shocked Daredevil's grasp, rushing to the fallen Spider-Man's side, who's clutching at the mask that's jutting out of his costume and neck, as if fused. In the background, Francis is crawling to the edge of the bridge-top.

SPIDER-MAN
UHHHNNN!

BLACK CAT
Oh my God, no!

SPIDER-MAN
I... I don't think... uhhhn... I don't think it hit... the carotid...

Panel Three:

The Black Cat holds Spider-Man in her arms, crying. She's screaming at Daredevil, who's heading for the edge of the bridge-top.

BLACK CAT
Get some help! Get a doctor!

SPIDER-MAN
No... Klum...

Panel Four:

In the background, Daredevil is leaping into the night sky, off to get a doctor. In the mid-ground, the Black Cat looks up from where she's holding Spider-Man to the foreground, where we see Francis' leg.

SPIDER-MAN
Uhhhhnnn... it's... uhhnnn...

BLACK CAT
Francis... help him! Take it out! Please!

Panel Five:

Francis, trying to stand, by the edge of the bridge, looking bloody and beaten -- just plain broken. A sniveling, sad mess.

FRANCIS
I trusted you, Felicia! And you lied to me! You... you somehow called your friends here! To kill me!

PAGE TWENTY

Panel One:

Black Cat stands, trying to approach Francis, leaving Spider-Man laying/leaning on his side, clutching at the mask in his neck.

BLACK CAT
Francis, no. I swear to God, that's not true. I would never betray you -- not after what you did for me!

Panel Two:

Over Black Cat, onto Francis.

FRANCIS
You lied to me! You were lying the whole time! To keep me here, until your friends could get here!

BLACK CAT
No, Francis! That's not true!

Panel Three:

Close on Francis, screaming, bloody spittle flying from his mouth.

FRANCIS
YOU'RE A LYING ▮▮▮▮▮▮

Panel Four:

Over Francis, onto Black Cat. Francis' hand is prominent in the foreground, the rest of him, from the wrist up, is off-panel.

BLACK CAT
Please, Francis! I wouldn't lie to you! I want to help you! We can break the cycle of violence! Together!

FRANCIS
Y'know what I've got in my apartment, Felicia? In a drawer, next to my bed, where I laid out your things so neatly?

Panel Five:

Same set-up, but now a gun has BAMF'ed into Francis' hand in the foreground of the frame. Black Cat's reaction has changed to surprise.

SFX
BAMF!

BLACK CAT
Francis. Please. Don't.

Panel Six:

On Francis, pointing the gun at the Black Cat.

FRANCIS
You're just like Garrison! And that hooker! And the kids at school!

(balloon two)
You're all a pack of lies and hate.

(balloon three)
And like you said...

Panel Seven:

Extreme close up on Francis' eyes, dead, bloodied, bruised, tear streaked -- all signs of humanity now gone.

FRANCIS
Blood calls for blood.

PAGE TWENTY ONE

Panel One:

Suddenly, Francis' gun-hand is covered in webbing. The gun goes off inside the webbing. The webbing lights on fire from the aborted gun shot.

SFX
THWIP!

SFX
BLAM!

SFX
FWASH!

FRANCIS
UHN!

Panel Two:

Spider-Man stands, holding his neck, his wrist shooter aimed at us spraying webbing.

SFX
THWIP!

Panel Three:

Francis, his webbed hand aflame, moves to avoid the second blast of Spider-Man's webbing. He stumbles backwards, his foot coming off the edge of the bridge-top floor.

FRANCIS
NO!

Panel Four:

Tight on Black Cat's wide-eyed face, as she reaches out for the OP falling Francis.

BLACK CAT
FRANCIS!

Panel Five:

The largest on the page: a high, wide of Francis falling backwards off the bridge-top, toward the river below. Spider-Man and Black Cat are racing toward the edge of the bridge-top to save him.

PAGE TWENTY TWO

Panel One:

Looking up at the edge of the bridge-top, Spider-Man hangs over, shooting a web. Black Cat fires a line from her sleeve.

SFX
THWIP!

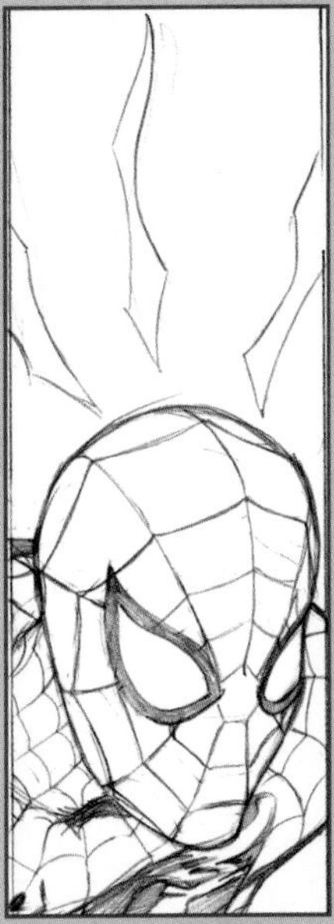

SFX
PAF!

Panel Two:

Looking down, over the heroes, as their lines chase the plummeting Francis, who faces up at us, scared, now almost in the river.

Panel Three:

Same exact shot, but now Francis is replaced by a puff of smoke, and a...

SFX
BAMF!

Panel Four:

Same exact shot, but now the smoke's clearing, and the lines -- both cat and web -- drop into the river.

Panel Five:

Looking back up at Spider-Man and the Black Cat, looking down at us, forlorn.

FELICIA VO
Do you think he's still alive?

PAGE TWENTY THREE

EXT WASHINGTON SQUARE PARK - DAY

Panel One:

A wide of the very familiar arch. Students and other New Yorkers move about. In the midst of it all, PETER PARKER and a FELICIA HARDY walk.

PETER
I don't know. Even though he teleported, he did it in mid-fall.

(balloon two)
Wherever he wound up, he still had to land, y'know?

FELICIA
He may have gotten off light if he did die. At least he doesn't have to live the rest of his life as a fugitive from the law.

PETER
We'll get you cleared, Leesh. It may take time, and you're gonna have to lay low, but sooner or later, we'll get you out from under the murder charge.

Panel Two:

Closer on the pair, walking. Felicia wears a long overcoat, jeans, a shirt and a hat. Her coat collar's pulled up, andher hat's pulled low. She's trying to obscure her identity. Peter's neck is bandaged.

FELICIA
God, it just sucks.

(balloon two)
No matter how hard we try to help, sometimes we only make things worse. For ourselves. For others.

(balloon three)
For Francis.

PETER
You can't think like that.

FELICIA
Why not?

PETER
Because no matter what the outcome, at the end of the day, we always help more people than not. The good outweighs the bad.

(balloon two)
Knowing that's the only way I can sleep at night.

Panel Three:

Felicia and Peter stop at the circle in the Square. She's indicating his neck.

FELICIA
And how are you sleeping at night now -- with the...

PETER
This? It's fine. Healing up nicely. Thank God Ma... Daredevil knows someone like the Night Nurse.

Panel Four:

Felicia smiles at Peter. Peter looks a little embarrassed.

FELICIA
You almost slipped, Peter Parker. You almost revealed another costume's name.

PETER
Lay off.

FELICIA
Isn't that you all over? Always rushing to unmask?

PETER
You loved it when I did it, and you know it.

Panel Five:

Felicia offers him a warm, small smile.

FELICIA
I did, actually.

PETER
S'not what you said then.

FELICIA
I was a kid then, Peter. I've grown up a lot since then.

(balloon two)
You telling me who you were... even though I didn't show it at the time...
(balloon three)
Well, it meant the world to me.

(balloon four)
You helped me.

Panel Six:

Peter, curious. Felicia, open.

PETER
Helped you how?

FELICIA
You helped me to trust again.

PETER
Really? Now you tell me -- when I'm all married and stuff.

(balloon two)
And trust what, exactly?

Panel Seven:

Wide on two old friends/former lovers, in the midst of the bustle of Washington Square Park.

FELICIA
Peter, I think it's time I told you about something that happened to me when I was in college...

PAGE TWENTY FOUR

Panel One:

EXT THE DOCKS - NIGHT

A warehouse situation, on the waterfront. There's light coming from coming from a crack beneath the roll-up, garage-style door of one of the units.

BOX
Epilogue...

BOX 2
Somewhere downtown...

FRANCIS OP
And how did you come into possession of this?

Panel Two:

INT WAREHOUSE - NIGHT

Somewhat wide. Surrounded by crates of various sizes, WILSON FISK stands beside FRANCIS -- his head covered in bandages like the Unknown Soldier. He sports a cast on his arm, and he leans on a crutch, missing a leg. The pair are looking into an opened, man-sized crate, the contents of which are obscured from the reader's view.

FISK
An associate acquired it from Jack-O-Lantern.

FRANCIS
The brown guy who rides that bat-thing?

FISK
You're thinking of Hobgoblin.

FRANCIS
Hard to keep them all straight.

Panel Three:

Fisk, talking to Francis, whose face is wrapped in bloody bandages, with slits for eyeholes. Francis stares at the off-panel crate.

FISK
You'll have to study up, if you truly intend to play the costume game, Mr. Klum.

(balloon two)
Even though many of them are histrionic psychotics, those lost souls will prove to be your best allies in your coming campaign.

FRANCIS
It's not a campaign, Mr. Fisk. It's not a game, and I don't intend to spend my life trading quips and blows with the man.

(balloon two)
I'm going to kill Spider-Man. Maybe the

Black Cat, too. That's it.

Panel Four:

Fisk and Francis.

FISK
Then why this, might I ask? I'm certainly not trying to talk you out of the purchase, but there're thousands of ways to reach your goal without wrapping yourself up in theatrics.

FRANCIS
I'm not in any shape to show my face to the world. The doctors say the wounds will never heal.

(balloon two)
I'll never look normal again.

Panel Five:

Francis.

FISK
If it's a question of the cosmetic, surely an original mask of your own design...

FRANCIS
That's only part of it, sir. I'll use this to draw out Spider-Man. And to get the edge.

(balloon two)
If he thinks he's dealing with the familiar, he'll approach me differently -- with his guard down. Why be wary of a foe you've trumped countless times, right?

(balloon three)
And when he does that? When he faces me in this guise, simply prepared to perform a rote ballet he's danced so many times before...

PAGE TWENTY FIVE

Panel One:

On Francis, studying the OP crate contents. Fisk stands behind him now.

FRANCIS
I'll teleport my fist into his brain.

FISK
That's certainly an advantage you'll have over the suit's original owner. He didn't have your... special abilities. He was all parlor tricks.
(balloon two)
With your powers, you could actually live up to the name.

Panel Two:

Francis dabs a handkerchief at the cheek of his bleeding bandages. Fisk stuffs a cigar in his mouth.

FRANCIS
How much?

FISK
Ah -- the uncomfortable discussion of money.

(balloon two)
Ten million.

FRANCIS
Seems kinda high for a suit that's been sitting in mothballs for awhile.

FISK
You're not just buying the suit, sir. You're buying all the accoutrements the designer of this identity created as well. His contraptions, which -- while admittedly rather childish -- do extend the mystique he afforded himself... just prior to his routine thrashings at the hands of Spider-Man.

(balloon two)
A fate I'm sure you'll not share.

Panel Three:

Fisk.

FISK
And aside from the history and the anonymity the suit provides, don't forget that you're also buying this entire warehouse.

(balloon two)
It's a turn-key operation, Mr. Klum. You hand me a briefcase, and I hand you the keys to a kingdom -- one you could rescue from ridicule.

Panel Four:

We're looking out at Francis and Fisk from inside the crate. Francis still stares at the OP contents.

FRANCIS
And ten million certainly puts you well on your way to rebuilding your empire, doesn't it, Mr. Fisk?

FISK
There's that, yes.

FRANCIS
Make it eight, and when I'm done killing the Arach-Knight, I'll do away with Daredevil for you as well.

Panel Five:

Fisk smiles.

FISK
A kind offer, to be sure.

(balloon two)
But there are some things a man has to do for himself, sir.

Panel Six:

Fisk and Francis, reflected in a curved glass that seems to hover in the darkness of the crate.

FISK
I'm afraid it's ten million or nothing.

(balloon two)
Such a small price to pay for revenge on your brother's killers, no?

FRANCIS
Hm.

FISK
So...

(balloon two)
Do we have a deal?

PAGE TWENTY TWO

SPLASH PAGE

A head-to-toe of the MYSTERIO SUIT, bubble-head and all, which hangs in the crate before the bandaged Francis (we're on his back).

FRANCIS
Yes.

(balloon two)
Yes, I believe we do.

FIN

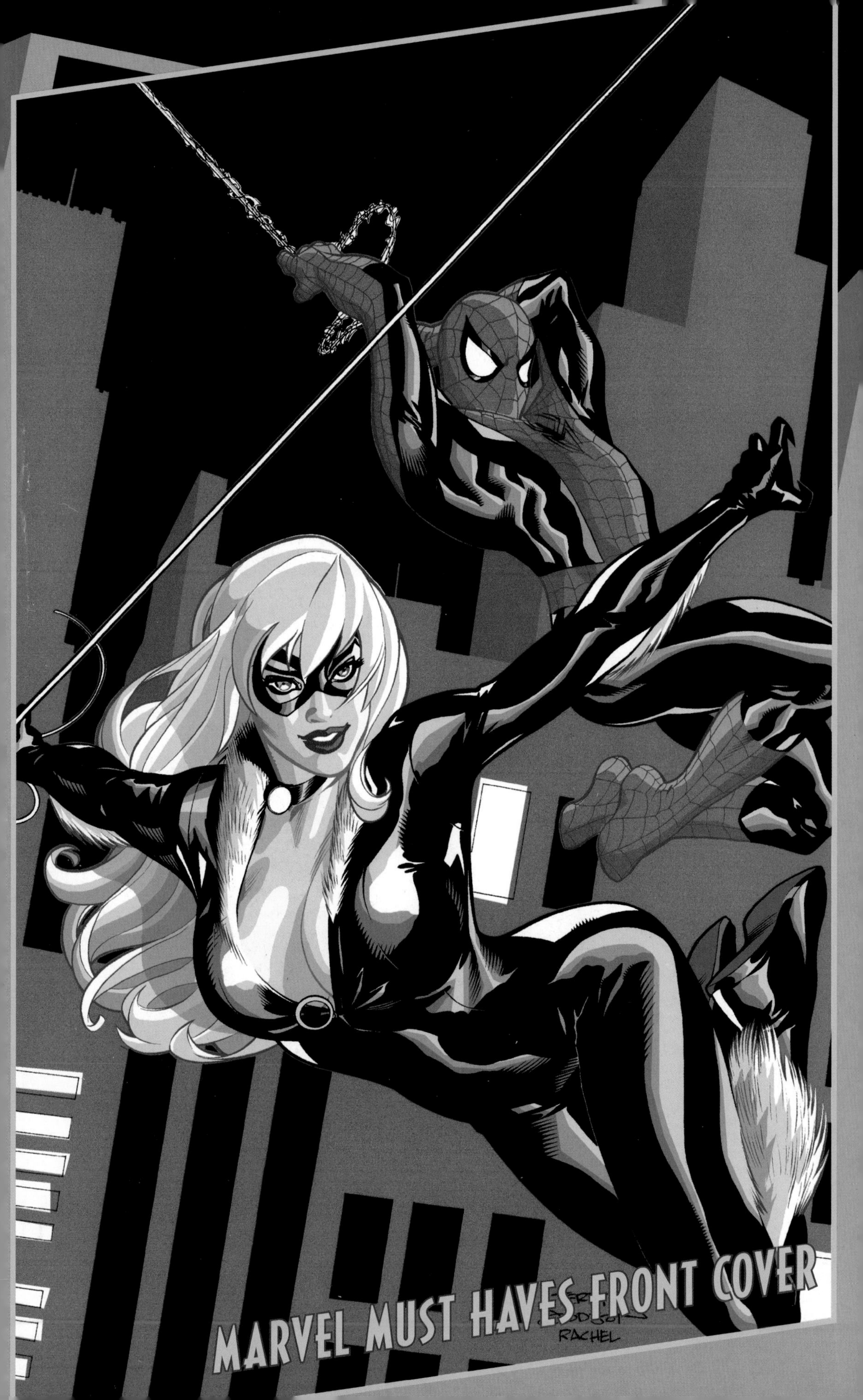
MARVEL MUST HAVES FRONT COVER
RACHEL

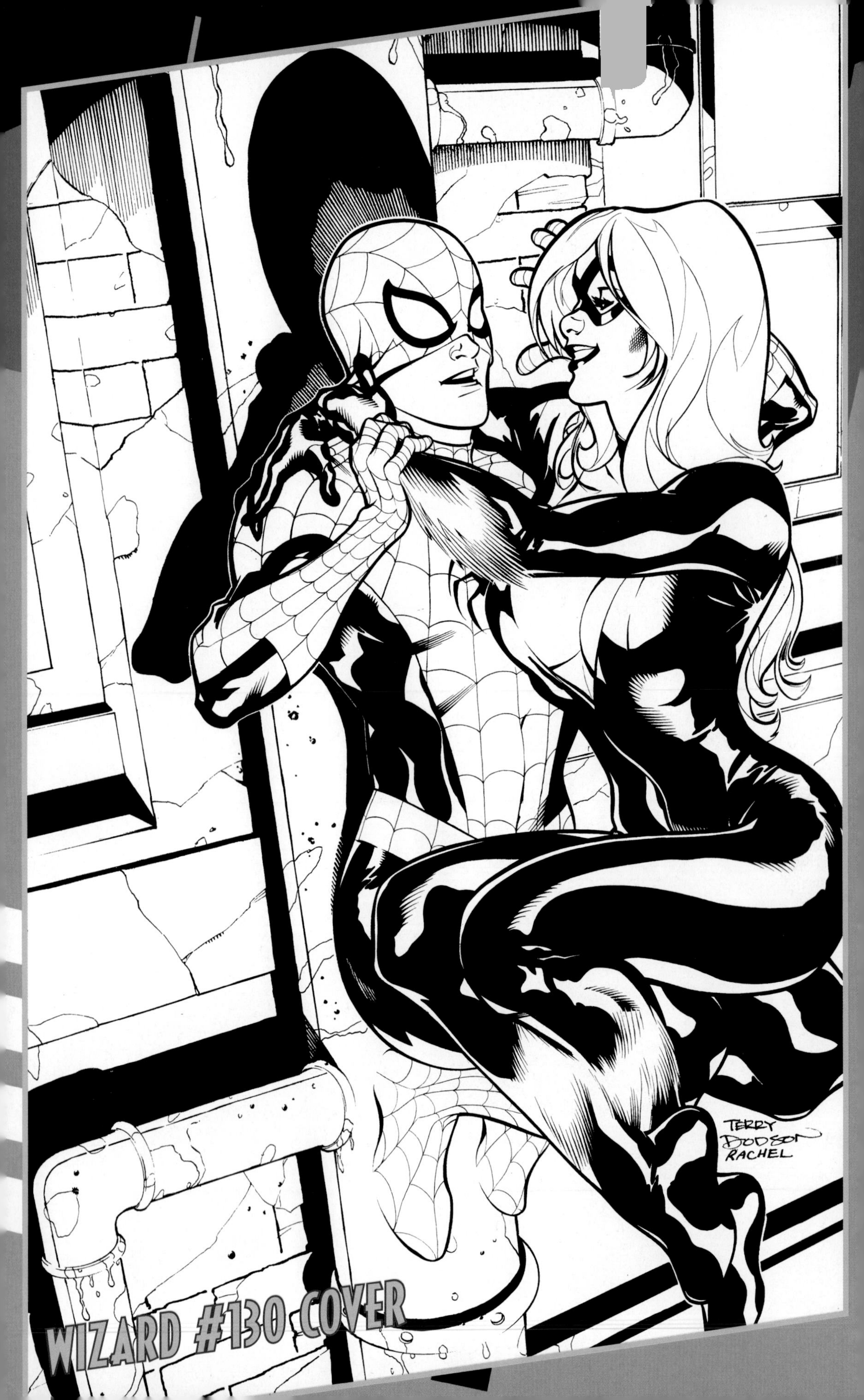
TERRY
DODSON
RACHEL

WIZARD #130 COVER

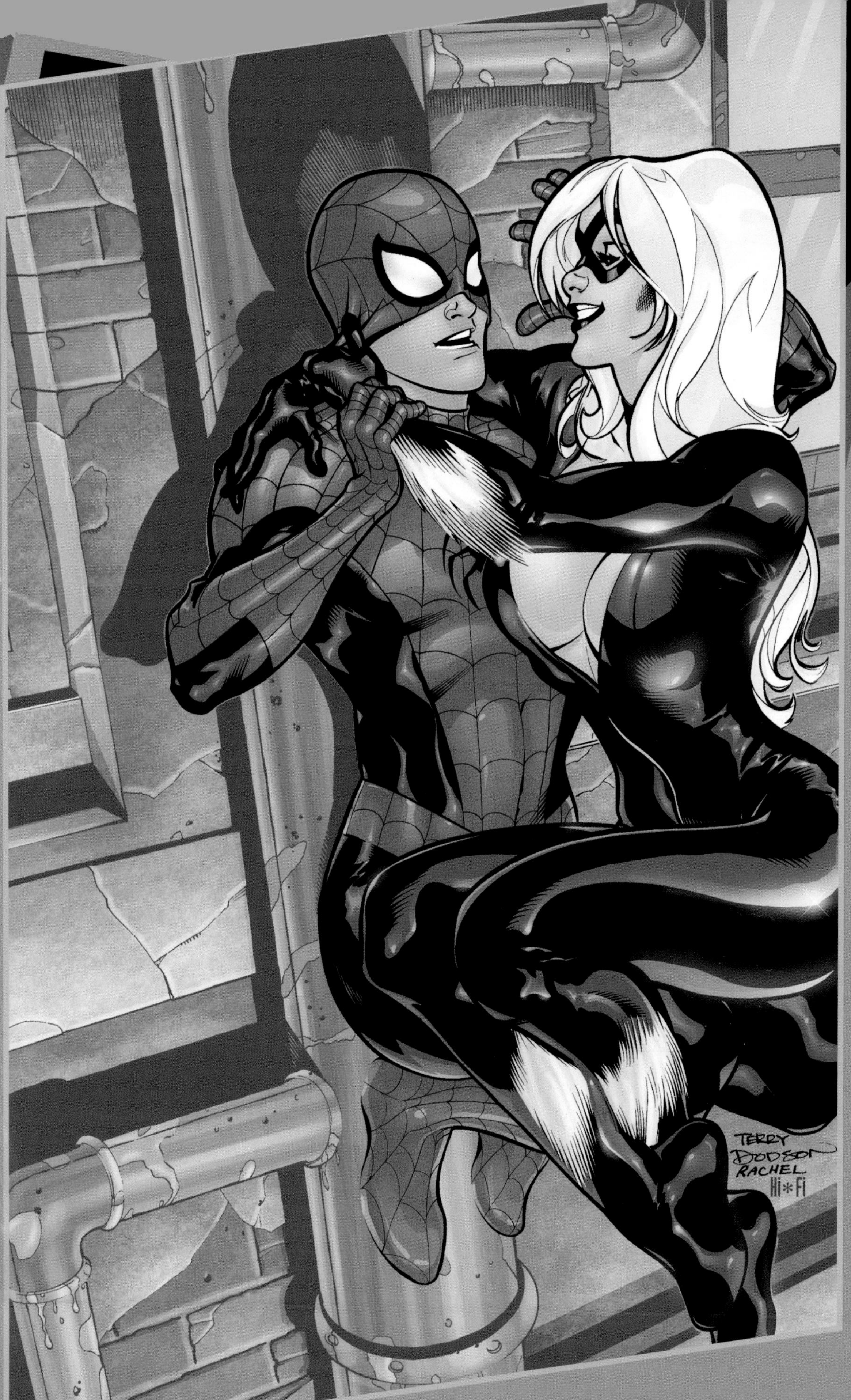
TERRY
DODSON
RACHEL
Hi*Fi

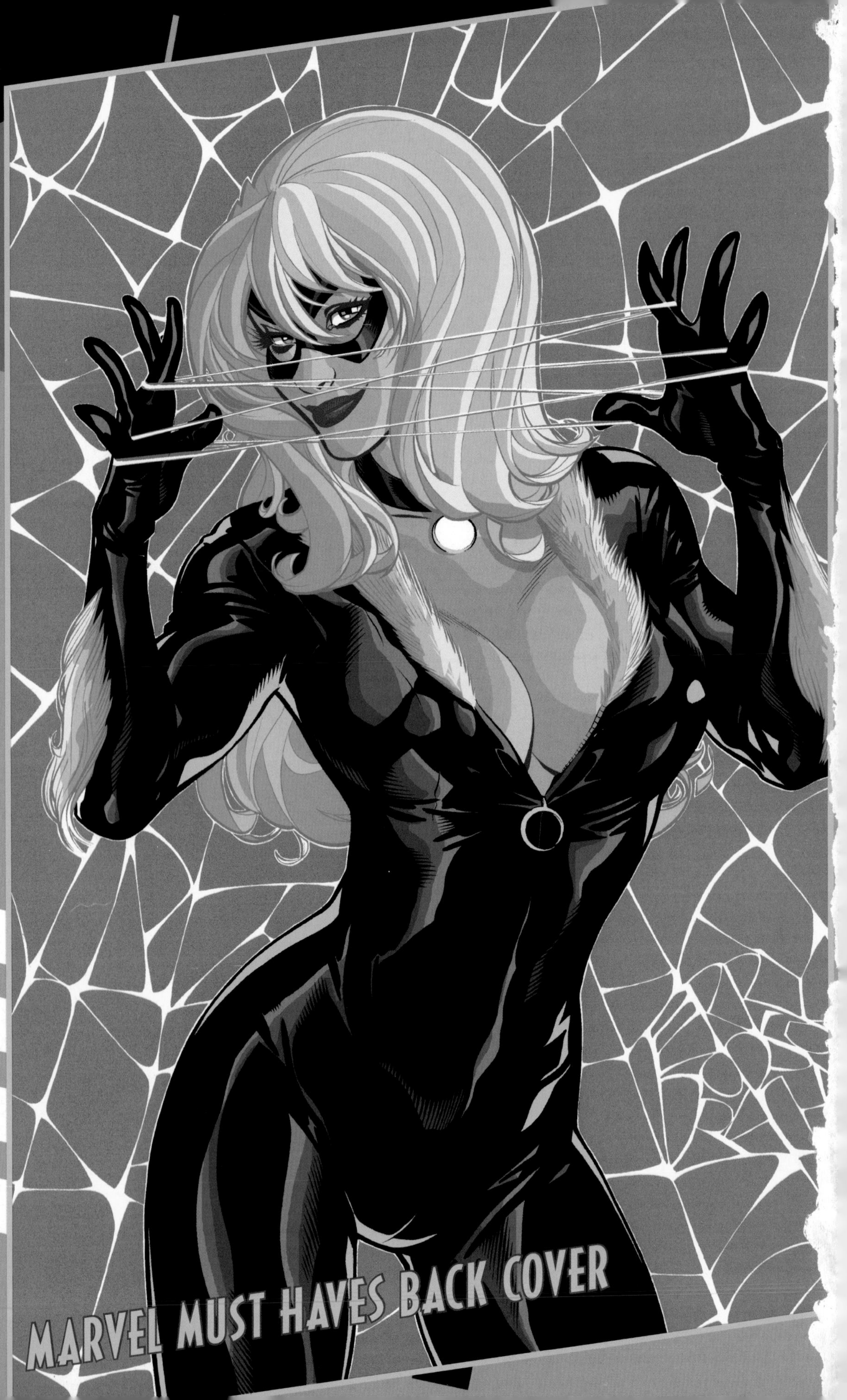
MARVEL MUST HAVES BACK COVER